Topics in Advanced Econometrics
Probability Foundations

Phoebus J. Dhrymes

Topics in
Advanced Econometrics

Probability Foundations

Springer-Verlag
New York Berlin Heidelberg
London Paris Tokyo Hong Kong

Phoebus J. Dhrymes
Department of Economics
Columbia University
New York, NY 10027
USA

Mathematics Classification Codes: 62P20, 60Axx, 60Fxx

Library of Congress Cataloging-in-Publication Data
Dhrymes, Phoebus J., 1932–
    Topics in advanced econometrics / Phoebus J. Dhrymes.
      p. cm.
    Contents: v. 1. Probability foundations.
    ISBN 0-387-97178-5 (v. 1 : alk. paper)
    1. Econometrics.   2. Probabilities.   I. Title.
  HB139.D49   1990
  330'.01'5195—dc20   89-27330

Printed on acid-free paper.

Camera-ready copy prepared by the author using LaTeX.
Printed and bound by R. R. Donnelley & Sons, Harrisonburg, Virginia.
Printed in the United States of America.

9 8 7 6 5 4 3 2 1

ISBN 0-387-97178-5 Springer-Verlag New York Berlin Heidelberg
ISBN 3-540-97178-5 Springer-Verlag Berlin Heidelberg New York

To Alexander
for his irrepressible energy

Preface

For sometime now, I felt that the evolution of the literature of econometrics had mandated a higher level of mathematical proficiency. This is particularly evident beyond the level of the general linear model (GLM) and the general linear structural econometric model (GLSEM).

The problems one encounters in nonlinear econometrics are not easily amenable to treatment by the analytical methods one typically acquires, when one learns about probability and inference through the use of density functions. Even in standard traditional topics, one is often compelled to resort to heuristics; for example, it is difficult to prove central limit theorems for nonidentically distributed or martingale sequences, solely by the use of characteristic functions. Yet such proofs are essential, even in only moderately sophisticated classroom exposition.

Unfortunately, relatively few students enter a graduate economics department ready to tackle probability theory in measure theoretic terms.

The present volume has grown out of the need to lay the foundation for such discussions. The motivating forces were, chiefly, (a) the frustration one encounters in attempting to communicate certain concepts to students wholly in analytic terms; and (b) the unwillingness of the typical student to sit through several courses in mathematics departments, in order to acquire the requisite background.

Chapter 1 of this volume provides a modicum of instruction in measure theory; chapter 2 introduces the fundamental aspects of probability theory in measure theoretic terms and covers, *inter alia*, such topics as the probability space, n-dimensional measureable (Borel) spaces, Kolmogorov's consistency requirements for infinite dimensional spaces, the Radon-Nikodym theorem and conditional probability; chapter 3 provides an introduction to properties of sequences, such as various forms of convergence, the relationship they bear to each other, and various criteria for the convergence of sequences of independent random variables; chapter 4, deals with the generalization of such results to random elements and discusses central limit theorems, similarly, for independent random elements; finally, chapter 5 introduces various types of dependent sequences such as martingale, mixing, stationary and ergodic sequences and discusses convergence properties of martingales, central limit theorems for martingales, and issues of convergence for ergodic, strictly stationary and covariance stationary sequences.

There is no overlap between this volume and my earlier work **Mathematics for Econometrics** which deals, essentially, with linear algebra and other tools useful in the context of linear econometrics.

It is anticipated that this work would be useful to graduate students with a reasonably strong mathematical background and to professionals who may be interested in acquiring at least a working knowledge of the fundamental probability theory underlying a great deal of nonstandard contemporary econometrics.

This volume was completed during my tenure of an NSF/ASA/Census Research Fellowship over the academic year 1988-89; I am grateful to these organizations for their support, particularly, to the Statistical Research Division of the Census Bureau, for providing a congenial working environment.

I would also like to acknowledge my intellectual debt to my colleague Y.S. Chow; his excellent book (with H. Teicher) **Probability Theory** has served as an inspiration for this work, and the unwillingess of economics students to attend his course as the goad for its production.

Last, but not least, I would like record my gratitude to my former student Dr. Myeongho Lee who has proofread the manuscript in its entirety and has prepared the index for this volume.

Phoebus J. Dhrymes
Bronxville, New York
September 1989

Contents

Chapter 1

Mathematical Foundations

1.1 Introduction

The purpose of this chapter is to provide a background on the results from probability theory required for the study of several of the topics of contemporary econometrics.

Increasingly, the formalism of measure theoretic arguments is finding its way into the literature of econometrics; moreover, the standard calculus approach does not really suffice in making clear the nature of such complex concepts as convergence with probability one, weak convergence, conditional probability, conditional expectations, the Kolmogorov consistency requirements, ergodic theorems, or martingale convergence theorems. For this reason, it is quite useful to collect in a convenient place a number of the salient results so as to make this volume as self contained as possible; a further, incidental, benefit is to make it considerably simpler for students of econometrics to acquire a modicum of literacy in topics of modern probability theory, which, from the viewpoint of economics, are still considered somewhat esoteric.

It is expected that the reader is familiar with such texts as Hogg and Craig (1970, or late editions), and has had an exposure to calculus, introductory analysis and matrix algebra.

An attempt will be made to give proofs for every proposition, except when to do so would not serve any educational purpose or when to do

1

so would entail arguments of such complexity so as to clearly lead us beyond the scope of this volume.

Finally, it should be stressed that this volume aims at providing the tools deemed necessary for the exposition of several topics in econometric theory; it is clearly **not our objective to provide a mathematical textbook of modern probability theory.**

1.2   Sets and Set Operations

Let Ω be a (nonempty) collection of objects (our universe of discourse); the nature of such objects need not specified. In most applications, the set Ω would be the set of all possible outcomes of an **experiment**, the sample space of probability theory, the real line, or the Cartesian product of a finite number of copies of the real line; for the moment, however, we treat Ω as an abstract collection of objects, and we shall refer to it as a **space** in this and subsequent sections. We denote its elements by ω, and as a matter of notation, we write

$$\omega \in \Omega.$$

A subset of Ω, say A, is simply a collection of elements of Ω; we denote it, as a matter of notation, by

$$A \subset \Omega,$$

which is to be read A is contained in Ω, or A is a subset of Ω. For completeness, we also define the null set, $\emptyset$, which has no elements; **by convention, the null set is a subset of every set.** As a matter of notation, we have that for every set, $A \subset \Omega$,

$$\emptyset \subset A.$$

A subset is described either by **enumeration**, i.e., by enumerating its elements, or by some property. For example, suppose

$$\Omega = \{1, 2, 3, \ldots\}.$$

One of its subsets might be $A = \{1, 2, 3, 4, 5\}$; or we may simply describe membership in a set, say B, by some property; for example,

$$B = \{n : n = 2k, \quad k = 1, 2, 3 \ldots\}.$$

In this case, B is the set of all even integers; it can also be easily specified by enumeration; thus, $B = \{2, 4, 6, 8, \ldots\}$. In most instances, the specification of subsets is done by the specification of the properties of their element(s) rather than by enumeration, since the latter is, typically, very difficult to accomplish.

We now begin our formal discussion.

Definition 1. Let A, $B \subset \Omega$; then, their **union** is defined by

$$A \cup B = \{\omega : \omega \in A \text{ or } \omega \in B\},$$

which is read the set of all points that belong **either to A or to B, (or both)**.

Definition 2. Let A, B be as in Definition 1; then, their **intersection** is defined by

$$A \cap B = \{\omega : \omega \in A \text{ and } \omega \in B\},$$

which is read the set of all points that belong to **both A and B**.

Definition 3. Let $A \subset \Omega$; then, the **complement** of A (relative to Ω) is given by

$$\bar{A} = \{\omega : \omega \in \Omega \text{ and } \omega \notin A\}.$$

In what follows, we shall drop repetitive and redundant statements, such as, for example, $A \subset \Omega$; any sets we consider will be understood to be subsets of Ω, which is the universe of discourse.

A consequence of the definitions above is

Proposition 1. Let A, B, be any two sets; then,

i. $\overline{(A \cup B)} = \bar{A} \cap \bar{B}$;

ii. $\overline{(A \cap B)} = \bar{A} \cup \bar{B}$.

Proof: If $\omega \in \overline{(A \cup B)}$, then $\omega \notin A$ and $\omega \notin B$; hence, $\omega \in \bar{A} \cap \bar{B}$. Conversely, if $\omega \in \bar{A} \cap \bar{B}$, then $\omega \notin A$ and $\omega \notin B$, i.e., $\omega \notin (A \cup B)$, which proves i.

To prove ii., we note that if $\omega \in \overline{(A \cap B)}$, then either $\omega \in \bar{A}$ or $\omega \in \bar{B}$; consequently, $\omega \in (\bar{A} \cup \bar{B})$. Conversely, if $\omega \in (\bar{A} \cup \bar{B})$, then either $\omega \in \bar{A}$ or $\omega \in \bar{B}$; hence, $\omega \notin (A \cap B)$, or $\omega \in \overline{(A \cap B)}$.

q.e.d.

Remark 1. The results above obviously extend by iteration to **finite** unions and intersections, i.e., the complement of a finite union is the intersection of the corresponding complements and the complement of finite intersections is the union of the corresponding complements.

It is simple to demonstrate that the results of Proposition 1 extend to **countable** unions and intersections, i.e., if

$$\{A_n : n = 1, 2, \ldots\}$$

is a sequence of sets (subsets of Ω), then

i. $\overline{\bigcup_{n=1}^{\infty} A_n} = \bigcap_{n=1}^{\infty} \bar{A}_n$;

ii. $\overline{\bigcap_{n=1}^{\infty} A_n} = \bigcup_{n=1}^{\infty} \bar{A}_n$.

1.3   Limits of Sequences

Let $\{a_n : n = 1, 2, 3, \ldots\}$ be a sequence of, say real numbers. We recall from calculus that the limit of the sequence, if one exists, is a real number, say a, such that given any $\epsilon \geq 0$ there exists some n_0 such that for all $n \geq n_0$

$$|a_n - a| \leq \epsilon.$$

We would like to express this concept in a way that would easily enable us to generalize it to the case where the sequence in question is not a sequence of real numbers but, say a sequence of sets (subsets of Ω).

Definition 4. Let $\{a_n : n \geq 1\}$ be a sequence of real numbers; then, the **supremum** of the sequence, denoted by

$$\sup_{n \to \infty} a_n,$$

is the **least upper bound (l.u.b.)** of the sequence, i.e., the smallest number, say α, such that

$$a_n \leq \alpha, \quad \text{for all } n.$$

The **infimum** of the sequence, denoted by

$$\inf_{n \to \infty} a_n,$$

is the **greatest lower bound (g.l.b.)** of the sequence, i.e., the largest number, say α, such that

$$a_n \geq \alpha, \quad \text{forall } n.$$

Remark 2. When dealing with a finite sequence, say $\{a_n : n = 1, 2, ..., N\}$, the supremum and infimum of a sequence coincide with the latter's maximum and mininimum, respectively. This is so since it is possible to find the largest (maximum) and the smallest (minimum) elements of the sequence, and these will obey the requirements, respectively, for the supremum and infimum. Contrast this to the case where the sequence is infinite, and the supremum and infimum need not be members of the sequence.

Example 1. Consider the sequence

$$\{a_n : a_n = 1 - \frac{1}{n}, \ n \geq 1\}.$$

It is easily shown that

$$\sup_{n \to \infty} a_n = 1.$$

Notice also that 1 is not a member of the sequence; on the other hand,

$$\inf_{n \to \infty} a_n = 0,$$

and here 0 is a member of the sequence. If we truncate the sequence at $n = N$ and consider the sequence to consist only of the first N elements, then both inf and sup are members of the sequence and correspond, respectively, to

$$\min a_n = 0, \quad \max a_n = 1 - \frac{1}{N}.$$

Consider further the sequence $\{a_n : a_n = 1 + (1/n), \ n \geq 1\}$. In this case we find

$$\inf_{n \to \infty} a_n = 1, \quad \sup_{n \to \infty} a_n = 2,$$

and note that the infimum is not a member of the sequence, while the supremum is.

Definition 5. The sequence $\{a_n : n \geq 1\}$ is said to be a **monotone nonincreasing** sequence if

$$a_{n+1} \leq a_n, \quad \text{for all } n,$$

and is said to be a **monotone nondecreasing** sequence if

$$a_{n+1} \geq a_n, \quad \text{for all } n.$$

Monotone nonincreasing or nondecreasing sequences are said to be **monotone** sequences.

Remark 3. It is clear that if we consider limits of sequences in the extended number system, $[-\infty, \ \infty]$, then all monotone sequences have a limit; this is so since, in the case of a monotone nonincreasing sequence either, there is a (finite) greatest lower bound or the sequence decreases to $-\infty$, while in the case of a monotone nondecreasing sequence, either there is a (finite) least upper bound or the sequence increases to $+\infty$.

Monotone sequences offer an important tool in studying the limiting behavior of general sequences. This is so since for a general sequence a limit, i.e., a point within a neighborhood of which are located all but a finite number of the elements of the sequence, may not exist. A simple example is the sequence

$$\{a_n : a_n = (-1)^n + (-1)^n \frac{1}{n}, \ n \geq 1\}.$$

Here, if we confine our attention to even numbered values of the index, we have a sequence with a limit at one; on the other hand, if we confine our attention to odd numbered values of the index, then we have a sequence with a limit at minus one. This sequence, then, has no limit in the sense that there is no point around which are located all but a finite number of the elements of the sequence; instead, there are two such points, each corresponding, however, to distinct subsequences of the original sequence. Occasionally, such points are called **limit, or cluster,** points of the sequence. Now, if we had a way in which we could determine more or less routinely the "largest" and "smallest" such point, then we would have a routine way of establishing whether the limit of a given sequence exists and, if it does, of identifying it.

Definition 6. Let $\{a_n : n \geq 1\}$ be a sequence of real numbers and put

$$b_n = \sup_{k \geq n} a_k, \quad c_n = \inf_{k \geq n} a_k.$$

Then, the sequences $\{b_n : n \geq 1\}$, $\{c_n : n \geq 1\}$ are, respectively, monotone nonincreasing and nondecreasing, and their limits are said to be the **limit superior** and **limit inferior** of the original sequence and are denoted, respectively, by

$$\limsup, \quad \liminf \quad \text{or} \quad \overline{\lim}, \quad \underline{\lim}.$$

Thus, we write

$$\lim_{n \to \infty} b_n = \lim_{n \to \infty} \sup_{k \geq n} a_k,$$

$$\lim_{n \to \infty} c_n = \lim_{n \to \infty} \inf_{k \geq n} a_k.$$

We immediately have

Proposition 2. Let $\{a_n : n \geq 1\}$ be a sequence of real numbers; then,

$$\limsup a_n \geq \liminf a_n.$$

Proof: Let

$$b_n = \sup_{k \geq n} a_k, \quad c_n = \inf_{k \geq n} a_k.$$

It is evident, by construction, that

$$b_n \geq c_n, \text{ for all } n. \tag{1.1}$$

Consequently,

$$\limsup a_n = \lim b_n \geq \lim c_n = \liminf a_n.$$

The validity of the preceding rests on the validity of the middle inequality; the latter in turn is implied by equation (1). For, suppose not; then, we can find $\epsilon \geq 0$ such that

$$b + \epsilon \leq c - \epsilon,$$

where, of course,

$$b = \lim b_n, \quad c = \lim c_n.$$

We may now select subsequences, say

$$\{b_{n_1} : b_{n_1} < b + \epsilon, \quad \text{for all} \quad n_1 \geq N_1\},$$

$$\{c_{n_2} : c_{n_2} > c - \epsilon, \quad \text{for all} \quad n_2 \geq N_2\},$$

and note that for all $n \geq N$, where $N \geq \max(N_1, N_2)$, we have, for the elements of the subsequences above,

$$b_n < b + \epsilon \leq c - \epsilon < c_n.$$

But, this states that there are infinitely many elements for which

$$b_n < c_n.$$

This is a contradiction.

q.e.d.

Definition 7. Let $\{a_n : n \geq 1\}$ be a sequence of real numbers; then, its limit exists, if and only if

$$\limsup a_n = \liminf a_n,$$

and it (the limit) is defined to be their common value.

Let us now consider sequences whose elements are sets, i.e., subsets of Ω.

Definition 8. Let $\{A_n : n \geq 1, \ A_n \subset \Omega\}$; define

$$B_n = \bigcup_{k=n}^{\infty} A_k, \quad C_n = \bigcap_{k=n}^{\infty} A_k,$$

and note that $\{B_n : n \geq 1\}$, $\{C_n : n \geq 1\}$ are, respectively, monotone nonincreasing and monotone nondecreasing. Let

$$A^* = \lim_{n \to \infty} B_n, \quad A_* = \lim_{n \to \infty} C_n,$$

where, for a monotone nonincreasing sequence,

$$\lim_{n \to \infty} B_n = \bigcap_{n=1}^{\infty} B_n,$$

and for a monotone nondecreasing sequence

$$\lim_{n \to \infty} C_n = \bigcup_{n=1}^{\infty} C_n.$$

Then, the **limit superior** of the sequence is defined to be A^*, the **limit inferior** of the sequence is defined to be A_*, and the limit of the sequence exists if and only if

$$A^* = A_* = A.$$

Moreover, we have the notation

$$\lim_{n \to \infty} \sup_{k \geq n} A_k = A^*, \quad \text{or} \quad \overline{\lim_{n \to \infty}} A_n = A^*,$$

$$\lim_{n \to \infty} \inf_{k \geq n} A_k = A_*, \quad \text{or} \quad \underline{\lim}_{n \to \infty} A_n = A_*,$$

and, whenever $A^* = A_* = A$,

$$\lim A_n = A.$$

Remark 4. The intuitive meaning of A^* is that if $\omega \in A^*$ then ω belongs to infinitely many sets, A_n, a fact also denoted by the notation

$$A^* = \{\omega : \omega \in A_n , \ i.o.\},$$

the abbreviation, *i.o.*, meaning **infinitely often**. To see this, pick any element $\omega \in A^*$; evidently, ω must belong to at least one set A_n; let this occur first for $n = n_1$, and consider B_n, for $n = n_1 + 1$. Clearly, this set, B_n, does not contain A_n, for $n = n_1$; however, since it must contain ω, there must be another set, say A_n, for $n = n_2 > n_1$, that contains ω. Continuing in this fashion, we can show that the elements of A^* are contained in infinitely many sets A_n.

Remark 5. The set A_* has the intuitive interpretation that its elements belong to all, except possibly a finite number, of the sets of the sequence. To see why this is so, note that if $\omega \in A_*$, then there exists an index, say n_0, such that for all $n \geq n_0$, $\omega \in A_n$.

We close this section with

Proposition 3. $A^* \supset A_*$.

Proof: Evidently, by construction,

$$B_n \supset C_n, \quad \text{for all} \quad n.$$

Thus,

$$A^* = \lim_{n \to \infty} B_n \supset \lim_{n \to \infty} C_n = A_*.$$

q.e.d.

1.4   Measurable Spaces, Algebras, and Sets

In previous sections, we introduced the abstract space Ω and dealt with operations on sets, which are subsets of Ω. Here, we wish to impart some structure on the class of subsets under consideration. Thus, we introduce

Definition 9. Let $\mathcal{A}$ be a nonempty class of subsets of Ω; then, $\mathcal{A}$ is said to be an algebra if

   i. for any $A \in \mathcal{A}$, we also have $\bar{A} \in \mathcal{A}$;

   ii. for any $A_i \in \mathcal{A}$, $i = 1, 2$, $A_1 \cup A_2 \in \mathcal{A}$.

Remark 6. A few implications of the definition of an algebra are worth pointing out. Since an algebra is a nonempty class of subsets of Ω, it contains at least one set, say A; since it is closed under complementation, it also contains the complement of A, in Ω. Since it is also closed under (finite) unions, it also contains the union of A and its complement; this is, of course, Ω! But, the complement of Ω, in Ω, is the null set, $\emptyset$. Thus, **any algebra must contain** the pair $(\Omega, \emptyset)$; moreover, one can easily verify that a class consisting solely of this pair is, indeed, an algebra.

Remark 7. Notice also that an algebra, $\mathcal{A}$, is closed under finite intersections as well. To see this, observe that if the sets A_i, $i = 1, 2, \ldots, n$, are in $\mathcal{A}$ then

$$\bigcup_{i=1}^{n} A_i \in \mathcal{A},$$

and consequently, since an algebra is closed under complementation,

$$\overline{\bigcup_{i=1}^{n} A_i} = \bigcap_{i=1}^{n} \bar{A}_i \in \mathcal{A}.$$

Remark 8. We may render the description of an algebra, verbally, as a nonempty class of subsets of Ω that is closed under complementation, finite unions, and intersections.

Definition 10. A nonempty class of subsets of Ω, say $\mathcal{A}$, is said to be a σ-algebra if

i. it is an algebra and, in addition,

ii. it is closed under countable unions, i.e., if $A_i \in \mathcal{A}$, $i \geq 1$, then $\bigcup_{i=1}^{\infty} A_i \in \mathcal{A}$.

Definition 11. Let Ω be a space and $\mathcal{A}$ a σ-algebra of subsets of Ω; the pair, $(\Omega, \mathcal{A})$, is said to be a **measurable space**, and the sets of $\mathcal{A}$ are said to be the **measurable sets**.

Remark 9. If Ω is the real line (in this case it is typically denoted by R) and $\mathcal{A}$ the σ-algebra generated by the open intervals (a, b), where a, b are real numbers, then $\mathcal{A}$ is said to be a **Borel σ-algebra** and is usually denoted by $\mathcal{B}$. The sets in $\mathcal{B}$ are said to be the **Borel sets**. The measurable space $(R, \mathcal{B})$ is typically referred to as a **Borel space** or a **one-dimensional Borel space**.

Definition 12. Let Ω_i , $i = 1, 2$, be two spaces; a function

$$X : \Omega_1 \longrightarrow \Omega_2$$

is a relation that associates to each element $\omega_1 \in \Omega_1$ an element, say $\omega_2 \in \Omega_2$, i.e., $X(\omega_1) = \omega_2$.

Definition 13. Let X, Ω_i, $i = 1, 2$, be as in Definition 12 and $A \subset \Omega_1$. The set (in Ω_2)

$$B = \{\omega_2 : \omega_2 = X(\omega_1), \ \omega_1 \in A\}$$

is said to be the **image** of A under X. Conversely, take any set $B \subset \Omega_2$. Then, the set (in Ω_1)

$$A = \{\omega_1 : \omega_1 = X^{-1}(\omega_2), \ \omega_2 \in B\}$$

is said to be the **inverse image** of B under X, and we have the notation

$$X(A) = B \ \text{ and } \ X^{-1}(B) = A,$$

i.e., B is the image of A under X, and A is the inverse image of B, under X.

The following question now arises: If $(\Omega_i, \ \mathcal{A}_i)$, $i = 1, 2$, are two measurable spaces and X is a function,

$$X : \Omega_1 \longrightarrow \Omega_2,$$

what can we say about the image of $\mathcal{A}_1$ under X and/or the inverse image of $\mathcal{A}_2$ under X? Denoting these entities by $X(\mathcal{A}_1)$, $X^{-1}(\mathcal{A}_2)$, respectively, we have

Proposition 4. Let $(\Omega_i, \ \mathcal{A}_i)$, $i = 1, 2$, be measurable spaces and suppose

$$X : \Omega_1 \longrightarrow \Omega_2.$$

Then, $X^{-1}(\mathcal{A}_2)$ is a σ-algebra on Ω_1, while $X(\mathcal{A}_1)$ is a σ-algebra on Ω_2, only if X is one to one and onto.

Proof: Let $\mathcal{A} = \{A : A = X^{-1}(B), \ B \in \mathcal{A}_2\}$ and suppose $A_i \in \mathcal{A}$, $i \geq 1$; we shall show that the complement and countable union of such sets are also in $\mathcal{A}$, thus showing that the latter is a σ-algebra. This, however, is quite evident, since if $A_i = X^{-1}(B_i)$, $i \geq 1$, for $B_i \in \mathcal{A}_2$, $i \geq 1$, then $\bigcup_{i=1}^{\infty} B_i \in \mathcal{A}_2$, as well. Consequently, $\bigcup_{i=1}^{\infty} A_i = \bigcup_{i=1}^{\infty} X^{-1}(B_i) = X^{-1}(\bigcup_{i=1}^{\infty} B_i)$, which shows that $\bigcup_{i=1}^{\infty} A_i \in \mathcal{A}$. Moreover, since $\overline{X^{-1}(B_i)} = X^{-1}(\bar{B_i})$, the proof of the first part of the proposition is complete.

As for the second part, to appreciate the need for the additional conditions, consider X such that it maps Ω_1 into a set $B \subset \Omega_2$. In such a case $B \in X(\mathcal{A}_1)$, but $\bar{B} \notin X(\mathcal{A}_1)$.' If X, however is **onto**, i.e., its range is Ω_2, and one to one, i.e., if for every $B \in \mathcal{A}_2$ there is one set, say $A \in \mathcal{A}_1$ such that $X(A) = B$ and if $X(\mathcal{A}_1) = X(\mathcal{A}_2)$, then $\mathcal{A}_1 = \mathcal{A}_2$, we may put forth the following argument. Let

$$\mathcal{C} = \{B : B = X(A), \ A \in \mathcal{A}_1\}$$

and suppose $B_i \in \mathcal{C}$, $i \geq 1$. We show that the the countable union and complements of such sets are also in $\mathcal{C}$. For each $B_i \in \mathcal{C}$, $i \geq 1$, there exist $A_i \in \mathcal{A}_1$, $i \geq 1$, such that $X(A_i) = B_i$. Since $A = \bigcup_{i=1}^{\infty} A_i \in \mathcal{A}_1$ and since $X(A) = \bigcup_{i=1}^{\infty} X(A_i) = \bigcup_{i=1}^{\infty} B_i = B$, we conclude that $B \in \mathcal{C}$. Moreover, since $\bar{B_i} = \overline{X(A_i)} = X(\bar{A_i})$, we conclude that $\bar{B_i} \in \mathcal{C}$.

q.e.d.

We now have

Definition 14. Let $(\Omega_i, \mathcal{A}_i)$, $i = 1, 2$, be measurable spaces and let

$$X : \Omega_1 \longrightarrow \Omega_2.$$

Then, X is said to be a **measurable** function, or $\mathcal{A}_1$-measurable, if and only if

$$X^{-1}(\mathcal{A}_2) \subset \mathcal{A}_1.$$

The connection between the mathematical concepts above and econometrics is, perhaps, most obvious in the following definition.

Definition 15. Let $(\Omega, \mathcal{A})$, $(R, \mathcal{B})$ be two measurable spaces, where R is the extended real line and $\mathcal{B}$ is the Borel σ-algebra. A random variable, X, is a function,

$$X : \Omega \longrightarrow R,$$

such that $X^{-1}(\mathcal{B}) \subset \mathcal{A}$, i.e., a **random variable is a real valued measurable function.**

A natural question of interest is: if X is a random variable, then what sort of "functions of X" are random variables? For example, if X is a random variable, are functions like $\sin X$, X^n, $\log X$, e^X, etc., also random variables? This is answered by

Proposition 5. Let $(\Omega,\ \mathcal{A})$, $(R,\ \mathcal{B})$ be measurable spaces and

$$X : \Omega \longrightarrow R$$

be as in Definition 15; let

$$\phi : R \longrightarrow R$$

be a $\mathcal{B}$-measurable function. Then,

$$\psi = \phi \circ X : \Omega \longrightarrow R$$

is a random variable (i.e., a measurable function), where

$$\psi(\omega) = \phi[X(\omega)].$$

Proof: We shall show that $\psi^{-1}(\mathcal{B}) \subset \mathcal{A}$. Let C be any set in $\mathcal{B}$; since ϕ is $\mathcal{B}$-measurable there exists a set, say $B \in \mathcal{B}$, such that $\phi^{-1}(C) = B$. On the other hand, since X is $\mathcal{A}$-measurable, there exists a set $A \in \mathcal{A}$ such that $X^{-1}(B) = A$. Consequently, for any set $C \in \mathcal{B}$, we have $\psi^{-1}(C) = X^{-1}[\phi^{-1}(C)] \in \mathcal{A}$. Thus, $\psi^{-1}(\mathcal{B}) \subset \mathcal{A}$.

q.e.d.

The result above is, also, applicable for functions that are defined over **sequences** of random variables. Since for the typical student in econometrics these functions are unfamiliar, we present an explicit discussion of them.

Proposition 6. Let $(\Omega,\ \mathcal{A})$, $(R,\ \mathcal{B})$ be measurable spaces, and let

$$X_n : \Omega \longrightarrow R,\ n \geq 1$$

be random variables. Then, the following are random variables, i.e., they are $\mathcal{A}$-measurable functions from Ω to R:

   i. $X_N^* = \sup_{n \leq N} X_n, \quad Y^* = \sup_n X_n$;

   ii. $X_{*N} = \inf_{n \leq N} X_n, \quad Y_* = \inf_n X_n$;

   iii. $Y_n = \sup_{k \geq n} X_k, \quad Z_n = \inf_{k \geq n} X_k$;

   iv. $X^* = \limsup X_n, \quad X_* = \liminf X_n$;

   v. $X^+ = \max(0, X), \quad X^- = \max(0, -X)$.

Proof: What is required here is to prove, in each case, that the inverse image of $\mathcal{B}$, under the appropriate function, is contained in $\mathcal{A}$; this will show that the corresponding function, say X_N^*, Y^*, X_*, Y_n, Z_n, etc., is measurable and, thus, a random variable according to Definition 15. Now, it can be shown that sets of the form (b, ∞), $b \in R$, generate $\mathcal{B}$, in the sense that the latter is simply the collection of complements, countable unions, and intersections, as well as limits of sequences of such sets. Consequently, if we can show that the inverse image of such sets (under the functions i. through iv. above) lies in $\mathcal{A}$, then we will have accomplished our task.

   To prove i., define

$$A_n = \{\omega : X_n(\omega) > b, \quad b \in R\}, \quad n = 1, 2, ..., N,$$

$$A_{1N} = \{\omega : X_N^*(\omega) > b, \quad b \in R,\}$$

$$A_{0N} = \bigcup_{n=1}^{N} A_n.$$

We shall now show that $A_{1N} = A_{0N}$, thus showing that X_N^* is measurable. Suppose $\omega \in A_{0N}$; then, for at least one n, $X_n(\omega) > b$. Since $X_N^*(\omega) \geq X_n(\Omega)$ for all n, we conclude that $\omega \in A_{1N}$; hence, $A_{0N} \subset A_{1N}$. Next, suppose that $\omega \in \bar{A}_{0N}$; this implies that $X_n(\omega) \leq b$ for all $n \leq N$. Consequently, $\omega \in \bar{A}_{1N}$, and thus, $\bar{A}_{0N} \subset \bar{A}_{1N}$. But this implies $A_{0N} = A_{1N}$, which completes the proof of i., since the argument for $\sup X_n$ is exactly the same, even though it involves a countable, instead of a finite, union.

To prove ii., define $A_{2N} = \bigcap_{n=1}^{N} A_n$ and $A_{3N} = \{\omega : X_{*N}(\omega) > b, \ b \in R\}$. We will show that $A_{2N} = A_{3N}$, thus showing that $A_{3N} \in \mathcal{A}$ and hence that X_{*N} is $\mathcal{A}$-measurable. Suppose $\omega \in A_{2N}$; then, $X_n(\omega) > b$ for all n. Consequently, $X_{*N}(\omega) > b$, which implies that $\omega \in A_{3N}$, and thus, $A_{2N} \subset A_{3N}$. Next, suppose that $\omega \in \bar{A}_{2N}$; this means that for some $n \leq N$, $X_n(\omega) \leq b$ and hence that $X_{*N}(\omega) \leq b$. Consequently, we must have $\bar{A}_{2N} \subset \bar{A}_{3N}$ or $A_{2N} \supset A_{3N}$. This proves ii., since the proof for $\inf_n X_n$ is exactly the same, except that instead of dealing with finite intersections we should be dealing with countable intersections.

To prove iii., define

$$B_n = \bigcup_{k=n}^{\infty} A_k, \quad B_n^* = \{\omega : Y_n(\omega) > b, \ b \in R\}.$$

We will show that $B_n = B_n^*$. Let $\omega \in B_n$; then, for some $k \geq n$, $X_k(\omega) > b$; hence, $Y_n(\omega) > b$, and consequently, $B_n \subset B_n^*$. Conversely, suppose $\omega \in \bar{B}_n$; then, for all $k \geq n$, $X_k(\omega) \leq b$; hence, $Y_n(\omega) \leq b$, which implies $\omega \in \bar{B}_n^*$. Thus, $\bar{B}_n \subset \bar{B}_n^*$, and consequently, $B_n \supset B_n^*$. This means that $B_n = B_n^*$.

For the second part of iii., define

$$C_n = \bigcap_{k=n}^{\infty} A_k, \quad C_n^* = \{\omega : Z_n(\omega) > b, \ b \in R\},$$

and let $\omega \in C_n$; then, for all $k \geq n$, $X_k(\omega) > b$; hence, $Z_n(\omega) > b$, which shows that $C_n \subset C_n^*$. Conversely, suppose $\omega \in \bar{C}_n$; then, for at least one $k \geq n$, $X_k(\omega) \leq b$. Hence, $Z_n(\omega) \leq b$, which means that $\omega \in \bar{C}_n^*$; thus, $\bar{C}_n \subset \bar{C}_n^*$ or, equivalently, $C_n \supset C_n^*$, which establishes that $C_n = C_n^*$.

To prove iv., it is sufficient to define

$$B = \bigcap_{n=1}^{\infty} B_n, \quad A^* = \{\omega : X^*(\omega) > b, \ b \in R\},$$

$$C = \bigcup_{n=1}^{\infty} C_n, \quad A_* = \{\omega : X_*(\omega) > b, \ b \in R\},$$

and to show that $B = A^*$, $C = A_*$. Now, if $\omega \in B$, then, for all n, $Y_n(\omega) > b$ and, consequently, $\omega \in A^*$; this means that $B \subset A^*$. Next, suppose that $\omega \in \bar{B}$; then, for at least one value of the index n, $Y_n(\omega) \leq b$. Consequently, $X^*(\omega) \leq b$, which shows that $\omega \in \bar{A}^*$. Hence, $\bar{B} \subset \bar{A}^*$, or $B \supset A^*$, which shows that $B = A_*$.

The proof that $C = A_*$ is entirely similar and is omitted in the interest of brevity.

To prove v., it is sufficient to prove only the first part. To that end, define, for $b \in R$,

$$A^+(b) = \{\omega : X^+(\omega) > b\}, \quad A(b) = \{\omega : X(\omega) > b\}.$$

For $b \geq 0$, $A^+(b) \subseteq A(b)$, while for $b < 0$, $A^+(b) = \Omega$. In either case, $A^+(b) \in \mathcal{A}$, which shows that X^+ is $\mathcal{A}$-measurable, i.e., it is a random variable.

q.e.d.

We close this section with two clarifications, whose meaning will become clear in the ensuing sections — although this is the natural place to present them.

Remark 10. The results of Propositions 5 and 6, although stated in terms of (scalar) random variables, are also applicable to vector random variables. For example, if $\{X_n : n \geq 1\}$ is a sequence of random variables and ϕ is a suitably measurable vector valued function, i.e., ϕ has, say k components, $(\phi_i : i = 1, 2, ..., k)$, then $\phi(Z_n)$ is also a random variable (vector), where $Z_n = (X_1, X_2, \ldots, X_n)$. In the literature of probability theory, entities like random vectors are referred to as *random elements*. We shall have occasion to study certain aspects of random elements in chapter 4.

Remark 11. The following convention will be observed throughout this volume: unless otherwise specified, a random variable will always mean an **a.c. finite random variable,** to be read as: an almost certainly finite random variable. Formally, what this means is that if X is a random variable and we define

$$A = \{\omega : \mid X(\omega) \mid = \infty\}$$

then $P(A) = 0$, where $P(\cdot)$ is the probability measure. What this means, roughly speaking, is that the probability of the random variable assuming the values $\pm\infty$ is zero. **All random variables routinely dealt with in econometrics are a.c. finite random variables and thus, no restriction is entailed by the adherence to the convention above.**

1.5   Measures and Probability Measures

1.5.1   Measures and Measurable Functions

Definition 16. Let Ω be a space and $\mathcal{A}$ be a nonempty class of subsets of Ω. A relation, μ, that associates with each set of $\mathcal{A}$ a real number is said to be a **set function**; thus,

$$\mu : \mathcal{A} \to R.$$

If for every $A \in \mathcal{A}$, $|\mu(A)| < \infty$ then, the set function, μ, is said to be finite.

Definition 17. Let $A \subset \Omega$ and suppose there exist pairwise disjoint sets A_i, i.e., $A_i \cap A_j = \emptyset$ for $i \neq j$, such that $A = \cup_{i=1}^n A_i$, then the collection

$$\mathcal{C}_n = \{A_i : i = 1, 2, \ldots, n\}$$

is said to be a **finite partition** of A in $\mathcal{A}$. If the collection above is countably infinite, i.e.,

$$\mathcal{C} = \{A_i : i \geq 1\},$$

the constituent sets are disjoint, and $A = \cup_{i=1}^\infty A_i$, then $\mathcal{C}$ is said to be a σ-partition of A in $\mathcal{A}$.

Definition 18. Let A and its partitions be as in Definition 17, and let μ be a finite set function as in Definition 16. Then, μ is said to be **finitely additive** if for any finite partition of A, say $\mathcal{C}_n$,

$$\mu(A) = \sum_{i=1}^n \mu(A_i).$$

If for any σ-partition of A, say $\mathcal{C}$,

$$\mu(A) = \sum_{i=1}^{\infty} \mu(A_i),$$

the set function μ is said to be σ-**additive**, provided the right member above is finite.

Definition 19. Let Ω, $\mathcal{A}$, and μ be as in Definition 16; the set function μ is said to be a **measure** if and only if

i. $\mu(\emptyset) = 0$;

ii. $\mu(A) \geq 0$, for any $A \in \mathcal{A}$;

iii. if $\mathcal{C}$, as in Definition 17, is a σ-partition (in $\mathcal{A}$) of a set $A \subset \Omega$, then

$$\mu(A) = \sum_{i=1}^{n} \mu(A_i).$$

Moreover, if μ is a measure and in addition $\mu(\Omega) = 1$, then μ is said to be a **probability measure**, or simply a **probability**, and is denoted by $P(\cdot)$.

Remark 12. To summarize the essentials: if Ω is a space and $\mathcal{A}$ a nonempty collection of its subsets containing at least $\emptyset$ and Ω, then a probability measure, or simply a probability $P(\cdot)$, is a real valued nonnegative nondecreasing set function, such that $P(\emptyset) = 0$, $P(\Omega) = 1$.

Definition 20. Let Ω be a space, $\mathcal{A}$ a σ-algebra of subsets of Ω, and μ a measure defined on $\mathcal{A}$. Then, the triplet $(\Omega, \mathcal{A}, \mu)$ is said to be a **measure space**; if μ is a probability, then the triplet $(\Omega, \mathcal{A}, P)$ is said to be a **probability space**.

Now that we have introduced measure spaces, it is desirable to elaborate, somewhat, on the concept of measurable functions. We have already defined measurable functions in an earlier section, in the context of two measurable spaces. The requirement imposed by that definition is that the inverse image of the σ-algebra of the range space be contained in the σ-algebra of the domain space. Thus, in order to exploit or establish the measurability of a function, we must rely on the fact that sets in the **range** σ-algebra have inverse images in the **domain** σ-algebra. Conseqently, it would be useful to establish just what kinds of sets in the range space have inverse images, under a measurable function, that belong to the domain σ-algebra. To this end, we have

Proposition 7. Let f be an extended real valued function, i.e., f may assume the values $\pm\infty$,

$$f : \Omega \longrightarrow R,$$

where the domain space is $(\Omega,\ \mathcal{A})$, and the range space is $(R,\ \mathcal{B})$. Then, the following statements are equivalent:

i. for each $a \in R$, the set

$$A = \{\omega : f(\omega) > a\}$$

is measurable;

ii. for each $a \in R$, the set

$$B = \{\omega : f(\omega) \geq a\}$$

is measurable;

iii. for each $b \in R$, the set

$$C = \{\omega : f(\omega) < b\}$$

is measurable;

iv. for each $b \in R$, the set

$$D = \{\omega : f(\omega) \leq b\}$$

is measurable.

Moreover, statements i. through iv. imply that for each **extended** real number, c, (i.e., one allows $c = \pm\infty$), the set

$$E = \{\omega : f(\omega) = c\}$$

is measurable.

Proof: It is evident that since the sets in i. are the complements of the corresponding sets in iv., and vice-versa, and $\mathcal{A}$ is a σ-algebra, then i. is true if and only if iv. is true; similarly, ii. is true if and only if iii. is true. Thus, to complete the proof of the first part of the proposition, we need only show that i. is true if and only if ii. is true. To this end, define the sets

$$A_n = \{\omega : f(\omega) > a - \frac{1}{n}, \ n = 1, 2, \ldots\}$$

and note that

$$B = \bigcap_{n=1}^{\infty} A_n,$$

which proves that i. implies ii. To prove that ii. implies i., define

$$B_n = \{\omega : f(\omega) \geq a + \frac{1}{n}, \ n = 1, 2, \ldots\},$$

and note that

$$A = \bigcup_{n=1}^{\infty} B_n.$$

As for the last statement of the proposition, note that if $a \in R$ is finite, and $c = b = a$, then $E = B \cap D$, and since B and D are measurable, then so is E. If $a = \infty$, then $E = \cap_{n=1}^{\infty} A_n^*$, where $A_n^* = \{\omega : f(\omega) \geq n\}$, $n = 1, 2, \ldots$. If $a = -\infty$, then $E = \cap_{n=1}^{\infty} D_n^*$, where $D_n = \{\omega : f(\omega) \leq -n\}, n = 1, 2 \ldots$. Since, the sets A_n^*, D_n^*, $n = 1, 2, \ldots$, are measurable, it follows that E is measurable whether a is finite or not.

q.e.d.

Proposition 8. Let $(\Omega, \ \mathcal{A})$, $(R, \ \mathcal{B})$ be measurable spaces and let $\{f_n.n \geq 1\}$, be a sequence of measurable functions

$$f_n : \Omega \longrightarrow R.$$

Then the following statements are true:

   i. if $c \in R$, then cf_n and $c + f_n$ are measurable;

   ii. for any n, m, $f_n + f_m$, $f_n - f_m$, and $f_n f_m$, are measurable;

   iii. the functions f_n^+, f_n^-, for all n are measurable, as are $\mid f_n \mid = f_n^+ + f_n^-$, where $f_n^+ = \max(0, \ f_n)$, $f_n^- = \max(0, -f_n)$;

iv. the functions

$$\sup_{n \leq N} f_n, \ \sup_{n \geq 1} f_n, \ \limsup_{n \to \infty} f_n$$

are measurable;

v. the functions

$$\inf_{n \leq N} f_n, \ \inf_{n \geq 1} f_n, \ \liminf_{n \to \infty} f_n$$

are measurable.

Proof: The proof of this proposition is left as an exercise for the reader, in view of the discussion in Propositions 5 and 6.

Definition 21. Let $(\Omega, \ \mathcal{A})$, $(R, \ \mathcal{B})$ be measurable spaces and

$$f : \Omega \to R$$

be a relation. We say that f is **simple** if and only if there exists a finite partition $\{A_i : i = 1, 2, ..., n\}$ of Ω in $\mathcal{A}$, such that

$$f(\omega) = \sum_{i=1}^{n} x_i I_i(\omega), \quad x_i \in R,$$

and $I_i(\cdot)$ is the indicator function of the set A_i, i.e.,

$$
\begin{aligned}
I_i(\omega) \ &= \ 1, \quad \text{if } \omega \in A_i, \ i = 1, 2, \ldots, n \\
&= \ 0, \quad \text{otherwise.}
\end{aligned}
$$

Proposition 9. Let $(\Omega, \mathcal{A}, \mu)$, $(R, \ \mathcal{B})$ be, respectively, a probability space and a (Borel) measurable space and suppose f is a function,

$$f : \Omega \to R.$$

If g is another function,

$$g : \Omega \to R,$$

which is $\mathcal{A}$-measurable and such that $\mu(A) = 0$, with

$$A = \{\omega : f(\omega) \neq g(\omega), \}$$

then f is also measurable and we have the notation, $f = g$ a.c.
(The notation a.c. means "almost certainly"; the notations a.s., to be
read "almost surely", or a.e., to be read "almost everywhere", are also
common in this connection).

Proof: Since $\mathcal{B}$ may be generated by sets of the form $(b, \infty]$, it will
suffice to show that $C \in \mathcal{A}$, for all $c \in R$, where

$$C = \{\omega : f(\omega) > c, \; c \in R\}.$$

Now, since g is measurable, then for any $c \in R$, $B \in \mathcal{A}$, where

$$B = \{\omega : g(\omega) > c, \; c \in R\}.$$

Next, note that we can always write

$$C = (C \cap \bar{A}) \cup (C \cap A).$$

But,

$$C \cap \bar{A} = (B \cap \bar{A}) \in \mathcal{A},$$

$$C \cap A \subset A,$$

and we conclude that for any set in $\mathcal{B}$, say (c, ∞), its inverse image
under f consists of a set in $\mathcal{A}$, viz., $(B \cap \bar{A})$, plus a set with measure
zero, viz., $(C \cap A) \in \mathcal{A}$. This is so since by the nondecreasing property
of measures

$$\mu(C \cap A) \leq \mu(A) = 0.$$

q.e.d.

Another useful fact about measurable functions is worth pointing out at
this stage.

Proposition 10. Let $(R, \mathcal{B}, \mu)$, $(R, \; \mathcal{B})$ be, respectively, a measure
space and a measurable space and let f be a measurable function,

$$f : R \to R,$$

such that for $A = \{\omega : f(\omega) = \pm\infty\}$, we have $\mu(A) = 0$. Then,

i. given any $\epsilon > 0$, however small, there exists $N > 0$ such that $|f| \le N$, except possibly on a set of measure less than ϵ;

ii. given any $\epsilon_1 > 0$, however small, there exists a simple function, g, such that $|f(\omega) - g(\omega)| < \epsilon_1$, except possibly on a set, say A_1, such that $A_1 = \{\omega : |f(\omega)| > N\}$, and $\mu(A_1) < \epsilon_1$;

iii. given any $\epsilon_2 > 0$, however small, there exists a continuous function, h, such that $|f(\omega) - h(\omega)| < \epsilon_2$, except possibly on a set, say $A_2 = \{\omega : |f(\omega) - h(\omega)| \ge \epsilon_2\}$, such that $\mu(A_2) < \epsilon_2$.

Proof: Define the sets $A_n = \{\omega : |f(\omega)| > n, n \ge 1\}$. By the conditions of the proposition,

$$\lim_{n \to \infty} \mu(A_n) = 0.$$

Hence, given $\epsilon > 0$, there exists n_0 such that for all $n \ge n_0$, $\mu(A_n) < \epsilon$. Choose $N > n_0$; then, $|f(\omega)| \le N$, except possibly on the set A_N, with $\mu(A_N) < \epsilon$.

To prove ii., suppose, without loss of generality, that there exist numbers, m, M such that $m < f(\omega) < M$ (this is possible by i.). Put $d = (M - m)/n$ such that $d < \epsilon_1$, and define

$$y_0 = m, \quad y_i = y_0 + di, \quad i = 1, 2, \ldots, n$$

$$B_i = \{\omega : y_i \le y_{i+1}\}, \quad i = 0, 1, 2, \ldots, n-1,$$

$$g(\omega) = \sum_{i=0}^{n-1} y_i I_i(\omega),$$

where I_i is the indicator function for B_i, i.e., $I_i(\omega) = 1$, if $\omega \in B_i$, and is equal to zero otherwise. By construction, g is a simple function; moreover, for any ω such that $m < f(\omega) < M$, we have that

$$f(\omega) - g(\omega) \le \epsilon_1.$$

To prove iii., note that if g is the simple function of ii. and h is the desired continuous function, then since

$$|f(\omega) - h(\omega)| \le |f(\omega) - g(\omega)| + |g(\omega) - h(\omega)|,$$

it will suffice to show that if g is a simple function, there exists a continuous function, say h, which approximates it, arbitrarily closely. Now, consider again the sets B_i of ii. above and suppose they are simple disjoint intervals, as, in fact, they would be if f were specified to be a **simple** function. For these sets, define

$$\omega_i^* = \sup_{\omega \in B_i} \omega, \quad \omega_{*i+1} = \inf_{\omega \in B_{i+1}} \omega,$$

and, for $\omega \in (x_{i1}, x_{i2})$, define the function h by

$$
\begin{aligned}
h(\omega) &= y_i + (y_{i+1} - y_i)/(x_{i2} - x_{i1})(\omega - x_{i1}), \\
&\quad \text{where } x_{i1} = \omega_i^* - \delta, \ x_{i2} = \omega_{*i+1} + \delta, \\
&= y_i, \text{ for } \omega \in B_i \text{ and } \omega \leq x_{i1}, \\
&= y_{i+1}, \text{ for } \omega \in B_{i+1} \text{ and } \omega > x_{i2}.
\end{aligned}
$$

It is apparent that, thus defined, h is a continuous function and for $m < f(\omega) < M$, we have

$$\mid f(\omega) - h(\omega) \mid \ \leq \ \mid f(\omega) - g(\omega) \mid + \mid g(\omega) - h(\omega) \mid < 2\epsilon_1.$$

If the B_i above are not intervals, they may, of course, be expressed as countable unions of intervals, say D_i, $i \geq 1$. Consequently, we may rewrite the function g in the required form,

$$g(\omega) = \sum_{i=1}^{\infty} z_i I_i(\omega),$$

where, now, I_i is the indicator function of the set D_i, and the z_i need no longer be distinct. Repeating the argument with g as just expressed above, we obtain the desired result, since now the D_i are contiguous disjoint intervals.

q.e.d.

Remark 13. The preceding discussion may be summarized loosely as follows. Any function that is closely approximated by a measurable function is measurable; measurable functions that are almost bounded, i.e., the set over which they assume the values, say $f(\omega) = \pm\infty$, has measure zero, can be closely approximated by bounded functions. Measurable functions that are bounded can be approximated, arbitrarily closely, by simple functions, i.e., functions that are constant over the sets of a finite (or countable) partition of the space. Finally, bounded measurable functions defined on $(R, \mathcal{B})$ are "almost" continuous, i.e., they can be arbitrarily closely approximated by continuous functions.

We are now in a position to deal with integration in measure spaces.

1.6 Integration

We begin with a brief review of the **Riemann integral**. It is assumed that the reader is thoroughly familiar with the Riemann integral, the point of the review being to set forth notation and the context of the discussion. Let

$$f : R \longrightarrow R$$

and let it be desired to find the **integral** of f over the interval $[a, b] \subset (-\infty, +\infty)$. To this effect, partition the interval

$$a = x_0 < x_1 < x_2 < \cdots < x_n = b,$$

put

$$c_i = \inf_{x \in (x_i,\ x_{i+1})} f(x), \quad C_i = \sup_{x \in (x_i,\ x_{i+1})} f(x), \quad i = 0, 1, 2, \ldots, n-1,$$

and define the sums

$$s_R = \sum_{i=0}^{n-1} c_i \Delta x_{i+1}, \quad S_R = \sum_{i=0}^{n-1} C_i \Delta x_{i+1},$$

with $\Delta x_{i+1} = x_{i+1} - x_i$. Take

$$\bar{s}_R = \sup s_R, \quad \underline{S}_R = \inf S_R,$$

where sup and inf are taken over all possible partitions of $[a, b]$. The entities $\bar{s}_R,\ \underline{S}_R$ always exist and, evidently, $\bar{s}_R \le \underline{S}_R$.

We say that the **Riemann integral exists**, if and only if $\bar{s}_R = \underline{S}_R$, and we denote the Riemann integral by

$$I_R = \int_a^b f(x)dx.$$

The **Riemann-Stieltjes** (RS) integral is defined similarly, except that f is weighted by another function, say G. Let it be desired to obtain the integral of f with respect to G, over the interval $[a, b]$. To this effect partition the interval as above and obtain the upper and lower sums

$$s_{RS} = \sum_{i=0}^{n-1} c_i [G(x_{i+1}) - G(x_i)], \quad S_{RS} = \sum_{i=0}^{n-1} C_i [G(x_{i+1}) - G(x_i)].$$

Again, determine the sup and inf of these quantities over all possible partitions of the interval, thus obtaining

$$\bar{s}_{RS} = \sup s_{RS}, \quad \underline{S}_{RS} = \inf \underline{S}_{RS}.$$

If

$$\bar{s}_{RS} = \underline{S}_{RS},$$

we say that the Riemann-Stieltjes integral exists, and we denote it by

$$I_{RS} = \int_a^b f(x) \, dG(x).$$

Remark 14. Note that if G is differentiable with derivative g then the RS integral reduces to the ordinary Riemann integral

$$I_R = \int_a^b f(x) g(x) dx.$$

To tie the development above with the discussion to follow, let us give the RS integral a slightly different formulation. Thus, we deal with the problem of defining the integral of f over $[a, b]$, and we subdivide the interval by the points,

$$a = x_0 < x_1 < x_2 < \ldots < x_n = b.$$

On these subintervals, we then define the **step functions**

$$f_n(x) = c_i, \quad F_n(x) = C_i, \quad x \in (x_i, \quad x_{i+1}), \quad i = 0, 1, 2, \cdots, n - 1,$$

where c_i and C_i, are as above; i.e., they represent, respectively, the inf and sup of f over the subinterval (x_i, x_{i+1}). It is easily verified that, by construction,

$$f_n(x) \le f(x), \quad F_n(x) \ge f(x), \quad \text{for all } x \in [a, b].$$

Moreover, in terms of the definition of **any** integral, it certainly makes sense to write

$$\sum_{i=0}^{n-1} c_i \Delta x_{i+1} = \int_a^b f_n(x)dx.$$

Similarly, we may put

$$\sum_{i=0}^{n-1} C_i \Delta x_{i+1} = \int_a^b F_n(x)dx.$$

Consequently, in this framework, the Riemann integral may be defined as

$$I_R = \int_a^b f(x)\,dx = \inf_{F_n \geq f} \int_a^b F_n(x)\,dx = \sup_{f_n \leq f} \int_a^b f_n(x)\,dx.$$

A similar idea is employed in the construction of the **Lebesgue** integral in measure space. The context in which we have operated in the preceding section (i.e., the context of abstract measure space) is unnecessarily general from the point of view of a basic review and thus, in discussing the elementary aspects of (Lebesgue) integration, we shall take measure to be Lebesgue outer measure, a concept to be explained below, and we shall take Ω to be the set of real numbers. By way of clarifying the meaning of Lebesgue outer measure, it is sufficient to note, for the moment, that in this context the outer measure of an interval is simply its length. Thus, if μ is measure and (x_i, x_{i+1}) are the (sub) intervals, which we denote conveniently by D_i, then

$$\mu(D_i) = x_{i+1} - x_i.$$

Remark 15. The basic difference between the Riemann and Lebesgue approaches to integration is the following: in the Riemann approach we look at the domain of the function, i.e., the "x-axis" and obtain a finite partition of the domain. Within each (disjoint) interval we choose an appropriate value assumed by the function in this interval. The integral, then, is simply the weighted sum of such values, the weights being functions of the reference (sub) intervals. In the Lebesgue approach we look at the range of the function, i.e., the "y-axis", and obtain a finite partition of it. We then ask: what is the inverse image of each (sub) interval in the range of the function, i.e., what (sub) interval in the domain of the function corresponds to the reference (sub) interval in the range. The integral is then obtained as a weighted sum of the values assumed by the function, the weights being a function of the measure of the (domain) subinterval corresponding to the reference (range) subinterval.

Remark 16. We note that Lebesgue measure may be defined on R as follows. Let A be a subset of R; then its Lebesgue (outer) measure is given by

$$\mu(A) = \inf_{A \subset \cup_{i \in I} D_i} \sum_{i \in I} l(D_i),$$

where I is at most a countable index set; $\{D_i : i \in I\}$ is at most a countable collection of open sets that cover A, i.e., whose union contains A, and $l(D_i)$ indicates the length of an interval, i.e., if, for example, $D_i = (x_i, x_{i+1})$, then, $l(D_i) = x_{i+1} - x_i$.

Note that Lebesgue measure, defined as (essentially) the length of an interval, is not a finite measure according to Definitions 16 through 19. In particular, consider the sets $[-\infty, a)$, $a \in (-\infty, \infty)$, which generate $\mathcal{B}$. The (Lebesgue) measure of such sets is unbounded. On the other hand, if we confine our attention to, say $[-N, N]$, $N < \infty$, measure, defined as length, is clearly finite.

Example 2. This example will help clarify the similarities and differences between the Riemann and Lebesgue approaches to integration. Consider the function f, which is defined to be zero for $x \notin [0, 1]$, while for $x \in [0, 1]$, is defined by

$$
\begin{aligned}
f(x) &= 1, \text{ if } x \text{ is irrational}, \\
&= 0, \text{ otherwise}.
\end{aligned}
$$

One feels intuitively that the integral of this function over $[0, 1]$ must be unity since the set of rationals in $[0, 1]$ is only countably infinite, while the set of irrationals is far larger. If we apply the Riemann definition, obtaining, for example, the partition $a = 0$, $x_1 = (1/n)$, $x_2 = (2/n), \ldots, x_n = 1$, then we find $c_i = 0$, $C_i = 1$ for all i. Thus, for all partitions $s_R \neq S_R$, and consequently, the Riemann integral does not exist. If we follow the Lebesgue approach, then we ask what is the inverse image of $\{0\}$; evidently, this is the set of rationals in the interval $[0, 1]$, i.e., the set of distinct elements in $\{(p/q) : p \leq q,\ p,\ q\ \text{positive integers}\}$. One may show that this set has measure zero, and, consequently, that its complement in $[0, 1]$ has measure one. But, its complement is precisely the inverse image of $\{1\}$ under f. Thus, by the definition of a Lebesgue integral,

$$I_L = 1, \quad \text{since } \mu(A) = 0 \text{ and } \mu(B) = 1,$$

where, evidently, μ denotes the measure, which is here length, and A is the set of rationals in $[0, 1]$, while B is the set of all irrationals in that interval. Let us now examine (Lebesgue) integration in measure space a bit more formally. We remind the reader, however, that when using the term measure we shall mean **Lebesgue outer measure**, and to facilitate this recognition, we shall, in this discussion, designate measure by λ. We shall retain the use of the symbol Ω for the space although it should be clear from the context that when dealing with the elementary concepts of integration we shall have in mind not an abstract space, but R, the set of real numbers.

Definition 22. Let $(\Omega,\ \mathcal{A},\ \lambda)$, $(R,\ \mathcal{B})$ be measure and measurable space, respectively. A function

$$f : \Omega \longrightarrow R$$

is said to be **simple, or elementary**, if there exists a set $A \subset \Omega$, of finite measure, such that $f(\omega) = 0$, for $\omega \notin A$, and there exists a finite partition of A (in $\mathcal{A}$) such that

$$f(\omega) = y_i, \quad \omega \in A_i, \quad \text{and} \quad y_i \neq 0, \quad y_i \neq y_j, \quad \text{for } i \neq j.$$

Definition 23. Let A be a set in the context of Definition 22. The function

$$I_A : \Omega \longrightarrow R$$

such that

$$I_A(\omega) \quad = \quad 1, \quad \text{if } \omega \in A,$$

$$= \quad 0, \quad \text{otherwise},$$

is said to be an **indicator function**, more precisely the indicator function of the set A.

Definition 24. In the context of Definition 22, let f be a simple function such that

$$f(\omega) = 0, \text{ if } \omega \notin A,$$

where A is a set of finite measure. Let $\{A_i : i = 1, 2, \dots, n\}$ be a finite partition of A, in $\mathcal{A}$, let y_i be the (distinct) values assumed by f on A_i and let I_i be the indicator function for A_i. Then, the **canonical representation** of f is given by

$$f(\omega) = \sum_{i=1}^{n} y_i I_i(\omega).$$

Remark 17. In terms of our earlier discussion, it is evident that the Lebesgue integral of the simple function f, above, is $\sum_{i=1}^{n} y_i \lambda(A_i)$, and we have the notation

$$\int_A f d\lambda, \text{ or simply } \int_A f.$$

It is evident from the definitions above that the Lebesgue integral is a linear operator relative to the class of simple functions as is argued in

Proposition 11. Let $(\Omega, \mathcal{A}, \lambda)$, $(R, \mathcal{B})$ be a measure and measurable space, respectively, and suppose f, g are simple functions,

$$f, \ g : \Omega \longrightarrow R,$$

which vanish outside a set $A \in \mathcal{A}$, with $\lambda(A) < \infty$. Then, for $a, \ b \in R$,

$$\int_A (af + bg) d\lambda = a \int_A f d\lambda + b \int_A f \, d\lambda.$$

Moreover, if $f \leq g$, a.e. (almost everywhere), then

$$\int_A f d\lambda \leq \int_A g d\lambda.$$

Proof: Let $\mathcal{P}_A = \{A_i . i = 1, 2, \dots, n\}$, $\mathcal{P}_B = \{B_i . i = 1, 2, \dots, n\}$ be finite partitions of $A \in \mathcal{A}$, corresponding to f and g, respectively, i.e.,

$$f(\omega) = \sum_{i=1}^{n} y_i I_i(\omega), \quad g(\omega) = \sum_{j=1}^{n} z_j I_j^*(\omega),$$

where I_i, $i = 1, 2, \ldots, n$, are the indicator functions of the sets A_i, while I_j^*, $j = 1, 2, \ldots, n$ are indicator functions of the sets B_j, $j = 1, 2, \ldots, n$. Consider now

$$\mathcal{P}_C = \{C_{ij} : C_{ij} = A_i \cap B_j\}$$

and note that this is a finite collection of disjoint sets, owing to the fact that $\mathcal{P}_A$ and $\mathcal{P}_B$ are disjoint collections. Denote, for notational convenience, the sets in $\mathcal{P}_C$ by C_k and write the functions f and g as step functions, where I_k are indicator functions for the sets C_k, $k = 1, 2, \ldots, m$:

$$f(\omega) = \sum_{k=1}^m a_k I_k(\omega), \quad g(\omega) = \sum_{k=1}^m b_k I_k(\omega).$$

Define

$$h(\omega) = af(\omega) + bg(\omega) = \sum_{k=1}^m (aa_k + bb_k) I_k(\omega)$$

and note that this is a step function whose (Lebesgue) integral is given by

$$
\begin{aligned}
\int_A h d\lambda &= \sum_{k=1}^m (aa_k + bb_k)\lambda(B_k) \\
&= a \sum_{k=1}^m a_k \lambda(B_k) + b \sum_{k=1}^m b_k \lambda(B_k) \\
&= a \int_A f\lambda + b \int_A g d\lambda.
\end{aligned}
$$

Now, suppose that $f \le g$, a.e., then $(g - f) \ge 0$, a.e., and $g - f$ is a step function; hence, from the definition of an integral

$$\int_A (g - f) d\lambda \ge 0 \quad \text{or} \quad \int_A f d\lambda \le \int_A g d\lambda.$$

q.e.d.

Remark 18. We recall that a property is said to hold *a.e.* if the set over which it fails to hold has measure zero. Thus, in the proof of the preceding proposition, we "should" have begun our discussion by defining the set

$$D = \{\omega : f(\omega) - g(\omega) > 0\}$$

and restricting the definition of f and g over the set

$$A \cap \bar{D}.$$

Let us now consider the class of bounded functions, i.e., real valued functions defined on a measure space for which there exists a number $M < \infty$, such that $|f(\omega)| \le M$; in this context, it is understood that f vanishes outside a set, say A, of finite measure.

Definition 25. Let $(\Omega, \mathcal{A}, \lambda)$, $(R, \mathcal{B})$ be a measure and measurable space, respectively, and let f be a bounded function,

$$f : \Omega \longrightarrow R,$$

which vanishes outside a set A, for which $\lambda(A) < \infty$. The function f is said to be **integrable** if its integral (over A) exists, i.e., for simple functions f_n, F_n such that

$$f_n(\omega) \le f(\omega) \le F_n(\omega), \quad \omega \in A,$$

we have

$$\sup_n \int_A f_n d\lambda = \inf_n \int_A F_n d\lambda.$$

We now ask what is the class of integrable bounded functions defined over a set of finite measure? This is answered by

Proposition 12. Let f be a bounded function as in Definition 25. Then, f is integrable (over the set A) if and only if f is **measurable**.

Proof: We recall that integrability in this context means

$$\inf_{f \le h} \int_A h \, d\lambda = \sup_{f \ge g} \int_A g d\lambda$$

for all simple functions h and g. Since f is bounded suppose $|f| \le M$. Define the sets, for $k = -n, -n+1, \ldots, 0, 1, 2, \ldots, n$,

$$A_k = \{\omega : \frac{(k-1)M}{n} < f(\omega) \le \frac{kM}{n}\}$$

and note that these sets are measurable. Further, define the simple functions

$$f_n(\omega) = \frac{M}{n} \sum_{k=-n}^{n} (k-1) I_k(\omega),$$

$$F_n(\omega) = \frac{M}{n} \sum_{k=-n}^{n} k I_k(\omega),$$

and note that

$$f_n(\omega) \leq f(\omega) \leq F_n(\omega).$$

Consequently,

$$\int_A f_n d\lambda = \frac{M}{n} \sum_{k=-n}^{n} (k-1)\lambda(A_k), \quad \int_A F_n d\lambda = \frac{M}{n} \sum_{k=-n}^{n} k\lambda(A_k).$$

Hence, if g is any simple function such that $g \leq f$, we have

$$\sup_{g \leq f} \int_A g d\lambda \geq \int_A f_n d\lambda = s,$$

and if h is any function such that $h \geq f$,

$$\inf_{h \geq f} \int_A h d\lambda \leq \int_A F_n d\lambda = S.$$

Thus, $S - s \leq (M/n)\lambda(A)$, which evidently converges to zero with n, and we conclude that

$$\sup_{g \leq f} \int_A g d\lambda = \inf_{h \geq f} \int_A h d\lambda. \tag{1.2}$$

This means, of course, that f is integrable. Next, suppose that equation (1.2) holds; we shall show that f is measurable. Given n, there exist simple functions f_n, F_n, not necessarily those constructed above, such that

$$f_n \leq f \leq F_n, \quad \text{and}$$

$$\int_A F_n d\lambda - \int_A f_n d\lambda < \frac{1}{n}. \tag{1.3}$$

Consider now

$$f_{*n} = \sup f_n, \quad F_{*n} = \inf F_n.$$

By Proposition 6, f_*, F_* are both measurable functions such that $f_* \leq f \leq F_*$. Consider now the sets

$$C_m = \{\omega : f_*(\omega) - F_*(\omega) < -\frac{1}{m}\}$$

and note that

$$C = \{\omega : f_*(\omega) - F_*(\omega) < 0\} = \bigcup_{m=1}^{\infty} C_m.$$

Moreover, since $f_n - F_n \leq f_* - F_*$, we conclude that $C_m \subset D_m$, where

$$D_m = \{\omega : f_n(\omega) - F_n(\omega) < -\frac{1}{m}\}.$$

Evidently, we have, using equation (1.3),

$$-\frac{1}{n} < \int_{D_m} f_n d\lambda - \int_{D_m} F_n d\lambda < -\frac{1}{m}\lambda(D_m),$$

or alternatively, $\lambda(D_m) < (m/n)$. Since n is arbitrary, we conclude that, for every m, $\lambda(C_m) = 0$, and thus, $f_* = F_*$, which shows that f is measurable.

q.e.d.

Before we proceed with the theory of Lebesgue integration, it is useful to demonstrate another important property of measurable functions.

Proposition 13 (Egorov's Theorem). Let $(\Omega, \mathcal{A}, \lambda)$, $(R, \mathcal{B})$, be a measure and (Borel) measurable space, respectively, and let

$$f_n : \Omega \longrightarrow R, \ n \geq 1,$$

be a sequence of measurable functions such that

$$f_n \longrightarrow f, \ \text{a.e.}$$

on a set A with $\lambda(A) < \infty$. Then, given any $\delta > 0$, there exists a (measurable) set $C \subset A$, with $\lambda(C) < \delta$ such that

$$f_n \longrightarrow f$$

uniformly on $A \cap \bar{C}$.

Proof: First note that the set

$$D = \{\omega : \lim_{n \longrightarrow \infty} |f_n(\omega) - f(\omega)| \neq 0\}$$

obeys $\lambda(D) = 0$ by the conditions of the proposition; accordingly, we shall henceforth interpret A as $A \cap \bar{D}$. To prove the result, we shall show that, given any $\epsilon > 0$, for all $\omega \in A \cap \bar{C}$ there exists N such that $|f_n(\omega) - f(\omega)| < \epsilon$, for all $n \geq N$. To see this, define the sets

$$B_{k,r} = \{\omega : |f_k(\omega) - f(\omega)| \geq \frac{1}{r}, \ \omega \in A\}, \quad k \geq 1,$$

and note that

$$C_{n,r} = \{\omega : \sup_{k \geq n} |f_k(\omega) - f(\omega)| \geq \frac{1}{r}, \ \omega \in A\} = \bigcup_{k=n}^{\infty} B_{k,r}.$$

Moreover, since the sequence converges pointwise, for any r, we have

$$C_r = \bigcap_{n=1}^{\infty} C_{n,r} = \emptyset.$$

Consequently,

$$\lim_{n \to \infty} \lambda(C_{n,r}) = 0,$$

and given $\delta > 0$, there exists $N(r)$ such that

$$\lambda(C_{n,r}) < 2^{-r}\delta.$$

Define

$$C = \bigcup_{r=1}^{\infty} C_{N(r),r}$$

and note that

$$\lambda(C) \leq \sum_{r=1}^{\infty} \lambda(C_{N(r),r}) < \delta.$$

The construction above shows, quite clearly, that $f_n \longrightarrow f$ uniformly on the set $A \cap \bar{C}$. For, suppose not; let $\epsilon > 0$ be given and suppose there exists

$$\omega \in A \cap \bar{C}$$

for which

$$|f_n(\omega) - f(\omega)| \geq \epsilon, \quad \text{for all} \quad n > N(\epsilon).$$

Now, given ϵ, there exists an $r*$ such that $(1/r*) < \epsilon$; consequently, for all $n \geq N(r*)$ we have that this ω is contained in $C_{N(r*),r*}$. This is a contradiction.

q.e.d.

A number of other useful results may be obtained for bounded functions; such results follow, essentially, from arguments that involve approximating such functions by simple functions and then applying Proposition 11. We have

Proposition 14. Let f, g be measurable functions,

$$f,\ g : \Omega \longrightarrow R,$$

in the context of Proposition 13. Suppose further that they are bounded and that they vanish outside a set, A, with $\lambda(A) < \infty$:

i. for any $a, b \in R$,

$$\int_A (af + bg)d\lambda = a\int_A fd\lambda + b\int_A gd\lambda;$$

ii. if $f = g$ a.e., then

$$\int_A fd\lambda = \int_A gd\lambda;$$

iii. if $f \leq g$ a.e., then

$$\int_A fd\lambda \leq \int_A gd\lambda;$$

iv. if $m \leq f(\omega) \leq M$, for all $\omega \in A$, then

$$m\lambda(A) \leq \int_A fd\lambda \leq M\lambda(A);$$

v. if $A = A_1 \cup A_2$ and A_1, A_2 are disjoint, then

$$\int_A fd\lambda = \int_{A_1} fd\lambda + \int_{A_2} fd\lambda.$$

Proof: For i., we note that if $a > 0$, and if h is a simple function, then so is ah, so that

$$\int afd\lambda = \inf_{ah \geq af} \int ahd\lambda = a\inf_{h \geq f} \int hd\lambda = a\int fd\lambda.$$

If $a < 0$, then for simple h, ah is also simple, and

$$\int afd\lambda = \inf_{ah \geq af} \int ahd\lambda = a\sup_{h \leq f} \int hd\lambda = a\int fd\lambda,$$

since

$$\int f d\lambda = \sup_{h \leq f} \int g d\lambda = \inf_{h \geq f} \int h d\lambda.$$

Hence, to complete the proof of i., we need only show that if f_1 and f_2 are integrable then so is $(f_1 + f_2)$. But this is simple since if we take $h_i \geq f_i$, $g_i \leq f_i$, and h_i, g_i simple, $i = 1, 2$, we can show that

$$\int (f_1 + f_2) d\lambda \leq \left[\inf_{h_1 \geq f_1} \int h_1 d\lambda + \inf_{h_2 \geq f_2} \int h_2 d\lambda \right].$$

Similarly, working with the simple functions f_i, g_i, $i = 1, 2$, we can establish that

$$\int (f_1 + f_2) d\lambda \geq \left[\sup_{g_1 \leq f_1} \int g_1 d\lambda + \sup_{g_2 \leq f_2} \int g_2 d\lambda \right].$$

Since f_i, $i = 1, 2$, are integrable functions, we conclude

$$\int (f_1 + f_2) d\lambda = \int f_1 d\lambda + \int f_2 d\lambda,$$

which proves i.

For ii., define

$$D = \{\omega : g(\omega) - f(\omega) \neq 0\}.$$

By assumption, $\lambda(D) = 0$; write $A = A_1 \cup A_2$, $A_2 = A \cap D$, and note that $A_2 \subset D$; hence, $\lambda(A_2) = 0$. Thus,

$$\int_A (g - f) d\lambda = \int_{A_1} (g - f) d\lambda + \int_{A_2} (g - f) \, d\lambda = \int_{A_1} (g - f) d\lambda,$$

owing to the fact the integral over A_2 is bounded by, say $M\lambda(D)$, which is simply null. Since $(g - f) = 0$ over A_1, the last integral above is null, and consequently, ii. is proved.

For iii., we employ a similar construction, except we define the set D by

$$D = \{\omega : g(\omega) - f(\omega) < 0\},$$

and note that the argument above implies that the integral in the rightmost member of the relation above is nonnegative. Consequently, iii. is proved.

Item iv. is obvious by the preceding.

Item v. has, in a sense, been employed in previous arguments, so let us give it an independent proof. Define I_i, to be the indicator functions of the sets A_i, $i = 1, 2$, as defined in the statement of item v. Note, as a consequence, that

$$f(\omega) = f(\omega)I_1(\omega) + f(\omega)I_2(\omega), \quad \text{for all} \ \ \omega \in A,$$

so that the first component consists of f restricted to A_1, and the second component consists of f restricted to A_2. By i. of this proposition,

$$\int_A f d\lambda = \int_{A_1} f d\lambda + \int_{A_2} f d\lambda.$$

q.e.d.

We shall complete the discussion of this section by extending the definition of the Lebesgue integral to nonnegative functions, which are not necessarily bounded, and finally to unrestricted functions. The technique is basically similar to that employed above: first we shall use bounded functions to approximate the nonnegative function and then use nonnegative functions to approximate an unrestricted function. We begin with the proper definition of integrability, where boundedness is no longer assumed.

Definition 26. Let f be a nonnegative measurable function

$$f : \Omega \longrightarrow R$$

which vanishes outside a set A, with $\lambda(A) < \infty$. Let h be a bounded measurable function obeying $h(\omega) \leq f(\omega)$ for $\omega \in A$ and otherwise $h(\omega) = 0$. The integral of f over A is defined by

$$I_L = \int_A f d\lambda = \sup_{h \leq f} \int_A h d\lambda,$$

and when $I_L < \infty$, the function f is said to be (Lebesgue) integrable over the set A.

Remark 19. The reader might ask, what if the function is not nonnegative? This is handled by noting that if f is an unrestricted function it can be written in a form involving **two nonnegative** functions as follows: define

$$f^+ = \max(f, 0), \quad f^- = \max(-f, 0),$$

and note that both entities above are nonnegative, and moreover,

$$f = f^+ - f^-.$$

A direct consequence of the remark above is

Definition 27. Let f be a measurable function

$$f : \Omega \longrightarrow R,$$

that vanishes except on a measurable set A with $\lambda(A) < \infty$. Define

$$f^+ = \max(f, \ 0), \quad f^- = \max(-f, \ 0),$$

and note that we can write

$$f = f^+ - f^-, \quad |f| = f^+ + f^-.$$

The functions f^+, f^- are nonnegative and measurable over A. If they are integrable (over A), then f is integrable, and its integral is defined to be

$$\int_A f d\lambda = \int_A f^+ d\lambda - \int_A f^- d\lambda.$$

Remark 20. In some contexts, it is convenient to extend the notion of integrability to the case where

$$\sup_{h \leq f} \int_A h d\lambda = \infty.$$

When this is so, if we can approximate a nonnegative function f by a nonnegative nondecreasing sequence $\{f_n : n \geq 1\}$, such that $f_n \leq f$, then

$$\int_A f d\lambda = \lim_{n \longrightarrow \infty} \int_A f_n d\lambda,$$

and the integral will always exist, since we are dealing with nonnegative functions. For unrestricted functions, f, the integral will fail to exist only if we have simultaneously

$$\int_A f^+ d\lambda = \infty, \quad \int_A f^- d\lambda = \infty.$$

If only one of the equalities above holds, then the integral of f will be either ∞ or $-\infty$.

As in the more restricted cases considered above, Lebesgue integration, in this context, is a linear operation; this is made clear in

Proposition 15. Let f, g be integrable functions over a set A with $\lambda(A) < \infty$. Then,

   i. for $a, b \in R$,

$$\int_A (af + bg)d\lambda = a\int_A fd\lambda + b\int_A gd\lambda;$$

  ii. if $f \leq g$ a.e., then

$$\int_A fd\lambda = \int_A gd\lambda;$$

 iii. if $A = A_1 \cup A_2$ and the A_i, $i = 1, 2$, are disjoint, then

$$\int_A fd\lambda = \int_{A_1} fd\lambda + \int_{A_2} fd\lambda.$$

Proof: Without loss of generality, we shall assume that a, b are both positive; for, if not, we simply change f and g, respectively, to $-f$ and $-g$. For the proof of i., it will suffice to show that

$$\int_A (af^+ + bg^+)d\lambda = a\int_A f^+d\lambda + b\int_A g^+d\lambda.$$

Let h_i, $i = 1, 2$, be bounded measurable functions such that

$$h_1 \leq f^+, \quad h_2 \leq g^+,$$

and note that, by assumption,

$$\int_A f^+d\lambda = \sup_{h_1 \leq f^+}\int_A h_1d\lambda, \quad \int_A g^+d\lambda = \sup_{h_2 \leq g^+}\int_A h_2d\lambda.$$

Since

$$ah_1 + bh_2 \leq (af^+ + bg^+),$$

we have

$$a\int_A h_1d\lambda + b\int_A g^+d\lambda \leq \int_A (af^+ + bg^+)d\lambda.$$

Thus, taking suprema, we find

$$a\int_A f^+d\lambda + b\int_A g^+d\lambda \leq \int_A (af^+ + bg^+)d\lambda. \tag{1.4}$$

Next, let v be a bounded measurable function that vanishes outside a set of finite measure, say $B \subset A$, and such that for all $\omega \in A$

$$v \le af^+ + bg^+.$$

Define

$$ar(\omega) = \min(v, \ af^+), \quad bk(\omega) = v(\omega) - r(\omega),$$

and note that

$$ar(\omega) \le af^+, \quad bk(\omega) \le bg^+.$$

Hence, r and k are bounded measurable functions such that

$$v(\omega) = ar(\omega) + bk(\omega).$$

Thus,

$$\int_A v d\lambda = a \int_A r d\lambda + b \int_A k d\lambda \le a \int_A f^+ d\lambda + b \int_A g^+ d\lambda.$$

Putting, for notational convenience,

$$p = af^+ + bg^+,$$

we find

$$\int_A p d\lambda = \sup_{v \le p} \int_A v d\lambda \le a \int_A f^+ d\lambda + b \int_A g^+ d\lambda.$$

Consequently,

$$\int_A (af^+ + bg^+) d\lambda \le a \int_A f^+ d\lambda + b \int_A g^+ d\lambda. \tag{1.5}$$

But equations (1.4) and (1.5) together imply

$$\int_A (af^+ + bg^+) d\lambda = a \int_A f^+ d\lambda + \int_A g^+ d\lambda,$$

which completes the proof of part i.

For part ii., define

$$C = \{\omega : g(\omega) - f(\omega) < 0\}.$$

By assumption $\lambda(C) = 0$; write $A_1 = A \cap \bar{C}$, $A_2 = A \cap C$ and note that $\lambda(A_2) = 0$ and the A_i are disjoint. But on A_1, $g \ge f$ everywhere, and hence by part i. of this proposition

$$0 \le \int_A (g - f) d\lambda = \int_{A_1} (g - f) d\lambda = \int_{A_1} g d\lambda - \int_{A_1} f d\lambda = \int_A g d\lambda - \int_A f d\lambda.$$

which proves part ii.

For part iii., let A_i, $i = 1, 2$, be two disjoint sets (not those used in the proof of part ii.) such that $A = A_1 \cup A_2$; define

$$f_1 = f I_1, \quad f_2 = f I_2,$$

where I_i is the indicator function of A_i, $i = 1, 2$; evidently, the functions above are integrable since $f_i \leq f$. By part i., we conclude that

$$\int_A f d\lambda = \int_{A_1} f d\lambda + \int_{A_2} f d\lambda.$$

q.e.d.

1.6.1 Miscellaneous Convergence Results

In this section, we present several important results involving issues of convergence of sequences of measurable functions or integrals of measurable functions. The context is still essentially that of the previous section, so that the underlying space, Ω, is simply R, and the measure, λ, is not necessarily such that $\lambda(\Omega) < \infty$. Otherwise, we deal with measurable functions that are defined on a measure space and take values in a measurable space, specifically the one-dimensional Borel space.

Proposition 16 (Bounded Convergence Theorem). Let $\{f_n : n \geq 1\}$ be a sequence of measurable functions,

$$f_n : \Omega \longrightarrow R, \ n \geq 1,$$

defined on a set A, such that $\lambda(A) < \infty$. Suppose further that they are uniformly bounded, i.e., there exists $M \in R$ such that, for all n, $| f_n(\omega) | < M < \infty$. If the seqence converges to a measurable function, f, pointwise, i.e., for each $\omega \in A$,

$$f_n(\omega) \longrightarrow f(\omega),$$

then

$$\int_A f d\lambda = \lim_{n \to \infty} \int_A f_n d\lambda.$$

Proof: By Proposition 13 (Egorov's theorem), given $\epsilon > 0$, there exists $n(\epsilon)$ and a measurable set C with $\lambda(C) < (\epsilon/4M)$ such that for all $n \geq N$ and $\omega \in A \cap \bar{C}$, we have

$$| f_n(\omega) - f(\omega) | < \frac{\epsilon}{2} \lambda(A).$$

Define $A_1 = A \cap \bar{C}$, $A_2 = A \cap C$, and note that $A_1 \cup A_2 = A$, $\lambda(A_2) < (\epsilon/4M)$. Consequently,

$$
\begin{aligned}
| \int_A f_n d\lambda - \int_A f d\lambda | &= | \int_A (f_n - f)d\lambda | \leq \int_A | f_n - f | \, d\lambda \\
&= \int_{A_1} | f_n - f | \, d\lambda + \int_{A_2} | f_n - f | \, d\lambda \\
&\leq \frac{\epsilon}{2} + \frac{\epsilon}{2} = \epsilon.
\end{aligned}
$$

q.e.d.

Proposition 17 (Monotone Convergence Theorem). Let $\{f_n : n \geq 1\}$ be a sequence of measurable functions,

$$f_n : \Omega \longrightarrow R, \quad n \geq 1,$$

which vanish outside a set A with $\lambda(A) < \infty$. Then, the following statements are true:

i. if $f_n \geq g$, for all n, where g is an integrable function and, moreover, $\{f_n : n \geq 1\}$ is a sequence of monotone nondecreasing functions that converge pointwise on A, i.e., if there exists a (measurable) function f such that

$$\lim_{n \to \infty} f_n(\omega) = f(\omega), \quad \text{for } \omega \in A,$$

then

$$\lim_{n \to \infty} \int_A f_n d\lambda = \int_A f d\lambda;$$

ii. if $\{f_n.n \geq 1\}$ is a monotone nonincreasing sequence that converges pointwise to f on a set A with $\lambda(A) < \infty$ and $f_n \leq g$, where g is an integrable function, then

$$\lim_{n \to \infty} \int_A f_n d\lambda = \int_A f d\lambda.$$

In either case, the convergence of integrals is monotone (in i., $\int_A f_n d\lambda \uparrow$ $\int_A f d\lambda$, while in ii., $\int_A f_n d\lambda \downarrow \int_A f d\lambda$).

Proof: To prove i., suppose $g \geq 0$; let $\{f_{nk} : k \geq 1\}$ be a sequence of simple nondecreasing functions converging to f_n and put

$$h_k = \max_{1 \leq n \leq k} f_{nk}.$$

It is clear that $\{h_k : k \geq 1\}$ is a nondecreasing sequence that converges pointwise on A, i.e., there is a function, say h, such that $\lim_{k \to \infty} h_k(\omega) = h(\omega)$ for $\omega \in A$, and moreover, $f_{nk} \leq h_k \leq f_k$. Letting $k \longrightarrow \infty$, we find

$$f_n \leq h \leq f.$$

Since $f_n \longrightarrow f$, we conclude that $h = f$, and since $\{h_k : k \geq 1\}$ is a monotone sequence of simple functions converging to h, we obtain

$$\lim_{k \to \infty} \int_A h_k d\lambda = \int_A h d\lambda = \int_A f d\lambda.$$

In addition, since $f_k \geq h_k$,

$$\lim_{k \to \infty} \int_A f_k d\lambda \geq \lim_{k \to \infty} \int_A h_k d\lambda = \int_A f d\lambda.$$

Finally, in view of the fact that $f_n \leq f_{n+1} \leq f$, we also have

$$\lim_{n \to \infty} \int_A f_n d\lambda = \int_A f d\lambda.$$

We therefore conclude

$$\lim_{n \to \infty} \int_A f_n d\lambda = \int_A f d\lambda.$$

Next, suppose that g is not restricted to be nonnegative. Thus, if $\int_A g d\lambda = \infty$, there is nothing to prove; so, let us suppose $\int_A g d\lambda < \infty$. Consider then

$$\{s_n : s_n = f_n - g,\ n \geq 1\},$$

and note that it is a nonnegative nondecreasing sequence of measurable functions converging pointwise to $f - g$ on the set A. By the discussion immediately preceding, we conclude

$$\lim_{n \to \infty} \int_A (f_n - g) d\lambda = \int_A (f - g) d\lambda,$$

or

$$\lim_{n\to\infty}\left[\int_A f_n d\lambda - \int_A g d\lambda\right] = \int_A f d\lambda - \int_A g d\lambda.$$

Since $\int_A g d\lambda < \infty$, we conclude

$$\lim_{n\to\infty}\int_A f_n d\lambda = \int_A \lim_{n\to\infty} f_n d\lambda = \int_A f d\lambda,$$

thus completing the proof of i.

The proof of ii. follows immediately from the proof of i. if we replace the functions f_n by their negatives.

q.e.d.

Proposition 18 (Fatou's Lemma). Let $\{f, g, f_n : n \geq 1\}$,

$$f, \ g, \ f_n : \ \Omega \longrightarrow R,$$

be a sequence of measurable functions, vanishing outside a set A and such that

$$f_n \longrightarrow f \text{ a.e., on a set } A \text{ with } \lambda(A) < \infty.$$

Then, the following statements are true:

i. if $f_n \geq g$ and $\int_A g d\lambda > -\infty$, then

$$\int_A \liminf_{n\to\infty} f_n d\lambda \leq \liminf_{n\to\infty} \int_A f_n d\lambda;$$

ii. if $f_n \leq g$, $n \geq 1$, and $\int_A g d\lambda < \infty$, then

$$\limsup_{n\to\infty} \int_A f_n d\lambda \leq \int_A \limsup_{n\to\infty} f_n d\lambda;$$

iii. if $|f_n| \leq g$, $n \geq 1$, and $\int_A g d\lambda < \infty$, then

$$\int_A \liminf_{n\to\infty} f_n d\lambda \leq \liminf_{n\to\infty} \int_A f_n d\lambda \leq \limsup_{n\to\infty} \int_A f_n d\lambda \leq \int_A \limsup_{n\to\infty} f_n d\lambda.$$

Proof: Let $C = \{\omega : \lim_{n\to\infty} |f_n(\omega) - f(\omega)| \neq 0\}$ and note that, by assumption, $\lambda(C) = 0$. In all arguments below, we shall interpret A as $A \cap \bar{C}$.

To prove i., define $h_n = \inf_{k \geq n} f_k$ and note that

$$h_n \leq f_n, \quad \lim_{n \to \infty} h_n = \lim_{n \to \infty} \inf_{k \geq n} f_n = \liminf_{n \to \infty} f_n.$$

From the first relation above, we infer $\int_A h_n d\lambda \leq \int_A f_n d\lambda$, and consequently,

$$\lim_{n \to \infty} \int_A h_n d\lambda \leq \liminf_{n \to \infty} \int_A f_n d\lambda.$$

Moreover, since $\{h_n : n \geq 1\}$ is a monotone nondecreasing sequence, we have

$$\lim_{n \to \infty} \int_A h_n d\lambda = \int_A \lim_{n \to \infty} h_n d\lambda = \int_A \liminf_{n \to \infty} f_n d\lambda.$$

This, in conjunction with the preceding result, implies

$$\int_A \liminf_{n \to \infty} f_n d\lambda \leq \liminf_{n \to \infty} \int_A f_n d\lambda,$$

which proves i.

To prove ii., define $h_n = \sup_{k \geq n} f_k$ and note that

$$h_n \leq g, \quad h_n \geq f_n, \quad \text{and} \quad \int_A h_n d\lambda \geq \int_A f_n d\lambda, \quad \text{for all} \ n.$$

As a matter of notation, we also have $\lim_{n \to \infty} h_n = \lim_{n \to \infty} \sup_{k \geq n} f_k = \limsup_{n \to \infty} f_n$. Since, for all n, $\int_A h_n d\lambda \geq \int_A f_n d\lambda$, we obtain

$$\lim_{n \to \infty} \int_A h_n d\lambda \geq \limsup_{n \to \infty} \int_A f_n d\lambda.$$

On the other hand, because h_n is a monotone sequence, we have

$$\lim_{n \to \infty} \int_A h_n d\lambda = \int_A \lim_{n \to \infty} h_n d\lambda = \int_A \limsup_{n \to \infty} f_n d\lambda,$$

which together with the result above implies

$$\int_A \limsup_{n \to \infty} f_n d\lambda \geq \limsup_{n \to \infty} \int_A f_n d\lambda;$$

this completes the proof of ii.

The proof of iii. follows easily from i. and ii.

q.e.d.

Proposition 19 (Lebesgue Dominated Convergence Theorem). Let g, $\{f_n : n \geq 1\}$ be integrable functions over a measurable set A, such that

$$|\, f_n(\omega)\,| \leq g(\omega), \ \omega \in A,$$

and

$$\lim_{n \to \infty} f_n(\omega) = f(\omega), \ \text{a.e., on } A.$$

Then,

$$\int_A f d\lambda = \lim_{n \to \infty} \int_A f_n d\lambda.$$

Proof: Consider the sequence $\{(g - f_n) : n \geq 1\}$. This is a sequence of nonnegative measurable functions that converge pointwise to $(g - f)$. Hence, by Proposition 18,

$$\int_A (g - f)\, d\lambda \leq \liminf_{n \to \infty} \int_A (g - f_n)\, d\lambda = \int_A g\, d\lambda - \limsup_{n \to \infty} \int_A f_n d\lambda.$$

Since f is, evidently, integrable, we have

$$\int_A f d\lambda \geq \limsup_{n \to \infty} \int_A f_n d\lambda.$$

Consider now $\{g + f_n : n \geq 1\}$. This is also a sequence of nonnegative functions such that

$$g(\omega) + f_n(\omega) \longrightarrow g(\omega) + f(\omega)$$

pointwise, for $\omega \in A$. Hence, again by Proposition 18,

$$\int_A (g + f) d\lambda \leq \liminf_{n \to \infty} \int_A (g + f_n) d\lambda = \int_A g d\lambda + \liminf_{n \to \infty} \int_A f_n d\lambda.$$

Since

$$\liminf_{n \to \infty} \int_A f_n d\lambda = \int_A \liminf_{n \to \infty} f_n d\lambda \leq \int_A \limsup_{n \to \infty} f_n d\lambda = \limsup_{n \to \infty} \int_A f_n d\lambda,$$

we have the result

$$\int_A f d\lambda \leq \liminf \int_A f_n d\lambda \leq \limsup \int_A f_n d\lambda \leq \int_A f d\lambda,$$

or

$$\lim \int_A f d\lambda = \int_A f d\lambda.$$

q.e.d.

Proposition 20 (Continuity of Lebesgue Integral). Let f be a nonnegative measurable function, integrable over a set A. Then, given $\epsilon > 0$, there exists $\delta > 0$ such that for every $C \subset A$, with $\lambda(C) < \delta$, we have

$$\int_C f \, d\lambda < \epsilon.$$

Proof: Suppose not; then, given $\epsilon > 0$ we can find sets C such that

$$\lambda(C) < \delta \quad \text{and} \quad \int_C f \, d\lambda \geq \epsilon.$$

In particular, choose the sets

$$\{C_n : \lambda(C_n) < 2^{-n}\}.$$

Define

$$g_n(\omega) = f(\omega) I_n(\omega),$$

where I_n is the indicator function of the set C_n. It is clear from the definition of the functions g_n that $g_n \longrightarrow 0$, a.e., except possibly for the sets $\liminf C_n$ or $\limsup C_n$. Since

$$\limsup C_n = \bigcap_{n=1}^{\infty} \bigcup_{k=n}^{\infty} C_n,$$

$$\lambda \left(\bigcup_{k=n}^{\infty} C_k \right) \leq \sum_{k=n}^{\infty} 2^{-k} = 2^{-(n-1)},$$

it follows that

$$\limsup \lambda(C_n) = 0.$$

Hence, by Proposition 18, with $f_n = f - g_n$,

$$\int_A f \, d\lambda \leq \liminf \int_A f_n \, d\lambda = \int_A f \, d\lambda - \limsup \int_A g_n \, d\lambda \leq \int_A f \, d\lambda - \epsilon.$$

This, however, is a contradiction.

q.e.d.

In the next proposition, we give a number of results that follow easily from Propositions 10 through 20.

Proposition 21. The following statements are true.

i. Let $\{g_n : n \geq 1\}$ be a sequence of nonnegative measurable functions defined on a measurable set A, with $\lambda(A) < \infty$ and let $g = \sum_{n=1}^{\infty} g_n$. Then,

$$\int_A g d\lambda = \sum_{n=1}^{\infty} \int_A g_n d\lambda.$$

ii. Let f be a nonnegative measurable function and $\{A_i : i \geq 1\}$ be a countable partition of the measurable set A. Then,

$$\int_A f d\lambda = \sum_{i=1}^{\infty} \int_{A_i} f d\lambda.$$

iii. Let f, g be two nonnegative measurable functions; if f is integrable and $g < f$ (both statements valid on a measurable set A), then g is also integrable, and

$$\int_A (f - g) d\lambda = \int_A f d\lambda - \int_A g d\lambda.$$

Proof: Define

$$h_n = \sum_{k=1}^{n} g_k$$

and note that $\{h_n : n \geq 1\}$ is a sequence of nonnegative nondecreasing measurable functions, defined on a measurable set A such that

$$h_n \longrightarrow g \text{ a.e. on } A.$$

Consequently, by Proposition 18,

$$\int_A g d\lambda = \lim_{n \to \infty} \int_A h_n d\lambda = \sum_{n=1}^{\infty} \int_A g_n d\lambda$$

which proves i. To prove ii., let I_n be the indicator function of A_n and define $g_n(\omega) = f(\omega) I_n(\omega)$. Note that on A

$$f = \sum_{n=1}^{\infty} g_n.$$

Consequently, by i. above, we have

$$\int_A f d\lambda = \sum_{n=1}^{\infty} \int_A g_n d\lambda = \sum_{n=1}^{\infty} \int_{A_n} f d\lambda,$$

which proves ii. To deal with iii., write $f = (f - g) + g$ and note that both $(f - g)$ and g are nonnegative measurable functions defined on a measurable set A; moreover, $(f - g) \leq f$ on A and thus integrable over A. Consequently,

$$\int_A g d\lambda = \int_A f d\lambda - \int_A (f - g) d\lambda < \infty,$$

which shows that g is integrable over A.

q.e.d.

We close this section by introducing and (partially) characterizing a form of convergence of sequences of measurable functions that is closely related to convergence in probability, a property widely discussed in econometrics.

Definition 28. Let f be a measurable function and $\{f_n : n \geq 1\}$ be a sequence of measurable functions defined on a measurable set A. For given $\epsilon > 0$, define the set

$$C_{n,\epsilon} = \{\omega : |f_n(\omega) - f(\omega)| \geq \epsilon\}.$$

The sequence is said to **converge in measure** to f on the set A if $C_{n,\epsilon} \subset A$ and $\lambda(C_{n,\epsilon}) < \epsilon$ for all $n \geq N(\epsilon)$.

We have the following partial characterization of convergence in measure.

Proposition 22. Let $\{f_n : n \geq 1\}$ be a sequence of measurable functions defined on the measurable set A; let f be a measurable function and suppose that f_n converges in measure to f on the set A. Then,

   i. every subsequence of $\{f_n : n \geq 1\}$ converges to f in measure;

   ii. there exists a subsequence, say $\{f_{n(r)} : r \geq 1\}$ that converges to f a.e.

Proof: Let $f_{n(k)}$ be any subsequence such that $n(k) \longrightarrow \infty$ with k, and let $\epsilon > 0$ be given; by the conditions of the proposition, there exists an $N(\epsilon)$ such that for all $n \geq N$ the set

$$C_{n,r} = \{\omega : |f_n(\omega) - f(\omega)| \geq \frac{1}{r}\}$$

has measure $\lambda(C_{n,r}) < (1/r)$, where r is an integer (the smallest), for which $(1/r) \leq \epsilon$. Let k_0 be such that $n(k_0) \geq N(\epsilon)$; then, by construction, we have that given $\epsilon > 0$ the set

$$B_k = \{\omega : \mid f_{n(k)} - f(\omega) \mid \geq \epsilon\}$$

for $k \geq k_0$ is contained in the set $C_{n,r}$, and thus

$$\lambda(B_k) < \frac{1}{r} \leq \epsilon.$$

This shows that any subsequence converges, in measure, to f, thus proving part i.

To prove part ii., consider the sets $\{C_{n,r}\}$ and choose the subsequence $\{f_{n(r)} : r \geq 1\}$, where, for each r, $n(r)$ is chosen by the condition that for $n \geq n(r)$, $\lambda(C_{n,r}) < 2^{-r}$; evidently, given any $\epsilon > 0$, there exists r_0 such that for all $n(r) \geq n(r_0)$ we have

$$\lambda\left(C_{n(r),r}\right) < \epsilon.$$

Thus, we conclude that this subsequence converges, in measure, to f. To show that it converges a.e. on A, we consider

$$C^* = \limsup C_{n(r),r} = \bigcap_{r=1}^{\infty} \bigcup_{k=r}^{\infty} C_{n(k),k},$$

and note that

$$\lambda(C^*) = \lim_{r \to \infty} \lambda\left(\bigcup_{k=r}^{\infty} C_{n(k),k}\right) \leq \lim_{r \to \infty} \sum_{k=r}^{\infty} \lambda\left(C_{n(k),k}\right)$$

$$= \lim_{r \to \infty} 2^{-(r-1)} = 0.$$

But this shows that $\{f_{n(r)} : r \geq 1\}$ converges to f a.e. on A.

q.e.d.

1.7   Extensions to Abstract Spaces

In the preceding section, we have essentially used the device of dealing with **bounded** measurable functions and in obtaining integrals, we have always operated with a set, A, that was specified to have finite Lebesgue measure. This has simplified the presentation considerably, but at the cost of producing results of seemingly restricted relevance; in point of fact, however, the results we have obtained in the preceding sections remain valid under a broader set of conditions as well. Taking the case of bounded functions, we recall from Proposition 10 that if f is a measurable function and the set over which it assumes the values $\pm\infty$ has measure zero then it can be closely approximated by a **bounded** measurable function, say g; moreover, g coincides with f, almost everywhere, i.e., $g = f$ a.e., and consequently, the integrals of the two functions over a set, A, of finite measure are equal.

We shall complete the discussion of (Lebesgue) integration by extending the definition of the Lebesgue integral to nonnegative functions, which are not necessarily bounded, and finally to unrestricted functions. The technique is basically similar to that employed earlier: first, we use bounded functions to approximate nonnegative functions and then use nonnegative functions to approximate unrestricted functions.

In addition, we shall establish the necessary modifications, if any, to the integration results presented above; we recall that in our initial discussion of Lebesgue integration we have dealt with measurable functions defined over a simple Borel space with measure defined as the length of the (bounded) interval in question. If we define functions over a more general measure space, it is not apparent from our earlier discussion under what conditions the results obtained earlier will continue to hold in the broader context.

We begin with the proper definition of integrability, where **boundedness is no longer assumed**.

Definition 29. Let f be a nonnegative measurable function,

$$f : \Omega \longrightarrow R,$$

which vanishes outside a set, A, with $\lambda(A) < \infty$; let h be a bounded measurable function obeying $h(\omega) \leq f(\omega)$, for $\omega \in A$, and otherwise $h(\omega) = 0$. The integral of f over A is defined by

$$I_L = \int_A f \, d\lambda = \sup_{h \leq f} \int_A h \, d\lambda,$$

and when $I_L < \infty$, the function f is said to be (Lebesgue) integrable over the set A.

Remark 21. The reader might ask what if the function is not nonnegative? This is handled by noting that if f is an unrestricted function it can be written in a form involving **two nonnegative** functions as follows. Define

$$f^+ = \max(f, 0), \quad f^- = \max(-f, 0);$$

note that both entities above are nonnegative, and moreover,

$$f = f^+ - f^-, \quad |f| = f^+ + f^-.$$

A direct consequence of the remark above is

Definition 30. Let f be a measurable function,

$$f : \Omega \longrightarrow R,$$

which vanishes except on a measurable set, A, with $\lambda(A) < \infty$. Define

$$f^+ = \max(f, 0), \quad f^- = \max(-f, 0)$$

and note that we can write $f = f^+ - f^-$. The functions f^+, f^- are nonnegative and measurable over A. If they are also integrable (over A), then f is integrable, and its integral is defined to be

$$\int_A f \, d\lambda = \int_A f^+ \, d\lambda + \int_A f^- \, d\lambda.$$

Remark 22. In some contexts, it is convenient to extend the notion of integrability to the case where

$$\sup_{h \leq f} \int_A h \, d\lambda = \infty.$$

In such a context, we can always approximate a nonnegative function f by a nonnegative nondecreasing sequence $\{f_n : n \geq 1\}$ such that $f_n \leq f$; for example,

$$f_n(\omega) = f(\omega), \quad \text{for } f(\omega) \leq n$$
$$= 0, \quad \text{for } f(\omega) > n.$$

We may then define the integral by

$$\int_A f d\lambda = \lim_{n\to\infty} \int_A f_n d\lambda,$$

since the limit, in the right member, will always exist for nonnegative functions. Note that this device "works" for (nonnegative) measurable functions, f, **even if they are unbounded and the set over which they are unbounded does not have measure zero**. When it does have measure zero, then, of course, the integral will be finite and there is no need for this extension of the definition of integrability. For unrestricted functions, f, the integral will fail to exist only if we have, simultaneously,

$$\int_A f^+ d\lambda = \infty \quad \text{and} \quad \int_A f^- d\lambda = \infty.$$

If only one of the equalities above holds, then the integral of f will be either $+\infty$ or $-\infty$. As in the more restricted cases considered earlier, Lebesgue integration, in this context, is a linear operation, a fact that is made clear in

Proposition 23. Let f, g be integrable functions over a set, A, with $\lambda(A) < \infty$. Then,

    i. for any $a, b \in R$,

$$\int_A (af + bg)d\lambda = a\int_A f d\lambda + b\int_A g d\lambda;$$

    ii. if $f \le g$ a.e.,

$$\int_A f d\lambda \le \int_A g d\lambda;$$

    iii. if $A = A_1 \cup A_2$ and the A_i, $i = 1, 2$, are disjoint,

$$\int_A f d\lambda = \int_{A_1} f d\lambda + \int_{A_2} f d\lambda.$$

Proof: Without loss of generality, we shall assume that a, b are both positive; for, if not, we simply change f and g, respectively, to $-f$ and $-g$. For the proof of i., it will suffice to show that

$$\int_A (af^+ + bg^+)d\lambda = a\int_A f^+ d\lambda + b\int_A g^+ d\lambda.$$

Let h_i, $i = 1, 2$, be bounded measurable functions such that

$$h_1 \le f^+, \qquad h_2 \le g^+,$$

and note that, by assumption,

$$\int_A f^+ d\lambda = \sup_{h_1 \le f^+} \int_A h_1 d\lambda, \quad \int_A g^+ d\lambda = \sup_{h_2 \le g^+} \int_A h_2 d\lambda.$$

Since

$$ah_1 + bh_2 \le (af^+ + bg^+),$$

we have

$$a \int_A h_1 d\lambda + b \int_A h_2 d\lambda \le \int_A (af^+ + bg^+) d\lambda .$$

Thus, taking suprema, we find

$$a \int_A f^+ d\lambda + b \int_A g^+ d\lambda \le \int_A (af^+ + bg^+) d\lambda . \qquad (1.6)$$

Next, let v be a bounded measurable function that vanishes outside a set of finite measure, say $B \subset A$, and such that for all $\omega \in A$, $v \le af^+ + bg^+$. Define

$$ar(\omega) = \min \left[af^+(\omega), \; v(\omega) \right], \quad bk(\omega) = v(\omega) - ar(\omega),$$

and note that

$$r(\omega) \le f^+(\omega), \quad k(\omega) \le g^+(\omega).$$

Hence, r and k are bounded measurable functions such that

$$v(\omega) = ar(\omega) + bk(\omega).$$

Thus,

$$\int_A v d\lambda = a \int_A r d\lambda + b \int_A k d\lambda \le a \int_A f^+ d\lambda + b \int_A g^+ d\lambda.$$

Putting, for notational convenience, $p = af^+ + bg^+$ we find

$$\int_A p d\lambda = \sup_{v \le p} \int_A v d\lambda \le a \int_A f^+ + b \int_A g^+ d\lambda.$$

Consequently,

$$\int_A (af^+ + bg^+) d\lambda \le a \int_A f^+ d\lambda + b \int_A g^+ d\lambda. \qquad (1.7)$$

But equations (1.7) and (1.8) together imply

$$\int_A (af^+ + bg^+)d\lambda = a \int_A f^+ d\lambda + b \int_A g^+ d\lambda,$$

which completes the proof of part i.

The remainder of the proof, just as the preceding, follows the lines of the proof of Proposition 15 and is thus omitted.

Next, we ask what difference does it make, in the proofs of the results of the previous sections, whether we are dealing with Lebesgue (outer) measure, or with more general versions of measure, as, simply, a nonnegative σ-additive set function defined on a σ-algebra. A little thought will convince us that nowhere in the proofs did we essentially use the fact that measure is defined as length. However, there is a technical difference that is not so manifest. This is the fact that while Lebesgue measure is **complete**, Lebesgue measure restricted to the σ-algebra of Borel sets is not. The term is explained in

Definition 31. A measure space, $(\Omega, \mathcal{B}, \mu)$, is said to be complete if $\mathcal{B}$ contains all subsets of sets of measure zero; i.e., if $B \subset A$, $A \in \mathcal{B}$, and $\mu(A) = 0$, then $B \in \mathcal{B}$.

Remark 23. It is for the reason implied in Definition 31 that, in discussing integration at an earlier stage, we were somewhat vague in specifying the precise σ-algebra involved, although we had made several references to Borel space. The reason why the previous definition may create conceptual problems is that, without taking account of its implications, we may negate the measurability of a function by simply changing its values over a set of measure zero. For example, suppose f is a measurable function on such a space and E is a measurable set of measure zero. Let $B \subset E$ and suppose the values assumed by f on B are "changed"; suppose, further, that the values assumed by f on B are in the range σ-algebra. Then, the inverse image of the set in question would not be measurable, i.e., it will not belong to the domain σ-algebra; consequently, the measurability of the function will be negated. We can obviate this problem by insisting that if $A \in \mathcal{B}$, where $\mathcal{B}$ is the σ-algebra of the space above, and if $\mu(A) = 0$ then all subsets of A are also in $\mathcal{B}$. This would mean, of course, that when we speak of a function we will really be speaking about an equivalence class, i.e., of a collection of such functions that are identical except possibly on sets of measure zero. In this connection, we have

Proposition 24. Let $(\Omega, \mathcal{A}, \mu)$ be a measure space; then there exists a complete measure space, say $(\Omega_0, \mathcal{A}_0, \mu_0)$, such that

i. $\mathcal{A} \subset \mathcal{A}_0$;

ii. $A \in \mathcal{A}$ implies $\mu(A) = \mu_0(A)$;

iii. $C \in \mathcal{A}_0$ if, and only if, $C = A \cup B$, where $A \in \mathcal{A}$, $B \subset D$, $D \in \mathcal{A}$, and $\mu(D) = 0$.

Proof: We first show that $\mathcal{A}_0$, as defined in iii. is, indeed, a σ-algebra. Let

$$\mathcal{A}_0 = \{C : C = A \cup B, \ A \in \mathcal{A}, \ B \subset D, \ D \in \mathcal{A}, \text{ and } \mu(D) = 0\}.$$

To show that this is a σ-algebra, we show that it is closed under complementation and countable unions. Thus, let $C \in \mathcal{A}_0$ and consider its complement $\bar{C} = \bar{A} \cap \bar{B}$. Since $B \subset D$, it is clear that $\bar{B} = \bar{D} \cup B_1$, where $B_1 = D - B$, i.e., $D - B$ is that subset of D which is not B. Consequently, $\bar{C} = (\bar{A} \cap \bar{D}) \cup (\bar{A} \cap B_1) \in \mathcal{A}$. This is so since the first component of $\bar{C}$ consists of a set in $\mathcal{A}$, while the second component is a subset of B_1, which is a subset of $D \in \mathcal{A}$, with $\mu(D) = 0$. Next, we show closure under countable unions. Let $C_i \in \mathcal{A}_0$, $i \geq 1$. This means that $C_i = A_i \cup B_i$ and that $\bigcup_{i=1}^{\infty} A_i \in \mathcal{A}$, $B_i \subset D_i$, with $D_i \in \mathcal{A}$ and $\mu(D_i) = 0$, for all i. But, $C = \bigcup_{i=1}^{\infty} C_i = A \cup B$, where $A = \bigcup_{i=1}^{\infty} A_i \in \mathcal{A}$, $B = \bigcup_{i=1}^{\infty} B_i$, $B \subset D$, and $D = \bigcup_{i=1}^{\infty} D_i$, with $\mu(D) = 0$, which completes the proof that $\mathcal{A}_0$ is, indeed, a σ-algebra. The proof of i. is, of course, quite obvious by simply taking, in the characterization of the sets of $\mathcal{A}_0$ as given in iii. of the proposition, $C = A \cup \emptyset$. Next, we define the measure μ_0 by

$$\mu_0(C) \quad = \quad \mu(C), \text{ if } C \in \mathcal{A}$$

$$= \quad \mu(A), \text{ if } C = A \cup B, \text{ such that } A \in \mathcal{A}, \quad B \subset D$$

$$\text{and } D \in \mathcal{A} \text{ with } \mu(D) = 0.$$

This is clearly a nonnegative set function that assigns to the null set the measure zero; it only remains to prove that μ_0 is also σ-additive. To this effect consider A, B, and C as defined in the preceding argument. We obtain

$$\mu_0 \left(\bigcup_{i=1}^{\infty} C_i \right) = \mu_0(C) = \mu(A) = \lim_{n \to \infty} \sum_{i=1}^{n} \mu_0(C_i).$$

q.e.d.

The next objective, in this discussion, is to show that although in the preceding sections we have dealt with a specific kind of measure on R the results obtained are valid over a wide range of spaces and measures, provided certain minimal conditions are satisfied. In the course of this discussion, we shall need an additional concept.

Definition 32. Let $(\Omega, \mathcal{A}, \mu)$ be a measure space, and let $A \in \mathcal{A}$; then A is said to be of **finite measure** if $\mu(A) < \infty$; it is said to be of σ-**finite measure** if there exists a partition of $A \in \mathcal{A}$, say $\{A_i : A_i \in \mathcal{A}, \mu(A_i) < \infty, i \geq 1\}$.

Definition 33. Let μ be a measure, as in Definition 32. Then, μ is said to be **finite** if $\mu(\Omega) < \infty$. It is said to be σ-finite if Ω is of σ-finite measure.

Remark 24. Note that a probability measure is simply a normalized finite measure. Note also that every finite measure is also σ-finite, but that the converse is not true. In particular, Lebesgue measure, λ, on R is σ-finite, but it is, clearly, not finite since the λ-measure of the set $(-\infty, \infty)$ is infinite.

Proposition 25. Let $(\Omega, \mathcal{A}, \mu)$ be a measure space and f a nonnegative measurable function,

$f : \Omega \longrightarrow R$.

Then, the following statements are true.

   i. A necessary condition for $J = \int_{\Omega} f d\mu < \infty$, is that A is of σ-finite measure and $\mu(B) = 0$, where $A = \{\omega : f(\omega) > 0\}$, $B = \{\omega : f(\omega) = \infty\}$.

ii. If A is of σ-finite measure, but $\mu(B) = 0$ does not hold, then we can only assert that

$$\int_\Omega f d\mu = \sup_{g \leq f} \int_\Omega g d\mu,$$

where the *sup* is taken over all **bounded** mesurable functions, g, such that $g \leq f$ and g vanishes outside a set, say A, of finite measure.

Proof: Suppose $J < \infty$ and $\mu(B) > 0$; define a function g such that $g = f$ on B and zero elsewhere. Then, it is clear that $g \leq f$ and, moreover, that $\int_\Omega g d\mu = \infty \mu(B) = \infty$. This is a contradiction; hence, $\mu(B) = 0$. Similarly, let $A_n = \{\omega : f(\omega) > (1/n)\}$ and note that, by construction, $n f(\omega) > 1$ on A_n; if I_n is the latter's indicator function, we easily stablish that, for each n, A_n is of finite measure and, in addition, that $\mu(A_n) = \int_\Omega I_n d\mu \leq n \int_{A_n} f d\mu < \infty$. Moreover, since $A_n \subset A_{n+1}$ for all $n \geq 1$ and $A = \bigcup_{i=1}^\infty A_i$, we conclude that

$$\mu(A) = \lim_{n \to \infty} \mu(A_n) < \infty,$$

which shows that A is not only of σ-finite measure, but also of finite measure, thus proving i.

To prove ii., suppose $\mu(A) < \infty$ and define g to be a (family of) nonnegative bounded function that vanishes outside A; hence, $g \leq f$, and consequently, we have $\int f d\mu \geq \sup_{g \leq f} \int g d\mu$. Now, if h is a nonnegative **simple function** such that $h \leq f$ and its integral is finite, then by i. above, it vanishes outside a set A, of σ-finite measure. Thus, if there is no simple nonnegative function $h \leq f$, with infinite integral, then, by the standard definition of the Lebesgue integral, we must have

$$\int f d\mu = \sup_{h \leq f} \int h d\mu \leq \sup_{g \leq f} \int g d\mu. \tag{1.8}$$

We note that the last inequality is due to the fact that h belongs to a more restricted class of approximating functions than g. If, on the other hand, there is a simple function, say $h(\omega) = \sum_{i=1}^n c_i I_i(\omega)$, where I_i is the characteristic function of the set A_i defined above, such that $h \leq f$ and $\int_\Omega h d\mu = \infty$, then $\int_\Omega f d\mu = \infty$. This means that at least one of the sets, say A_{i_0}, has infinite measure; since it is also true that $A_{i_0} \subset A$, we conclude that the former, i.e., A_{i_0}, is of σ-finite measure as well. Consequently, there exists a countable collection of sets, say $\{B_k : \mu(B_k) < \infty, \ k \geq 1\}$, such that A_{i_0} is their union. Let v_n be the characteristic function of the set $\bigcup_{k=1}^{n} B_k$ and note that the function $c_{i_0} v_n$ has the following properties: $c_{i_0} \leq f$; it is bounded; it vanishes outside a set of finite measure; and moreover,

$$K_n = \int_{\Omega} c_{i_0} v_n d\mu = c_{i_0} \mu \left(\bigcup_{k=1}^{n} B_k \right).$$

Since it is easily established that

$$\lim_{n \to \infty} K_n = \mu(A_{i_0}) = \infty,$$

we conclude $\sup_{g \leq f} \int_{\Omega} g d\mu = \infty = \int_{\Omega} f d\mu$.

q.e.d.

Remark 25. The preceding discussion concludes the demonstratation that the results obtained in Propositions 12 through 23 remain valid even when dealing with abstract measure spaces.

We now turn to the discussion of another topic, which will play an important role when we consider conditional probability and conditional expectation. We have

Definition 34. Let μ, ν be measures defined on a measurable space $(\Omega, \mathcal{A})$; then ν is said to be **absolutely continuous** with respect to (or relative to) μ if and only if $\nu(A) = 0$ for every set $A \in \mathcal{A}$ such that $\mu(A) = 0$. This is denoted by $\nu \ll \mu$.

Definition 35. Let ν be a set function defined on the measurable space $(\Omega, \mathcal{A})$; then ν is said to be a **signed measure** if $\nu = \nu^+ - \nu^-$ and each of the set functions ν^+ and ν^- is a measure. Moreover, the signed measure is absolutely continuous with respect to the measure μ if and only if the two measures ν^+ and ν^- are absolutely continuous with respect to μ.

The preceding discussion immediately suggests

Proposition 26. Let $(\Omega, \mathcal{A}, \mu)$ be a measure space and f a nonnegative $\mathcal{A}$-measurable function,

$$f : \Omega \longrightarrow R,$$

whose integral exists and define the set function

$$\nu(A) = \int_A f d\mu.$$

Then, the following statements are true:

i. $\nu(A)$ is a measure, and

ii. it is absolutely continuous with respect to μ.

Proof: To prove i., we note that, by the elementary properties of the Lebesgue integral, ν is a nonnegative nondecreasing function obeying $\nu(\emptyset) = 0$. Again, using the elementary properties of the Lebesgue integral, if $A \in \mathcal{A}$ and $\{A_i : i \geq 1\}$ is a partition of A in $\mathcal{A}$, then $\nu(A) = \sum_{i=1}^{\infty} \nu(A_i)$, which proves i.

   To prove ii., let $A \in \mathcal{A}$ and $\mu(A) = 0$; let h be a nonnegative simple function, $h(\omega) = \sum_{i=1}^{n} c_i I_i(\omega)$, where I_i are the characteristic functions of the sets of the partition of A in $\mathcal{A}$. Then,

$$\int_A h d\mu = \sum_{i=1}^{n} c_i \mu(A_i \cap A) = 0.$$

Accordingly, let $\{f_n . f_n \leq f, i \geq 1\}$ be a sequence of nonnegative simple functions converging to f; by the monotone convergence theorem, we conclude

$$\nu(A) = \int_A f d\mu = \lim_{n \to \infty} \int_A f_n d\mu = 0.$$

q.e.d.

Corollary 1. Let $(\Omega, \mathcal{A}, \mu)$ be a measure space and let f be a measurable function,

$$f : \Omega \longrightarrow R,$$

whose integral exists in the extended sense. Then, the set function

$$\nu(A) = \int_A f d\mu$$

is a signed measure that is absolutely continuous with respect to μ.

Proof: By the conditions of the corollary, putting $f = f^+ - f^-$, we have that, at least, one of the integrals of the right member below

$$\int_A f d\mu = \int_A f^+ d\mu - \int_A f^- d\mu$$

is finite. Denoting the first integral, on the right, by $\nu^+(A)$ and the second by $\nu^-(A)$, we observe that each is a measure absolutely continuous with respect to μ. Putting

$$\nu(A) = \nu^+(A) - \nu^-(A),$$

we note that it is a well defined entity since at least one of the two right measures are finite; moreover, it is a signed measure that is absolutely continuous with respect to μ.

q.e.d.

It is remarkable that the converse of Proposition 26 is also valid, a fact that forms the basis of the abstract development of conditional probability and conditional expectation. We state the result without proof, since its proof will take us well beyond the objectives of this volume.

Proposition 27 (Radon-Nikodym Theorem). Let $(\Omega, \mathcal{A}, \mu)$ be a measure space, where μ is σ-finite, and let ν be a signed measure that is absolutely continuous with respect to μ; then there exists an extended measurable function (i.e., a measurable function taking values in $[-\infty, \infty]$) such that for any $A \in \mathcal{A}$

$$\nu(A) = \int_A f d\mu.$$

The function f is unique up to sets of μ-measure zero, i.e., if g is another such function, then the set $C = \{\omega : f \neq g\}$ obeys $\mu(C) = 0$. If ν is a measure, then the function f is nonnegative, i.e., it takes values only in $[0, \infty]$.

Remark 26. The function f, of Proposition 27, is said to be the **Radon-Nikodym derivative of the measure ν with respect to the measure μ** and is denoted by

$$\frac{d\nu}{d\mu}.$$

1.8 Miscellaneous Concepts

We close this chapter by providing a review of certain mathematical concepts, which, although not directly relevant to the econometric problems we shall be dealing with, are nonetheless useful in dealing with the mathematical issues we wish to consider in this volume.

Definition 36. Let Ω_i, $i = 1, 2$, be (abstract) spaces; their Cartesian product, $\Omega_1 \times \Omega_2$, consists of all ordered pairs, (ω_1, ω_2), such that $\omega_i \in \Omega_i$, $i = 1, 2$; i.e., the elements of the Cartesian product are the ordered pairs above such that the first component of the pair is an element of the first space and the second component is an element of the second space. Similarly, the subsets of the Cartesian product, say A, are of the form $A = A_1 \times A_2$ such that $A_i \subset \Omega_i$, $i = 1, 2$.

Remark 27. If we are dealing with two independent random variables defined on the probability spaces $(\Omega_i, \mathcal{A}_i, P_i)$, respectively, it may be convenient to think of them as being defined on the space $\Omega_1 \times \Omega_2$; it turns out that the appropriate σ-algebra on this space is $\sigma(\mathcal{A}_1 \times \mathcal{A}_2)$, and the appropriate probability measure is $P_1 \times P_2$, where the last two entities will be explained at a later stage.

Definition 37. Let Ω be a space; a function ρ,

$$\rho : \Omega \longrightarrow R,$$

is said to be a **metric** if and only if for any three elements, $x, y, z \in \Omega$,

    i. $\rho(x, y) \geq 0$;

    ii. $\rho(x, y) = \rho(y, x)$;

    iii. $\rho(x, y) \leq \rho(x, z) + \rho(z, y)$;

iv. $\rho(x,\ y) = 0$, if and only if $x = y$.

The pair $(\Omega,\ \rho)$ is said to be a **metric space**.

A closely related concept is that of a **norm**, which is defined on a linear space. We have the definitions,

Definition 38. A set of elements, Ω, is said to be a **linear space**, (or a **vector space** or a **linear vector space**) over the set of real numbers, if there exists a function $+$, called vector addition,

$$+ : \Omega \times \Omega \longrightarrow \Omega,$$

and a function $\cdot$, called scalar multiplication,

$$\cdot : R \times \Omega \longrightarrow \Omega,$$

such that the following conditions hold for all $x, y, z \in \Omega$ and $\alpha,\ \beta \in R$:

i. $x + y = y + x$;

ii. $(x + y) + z = x + (y + z)$;

iii. there exists a unique **zero vector** in Ω, denoted by 0, such that for all $x \in \Omega,\ \ x + 0 = x$;

iv. scalar multiplication is distributive over vector addition, i.e., for all $x, y \in \Omega$ and $\alpha \in R$, $\alpha \cdot (x + y) = \alpha \cdot x + \alpha \cdot y$;

v. $(\alpha + \beta) \cdot x = \alpha \cdot x + \beta \cdot y$;

vi. scalar multiplication is associative, i.e., $\alpha(\beta \cdot x) = (\alpha\beta) \cdot x$;

vii. $0 \cdot x = 0$ (zero vector) and $1 \cdot x = x$.

The elements of a linear space are typically called **vectors**.

Remark 28. The notation $\cdot$, indicating the operation of **scalar multiplication**, is often suppressed, and one simply writes, for example, $c(x + y) = cx + cy$, it being understood that c is a scalar and $x,\ y$ are vectors.

Definition 39. Let Ω be a linear space; the function

$$\| \cdot \| : \Omega \longrightarrow R$$

is said to be a norm if and only if it satisfies the following conditions for all $x, y \in \Omega$ and $\alpha \in R$:

   i. $\| x \| \geq 0$;

   ii. $\| x + y \| \leq \| x \| + \| y \|$ (triangle inequality);

   iii. $\| \alpha x \| = | \alpha | \| x \|$;

   iv. $\| x \| = 0$, if and only if $x = 0$.

A linear space with a norm defined on it is said to be a **normed linear space**.

Definition 40. Let (Ω, ρ) be a metric space and let A be a set in Ω, i.e., $A \subset \Omega$. A point $w \in \Omega$ is said to be a **point of closure** of A if for any $\epsilon > 0$ there exists at least one point $y \in A$ such that $\rho(w, y) < \epsilon$. The set of all points that are points of closure of a set A is termed the **closure** of A and is denoted by $C(A)$.

Remark 29. Note that a normed linear space becomes a **metric space** if we define on it the metric $\rho(x, y) = \| x - y \|$. Moreover, observe that if $x \in A$ then $x \in C(A)$ and that if $\{x_i : i \geq 1\}$ is a sequence of points in A then all the cluster points of the sequence, (as well as its limit, if one exists,) are in $C(A)$.

We can now define the important topological concepts of open and closed sets.

Definition 41. Let (Ω, ρ) be a metric space. A set $A \subset \Omega$ is said to be **open** if for any $w \in A$ there exists $\delta > 0$ such that

$$S \subset A \quad \text{where} \quad S = \{x : \rho(w, x) < \delta\}.$$

Definition 42. Let (Ω, ρ) be a metric space. A set A is said to be **closed** if and only if $C(A) = A$.

We set forth below a number of the elementary properties of open and closed sets in the context of a metric space.

Proposition 28. Let (Ω, ρ) be a metric space. The following statements are true:

i. Ω and $\emptyset$ are both open and closed;

ii. let $A, B \subset \Omega$ be open sets; then $A \cap B$ is an open set;

iii. let $S = \{S_\nu : \nu \in \mathcal{N}\}$, where $\mathcal{N}$ is an index set, not necessarily countable, and suppose that S is a collection of open sets; then $\bigcup_\nu S_\nu$ is **open**;

iv. for $A, B \subset \Omega$, $C(A \cup B) = C(A) \cup C(B)$, and $C(A \cap B) \subset C(A) \cap C(B)$;

v. let $A, B \subset \Omega$ be closed sets; then, $A \cup B$ is closed;

vi. let $S = \{S_\nu : \nu \in \mathcal{N}\}$, where $\mathcal{N}$ is an index set, not necessarily countable, and suppose that S is a collection of **closed** sets; then $\bigcap_\nu S_\nu$ is **closed**;

vii. the closure of a closed set is closed, i.e., if F is a closed set then $C(F)$ is also closed; moreover, if G is any set (i.e., not necessarily a closed set), then $C[C(G))] = C(G)$;

viii. the complement, (in Ω), of an open set is closed and the complement of a closed set is open.

Proof: To prove i., we note that the two sets in question are **not** open if we can find a point, say x, for which it is not true that the set $S = \{\omega : \rho(\omega, x) < \delta\}$ is a subset of Ω or $\emptyset$, as the case may be, for some $\delta > 0$. It is clear that this cannot be so for Ω, while in the case of $\emptyset$, S is itself empty! That Ω is closed is rather obvious; as for $\emptyset$, we note that the set containing its **points of closure** is empty; consequently, $C(\emptyset) = \emptyset$, which shows it to be closed.

To prove ii., we note that if $x \in A \cap B$, then $x \in A$ and $x \in B$. Consequently, there exists some $\delta > 0$ such that the set $S = \{\omega : \rho(x, \omega) < \delta\}$ is a subset of **both** A and B; consequently, $S \subset A \cap B$.

The proof of iii. is fairly obvious, since if $x \in \cup_\nu S_\nu$ then $x \in S_\nu$, for at least one ν, say S_{ν_0}; since the latter is open, it totally contains a sphere around x of radius δ, for some $\delta > 0$.

To prove iv., let $x \in C(A \cup B)$; then, there exists a point $\omega \in (A \cup B)$ such that $\rho(x, \omega) < \delta$, for all $\delta > 0$. But, this means that $\omega \in C(A) \cup C(B)$, so that $C(A \cup B) \subset C(A) \cup C(B)$. Conversely, suppose that $x \in C(A) \cup C(B)$; then, by definition, there exists $\omega \in A \cup B$ such that $\rho(x, \omega) < \delta$, for all $\delta > 0$. But, this means that $C(A) \cup C(B) \subset C(A \cup B)$. As for the second part, suppose that $x \in C(A \cap B)$; then, by definition, there exists $\omega \in A \cap B$ such that $\rho(x, \omega) < \delta$, for all $d > 0$. This, however, implies that $x \in C(A) \cap C(B)$, which completes the proof of iv.

The proof of v. is immediate from iv. since

$$C(A \cup B) = C(A) \cup C(B) = A \cup B,$$

and the fact that $A \cup B$ is closed follows from the definition of closed sets.

To prove vi., we note that for any $x \in C(S)$, we have that for all $\delta > 0$ there exists a point, say $\omega \in S$, such that $\rho(x, \omega) < \delta$. This, of course, means that $\omega \in S_\nu$, **for every** ν; consequently, x is a point of closure for every set S_ν; it follows then that $x \in S$, which shows S to be closed.

The proof of vii. is quite obvious and is, thus, omitted.

To prove viii., we proceed as follows: let A be an open set and consider its complement $\bar{A}$. Let x be a point of closure of $\bar{A}$; we shall show that $x \in \bar{A}$. By definition, this means that there exists a point $\omega \in \bar{A}$ such that for all $\delta > 0$, $\rho(x, \omega) < \delta$. But, $x \notin A$, since if it were there would exist some δ_0 such that the sphere $S = \{y : \rho(x, y) < \delta_0\}$ is contained in A. This entails a contradiction; consequently, $x \in \bar{A}$, which shows $\bar{A}$ to be closed, i.e., that $C(\bar{A}) = \bar{A}$. The remainder of this part is proved by an entirely similar argument and is, thus, omitted.

q.e.d.

The important concept of a separable metric space is given in the definition below.

Definition 43. A metric space (Ω, ρ) is said to be **separable** if and only if it contains a countable subset D (i.e., one that has a countable number of elements), which is dense in Ω, i.e., $C(D) = \Omega$.

Remark 30. The set of real numbers, R, is a separable metric space under the usual metric $\rho(x, y) = \mid x - y \mid$; this is so, since the set of rational numbers is a countable subset of R; moreover, it is shown in analysis that the closure of the rationals is R.

A characterization of the separability property is given by

Proposition 29. A metric space, (Ω, ρ), is **separable** if and only if it contains **a countable collection of open sets**, $S = \{S_i : i = 1, 2, \ldots\}$, such that (the sets S_i are open and) for any open set $A \subset \Omega$, we have

$$A = \bigcup_{S_i \subset A} S_i.$$

Proof: Suppose it is separable; then there exists a countable dense set, say D, i.e., such that $C(D) = \Omega$. Let $x \in \Omega$ and define the sphere about x, $S_{x,r} = \{\omega : \rho(x, \omega) < r\}$, where r is a rational number. Define, further, $S_r^* = \{S_{x,r} : x \in D\}$ and note that $S = \{S_r^* : r$ is rational$\}$ is a countable collection of open sets. Let $y \in A$ and suppose A is an open set. Then, for some $\delta > 0$, the sphere $S_{y,\delta} = \{\omega : \rho(y, \omega) < \delta\}$ is totally contained in A. Moreover, since $y \in C(D)$, there exists a point $x \in D$ such that $\rho(x, y) < \delta$; in addition, there exists a rational number, say r_0, such that $\rho(x, y) < r_0$. But, this means that given any $y \in A$ there exists an element of S, say S_{x,r_0}, such that $y \in S_{x,r_0}$.

Since the collection S is countable, it can be put into one to one correspondence with the set of integers, so that we can write more simply $S = \{S_i : i = 1, 2, \ldots\}$. Consequently, for every open set A, we may write

$$A = \bigcup_{S_i \subset A} S_i.$$

Conversely, suppose we are given a countable collection of open sets $S = \{S_i : i = 1, 2, \ldots\}$ such that every open set $A \subset \Omega$ can be written as a countable union of sets in S; we shall show that the space is separable. To this effect, let $D = \{x_i : x_i \in S_i, \ i = 1, 2, \ldots\}$; we show that this is dense in Ω, i.e., that $C(D) = \Omega$. Choose any point $x \in \Omega$; since Ω is open, the sphere $S_{x,\delta} = \{\omega : \rho(x, \omega) < \delta\}$ is an open set for every $\delta > 0$. Consequently, for every $\delta > 0$, there exists at least one set, say S_{i_0}, such that $S_{i_0} \subset S_{x,\delta}$. Consequently, $x_{i_0} \in S_{x,\delta}$; but this shows that given **any** $x \in \Omega$ there exists a point, say $x_{i_0} \in D$, such that $\rho(x, x_{i_0}) < \delta$, for any $\delta > 0$. This implies that $x \in C(D)$ and, consequently, that $\Omega \subset C(D)$, or that $\Omega = C(D)$.

q.e.d.

Before closing this chapter, it is useful to introduce a few topological concepts. Roughly speaking, topology involves the study of spaces in which the notion of an open set is a **logical primitive**, rather than the construct we had considered in the context of metric spaces.

Definition 44. A topological space $(\Omega, \mathcal{T})$ is a nonempty set, Ω, together with a collection, $\mathcal{T}$, of subsets of Ω, called a **topology**, having the following properties:

    i. $\Omega \in \mathcal{T}$, and $\emptyset \in \mathcal{T}$;

    ii. if $S_1, S_2 \in \mathcal{T}$ then $S_1 \cap S_2 \in \mathcal{T}$;

    iii. if $S_\nu \in \mathcal{T}$ then $\bigcup_\nu S_\nu \in \mathcal{T}$ for $\nu \in \mathcal{N}$, $\mathcal{N}$ being an index set, not necessarily countable.

Remark 31. The elements (sets) of the topology $\mathcal{T}$ are said to be the **open sets**. Note further that, given any **normed** space, we can generate a **metric** space by defining the metric as

$$\rho(x, y) = \| x - y \|, \quad \text{for } x, y \in \Omega.$$

Moreover, given a metric space, we can generate a topological space by defining the open sets as the spheres generated about every point of Ω. Thus, to each metric space, we can always associate a topological space; such a topological space is said to be **metrizable**. On the other hand, the same topological space may be associated with more than one metric spaces.

We give below several basic results regarding topological spaces.

Definition 45. Let $(\Omega, \mathcal{T})$ be a topological space; a collection of open sets, $\mathcal{B}_x$, (each) containing the point $x \in \Omega$, is said to be a **base at** x if for each open set A containing x there is a set $B_x \in \mathcal{B}_x$ such that $x \in B_x \subset A$. A collection of open sets $\mathcal{B}$ is a **base for the topology** $\mathcal{T}$ if and only if it is a base at each point $x \in \Omega$.

Proposition 30. A collection, $\mathcal{B}$, of open subsets of a space, Ω, is a base for some topology on Ω if and only if for every point $\omega \in \Omega$ there is a set $B \in \mathcal{B}$ such that $\omega \in B$, and if $\omega \in B_1 \cap B_2$, then there exists $B_3 \subset B_1 \cap B_2$ and $\omega \in B_3$.

Proof: That these conditions are necessary follows directly from Definition 44 and the requirement, in a topology, that the intersection of (two) open sets be open. Next, suppose that $\mathcal{B}$ satisfies these conditions. Define now the collection of (open) sets

$$\mathcal{T} = \{A : \text{such that if } x \in A, \text{ there exists } B \in \mathcal{B} \text{ and } x \in B \subset A\}.$$

We now show that $\mathcal{T}$ is a topology. Since for every $\omega \in \Omega$, there exists a set in $\mathcal{B}$ containing ω, it follows that $\Omega \in \mathcal{T}$. Evidently, $\emptyset \in \mathcal{T}$; moreover, if $A_1, A_2 \in \mathcal{T}$, then $A_1 \cap A_2 \in \mathcal{T}$, since for any $\omega \in A_1 \cap A_2$, there exist B_1, B_2, with $\omega \in B_1$ and $\omega \in B_2$. Consequently, there exists $B_3 \in \mathcal{B}$ such that $\omega \in B_3 \subset B_1 \cap B_2 \subset A_1 \cap A_2$, and thus, $A_1 \cap A_2 \in \mathcal{T}$. Finally, the third condition of Definition 42 (defining a topology) is, evidently, satisfied. Hence, $\mathcal{T}$ is a topology.

q.e.d.

Definition 46. Let $(W, \mathcal{T})$ be a topological space. It is said to satisfy the **first axiom of countability**, if at every point $\omega \in \Omega$ there is a countable base. It is said to satisfy **the second axiom of countability** if there exists a countable base for its topology.

Remark 32. Note that every **metric space** defines a topological space that satisfies the first axiom of countability. This is so since, at each point, the spheres about this point with **rational radii** will define a

countable base at this point. However, the topological space induced by
the metric of a metric space does not necessarily satisfy the second axiom
of countability. Indeed, a little reflection will convince the reader that
the second axiom of countability will be satisfied if and only if the metric
space is **separable**.

In dealing with topological spaces, one usually imposes additional
conditions that hold in metric spaces but would not in topological spaces
unless explicitly asserted.

Definition 47. Let (W, T) be a topological space and consider the
additional conditions.

C_1: Given two distinct points $\omega_i \in \Omega$, $i = 1, 2$, there is an open set
that contains ω_1 but not ω_2.

C_2: Given two distinct points $\omega_i \in \Omega$, $i = 1, 2$, there exist **disjoint
open** sets, A_i, $i = 1, 2$, such that $\omega_i \in A_i$, $i = 1, 2$.

C_3: The condition C_1 holds, and in addition, if G is a closed set and
$\omega \notin G$, then there exist **disjoint open** sets A_1, A_2 such that $\omega \in$
A_1 and $G \subset A_2$.

C_4: The condition C_1 holds, and in addition, if G_i, $i = 1, 2$, are
disjoint closed sets, there exist **disjoint open** sets, A_i, $i = 1, 2$,
such that $G_i \subset A_i$, $i = 1, 2$.

Remark 33. The four conditions of Definition 47 are known as **sepa-
ration axioms** and are valid in metric spaces. For topological spaces,
condition C_1 has as its only implication that sets consisting of a single
element (singletons) are **closed**.

A topological space satisfying C_2 is said to be a **Hausdorff space**.
One that satisfies C_3 is said to be a **regular space**, and one that satisfies
C_4 is said to be a **normal space**.

Moreover, it may be shown that C_4 implies C_3, that C_3 implies C_2
and that C_2 implies C_1.

We now introduce a number of concepts informally since we shall not employ them, in any essential way, in the exposition of econometric theory.

On the other hand, knowing what the terms mean is undeniably useful.

Definition 48. A normed linear space is said to be **complete**, if every Cauchy sequence converges; more precisely, suppose we have the Cauchy sequence $\{p_n : n \geq 1\}$, i.e., given any $\epsilon > 0$, there exists $N(\epsilon)$, such that $| p_n - p_m | < \epsilon$, for all $n, m > N(\epsilon)$. In a **complete normed linear space**, such sequences will converge, i.e., there will exist an element of the space, say p, such that given any $\epsilon > 0$, $| p_n - p | < \epsilon$, for all $n \geq N(\epsilon)$. A complete normed linear space is said to be a **Banach space**.

Definition 49. A metric space is said to be complete if and only if all Cauchy sequences converge (to an element of the space). If $\{z_n : n \geq 1\}$ is a Cauchy sequence in a metric space, it means that given any $\epsilon > 0$, there exists $N(\epsilon)$ such that for $n, m > N(\epsilon)$, $\rho(z_n, z_m) < \epsilon$.

Definition 50. A **Hilbert space**, H, is simply a Banach space on which we have defined an additional entity, (x, y), termed the **inner product**, obeying the following conditions, for $x, y, z \in H$ and $\alpha, \beta \in R$:

i. $(\alpha x + \beta y, z) = \alpha(x, z) + \beta(y, z)$;

ii. $(x, y) = (y, x)$;[1]

iii. $(x, x) = \| x \|^2$;

iv. $(x, x) > 0$ if and only if $x \neq 0$.

---

[1] For complex spaces this should read $(x, y) = \overline{(y, x)}$.

Chapter 2

Foundations of Probability

2.1 Discrete Models

Consider the problem of constructing a model of the process (experiment) of throwing a die and observing the outcome; in doing so, we need to impose on the experiment a certain probabilistic framework, since the same die thrown under ostensibly identical circumstances generally yields different outcomes. The framework represents, primarily, the investigator's view of the nature of the process, but it must also conform to certain logical rules. In dealing with the experiment above, we shall employ the mathematical framework we have created in Chapter 1. This is done not because the complexity of the problem requires it, but only in order to demonstrate, in a totally transparent fashion, the use to which such a framework may be put.

Example 1. Suppose the "experiment" consists of throwing a single die and recording the face showing; thus, the "outcomes" of the experiment consist of the set $\Omega = \{1, 2, 3, 4, 5, 6\}$. The collection

$(\emptyset); (1), (2), \ldots, (6);$
$(1,2), (1,3), \ldots, (1,6); (2,3), \ldots, (2,6); (3,4), \ldots, (3,6); \ldots; (5,6);$
$(1,2,3), (1,2,4), \ldots, (1,2,6); \ldots; (4,5,6);$
$\vdots$
$(1,2,3,4,5,6)$

consists of all subsets of Ω, including the null set; this collection, say

$\mathcal{A}$, is finite and is the equivalent of the σ-algebra for discrete models.

Sets containing multiple elements may be considered as unions of the **singletons**, i.e., the sets containing a single element. Thus, the pair $(\Omega, \mathcal{A})$, as above, is a rather simple measurable space. On this space, we may define the probability "measure", P, as follows: if $A \in \mathcal{A}$ and A contains $i \le 6$ elements, then $P(A) = i/6$. This reflects one's (the investigator's) view that all outcomes of this experiment are equally likely. The reader can verify that P is a nonnegative finitely additive set function with $P(\emptyset) = 0$ and $P(\Omega) = 1$. Notice that a set like $(2, 2)$ does not make sense, since it means that if we throw a die once "we observe a 2 or a 2" and this is not a very sensible way of putting things. Moreover, since, in general, $A \cup A = A$, sets with repeated elements do not make any sense in this context, or more precisely they are redundant.

Example 2. Let the experiment now consist of throwing the die twice and recording the outcomes in the order in which they have occurred. In this case, the sample space, or space Ω, consists of the collection of pairs

$$
\begin{aligned}
\Omega \quad = \quad & (1,1), (1,2), \ldots, (1,6); \\
& (2,1), (2,2), \ldots, (2,6); \\
& (3,1), (3,2), \ldots, (3,6); \\
& \vdots \\
& (6,1), (6,2), \ldots, (6,6).
\end{aligned}
$$

Again, the σ-algebra, $\mathcal{A}$, may be defined as the collection of all subsets of $\mathcal{A}$, including the null set, and it may be verified that it, too, contains a finite number of sets. On this σ-algebra, we may define the probability measure P as follows: if A is one of the elements of Ω, i.e., if $A = (i, j)$ with $i, j = 1, 2, 3, \ldots, 6$, then $P(A) = 1/36$. If A is a set that is made up of the union of, say k disjoint sets of the type above, then $P(A) = k/36$. Note that the elements of Ω, i.e., the sets (i, j), $i, j = 1, 2, \ldots, 6$, are disjoint. In the language of probability, these are also called **simple events**, while any member of the σ-algebra (the collection of subsets of Ω) is said to be an **event**, or sometimes a **compound event**. For example, if we wish to calculate the probability of the event

$$A = \{\text{the sum of the faces showing is less than 10}\},$$

we may proceed as follows: first, we write A, if possible, as the union of disjoint events, and then we write the latter as unions of simple events. Executing the first step, we have $A = \bigcup_{i=2}^{9} A_i$, where $A_i =$ the sum of the faces showing is i. Executing the second step, we reason as follows: since A_2 consists only of the simple event $(1,1)$, $P(A_2) = 1/36$; $A_3 = (1,2) \cup (2,1)$; hence, $P(A_3) = 2/36$; $A_4 = (1,3) \cup (2,2) \cup (3,1)$; hence, $P(A_4) = 3/36$; $A_5 = (1,4) \cup (2,3) \cup (3,2) \cup (4,1)$; hence, $P(A_5) = 4/36$; $A_6 = (1,5) \cup (2,4) \cup (3,3) \cup (4,2) \cup (5,1)$; hence, $P(A_6) = 5/36$; $A_7 = (1,6) \cup (2,5) \cup (3,4) \cup (4,3) \cup (5,2) \cup (6,1)$; hence, $P(A_7) = 6/36$; $A_8 = (2,6) \cup (3,5) \cup (4,4) \cup (5,3) \cup (6,2)$; hence, $P(A_8) = 5/36$; finally, $A_9 = (3,6) \cup (4,5) \cup (5,4) \cup (6,3)$; hence, $P(A_9) = 4/36$. Consequently, $P(A) = \sum_{i=1}^{6}(i/36) + (5/36) + (4/36)$.

Remark 1. The two simple examples above contain a great deal of the fundamental concepts of abstract probability theory. Let Ω_i, $i = 1, 2$, be two exact copies of the space Ω of Example 1 and notice that the space of Example 2 is simply the Cartesian (or direct) product of these spaces, i.e.,

$$\Omega = \{(\omega_1, \omega_2) : \omega_1 \in \Omega_1, \omega_2 \in \Omega_2\}.$$

The notation for a Cartesian product is $\Omega = \Omega_1 \times \Omega_2$. Similarly, if we put $\mathcal{A}_i$, $i = 1, 2$, for the σ-algebras of the two copies, then

$$\mathcal{A} = \mathcal{A}_1 \otimes \mathcal{A}_2$$

is the σ-algebra of the measurable space of Example 2. This notation is nonstandard, and $\otimes$ usually denotes the direct product of two entities, such as matrices, for example. In the usage above, **it simply denotes the smallest σ-algebra containing the collection** [1]

$$\mathcal{J} = \{A : A = A_1 \times A_2, \; A_i \in \mathcal{A}_i, \; i = 1, 2\}.$$

The reader ought to verify the claims just made; in doing so he ought to consider the term σ-algebra to mean, just for this space, "the class of all subsets" of the space. Nearly all of the concepts introduced through

---

[1] Certain other usages are also common; thus the collection $\mathcal{J}$ is also denoted by $\mathcal{J} = \mathcal{A}_1 \times \mathcal{A}_2$, which is to be distinguished from $\mathcal{A}_1 \otimes \mathcal{A}_2$, the latter being equal to $\sigma(\mathcal{J})$. This topic is further discussed in the following section.

Examples 1 and 2, generalize easily to abstract spaces, except, obviously, for the manner in which the σ-algebra is generated. For a general space the class of all subsets of Ω is too large a collection on which to define a measure. We shall take up the discussion of such issues in the next section, beginning with the case where $\Omega = R = (-\infty, \infty)$.

2.2   General Probability Models

2.2.1   The Measurable Space (R^n, $\mathcal{B}(R^n)$)

We consider the space $\Omega = R$ and a certain collection of subsets of R. The collection in question is one that consists of what we shall call the **basic or elementary sets** of the space; they are of the form $(a, b]$, where $a, b \in R$, and others, which can be expressed as a finite union of the basic intervals, together with the null set. As a matter of convention, we consider $(b, \infty]$ to be the same as (b, ∞); this is necessary in order to enforce the property that the complement of a set of the form $(-\infty, b]$ is a set of the same form, i.e., open on the left and closed on the right. Let this collection be denoted by $\mathcal{A}$; it is easy to verify that $\mathcal{A}$ is an algebra. This is so since if $A_i \in \mathcal{A}$, $i = 1, 2, \ldots, n$, then $A = \bigcup_{i=1}^{n} A_i \in \mathcal{A}$, where $n < \infty$ and $A_i = (a_i, b_i]$, so that the collection is closed under finite unions. Moreover, the complement of a set of the form $(a_i, b_i]$ is simply $(-\infty, a_i] \cup (b_i, \infty]$; consequently, the complement of any set in $\mathcal{A}$ is also in $\mathcal{A}$, so that the latter is closed under complementation and thus it is an algebra.

Remark 2. Given a collection of sets, say $\mathcal{J}$, there is always a smallest σ-algebra that contains $\mathcal{J}$. This is proved as follows: clearly, the set of all subsets of the space is a σ-algebra that contains $\mathcal{J}$; consider now the collection of all σ-algebras containing $\mathcal{J}$. As we have just shown, this collection is nonempty. Define the desired smallest σ-algebra to be the intersection of all σ-algebras containing $\mathcal{J}$. This σ-algebra is denoted by $\sigma(\mathcal{J})$ and is said to be the σ-algebra **generated by** $\mathcal{J}$. The elements of the set $\mathcal{J}$, i.e., the set "generating" the σ-algebra are said to be **the elementary sets**.

Although, in general, it is not possible to describe the process of constructing the σ-algebra generated by any **arbitrary** collection of sets, we may do so in particualr cases. In point of fact, if $\mathcal{J}$ **is an algebra**, it means that it is already closed under complementation and finite unions. Thus, if we add to it all sets that are limits of sets in $\mathcal{J}$, we shall have the desired σ-algebra. A similar argument will describe the **algebra generated** by a (nonempty) collection of subsets of Ω as simply the smallest algebra containing the class of subsets in question. The following proposition establishes a relation between the "size" of the collection and the "size" of the algebra or σ-algebra it generates.

Proposition 1. Let $\mathcal{C}$, $\mathcal{D}$ be two nonempty collections of the subsets of Ω. Denote by $\mathcal{A}(\mathcal{C})$, $\mathcal{A}(\mathcal{D})$ the algebras generated by the two collections, respectively, and by $\sigma(\mathcal{C})$, $\sigma(\mathcal{D})$ the σ-algebras generated by the two collections, respectively. If $\mathcal{C} \subset \mathcal{D}$, then $\mathcal{A}(\mathcal{C}) \subset \mathcal{A}(\mathcal{D})$, and $\sigma(\mathcal{C}) \subset \sigma(\mathcal{D})$.

Proof: We shall give a proof for the case of σ-algebras; the proof for algebras is entirely similar and is left to the reader. Let

$$Z_{\mathcal{C}} \;=\; \{\mathcal{B} : \mathcal{B} \supset \mathcal{C},\; \mathcal{B} \text{ a } \sigma\text{--algebra}\};$$

$$Z_{\mathcal{D}} \;=\; \{\mathcal{G} : \mathcal{G} \supset \mathcal{D},\; \mathcal{G} \text{ a } \sigma\text{--algebra}\}.$$

It is easy [2] to see that if $\mathcal{G} \in Z_{\mathcal{D}}$, then $\mathcal{G} \in Z_{\mathcal{C}}$, since $\mathcal{G}$ **is a σ-algebra** and $\mathcal{G} \supset \mathcal{D} \supset \mathcal{C}$. By definition,

$$
\begin{aligned}
\sigma(\mathcal{C}) \;&=\; \bigcap_{\mathcal{B} \in Z_{\mathcal{C}}} \mathcal{B} \\
&\subset\; \bigcap_{\mathcal{G} \in Z_{\mathcal{D}}} \mathcal{G} \\
&=\; \sigma(\mathcal{D}).
\end{aligned}
$$

This is so since $Z_{\mathcal{D}} \subset Z_{\mathcal{C}}$, and thus, the intersection of all the elements in $Z_{\mathcal{D}}$ **contains** the intersection of all the elements in $Z_{\mathcal{C}}$.

q.e.d.

---

[2] In this argument, it is assumed that the collections $Z_{\mathcal{C}}$, $Z_{\mathcal{D}}$ are nonempty; otherwise, there is nothing to prove. Evidently, if the collections $\mathcal{C}$, $\mathcal{D}$ are **algebras**, then it is easy to see that $Z_{\mathcal{C}}$, $Z_{\mathcal{D}}$ are nonempty collcetions.

Definition 1. Let $\mathcal{J}$ be the collection of intervals $(a, b]$, with $a, b \in R$, as above. Then, the σ-algebra $\sigma(\mathcal{J})$, generated by $\mathcal{J}$, is said to be the **Borel** σ-algebra and is usually denoted by $\mathcal{B}$, or $\mathcal{B}(R)$. The sets of this σ-algebra are said to be the **Borel** sets, and the pair $(R, \mathcal{B}(R))$ is said to be the **Borel** measurable space, or simply the one dimensional Borel space.

Now, suppose we are dealing with the Cartesian product of two real lines, which we denote, for clarity, by R_i, $i = 1, 2$. As a matter of notation, put $R^2 = R_1 \times R_2$, and on this space define, by analogy with the one dimensional case, rectangles, say $T^2 = T_1 \times T_2$, where $T_i \in R_i$ is a set of the form $(a_i, b_i]$, $i = 1, 2$. If $\mathcal{J}$ is the collection of all such rectangles in R^2, then the σ-algebra generated by $\mathcal{J}$, i.e. $\sigma(\mathcal{J})$, is also denoted by $\mathcal{B}(R^2)$; this is read the σ-algebra generated by the (half open) rectangles of R^2. As an alternative, consider the collection $\mathcal{J}^*$ of rectangles with "Borel sides", i.e. sets of the form $B = B_1 \times B_2$, where $B_i \in \mathcal{B}(R_i)$, $i = 1, 2$.

Definition 2. Let $\mathcal{J}^* = \{B : B = B_1 \times B_2, \; B_i \in \mathcal{B}(R_i), \; i = 1, 2\}$, i.e., the set of all (two dimensional) rectangles with Borel sides; the σ-algebra generated by this collection, $\sigma(\mathcal{J}^*)$, is said to be the **direct product** of the σ-algebras $\mathcal{B}(R_i)$, $i = 1, 2$, and is often denoted by $\mathcal{B}(R_1) \otimes \mathcal{B}(R_2)$.

Remark 3. Note that if B, C are any two sets in $\mathcal{J}^*$, their union is not necessarily in $\mathcal{J}^*$; this is so since $B \cup C \neq (B_1 \cup C_1) \times (B_2 \cup C_2)$, and consequently, it is not necessarily a set of the form $(D_1 \times D_2)$, with $D_i \in \mathcal{B}(R_i)$, $i = 1, 2$. On the other hand, $B \cap C = (B_1 \cap C_1) \times (B_2 \cap C_2) \in \mathcal{J}^*$. Considering the complement of B, a little reflection will show that

$$\bar{B} = (\bar{B}_1 \times B_2) \cup (B_1 \times \bar{B}_2) \cup (\bar{B}_1 \times \bar{B}_2),$$

which is, evidently, the union of disjoint sets (in $\mathcal{J}^*$), and as such it is in $\mathcal{J}^*$.

The observation above leads to

Definition 3. Let $\mathcal{J}$ be a collection of subsets of a space Ω. If (a) $\Omega \in \mathcal{J}$; (b) the complement of a set in $\mathcal{J}$ is the union of **disjoint sets** in $\mathcal{J}$, and (c) $\mathcal{J}$ is closed under (finite) intersections, then $\mathcal{J}$ is said to be a **semi-algebra**.

Remark 4. Note first that the collection $\mathcal{J}^*$ of Remark 3 is a semi-algebra. Note, also, that if, in general, $\mathcal{H}$ is a semi-algebra and is augmented by adding to it the null set and all sets that are finite disjoint unions of sets in $\mathcal{H}$, the resulting collection, $\mathcal{H}^*$, may be shown to be an **algebra**. This is so since, if $A \in \mathcal{H}$, its complement, $\bar{A}$, is the union of disjoint sets in $\mathcal{H}$, and hence, $\bar{A} \in \mathcal{H}^*$; if $A \in \mathcal{H}^*$, but $A \notin \mathcal{H}$, then it is the union of disjoint sets in $\mathcal{H}$, and by a similar argument we may establish that its complement is also in $\mathcal{H}^*$. Evidently, the augmented set is closed under finite unions. Moreover, $\sigma(\mathcal{H}^*) = \sigma(\mathcal{H})$. The argument for this is quite simple. Since $\mathcal{H}^* \supset \mathcal{H}$ it follows, by Proposition 1, that $\sigma(\mathcal{H}^*) \supset \sigma(\mathcal{H})$. Let $\mathcal{A}(\mathcal{H})$ be the algebra generated by $\mathcal{H}$. If $A \in \mathcal{H}^*$, then it is the union of disjoint sets in $\mathcal{H}$, and hence, $A \in \mathcal{A}(\mathcal{H})$; this shows that $\mathcal{H}^* \subset \mathcal{A}(\mathcal{H})$. Thus, again by Proposition 1, $\sigma(\mathcal{H}^*) \subset \sigma(\mathcal{A}(\mathcal{H}))$; but $\sigma(\mathcal{A}(\mathcal{H})) = \sigma(\mathcal{H})$. We thus conclude that $\sigma(\mathcal{H})^* = \sigma(\mathcal{H})$.

Referring the contents of Remark 4 to the earlier discussion, we note that the two collections of elementary sets, say

$$\mathcal{J}_1 = \{T^2 : T^2 = T_1 \times T_2, \ T_i = (a_i, \ b_i], \ i = 1, 2\}$$

and

$$\mathcal{J}_2 = \{B^2 : B^2 = B_1 \times B_2, \ B_i \in \mathcal{B}(R_i), \ i = 1, 2\}$$

are both semi-algebras. Thus, to show that their respective σ-algebras are the same, it will be sufficient to show that that the elementary sets of one are contained in the σ-algebra of the other. Now, it is evident that $\mathcal{J}_1 \subset \mathcal{J}_2$, since, evidently, $T_i \in \mathcal{B}(R_i)$, $i = 1, 2$. By Proposition 1, then, $\sigma(\mathcal{J}_1) \subset \sigma(\mathcal{J}_2)$. Conversely, consider $\sigma(\mathcal{J}_1)$ and note that it contains the sets $B_1 \times R_2$, $R_1 \times B_2$, for arbitrary $B_i \in \mathcal{B}(R_i)$, $i = 1, 2$. Hence, it contains, also, their intersection, which is nothing more than $B_1 \times B_2$, for arbitrary $B_i \in \mathcal{B}(R_i)$, $i = 1, 2$. This implies that $\sigma(\mathcal{J}_2) \subset \sigma(\mathcal{J}_1)$; we, thus, conclude that $\sigma(\mathcal{J}_1) = \sigma(\mathcal{J}_2)$. In fact, it may be shown that

$$\mathcal{B}(R^2) = \sigma(\mathcal{J}_1) = \sigma(\mathcal{J}_2) = \mathcal{B}(R_1) \otimes \mathcal{B}(R_2).$$

Remark 5. The import of the preceding discussion is that given n identical unidimensional Borel (measurable) spaces, we can routinely construct the n-dimensional Borel (measurable) space, $(R^n, \mathcal{B}(R^n))$, where $R^n = R_1 \times R_2 \times \cdots \times R_n$, and $\mathcal{B}(R^n) = \mathcal{B}(R_1) \otimes \mathcal{B}(R_2) \otimes \cdots \otimes \mathcal{B}(R_n)$.

We close this section by considering the infinite dimensional Borel space. This is an extremely important space, in that it is the space of (infinite) ordered sequences; as such, or in suitably generalized fashion, it plays an important role in the asymptotic theory of econometrics. Note that the space in question is

$$R^\infty = \{x : x = (x_1, x_2, x_3, \ldots)\}, \text{ where } x_i \in R_i, \ i = 1, 2, 3, \ldots,$$

i.e., the i_{th} real line R_i is the space of the i_{th} coordinate of the infinite sequence. To complete the construction of the infinite dimensional Borel space, $(R^\infty, \mathcal{B}(R^\infty))$, we need to specify its measurable sets, i.e., its σ-algebra. From our previous discussion, it is clear that this "should" be $\otimes_{i=1}^\infty \mathcal{B}(R_i)$; as pedagogical reinforcement, let us proceed to this task from first principles, i.e., by first specifying a certain collection of "elementary sets", usually a semi-algebra, and then obtaining the σ-algebra it generates. On the real line, this is the collection of intervals $\{T : (a, b], \ a, b \in R\}$. On R^2, it is the collection of rectangles $T_1 \times T_2$, and on R^n, it is the collection

$$\mathcal{T}_n = \{T^n : T^n = T_1 \times T_2 \times \cdots \times T_n, \ T_i = (a_i, b_i], \ a_i, b_i \in R_i, i = 1, 2, \ldots, n\}.$$

The obvious extension of this procedure is to specify the collection $T_1 \times T_2 \times \cdots$, but this does not offer an operational framework, i.e., it does not afford us the means of carrying out the required operations. Instead, we define the collection of basic or elementary sets by

$$\mathcal{G}(T^n) = \{x : x = (x_1, x_2, \ldots, x_n, \ldots), \ x_i \in T_i, \ T_i = (a_i, b_i]\},$$

i.e., the elementary sets consist of all infinite sequences, the first n elements of which lie in the intervals T_i, $i = 1, 2, \ldots, n$, for a_i, $b_i \in R_i$. Such sets, i.e., sets that require a finite number of elements (of an infinite sequence) to lie in certain subsets of the appropriate coordinate space and leave all others free, are said to be **cylinder sets**.

Thus, the typical cylinder set above could, more carefully, be specified as $T_1 \times T_2 \times \cdots \times T_n \times R \times R \cdots$. The σ-algebra generated by the cylinder sets above is denoted by $\mathcal{B}(R^\infty)$. As before, we have the alternative of considering cylinder sets, where the first n elements of the infinite sequence are required to lie in the Borel sets of the appropriate coordinate space. Thus, we consider the elementary sets to be the collection

$$\mathcal{G}(B^n) = \{x : x = (x_1, x_2, \ldots, x_n, \ldots), \quad x_i \in B_i \in \mathcal{B}(R_i), \quad i = 1, 2, \ldots n\}.$$

The smallest σ-algebra that contains this collection, i.e., the σ-algebra generated by $\mathcal{G}(B^n)$, for arbitrary n, is the (infinite) direct product of the constituent σ-algebras, viz., $\mathcal{B}(R_1) \otimes \mathcal{B}(R_2) \otimes \mathcal{B}(R_3) \otimes \cdots$. Finally, we may consider the elementary sets to be the collection of cylinders $\mathcal{G}(\mathcal{B}^n) = \{x : x = (x_1, x_2, x_3, \ldots, x_n, \ldots), (x_1, x_2 \ldots, x_n) \in B^n \in \mathcal{B}(R^n)\}$.

It may be shown that the σ-algebras generated by all three such collections of elementary sets are the same. The formal proof of this is somewhat tedious, but an intuitive understanding can be easily obtained by noting that if T^n is an n dimensional rectangle with (basic) interval sides then clearly it is a special form of an n dimensional rectangle with Borel sides, and the latter is clearly a special case of a set in $\mathcal{B}(R^n)$. On the other hand, any rectangle with Borel sides can be approximated by unions and/or intersections of rectangles with interval sides. As to the unspecified components of the sequences, note that the σ-algebra generated by the sets $T^n = T_1 \times T_2 \times \cdots \times T_n$, i.e., the collection $\mathcal{G}(T^n)$, is the same as that generated by the collection, $T^n \times R$, which is the same as that generated by the collection $T^n \times R \times R$, etc. This is so since the "character" of the set is determined by the intervals T_i, $i = 1, 2, \ldots, n$, while the additional dimensions occupied by the real lines only determine the "position" of the set in the higher dimension. This is so whether we are dealing with the first or the second or the third type of elementary cylinder sets.

2.2.2   Specification of Probability Measures

The purpose of this section is to elucidate some of the basic properties of the probability measure (whose definition was given in the preceding

chapter) and to show its connection with distribution functions. We
recall that a distribution function,

$$F : R \longrightarrow [0, \ 1],$$

has the following properties:

    i. $F(-\infty) = 0$;

    ii. $F(\infty) = 1$;

    iii. it is nondecreasing;

    iv. it is right continuous, i.e., if $x_n \downarrow x$, then $\lim_{x_n \downarrow x} F(x_n) = F(x)$,
        and moreover, for each $x \in R$, the $\lim_{x_n \uparrow x} F(x_n) = F(x-)$ exists.

We repeat, for convenience, the definition of a probability measure given
earlier in Chapter 1.

Definition 4. Let $(\Omega, \ \mathcal{A})$ be a measurable space; the set function,

$$P : \mathcal{A} \longrightarrow R,$$

is said to be a probability measure if and only if

    i. $P(\emptyset) = 0$;

    ii. $P(\Omega) = 1$;

    iii. for $\{A_i : i \geq 1, \ A_i \in \mathcal{A}\}$, a collection of pairwise disjoint sets,

$$P(\bigcup_{i=1}^{\infty} A_i) = \sum_{i=1}^{\infty} P(A_i),$$

i.e., if and only if it is nonnegative, σ-additive and satisfies property ii.

A few basic properties of the probability measure follow immediately.

Proposition 2. Let $(\Omega, \ \mathcal{A}, \ P)$ be a probability space:

    i. if $A, \ B \in \mathcal{A}$, then $P(A \cup B) = P(A) + P(B) - P(A \cap B)$;

    ii. if $A, \ B \in \mathcal{A}$ and $A \subset B$, then $P(A) \leq P(B)$;

iii. if $A_i \in \mathcal{A}$, $i \geq 1$, and $A = \bigcup_{i=1}^{\infty} A_i$, then $P(A) \leq \sum_{i=1}^{\infty} P(A_i)$.

Proof: For the proof of i., we note that since $(A \cup B) = A \cup (\bar{A} \cap B)$ and the two sets in the right member above are disjoint,

$$P(A \cup B) = P(A) + P(\bar{A} \cap B).$$

On the other hand, $B = (\bar{A} \cap B) \cup (A \cap B)$, and again because the two sets on the right are disjoint, $P(B) = P(\bar{A} \cap B) + P(A \cap B)$. Thus, $P(A \cup B) = P(A) + P(B) - P(A \cap B)$. For ii., suppose $A \subset B$; then, we can write $B = A \cup (\bar{A} \cap B)$, so that the two components of B (in the right member of the equation above) are disjoint; consequently,

$$P(B) = P(A) + P(\bar{A} \cap B) \geq P(A).$$

For iii., we employ essentially the same construction as above, viz., we define $B_1 = A_1$, $B_2 = A_2 \cap \bar{A}_1$, $B_3 = A_3 \cap \bar{A}_2 \cap \bar{A}_1 \ldots$, so that the sequence $\{B_i : i \geq 1\}$ consists of disjoint sets. Then,

$$P\left(\bigcup_{i=1}^{\infty} A_i\right) = P\left(\bigcup_{i=1}^{\infty} B_i\right) = \sum_{i=1}^{\infty} P(B_i) \leq \sum_{i=1}^{\infty} P(A_i).$$

q.e.d.

A number of other fundamental properties, which will be needed in subsequent discussion, are most conveniently exposited at this juncture.

Proposition 3. Let $(\Omega, \mathcal{A})$ be a measurable space and P a nonnegative, finitely additive set function defined on $\mathcal{A}$, with $P(\Omega) = 1$; then, the following four conditions are equivalent:

i. P is σ-additive, i.e., P is a probability;

ii. P is continuous at $\emptyset$, i.e., if $A_i \supset A_{i+1}$ and $\bigcap_{i=1}^{\infty} A_i = \emptyset$, then $\lim_{i \to \infty} P(A_i) = 0$;

iii. P is continuous from above, i.e., for any sets $A_i \in \mathcal{A}$, $i \geq 1$ such that $A_i \supset A_{i+1}$, $\lim_{i \to \infty} P(A_i) = P(\bigcap_{i=1}^{\infty} A_i)$;

iv. P is continuous from below, i.e., for any sets $A_i \in \mathcal{A}$, $i \geq 1$ such that $A_i \subset A_{i+1}$, $\lim_{i \to \infty} P(A_i) = P(\bigcup_{i=1}^{\infty} A_i)$.

Proof: We shall show that i. implies iv.; iv. implies iii.; iii. implies ii.; and finally, that ii. implies i., thus completing the proof. To show that i. implies iv., let $\{A_i : i \geq 1\}$ be a nondecreasing sequence and define as before

$$B_1 = A_1, \ B_i = A_i \bigcap_{j=1}^{i-1} \bar{A}_j, \ i > 1.$$

Since the sets are nondecreasing, we may simplify the expression above to

$$B_1 = A_1, \ B_i = A_i \cap \bar{A}_{i-1}, \ i > 1$$

and still preserve the disjointness of the B_i. Moreover, we find

$$\sum_{i=1}^{n} P(B_i) \ = \ P(A_1) + P(A_2) - P(A_1) + P(A_3) - P(A_2)$$

$$+ \cdots + P(A_n) - P(A_{n-1}) = P(A_n).$$

Given the σ-additivity of P we obtain

$$P\left(\bigcup_{i=1}^{\infty} A_i\right) \ = \ \sum_{i=1}^{\infty} P(B_i) = \lim_{n \to \infty} \sum_{i=1}^{n} P(B_i)$$

$$= \ \lim_{n \to \infty} P(A_n),$$

which proves that i. implies iv. To show that iv. implies iii., define

$$B_n = A_1 \cap \bar{A}_n, \ n \geq 1,$$

note that $B_1 = \emptyset$, $B_n \subset B_{n+1}$ and, as required by iii., the sequence $\{A_n : n \geq 1\}$ is nonincreasing. Since $\{B_n : n \geq 1\}$ is, evidently, a nondecreasing sequence, we have, by iv.,

$$P\left(\bigcup_{i=1}^{\infty} B_i\right) = \lim_{n \to \infty} P(B_n).$$

But, from the definition of B_n we easily ascertain that $P(B_n) = P(A_1) - P(A_n)$, or more usefully, $P(A_n) = P(A_1) - P(B_n)$. Thus,

$$\lim_{n \to \infty} P(A_n) = P(A_1) - \lim_{n \to \infty} P(B_n),$$

and moreover,

$$\lim_{n\to\infty} P(B_n) = P\left[\bigcup_{n=1}^{\infty}(A_1 \cap \bar{A}_n)\right].$$

The set whose probability measure is taken in the right member of the equation above may also be rendered as

$$\bigcup_{n=1}^{\infty}(A_1 \cap \bar{A}_n) = A_1 \cap \left(\bigcup_{n=1}^{\infty}\bar{A}_n\right).$$

Since we can always write

$$A_1 = \left[A_1 \cap (\bigcup_{n=1}^{\infty}\bar{A}_n)\right] \cup \left[A_1 \cap (\bigcap_{n=1}^{\infty}A_n)\right]$$

we have the relation

$$P(A_1) = P\left[A_1 \cap \left(\bigcup_{n=1}^{\infty}\bar{A}_n\right)\right] + P\left(\bigcap_{n=1}^{\infty}A_n\right).$$

Thus,

$$\lim_{n\to\infty} P(A_n) = P(A_1) - \lim_{n\to\infty} P(B_n) = P(A_1) - P(A_1) + P\left(\bigcap_{n=1}^{\infty}A_n\right).$$

To show that iii. implies ii. is quite simple, since

$$\lim_{n\to\infty} P(A_n) = P\left(\bigcap_{n=1}^{\infty}A_n\right) = P(\emptyset) = 0.$$

Finally, to show that ii. implies i., define $B_i \in \mathcal{A}$, $i \geq 1$, to be pairwise disjoint, and further define $A_n = \bigcup_{k=n}^{\infty} B_k$. Note that

$$P\left(\bigcup_{k=1}^{\infty} B_k\right) = \sum_{k=1}^{n-1} P(B_k) + P(A_n)$$

and moreover that $\{A_n : n \geq 1\}$ is a monotone nonincreasing sequence obeying $\bigcap_{n=1}^{\infty} A_n = \emptyset$. Thus, we have by ii., and rearranging an argument just used above,

$$\sum_{k=1}^{\infty} P(B_k) = \lim_{n\to\infty} \sum_{k=1}^{n} P(B_k) = P\left(\bigcup_{k=1}^{\infty} B_k\right) - \lim_{n\to\infty} P(A_n) = P\left(\bigcup_{k=1}^{\infty} B_k\right).$$

q.e.d.

To see the connection between probability measures and distribution functions in the context of the measurable space $(R, \mathcal{B})$, let P be a probability measure defined on $\mathcal{B}$, let $A = (-\infty, x]$, and define

$$F(x) = P(A).$$

Clearly, the function F is nonnegative; it is also nondecreasing by iv. of Proposition 3; $F(-\infty) = P(\emptyset) = 0$ by i., and $F(\infty) = P(R) = 1$ by property iv. of that proposition. Moreover, it is right continuous by iii. of Proposition 3. Thus, it is a distribution function as claimed. Conversely, if F is a distribution function defined on the measurable space in question, there exists a unique measure, say $P : \mathcal{B}(R) \longrightarrow R$ such that for any set of $\mathcal{B}$, say $A = (x, y]$, $x,\ y \in R$, it obeys

$$P(A) = F(y) - F(x).$$

By way of explanation consider, the collection of intervals on the real line, i.e., sets of the form $T = (a, b]$, and suppose

$$A = \bigcup_{i=1}^{n} (a_i,\ b_i],$$

where the intervals involved are disjoint. Define the probability measure

$$P_0(A) = \sum_{i=1}^{n} [F(b_i) - F(a_i)]$$

and note that this defines uniquely a set function on the collection (semi-algebra) of the intervals of the real line, which is finitely additive. It turns out that P_0 is σ-additive on this semi-algebra and, moreover, that it can be extended to $\mathcal{B}(R)$. This demonstration involves arguments that are too technical for our purposes, and we give the result below without a complete proof.

Proposition 4: Let F be a distribution function defined on the real line. Then, there exists a unique probability measure on $(R,\ \mathcal{B}(R))$ such that, for any $x,\ y \in R$,

$$P((x,\ y]) = F(y) - F(x).$$

Proof: For the basic interval collection, i.e. for sets of the form $(a,\ b]$, define

$$P_0((a,\ b]) = F(b) - F(a),$$

and for unions of disjoint such sets, define

$$P_0(\bigcup_{i=1}^{n}(a_i,\ b_i]) = \sum_{i=1}^{n}[F(b_i) - F(a_i)].$$

One easily verifies that the preceding defines, uniquely, a nonnegative, nondecreasing finitely additive set function on the semi-algebra of the elementary sets of R. Moreover, $P_0(R) = 1$. The remainder of the proof makes use of Caratheodory's extension theorem, which is given below (in a somewhat generalized form).

Proposition 5 (Caratheodory Extension Theorem). Let Ω be a space, let $\mathcal{C}$ be a semi-algebra of its subsets, and let $\sigma(\mathcal{C})$ be the smallest σ-algebra containing $\mathcal{C}$. Let P_0 be a measure defined on $(\Omega,\ \mathcal{C})$; then, there exists a unique measure, P, on $(\Omega,\ \sigma(\mathcal{C}))$ that is an extension of P_0 to $\sigma(\mathcal{C})$, i.e., if $A \in \mathcal{C}$, then

$$P(A) = P_0(A).$$

The measure P_0 is said to be be the restriction of P to $\mathcal{C}$, denoted by $P \mid \mathcal{C}$. Moreover, if P_0 is a probability or a σ-finite measure, then so is P.

Proof: See Chow and Teicher (1988, Theorem 1, ch. 6.1).

Example 3. Consider the distribution function

$$F(x) \quad = \quad 0 \text{ if } x < 0$$
$$= \quad \frac{x}{N} \text{ if } 0 \le x \le N < \infty$$
$$= \quad 1 \text{ if } x > N.$$

Applying Proposition 3, we can assert that if $a,\ b \in [0,\ N]$ then there exists a measure, say P, such that

$$P((a,\ b]) = b - a.$$

Here, the space is $\Omega = [0, N]$, and the σ-algebra of (Borel) subsets of the space is given by

$$\mathcal{B}([0, N]) = \{B \cap [0, N], \ B \in \mathcal{B}(R)\}.$$

Clearly, for sets in $\mathcal{B}([0, N])$, P essentially defines the simple Lebesgue measure on $[0, N]$.

Remark 6. If the distribution function of Proposition 3 is **absolutely continuous**, i.e., if there exists an integrable function, say f, such that F is the (indefinite) integral of f, then the measure of that proposition is definable by

$$P((a, \ b]) = \int_a^b f \, dx = F(a) - F(b),$$

and it should be apparent to the reader that sets of the form $(a, \ b)$, $(a, \ b]$, $[a, \ b)$, $[a, \ b]$ all have the same measure.

Generalization of such results to the measurable space $(R^n, \ \mathcal{B}^n)$, for finite n, is straightforward. Incidentally, $\mathcal{B}^n$ is shorthand for $\mathcal{B}(R^n)$. Thus, if P is a probability measure on this space, let

$$T = T_1 \times T_2 \times \cdots \times T_n,$$

where $T_i = (-\infty, \ x_i]$, $i = 1, 2, ..., n$, and define

$$F(x) = P(T), \ x = (x_1, \ x_2, \ldots, x_n).$$

It can be routinely verified that F is indeed a distribution function. The converse result is also valid and can be proved essentially in the same manner as Proposition 4. In particular, if F is absolutely continuous and if T is as above, then the probability measure obeys

$$P(T) = \int_a^b f \, dx = \int_{a_1}^{b_1} \int_{a_2}^{b_2} \cdots \int_{a_n}^{b_n} f \, dx_n \ldots dx_1,$$

except that now we take $T_i = (a_i, \ b_i]$. The extension of these results to the space $(R^\infty, \ \mathcal{B}(R^\infty))$ is due to Kolmogorov and essentially involves the idea that if we can specify measures on $\mathcal{B}(R^n)$ in a consistent fashion then, in fact, we have established a measure on $\mathcal{B}(R^\infty)$. Proceeding in the same fashion as before, let us ask ourselves what do we want to take as the elementary sets in this space? A natural choice would be the **cylinder sets** with base on the Borel sets of $\mathcal{B}(R^n)$. Let A be a Borel set in R^n; we recall that the cylinder set with base A is defined by

$$C_n(A) = \{x : x \in R^\infty, (x_1, x_2, \ldots, x_n) \in A \in \mathcal{B}(R^n)\}.$$

A less precise, but perhaps more revealing, way of representing this (cylinder) set is to write it as $A \times R \times R \ldots$. Consider now another set, say $A^* = A \times R$, and the cylinder set associated with it, viz., $C_{n+1}(A^*)$; if we use the more revealing notation to represent it, we see that the two sets are indeed identical. Hence, we would expect that

$$P[C_n(A)] = P[C_{n+1}(A^*)].$$

Indeed, the basic character of such (cylinder) sets is determined by the set A, and the fact that they are "infinitely dimensional", creates only "bookkeeping" problems of properly dealing with the dimensionality of the sets to which various probability measures apply. Specifically, if P were a probability measure on $(R^\infty, \mathcal{B}(R^\infty))$, we would want it to satisfy the property above. However, in the context of $(R^\infty, \mathcal{B}(R^\infty))$, the operation $P(A)$ does not make any sense since A is, strictly speaking, not in that σ-algebra; if we want to "place" A therein, we have to represent it as $A \times R \times R \cdots$, i.e., as the cylinder set $C_n(A)$. If we denote by P_n a probability measure on $(R^n, \mathcal{B}(R^n))$, then we would want to have

$$P[C_n(A)] = P_n(A). \tag{2.1}$$

Thus, if we construct a sequence of probability measures, P_i, on the space $(R^i, \mathcal{B}(R^i))$, we would want them to satisfy the following consistency property for any set $A \in \mathcal{B}(R^i)$, $i \geq 1$:

$$P_{i+1}(A \times R) = P_i(A). \tag{2.2}$$

It is remarkable that the converse of this result also holds and, moreover, that it is valid for abstract measurable spaces as well.

Proposition 6 (Kolmogorov Extension Theorem). Let P_i, $i \geq 1$, be a sequence of probability measures defined on the measurable spaces

$(R^i, \ \mathcal{B}^i)$, $i = 1, 2, \ldots$, respectively, and satisfying the consistency property in Equation (2.2). Then, there exists a unique probability measure, say P, on $(R^\infty, \ \mathcal{B}(R^\infty))$ such that, for any cylinder set $C_n(A)$, with $A \in \mathcal{B}(R^n)$,

$$P[C_n(A)] = P_n(A).$$

Proof: See Chow and Teicher (1988, Theorem 2, ch. 6.4).

Remark 8. The reader may wonder: are the preceding results, which were developed for the case where $\Omega = R$, restricted to that space alone? In fact, they are not. The real number system possesses two types of properties: algebraic, i.e., those that have something to do with notions of addition, multiplication, etc., and **metric**, or **topological** properties, i.e., those that have something to do with the distance between two numbers or sets of numbers as well as those dealing with the concept of the limit. These metric or topological properties are not confined to R alone. In fact, we have the following generalization of the version of Kolmogorov's consistency theorem given above.

Proposition 7. Let $(\Omega_i, \ \mathcal{G}_i, \ P_i)$, $i \geq 1$, be a sequence of probability spaces; then, there exists a unique probability measure, say P, on the (infinite dimensional product) measurable space $(\Omega, \ \mathcal{G})$, where

$$\Omega = \Omega_1 \times \Omega_2 \times \cdots$$

$$\mathcal{G} = \mathcal{G}_1 \otimes \mathcal{G}_2 \otimes \cdots,$$

such that if $A \in \mathcal{G}_1 \otimes \cdots \otimes \mathcal{G}_n$, then

$$P[C_n(A)] = (P_1 \times P_2 \times \cdots \times P_n)(A).$$

Proof: See Chow and Teicher, (1988, Theorem 1, ch. 6.4).

Remark 9. While the results of interest to us are valid for copies of the measurable space $(R, \ \mathcal{B})$, as well as copies of $(\Omega, \ \mathcal{G})$, it must not be supposed that there are no differences between the two sets of structures. For example, if we consider the sequence of probability spaces $(R^i, \ \mathcal{B}(R^i), \ P_i)$ and $(\Omega_i, \ \mathcal{G}_i, \ P_i)$ such that $\mathcal{G}_i \subset \mathcal{G}_{i+1}$ and $P_i = P_{i+1} \mid \mathcal{G}_i$

(the equivalent of the consistency property for the infinite dimensional Borel space) then defining

$$P(A) = \lim_{n \to \infty} P_n(A)$$

for $A \in \bigcup_{n=1}^{\infty} \mathcal{G}_n$ does not yield a σ-additive measure on that algebra; on the other hand, if we consider the Borel probability spaces, the measure so defined will be σ-additive, as Proposition 6 asserts. In any event, the import of the discussions above is that if $(\Omega_i, \mathcal{G}_i, P_i)$, $i \geq 1$, is a sequence of probability spaces, as described in the proposition, and if A is a set of the form

$$A = A_1 \times A_2 \times \cdots \times A_n \times \Omega \times \Omega \cdots,$$

then there exists a unique probability measure, say P, such that

$$P(A) = \prod_{i=1}^{n} P_i(A_i).$$

2.2.3   Fubini's Theorem and Miscellaneous Results

We begin by repeating the definition of a product measure (space). If $(\Omega_i, \mathcal{G}_i, \mu_i)$, $i = 1, 2$, are two measure spaces, consider the space

$$\Omega = \Omega_1 \times \Omega_2$$

and the semi-algebra

$$\mathcal{G} = \mathcal{G}_1 \times \mathcal{G}_2.$$

We recall that the notation above indicates that the sets in $\mathcal{G}$, say A, are of the form $A = A_1 \times A_2$, such that $A_i \in \mathcal{G}_i$, $i = 1, 2$. On this semi-algebra, we may define a measure by the operation

$$\mu_0(A) = \prod_{i=1}^{2} \mu_i(A_i),$$

and for unions of disjoint such sets, we may further require that

$$\mu_0 \left(\bigcup_{i=1}^{n} B_i \right) = \sum_{i=1}^{n} \mu_0(B_i).$$

If by $\sigma(\mathcal{G})$ we denote the σ-algebra generated by the semi-algebra $\mathcal{G}$, we may extend μ_0 to $\sigma(\mathcal{G})$, using Caratheodory's extension theorem.

We finally recall that if μ_0 is a probability then so would be its extension. Thus, let μ be the desired extension and consider the space $(\Omega,\ \sigma(\mathcal{G}),\ \mu)$; this is a product space, and it is in the context of this space that we shall discuss Fubini's theorem. First, however, a few preliminaries.

Consider the set $A = A_1 \times A_2$, in the product space above, and let $\omega_i \in A_i$, $i = 1, 2$. Define now the sets

$$A^{(1)}_{\omega_2} = \{\omega_1 : (\omega_1,\ \omega_2) \in A,\ \text{for fixed } \omega_2\},$$

$$A^{(2)}_{\omega_1} = \{\omega_2 : (\omega_1,\ \omega_2) \in A,\ \text{for fixed } \omega_1\}.$$

Definition 5. Consider the product measure space $(\Omega, \sigma(\mathcal{G}), \mu)$, defined above, and the the set $A = A_1 \times A_2$, with $A_i \in \mathcal{G}_i$, $i = 1, 2$. Then, the sets $A^{(1)}_{\omega_2}$, $A^{(2)}_{\omega_1}$, are said to be the **sections** of A at ω_2 and ω_1, respectively. More generally, if $A \in \mathcal{G}$ (and not necessarily as above), then sets of the form $A^{(1)}_{\omega_2}$, $A^{(2)}_{\omega_1}$, are said to be **sections** of A at ω_2 and ω_1, respectively, (with $\omega_i \in \Omega_i$, $i = 1, 2$).

Remark 10. Note that, in the general definition of sections, if $A = A_1 \times A_2$ and $\omega_2 \in A_2$, then $A^{(1)}_{\omega_2} = A_1$; otherwise, it is the null set. If $\omega_1 \in A_1$, then $A^{(2)}_{\omega_1} = A_2$; otherwise, it is the null set. The development above leads to

Proposition 8. Let $(\Omega, \mathcal{G}, \mu)$ be the product measure space, where $\Omega = \Omega_1 \times \Omega_2$, $\mathcal{G} = \sigma(\mathcal{G}_1 \times \mathcal{G}_2)$, $\mu = \mu_1 \times \mu_2$, and all measures are σ-finite. Then,

i. for any measurable set A, the sections $A^{(1)}_{\omega_2}$, $A^{(2)}_{\omega_1}$ are $\mathcal{G}_1$-, $\mathcal{G}_2$-measurable, respectively;

ii. if $\mu(A) = 0$, then $\mu_1(A^{(1)}_{\omega_2}) = 0$ and $\mu_2(A^{(2)}_{\omega_1}) = 0$;

iii. if f is a measurable function from $(\Omega, \mathcal{G}, \mu)$ to $(R, \mathcal{B})$, then for every $\omega_1 \in \Omega_1$, $f(\omega_1,\ \omega_2)$ defines a measurable function from $(\Omega_2,\ \mathcal{G}_2,\ \mu_2)$ to $(R,\ \mathcal{B})$, and for every $\omega_2 \in \Omega_2$, $f(\omega_1, \omega_2)$ defines a measurable function from $(\Omega_1, \mathcal{G}_1, \mu_1)$ to $(R,\ \mathcal{B})$.

Proof: To prove i., let

$$\mathcal{A} \;=\; \{A : A \in \mathcal{G},\; A^{(1)}_{\omega_2} \in \mathcal{G}_1,\; \text{for every } \omega_2 \in \Omega_2\},$$

$$\mathcal{C} \;=\; \{C : C = C_1 \times C_2,\; C_i \in \mathcal{G}_i,\; i = 1, 2\},$$

and note that by Remark 10, $\mathcal{C} \subset \mathcal{A}$. Moreover, if $A_i \in \mathcal{A}$, $i \geq 1$, consider $A = \bigcup_{i=1}^{\infty} A_i$ and its section at ω_2, which we denote by $A^{(1)}$, for simplicity. An easy calculation will show that $A^{(1)} = \bigcup_{i=1}^{\infty} A_i^{(1)} \in \mathcal{G}_1$. Similarly, if $A \in \mathcal{A}$, its complement also belongs to $\mathcal{A}$, since it can be written as the countable union of sets of the form $B_1 \times B_2$, with $B_i \in \mathcal{G}_i$, $i = 1, 2$. Thus, by the previous argument, the section of this union is the union of sections and thus the complement of $A \in \mathcal{A}$. But, this shows that $\mathcal{A}$ is a σ-algebra that contains $\sigma(\mathcal{C}) = \mathcal{G}$.

To prove ii., let A be of the form $A = A_1 \times A_2$; clearly, for such a set, $\mu(A) = \mu_1(A_1)\mu_2(A_2)$, and its indicator (or characteristic) function obeys

$$I_{12}(\omega_1, \omega_2) = I_1(\omega_1)I_2(\omega_2),$$

where $I_i(\omega_i), i = 1, 2$, are the indicator functions of the sets A_i, $i = 1, 2$, respectively, i.e.,

$$I_{12}(\omega_1, \omega_2) \;=\; 1, \quad \text{if } (\omega_1, \omega_2) \in A_1 \times A_2$$

$$=\; 0, \quad \text{otherwise.}$$

Moreover,

$$\mu(A) = \int_{\Omega} I_{12}(\omega_1,\ \omega_2)\, d\mu = \int_{\Omega_2} \mu_1(A^{(1)})d\mu_2 = \int_{\Omega_1} \mu_2(A^{(2)})d\mu_1.$$

Hence, on the semi-algebra, say $\mathcal{A}$, of sets of the form $A = A_1 \times A_2$, the result in ii. holds since, evidently, $\mu(A) = 0$ implies both $\mu_1(A^{(1)}) = 0$ a.e., and $\mu_2(A^{(2)}) = 0$ a.e. Next, consider the restriction $\mu \mid \mathcal{A}$. This is a σ-finite measure on the semi-algebra $\mathcal{A}$, and thus, by the Caratheodory extension theorem, there exists a unique extension to the σ-algebra $\sigma(\mathcal{A})$. By uniqueness, this extension is μ since $\sigma(\mathcal{A}) = \mathcal{G}$, which completes the proof of ii.

To prove iii., note that setting

$$f(\omega_1,\ \omega_2) = I_{12}(\omega_1,\ \omega_2),$$

where $I_{12}(\cdot, \ \cdot)$ is, as in the proof of ii., the indicator function of the set $A = A_1 \times A_2$, with $A_i \in \mathcal{G}_i$, $i = 1, 2$, we may conclude, by the discussion immediately preceding, that

$$f(\omega_1, \ \omega_2) \ = \ 1, \ \text{if } (\omega_1, \ \omega_2) \in A$$

$$= \ 0, \ \text{otherwise.}$$

In particular, treating ω_2 as fixed, we have the indicator function for A_1, while treating ω_1 as fixed, we have the indicator function for A_2. Thus, clearly the result in iii. holds for indicator functions of sets of the form $A = A_1 \times A_2$. But, any measurable function on the space $(\Omega_1 \times \Omega_2, \ \sigma(\mathcal{G}_1 \times \mathcal{G}_2))$ can be approximated by simple functions that are constant on (disjoint) sets of the form $A_1 \times A_2$, i.e., by

$$f_n(\omega_1, \ \omega_2) = \sum_{i=1}^{n} c_i I_{12i}(\omega_1, \ \omega_2),$$

where I_{12i} is the indicator function of a set of the form $A_{1i} \times A_{2i}$. Thus, for fixed μ_1, f_n is $\mathcal{G}_2$-measurable, and for fixed ω_2, it is $\mathcal{G}_1$-measurable. The conclusion then follows by the convergence of such functions to f.

q.e.d.

Proposition 9 (Fubini's Theorem). Let $(\Omega, \mathcal{G}, \mu)$ be the product measure space above (with μ σ-finite) and let $(\Psi, \mathcal{C})$ be a measurable space. Let

$$f : \Omega \longrightarrow \Psi$$

be a measurable function which is μ-integrable $(\mu = \mu_1 \times \mu_2)$. Then, the following statements are true:

i. the integrals

$$\int_{\Omega_1} f(\omega_1, \ \omega_2) \, d\mu_1, \quad \int_{\Omega_2} f(\omega_1, \ \omega_2) \, d\mu_2$$

are well defined for all ω_2, ω_1, respectively;

ii. the integrals in i. are $\mathcal{G}_2$-, $\mathcal{G}_1$-measurable, respectively, and moreover, $\mu_2(D_2) = \mu_1(D_1) = 0$, where

$$D_2 = \left\{ \omega_2 : \int_{\Omega_1} f(\omega_1, \ \omega_2) \, d\mu_1 = \infty \right\}$$

$$D_1 = \left\{ \omega_1 : \int_{\Omega_2} f(\omega_1,\ \omega_2)\, d\mu_2 = \infty \right\}$$

iii.

$$
\begin{aligned}
\int_\Omega f\, d\mu &= \int_\Omega f(\omega_1,\ \omega_2)\, d(\mu_2 \times \mu_1) \\
&= \int_{\Omega_1} \left[\int_{\Omega_2} f(\omega_1,\ \omega_2)\, d\mu_2 \right] d\mu_1 \\
&= \int_{\Omega_2} \left[\int_{\Omega_1} f(\omega_1,\ \omega_2)\, d\mu_1 \right] d\mu_2 .
\end{aligned}
$$

Proof: The proof of i. is an immediate consequence of Proposition 8, since we have shown there that, for fixed ω_2, f is $\mathcal{G}_1$-measurable and for fixed ω_1, it is $\mathcal{G}_2$-measurable. To prove ii. and iii., we begin with the case of nonnegative (measurable) functions. Thus, consider the set $A = A_1 \times A_2$ with $A_i \in \mathcal{G}_i$, $i = 1, 2$, take

$$f(\omega_1,\ \omega_2) = I_{12}(\omega_1,\ \omega_2),$$

where I_{12} is the indicator function of the set A above, and observe that, in the obvious notation,

$$I_{12}(\omega_1,\ \omega_2) = I_1(\omega_1) I_2(\omega_2).$$

Consequently,

$$\int_{\Omega_2} f\, d\mu_2 = I_1(\omega_1)\mu_2(A_2),$$

and

$$\int_{\Omega_1} f\, d\mu_1 = I_2(\omega_2)\mu_1(A_1),$$

which are, evidently, $\mathcal{G}_1$- and $\mathcal{G}_2$-measurable functions, respectively. Now, every nonnegative measurable function, f, can be approximated by a sequence of simple (nondecreasing) functions, converging pointwise to f. As we recall, the simple functions are linear combinations of indicator functions of the type examined above, i.e.,

$$f_n = \sum_{i=1}^{n} c_i I_{12i}(\omega_1,\ \omega_2),$$

such that $f_n \le f$, and I_{12i} is the indicator function of a set of the form $A_{1i} \times A_{2i}$. Notice that in view of the inequality above we must also have, for fixed ω_1 or ω_2,

$$f_n(\omega_1,\ \omega_2) \le f(\omega_1,\ \omega_2).$$

Hence, by the Monotone Convergence Theorem

$$H_{ni} = \int_{\Omega_i} f_n \, d\mu_i \longrightarrow \int_{\Omega_i} f \, d\mu_i = H_i, \ i = 1, 2$$

and, similarly, since $H_{ni} \leq H_i$, again by the monotone convergence theorem, we obtain

$$\int_{\Omega_2} H_{n1}(\omega_2) \, d\mu_2 \longrightarrow \int_{\Omega_2} H_1(\omega_2) \, d\mu_2.$$

Moreover, the integral of H_{n2} converges to that of H_2. But, this demonstrates the validity of iii. It is obvious, then, that ii. must be valid as well. This is so, since the functions displayed there have finite integrals; a necessary condition for this to be so is that the set over which the function(s) become unbounded must have measure zero. Having shown the validity of the proposition for nonnegative (measurable) functions and noting that any (measurable) function, f, can be written as $f^+ - f^-$, the proof of the proposition is completed.

q.e.d.

2.3   Random Variables

2.3.1   Generalities

In this section, we shall gather a number of results, regarding random variables, some of which have been dealt with in the previous sections and some of which are entirely new. The purpose is to assemble in one location a number of useful characterizations and other pertinent information about random variables. First, we recall the definition that a random variable is **a real valued measurable function, defined on a probability space**. Thus, given the extensive discussion of measurable functions in chapter 1, we already know a great deal about random variables, since nearly everything discussed in that chapter dealt with measurable functions defined on general, or at worst σ-finite, measure spaces. Since a random variable is a real valued function defined on a probability space, which is certainly σ-finite, all results obtained therein are immediately applicable to random variables.

If a function is given, how can we determine whether it is measurable? This is answered unambiguously by

Proposition 10. Let $(\Omega, \mathcal{A})$, $(R, \mathcal{B})$ be measurable spaces and

$$f : \Omega \longrightarrow R,$$

be a relation. Let $\mathcal{C}$ be a collection of subsets of R such that

$$\sigma(\mathcal{C}) = \mathcal{B}(R).$$

Then, f is measurable if and only if

$$A \in \mathcal{A}, \ A = \{\omega : f(\omega) \in C\}$$

for all $C \in \mathcal{C}$.

Proof: If the condition holds, then evidently $A \in \mathcal{A}$; thus, consider the sufficiency part. Let

$$\mathcal{H} = \{B : B \in \mathcal{B}(R) \quad \text{and} \quad f^{-1}(B) \in \mathcal{A}\}$$

and consider the sequence B_i, $i \geq 1$, such that $B_i \in \mathcal{H}$. Since

$$f^{-1}(\bar{B}_i) = \overline{f^{-1}(B_i)}, \quad f^{-1}\left(\bigcup_{i=1}^{\infty} B_i\right) = \bigcup_{i=1}^{\infty} f^{-1}(B_i),$$

we conclude that $\mathcal{H}$ is a σ-algebra. Clearly $\mathcal{C} \subset \mathcal{H} \subset \mathcal{B}(R)$. Therefore, by Proposition 1, of this chapter, $\sigma(\mathcal{C}) \subset \mathcal{H} \subset \mathcal{B}(R)$. But, by the condition of the proposition, $\sigma(\mathcal{C}) = \mathcal{B}(R)$.

q.e.d.

Corollary 1. A necessary and sufficient condition for X to be a random variable is that $A_x \in \mathcal{A}$, where $A_x = \{\omega : X(\omega) \leq x\}$ or $\{\omega : X(\omega) < x\}$, for every $x \in R$.

Proof: Let $\mathcal{C}$ be the collection of intervals of the form $(-\infty, x)$, $x \in R$, and $\mathcal{C}^*$ the collection of intervals of the form $(-\infty, x]$. From Proposition 1, of this chapter we conclude that $\sigma(\mathcal{C}) = \sigma(\mathcal{C}^*) = \mathcal{B}(R)$.

q.e.d.

Remark 11. Notice, in the course of the proof above, that if $\sigma(\mathcal{C}) = \mathcal{B}(R)$ then putting

$$\mathcal{H} = \{H : H = X^{-1}(C),\ C \in \mathcal{C}\}$$

we easily conclude that $\mathcal{H}$ is a σ-algebra. This σ-algebra is often denoted by $\sigma(X)$ and is said to be the σ-algebra **induced by** X.

Remark 12. When dealing with random variables, it is occasionally convenient to allow the range of measurable functions to be

$$\bar{R} = [-\infty,\ \infty], \text{ instead of } R = (-\infty,\ \infty).$$

Since the set $[-\infty,\ \infty]$ is said to be the **extended** real line, such random variables are said to be **extended** random variables. When dealing with such random variables, it is crucial to bear in mind a number of important conventions as follows: if $a \in R$, then $a \pm \infty = \pm\infty$; $a \cdot \infty = \infty$ if $a > 0$, $a \cdot \infty = -\infty$ if $a < 0$ and $a \cdot \infty = 0$, if $a = 0$; $a/\pm\infty = 0$; $\infty + \infty = \infty$; $-\infty + (-\infty) = -\infty$. We must also recognize that, despite the conventions above, we are still left with the following indeterminate forms: ∞/∞, $\infty - \infty$, $0/0$.

In most of our discussion, we shall be dealing with a.c. finite random variables, i.e., if X is a random variable, then

$$P(A) = 0,\ A = \{\omega : X(\omega) = \pm\infty\}.$$

Note, further, that if X is integrable, i.e., if

$$\int X\, dP < \infty,$$

then for A, as defined above, we must also have $P(A) = 0$.

Definition 6. The expectation of a random variable, defined over the probability space $(\Omega, \mathcal{A}, P)$, is given by the integral above, whenever the latter exists; thus, the expectation of a random variable is

$$\int_{\Omega} X\, dP$$

and is denoted by $E(X)$, E being the expectation operator.[3]

---

[3] When the context is clear and no confusion is likely to arise, we shall also employ the notation $E X$.

Remark 13. Note that the use of the expectation operator, combined with the notation for indicator functions, virtually eliminates the need to write an integral sign. For purposes of notational ease, we shall frequently employ this procedure. For example, suppose we wish to take the integral of the square of a zero mean random variable over a set A. Instead of the notation

$$\int_A X^2 \, dP,$$

we can write simply $E[X^2 I_A]$.

The reader is no doubt very familiar with statements of the form: Let X be a random variable with distribution function, F; moreover, he is no doubt well aware of the fact that F is defined on the real line. This terminology might create the erroneous impression that random variables are defined on the real line, which is incompatible with our previous discussion. The following few words are meant to clarify these issues. Thus, we have

Definition 7. Let X be a random variable as in Definition 6. Then, its **probability distribution** is a **set function**

$$P_x : \mathcal{B}(R) \longrightarrow R$$

such that, for all sets $B \in \mathcal{B}$,

$$P_x(B) = P[X^{-1}(B)].$$

Remark 14. The probability function, P_x, of a random variable, X, is to be distinguished from its **distribution function**, say F, sometimes also termed the p.d.f. (probability distribution function), which is a **point function**

$$F : R \longrightarrow [0, 1]$$

and is defined, for all $x \in R$, by

$$F(x) = P\left(X^{-1}((-\infty, \ x])\right) = P_x\left((-\infty, \ x]\right).$$

2.3.2   Random Elements

Definition 8. Let $(\Omega,\ \mathcal{A})$, $(\Psi,\ \mathcal{G})$ be two measurable spaces and f a relation

$$f : \Omega \longrightarrow \Psi.$$

Then, f is said to be $\mathcal{A} \mid \mathcal{G}$-measurable if and only if for every $G \in \mathcal{G}$, $A \in \mathcal{A}$, where

$$A = \{\omega : f(\omega) \in G\}.$$

Definition 9. Let $(\Omega, \mathcal{A}, P)$, $(\Psi,\ \mathcal{G})$ be a probability and measurable space, respectively, and let

$$X : \Omega \longrightarrow \Psi.$$

Then, X is said to be a **random element** if and only if it is $\mathcal{A} \mid \mathcal{G}$-measurable.

Example 4. Let $\Psi = R^n$, $\mathcal{G} = \mathcal{B}(R^n)$, then a random element, say $X(\omega)$ from Ω to R^n, represents a "random point" in R^n; or, more precisely, if

$$X : \Omega \longrightarrow R^n$$

is a (real) vector valued measurable function, then it represents the ordered collection of points $\{X_1(\omega),\ X_2(\omega),\ \dots, X_n(\omega)\}$. In fact, if we define the function c_k by the operation

$$c_k(X(\omega)) = X_k(\omega),$$

so that it extracts the kth coordinate of the point (or the vector), then X_k can be shown to be a random variable, i.e., a real valued $\mathcal{B}(R_k)$-measurable function and its probability properties can easily be deduced from those of X, as follows. Given the measure P, let

$$H_k = \{\omega : X_k(\omega) \in B_k\},$$

where B_k is a (Borel) set in $(R_k,\ \mathcal{B}(R_k))$, and define a measure on this measurable space by the operation

$$P_k(H_k) = P(B_k^*),$$

where $B_k^* = R \times R \times \cdots R \times B_k \times R \times \cdots \times R$. Moreover, we can also define the σ-algebra, $\sigma(X_k)$, so that we can think of X_k as defined on $(\Omega,\ \sigma(X_k),\ P_k)$ and assuming values in $(R,\ \mathcal{B})$. This shows that given a random element we can deduce therefrom a set of (scalar) random variables. The converse is also true, i.e., given a sequence of random variables X_k, each defined on $(\Omega_k,\ \mathcal{A}_k,\ P_k)$ and assuming values in $(R,\ \mathcal{B})$, we can define a random element, say $X = (X_1, X_2, \ldots, X_n)$, which is defined on $(\Omega, \mathcal{A}, P)$ and assumes values in $(R^n,\ \mathcal{B}(R^n))$. For instance, we may take

$$\Omega \quad = \quad \Omega_1 \times \Omega_2 \times \cdots \times \Omega_n,$$

$$\mathcal{A} \quad = \quad \sigma(\mathcal{A}_1 \times \mathcal{A}_2 \times \cdots \times \mathcal{A}_n).$$

As for the measure to be defined on Ω, we may note that if $C \in \mathcal{A}$, then C has a representation as a countable union of sets of the form $A = A_1 \times A_2 \times \cdots \times A_n$ with $A_i \in \mathcal{A}_i$; for such sets, we then define P by the operation

$$P(A) = P_1(A_1) \cdot P_2(A_2) \cdot P_3(A_3) \cdot \cdots \cdot P_n(A_n).$$

Remark 15. An ordered set of random variables, $(X_1, X_2, \ldots, X_n)$, is said to be a **random vector**. Note further that in terms of our previous discussion, whether we deal with "scalar" or "vector" random variables, i.e. single random variables or ordered sets of random variables, does not make a great deal of difference in terms of the complexity of the concepts involved. The class of random elements is, of course, much richer than the class of vector random variables. We shall examine the theory of random elements more extensively in chapter 4.

We will close this section with a result regarding changing of variables.

Proposition 11 (Change of Variable). Let $(\Omega, \mathcal{A}, P)$, $(\Psi,\ \mathcal{G})$ be a probability and measure space, respectively, and let

$$X : \Omega \longrightarrow \Psi$$

be a $\mathcal{A} \mid \mathcal{G}$-measurable function (i.e., a random element); let P_x be the probability measure on $(\Psi,\ \mathcal{G})$ induced by X. Then, for any $\mathcal{G}$-

measurable function, g, and $A \in \mathcal{G}$,

$$\int_A g(x)\, dP_x = \int_{X^{-1}(A)} g[X(\omega)]\, dP.$$

Proof: Let A, $B \in \mathcal{G}$ and take $g(x) = I_B(x)$, the latter being the indicator function of the set B. Then, it is easy to see that

$$\int_A g(x)\, dP_x = \int_A I_B(x)\, dP_x = P_x(A \cap B).$$

Next, consider the integral

$$\int_{X^{-1}(A)} g[X(\omega)]\, dP = \int_{X^{-1}(A)} I_B[X(\omega)]\, dP.$$

Examining the last integral, we note that, given the set over which we integrate, the integrand is null except when ω is such that $X(\omega) \in A \cap B$, in which case it is unity; thus, the first integral obeys

$$\int_{X^{-1}(A)} g[X(\omega)]\, dP = \int_{X^{-1}(A) \cap X^{-1}(B)} dP = P\left(X^{-1}(A) \cap X^{-1}(B)\right)$$

$$= P\left(X^{-1}(A \cap B)\right).$$

In view of the definition of P_x, it is transparent that $P(X^{-1}[A \cap B]) = P_x(A \cap B)$. Thus, the conclusion of the proposition holds for simple nonnegative functions, and by the monotone convergence theorem, it holds for all nonnegative functions as well. But, given any function, g, we can alwasys write it in terms of a pair of nonnegative functions, i.e., $g = g^+ - g^-$. Consequently, the conclusion holds for all $\mathcal{G}$-measurable functions.

q.e.d.

Example 5. Let X be a random element defined on $(\Omega, \mathcal{A}, P)$, which takes values in $(R^n,\ \mathcal{B}(R^n))$. Consider the function

$$h : R^n \longrightarrow R,$$

given by $h(X) = a'X$, where $a \in R^n$. The measure induced by X, on $\mathcal{B}(R^n)$, is defined for all $A \in \mathcal{B}(R^n)$, by

$$P_x(A) = P(X^{-1}(A)).$$

Thus, by the results of the preceding proposition we have that

$$\int_A a' x \, dP_x = \int_{X^{-1}(A)} a' X(\omega) \, dP.$$

The operation above has shown the equivalence of integration over the spaces Ω and R^n. We may, however, show a further equivalence of integration over the spaces R and R^n, and thus an equivalence of integration over the spaces R, R^n, and Ω. To this effect, let $C \in \mathcal{B}$ define $B = \{x : h(x) \in C\}$ and also put $A = \{\omega : X(\omega) \in B\}$. Further, define the measure over R by the operation

$$P_y(C) = P_x(B) = P(A) = P\left(X^{-1}[h^{-1}(C)]\right).$$

Thus, we have the useful relation, with $y = h(X)$,

$$\int_C y \, dP_y = \int_{h^{-1}(C)} a' x \, dP_x = \int_{X^{-1}(h^{-1}[C])} a' X(\omega) \, dP.$$

2.3.3 Moments of Random Variables and Miscellaneous Inequalities

Let $(\Omega, \mathcal{A}, P)$, $(R, \mathcal{B})$ be a probability and measurable space, respectively, and let

$$X : \Omega \longrightarrow R$$

be a random variable.[4] We recall that the **expectation** or **mean** of a random variable, say X, is denoted by $E(X)$ and is given by

$$E(X) = \int_\Omega X(\omega) \, dP.$$

In all subsequent discussion, it will be understood that all random variables are integrable in the sense that the relevant integrals exist and are finite, i.e., we shall always be dealing with a.c. finite random variables. If X is a random variable, then so is X^k, and the kth **moment** of the random variable X is defined by

$$\int_\Omega X^k(\omega) \, dP = E(X^k) = \mu_k, \ k = 1, 2, \ldots$$

---

[4] In order to avoid this cumbersome phraseology, in the future, when we say that X is a random variable, it is to be understood that we have predefined the appropriate probability and measurable spaces. Thus, mention of them will be suppressed.

provided the integrals exist and are finite. The second moment about the mean, (μ_1), is of special significance; it is termed the **variance** of the random variable and is given by

$$\text{Var}(X) = E(X - \mu_1)^2.$$

If X is a random vector, then μ_1 is a vector of means and the concept of variance is generalized to that of the **covariance matrix**

$$\text{Cov}(X) = E(X - \mu)(X - \mu)' = \Sigma,$$

which is usually denoted by the capital greek letter Σ.

Proposition 12 (Generalized Chebyshev Inequality). If X be a non-negative integrable random variable, then given $\epsilon > 0$,

$$P(A) \leq \frac{E(X)}{\epsilon},$$

where $A = \{\omega : X(\omega) \geq \epsilon\}$.

Proof: Let I_A be the indicator function of the set A and note that $X \geq XI_A \geq \epsilon I_A$. Taking expectations, we find

$$E(X) \geq E(XI_A) \geq \epsilon E(I_A) = \epsilon P(A).$$

Noting that $P(A)$ is the proper notation for $P(X \geq \epsilon)$, we have the standard result for the general case.

$$\text{q.e.d.}$$

Corollary 2. If ξ is an unrestricted random variable with mean μ and variance σ^2, then

$$P(|\xi - \mu| \geq \epsilon) \leq \frac{\sigma^2}{\epsilon^2}.$$

Proof: Let $X = |\xi - \mu|^2$ and note that $E(X) = \sigma^2$; by Proposition 12,

$$P(X \geq \epsilon^2) \leq \sigma^2/\epsilon^2.$$

Next, consider the sets

$$A = \{\omega : X \geq \epsilon^2\} \quad \text{and} \quad A^* = \{\omega : X^{1/2} \geq \epsilon\};$$

we shall show that $A = A^*$. This is so since, if $\omega \in A$, then we must also have that $[X(\omega)]^{1/2} \geq \epsilon$, so that $\omega \in A^*$, which shows that $A \subset A^*$; similarly, if $\omega \in A^*$, then we must have that $X(\omega) \geq \epsilon^2$, so that $\omega \in A$, which shows that $A^* \subset A$. The latter, in conjunction with the earlier result, implies $A = A^*$, and thus, $P(A) = P(A^*)$.

q.e.d.

Corollary 3. Let ξ be a vector random variable with mean μ and covariance matrix Σ. Then,

$$P(\| \xi - \mu \|^2 \geq \epsilon^2) \leq \frac{\mathrm{tr}\Sigma}{\epsilon^2}.$$

Proof: Note that $\| \xi - \mu \|^2 = X$ is a nonnegative integrable random variable; hence, by Proposition 12,

$$P(X \geq \epsilon^2) \leq \frac{\mathrm{tr}\Sigma}{\epsilon^2},$$

where, evidently, $\mathrm{tr}\Sigma = E(\| \xi - \mu \|^2)$.

q.e.d.

Proposition 13 (Cauchy Inequality). Let X_i, $i = 1, 2$, be zero mean random variables and suppose that $\mathrm{Var}(X_i) = \sigma_{ii} \in (0, \infty)$; then,

$$(E \mid X_1 X_2 \mid)^2 \leq \sigma_{11}\sigma_{22}.$$

Proof: Since $\sigma_{ii} > 0$, $i = 1, 2$, define the variables $\xi_i = \frac{X_i}{\sigma_{ii}^{1/2}}$, and note that $\mathrm{Var}(\xi_i) = 1$. Moreover, since

$$(\mid \xi_1 \mid - \mid \xi_2 \mid)^2 \geq 0,$$

we have that

$$2E(\mid \xi_1 \xi_2 \mid) \leq E(\xi_1^2 + \xi_2^2).$$

But, this implies $E(\mid X_1 X_2 \mid) \leq (\sigma_{11}\sigma_{22})^{1/2}$.

q.e.d.

Corollary 4. The correlation between any two square integrable random variables lies in $[-1, 1]$.

Proof: Let X_i, $i = 1, 2$, be any two square integrable random variables as in the proposition and put $\sigma_{12} = E(X_1 X_2) = \text{Cov}(X_1, X_2)$. We recall that the correlation (or correlation coefficient) between two random variables is given by

$$\rho_{12} = \frac{\sigma_{12}}{(\sigma_{11}\sigma_{22})^{1/2}}.$$

Since from Proposition 13 we have $\sigma_{12}^2 \leq \sigma_{11}\sigma_{22}$, the result follows immediately.

q.e.d.

Proposition 14. Let h be a measurable function

$$h : R^n \longrightarrow R$$

and X be an integrable random vector, i.e., $\| E(X) \| < \infty$ for an appropriate norm; then,

    i. if h is a convex function, $h[E(X)] \leq E(h[X])$;

    ii. if h is a concave function, $h[E(X)] \geq E(h[X])$.

Proof: If h is a convex function,[5] then we can write for any point, x_0,

$$h(x) \geq h(x_0) + s(x_0)(x - x_0),$$

where x is an appropriate (row) vector valued function. Consequently, for $x = X$ and $x_0 = E(X)$, we have the proof of i. As for ii., we note that if h is a convex function then $-h$ is concave. The validity of ii. is, then, obvious.

q.e.d.

---

[5] For twice differentiable convex functions, the matrix of the second order partial derivatives is positive semidefinite; for concave functions, it is negative semidefinite; in both cases this is to be understood in an a.e. sense.

Proposition 15 (Liapounov's Inequality). Let X be a suitably integrable random variable and $0 < s < r$ be real numbers; then,

$$(E \mid X \mid^s)^{1/s} \le (E \mid X \mid^r)^{1/r}.$$

Proof: Define $\mid X \mid^s = \xi$, and consider ξ^k, where $k = (r/s)$. Since ξ^k is a convex function, by Jensen's inequality, we have

$$[E(\xi)]^k \le E(\xi^k).$$

Now, reverting to the original notation, this gives the result

$$(E \mid X \mid^s)^{1/s} \le (E \mid X \mid^r)^{1/r}.$$

q.e.d.

Corollary 5. Let X be a suitably integrable random variable; then, for any integer n, for which $\mid X \mid^n$ is integrable,

$$E \mid X \mid \le (E \mid X \mid^2)^{1/2} \le \cdots \le (E \mid X \mid^n)^{1/n}.$$

Proof: This is obvious by repeated application of Liapounov's inequality.

q.e.d.

Proposition 16 (Holder's Inequality). Let X_i, $i = 1, 2$, be suitably integrable random variables and let $p_i \in (1, \infty)$, such that $(1/p_1) + (1/p_2) = 1$. Then, provided the $\mid X_i \mid^{p_i}$ are integrable,

$$E \mid X_1 X_2 \mid \le (E \mid X_1 \mid^{p_1})^{1/p_1} (E \mid X_2 \mid^{p_2})^{1/p_2}.$$

Proof: Evidently, if $E \mid X_i \mid^{p_i} = 0$, then $X_i = 0$ a.c., and consequently, the result of the proposition is valid. Thus, we suppose that $E \mid X_i \mid^{p_i} > 0$. Define now $\xi_i = \mid X_i \mid / c_i$, where $c_i = (E \mid X_i \mid^{p_i})^{1/p_i}$, $i = 1, 2$. Since the logarithm is a concave function, it is easy to show that

$$\ln[ax + by] \ge a \ln x + b \ln y$$

for $x, y, a, b > 0$ such that $a + b = 1$. But, this implies that

$$x^a y^b \le ax + by.$$

Applying this inequality with $x = \xi_1^{p_1}$, $y = \xi_2^{p_2}$, $a = 1/p_1$, $b = 1/p_2$, we find

$$E(\xi_1 \xi_2) \leq \frac{1}{p_1} E(\xi_1^{p_1}) + \frac{1}{p_2} E(\xi_2^{p_2}),$$

and, reverting to the original notation, we have

$$E \mid X_1 X_2 \mid \, \leq (E \mid X_1 \mid^{p_1})^{1/p_1} (E \mid X_2 \mid^{p_2})^{1/p_2}.$$

q.e.d.

Proposition 17 (Minkowski's Inequality). Let X_i, $i = 1, 2$, be random variables, $p \in (1, \infty)$ such that $\mid X_i \mid^p$ is integrable. Then,

$$\mid X_1 + X_2 \mid^p \text{ is integrable,}$$

and moreover,

$$(E \mid X_1 + X_2 \mid^p)^{1/p} \leq (E \mid X_1 \mid^p)^{1/p} + (E \mid X_2 \mid^p)^{1/p}.$$

Proof: Consider the function $F(x) = (x + a)^p - 2^{p-1}(x^p + a^p)$ and note that $F'(x) = p(x + a)^{p-1} - 2^{p-1} p x^{p-1}$. From this, we easily deduce that the function has a maximum at $x = a$, provided a and x are restricted to be positive. But, we note that $F(a) = 0$; consequently, we have

$$(x + a)^p \leq 2^{p-1}(x^p + a^p).$$

Since

$$(\mid X_1 + X_2 \mid)^p \leq (\mid X_1 \mid + \mid X_2 \mid)^p \leq 2^{p-1}(\mid X_1 \mid^p + \mid X_2 \mid^p),$$

the validity of the first part of the proposition is evident. For the second part, note that

$$(\mid X_1 + X_2 \mid)^p \leq \mid X_1 \mid \mid X_1 + X_2 \mid^{p-1} + \mid X_2 \mid \mid X_1 + X_2 \mid^{p-1}.$$

Applying Holder's inequality to the two terms of the right member above, we find

$$E(\mid X_1 \mid \mid X_1 + X_2 \mid^{p-1}) \leq (E \mid X_1 \mid^p)^{1/p} (E \mid X_1 + X_2 \mid^{(p-1)q})^{1/q},$$

$$E(\mid X_2 \mid \mid X_1 + X_2 \mid^{p-1}) \leq (E \mid X_2 \mid^p)^{1/p} (E \mid X_1 + X_2 \mid^{(p-1)q})^{1/q},$$

where q is such that $(1/p) + (1/q) = 1$; this being so, note that $(p - 1)q = p$. Adding the two inequalities above we find

$$(E \mid X_1 + X_2 \mid^p)^{\frac{1}{p}} \leq (E \mid X_1 \mid^p)^{\frac{1}{p}} + (E \mid X_2 \mid^p)^{\frac{1}{p}}.$$

q.e.d.

2.4   Conditional Probability

2.4.1   Conditional Probability in Discrete Models

The reader is no doubt familiar with the general notion of conditional probability. Thus, for example, if $(\Omega, \mathcal{A}, P)$ is a probability space and A, $B \in \mathcal{A}$, then the conditional probability of A, given B, is given by the relation

$$P(A \mid B) = \frac{P(A \cap B)}{P(B)},$$

provided $P(B) \neq 0$. The underlying principle is that by conditioning we shift the frame of reference from the general space Ω to the conditioning entity, in this case the event B. Thus, the probability of the event A given the event B is the probability assigned by the (probability) measure P to that part of A that is also in the new frame of reference, viz., B; this, of course, is simply the intersection $A \cap B$; division by $P(B)$ is simply a bookkeeping devise to ensure that the probability of the "new" space is unity. This basic idea is easily transferable to discrete random variables, but its extension to general random variables, i.e., the case where the conditioning entity is a σ-algebra, is somewhat less transparent. Somewhat less familiar, although in some respects more fundamental, is the notion of conditional expectation.

We begin by considering conditional probability in the case of discrete probability models. First, an informal discussion by example. Suppose we have two random variables, X_i, $i = 1, 2$, which are independent, identically distributed, and assume the values $1, 2, ..., 6$, with equal probability, viz., $1/6$. These random variables may, for example, indicate the faces showing when two dice are thrown. Define, a new random variable, say $X = X_1 + X_2$. In the two independent dice model we had discussed above, the random variable X is simply the sum of the faces showing at each throw; it is clear that X assumes the values $2, 3, ..., 12$, with probabilities determined at an earlier stage. We note that if we condition on X_2, say by requiring that $X_2 = i$, $1 \leq i \leq \min(k - 1,\ 6)$, then

$$P(X = k \mid X_2 = i) = P(X_1 + i = k).$$

Moreover, since it is assumed that the two random variables are independent, then it follows, from the definition of conditional probability, that

$$P(X_1 + X_2 = k \mid X_2 = i) = P(X_1 = k - i).$$

The preceding has resolved the problem of calculating the probability that X will assume a specific value given that X_2 assumes a specific value, which is really a special case of conditioning one "event" in terms of another. But, what would we want to mean by $X \mid X_2$, i.e., by conditioning the random variable X in terms of the random variable X_2? Clearly, we can accomplish our task if we can determine the probability with which this new variable "assumes" values in its range. Now, let

$$D_i = \{\omega : X_2(\omega) = i\}, \quad i = 1, 2, \ldots, 6$$

and denote the indicator functions of the sets D_i by $I_i(\omega)$. It is, then, rather simple to establish that

$$P(X = k \mid X_2) = \sum_{i=1}^{\min(k-1,6)} p_{k-i} I_i(\omega),$$

where, of course, $p_{k-i} = P(X_1 = k - i)$. Consequently, we conclude that the random variable $X \mid X_2$ has the range $k = 2, 3, \ldots, 12$ and assumes the value k with probability $\sum_{i=1}^{\min(k-1,6)} p_{k-i} I_i$. For notational simplicity, we shall write the upper limit of the sum as 6, with the understanding that if, for some i, $k - i \leq 0$ then $p_{k-i} = 0$.

If we were dealing solely with discreet models, then perhaps there would be no need to abstract the salient aspects of the problem and seek to generalize the solution obtained. Unfortunately, however, this is not the case. By way of motivation, consider the following "experiment": choose a point, x, at "random" in the unit interval $(0, 1)$; then toss a coin whose "probability" of showing heads is x and of showing tails is $1 - x$. If we engage in such an experiment n times, what is the conditional probability that k of the tosses result in heads, conditional on the fact that the probability (of heads) is x? Since, in the context of the uniform distribution over the unit interval, the probability of chosing x is zero, the usual approach fails. Nonetheless, it makes perfectly good sense to expect that the required probability is given by the binomial distribution with $p = x$. More formally, the elementary definition of conditional probability of an event A, given another, B, requires that

$P(B) > 0$. We have just given a very real problem in which this condition is violated. Thus, there is need for abstraction, and we now turn to this task. A careful examination of the solution we have given to the two dice example indicates that the random variables as such do not play a direct intrinsic role; rather, the result depends on certain collections of sets, which, in that example, are, of course, determined by the random variables in question. To illuminate this aspect, let us augment our notation accordingly. The problem as posed is symmetric in X_1 and X_2, and thus, initially, the need for this notation did not arise. Here, let us denote by $D_{i,2}$ the sets earlier denoted by D_i (since they pertain to the variable X_2) and define, additionally, the sets $D_{i,1}$ relative to the variable X_1. Moreover, note that the probabilities p_i, as utilized in that example, are simply given by

$$p_i = P(D_{i1}), \quad i = 1, 2, \ldots, 6.$$

Thus, the probability structure of $X \mid X_2$ could as well be described by

$$P(X = k \mid X_2) = \sum_{i=1}^{6} P(D_{k-i,1}) I_{i2}(\omega),$$

and the **conditional expectation** of $X \mid X_2$ may be written in the natural notation as

$$E(X \mid X_2) = \sum_{k=2}^{12} k \sum_{i=1}^{6} P(D_{k-1,1}) I_{i2}(\omega).$$

Bearing in mind that $P(D_{k-i,1}) = P(D_{k-i,1} \mid D_{i,2})$, we can rewrite the conditional expectation above as

$$E(X \mid X_2) = \sum_{i=1}^{6} E(X \mid X_2 = i) I_{i2}(\omega).$$

This is so since $E(X \mid X_2 = i) = \sum_{k=2}^{12} k P(X = k \mid X_2 = i)$, with the understanding that for $k < i + 1$ the probability above is defined to be zero. Let us now examine the abstract elements of this procedure. First, note that the discrete random variable X_2, i.e., the conditioning variable, gives rise to the collection of sets: $\mathcal{D}_2 = \{D_{i2} : i = 1, 2, \ldots, 6\}$. Moreover, note that this is a **partition** of the space Ω, in the sense that the D_{i2} are **disjoint** and $\bigcup_{i=1}^{6} D_{i2} = \Omega$. Notice also that there is another partition of Ω in terms of the collection $\mathcal{D}_1 = \{D_{i1} : i = 1, 2, \ldots, 6\}$, and in fact that X is defined over the space $\Omega \times \Omega$; the σ-algebra of this space is generated by sets of the form $D_{i1} \times D_{j2}$ with $i, j = 1, 2, \ldots, 6$; the probability measure on this space is simply the product (probability) measure. Moreover, if we define the sets $D_k = \bigcup_{i+j=k}(D_{i1} \times D_{j2})$, we easily establish that $P(X = k) = P(D_k)$, where the notation P is used generically, in this context only, both for the measures over the (two) single die spaces, as well as the measure over the product space of the two dice. Thus, we can represent the variable X as

$$X(\omega) = \sum_{k=2}^{12} k I_k(\omega),$$

where I_k is the indicator set of D_k. Since by definition

$$E(X) = \sum_{k=2}^{12} k P(D_k),$$

it is natural, and it conforms to the earlier derivation, to define

$$E(X) = \sum_{k=2}^{12} k P(D_k \mid X_2 = j).$$

But, of course, $P(D_k \mid X_2 = j) = P(D_k \mid D_{j2})$. In this context, what would we want to mean by the notation $P(D_k \mid X_2)$? The notation alludes to the probability to be assigned to the set D_k **given** or **conditionally on** the variable X_2. Since the latter is a random variable, so should be the former. Moreover, for every value assumed by the random variable X_2, say j, a corresponding value ought to be assumed by $P(D_k \mid X_2)$, viz., $P(D_k \mid D_{j2})$. This leads us to define

$$P(D_k \mid X_2) = \sum_{j=1}^{6} P(D_k \mid D_{j2}) I_{j2}(\omega),$$

again it being understood that I_{j2} is the indicator function of the set D_{j2} and the conditional probability is defined to be zero whenever $k < j+1$. With the help of these redefinitions of the steps we had taken earlier based on elementary probability considerations, we can now write

$$E(X \mid X_2) = \sum_{k=2}^{12} k P(D_k \mid X_2) = \sum_{j=1}^{6} E(X \mid D_{j2}) I_{j2}(\omega),$$

where, evidently,

$$E(X \mid D_{j2}) = E(X \mid X_2 = j).$$

In addition, note that in some sense the notion of conditional expectation is somewhat more "fundamental" than the notion of conditional probability, in the sense that conditional probability can always be expressed as conditional expectation. For example, given any set A, we may define its indicator set to be the random variable associated with it; by analogy with the standard definition, we may then set

$$E(A \mid X_2) = \sum_{j=1}^{m} P(A \mid D_{j2}) I_{j2}(\omega),$$

as the conditional expectation of A with respect to the random variable X_2. In this framework, what would one want to mean by the conditional probability of $A \mid X_2$? Presumably, one would want the random variable that rearranges the mass assigned to A, over the constituent (elementary) sets of the partition induced by X_2. This is simply

$$P(A \mid X_2) = \sum_{j=1}^{m} P(A \mid D_{j2}) I_{j2}(\omega).$$

If we take the expectation of this random variable (i.e., if we take the expectation of the conditional probability), we have the standard formula for what is known as **total probability**. Specifically, we have

$$E[P(A \mid X_2)] = \sum_{j=1}^{m} P(A \mid D_{j2}) P(D_{j2}) = P(A),$$

and moreover,

$$E[E(A \mid X_2)] = P(A),$$

which exhibits the probability of an event A, as the expectation of a conditional probability, as well as the expectation of a conditional expectation. We now undertake the formal development of the subject.

Definition 10. Let $(\Omega, \mathcal{A}, P)$ be a probability space, $A \in \mathcal{A}$, and $\mathcal{D} = \{D_i : i = 1, 2, \ldots, n\}$ be a finite partition of Ω (i.e., the D_i

are disjoint sets whose union is Ω). The conditional probability of the "event" A, given the partition $\mathcal{D}$, is defined by

$$P(A \mid \mathcal{D}) = \sum_{i=1}^{n} P(A \mid D_i) I_i(\omega),$$

where, evidently, I_i is the indicator function of D_i.

Remark 16. It is important to realize just what the operation of conditioning with respect to a partition involves. It does not involve holding anything "constant" although this notion is useful in operations involving integration. What it does involve conceptually, however, is the rearrangement of the probability assigned to an event (or more generally a random variable) in terms of the conditioning entity. In terms of the definition above, the event A has probability in terms of the measure assigned to A by P, in the context of the space Ω. Conditioning in terms of the partition $\mathcal{D}$ shifts attention from Ω to $\mathcal{D}$. In this new framework, the probability of A is distributed over the constituent parts (i.e., the sets D_i of $\mathcal{D}$), and the **random variable** $P(A \mid \mathcal{D})$ takes on the value $P(A \mid D_i)$, whenever $\omega \in D_i$. Notice, further, that the expectation of this random variable yields the probability of the event A! Specifically, since $E(I_i) = P(D_i)$, we easily establish

$$E[P(A \mid \mathcal{D})] = \sum_{i=1}^{n} P(A \cap D_i) = P(A).$$

Thus, loosely speaking, conditioning an event A, in terms of a partition $\mathcal{D}$, means distributing the probability assigned to A over the constituent elements of the partition. It is evident from the definition above that the conditional probability of an event A, with respect to a decomposition, is a simple random variable that assumes a constant value over the elements of the decomposition; this value is simply the conditional probability of A given the element in question, say D_i. It also follows immediately that

$$P(A \mid \Omega) = P(A),$$

and that if A, B are two disjoint sets, then

$$P(A \cup B \mid \mathcal{D}) = P(A \mid \mathcal{D}) + P(B \mid \mathcal{D}).$$

Remark 17. It is now straightforward to apply to random variables the notion of conditional expectation with respect to a partition. Thus, let $\mathcal{D}$ be a partition as above and let X be a discrete (simple) random variable, say

$$X(\omega) = \sum_{j=1}^{m} x_j I_j(\omega),$$

where I_j is the indicator function of the set $B_j = \{\omega : X(\omega) = x_j\}$, $j = 1, 2, \ldots, m$. Since

$$E(X) = \sum_{j=1}^{m} x_j P(B_j),$$

it is natural to define the conditional expectation of X with respect to the partition $\mathcal{D}$ as

$$E(X \mid \mathcal{D}) = \sum_{j=1}^{m} x_j P(B_j \mid \mathcal{D}).$$

Notice that, as we have sought to explain above, the operation of **conditioning the expectation with respect to a partition** simply involves the **rearrangement of the probability mass** of the random variable, X, in terms of the conditioning entity. Particularly, the random variable X, originally, assumes constant values over the sets B_j and these values are x_j, respectively. Its conditional expectation with respect to $\mathcal{D}$, on the other hand, redistributes (or perhaps one should say rearranges) its probability mass over the constituent elements of the partition, so that $E(X \mid \mathcal{D})$ assumes constant values over the (elementary) constitutent sets of $\mathcal{D}$, say D_i, $i = 1, 2, \ldots, n$. These values are, respectively, $\sum_{j=1}^{m} x_j P(B_j \mid D_i)$. It should also be apparent that taking a second expectation, over the partition, restores us to the basic notion of expectation. This is so since the expectation of the indicator functions of the elements of the partition yields $P(D_i)$. The preceding discussion introduces

Definition 11. Let $(\Omega, \mathcal{A}, P)$ be a probability space, X a random variable defined thereon, and $\mathcal{D}$ a finite partition of Ω, as above. Then, the conditional expectation of X with respect to the partition $\mathcal{D}$ is given by

$$E(X \mid \mathcal{D}) = \sum_{j=1}^{m} x_j P(B_j \mid \mathcal{D}) = \sum_{i=1}^{n} E(X \mid D_i).$$

Finally, we formally introduce two common terms.

Definition 12. Let X be a (simple) random variable on the probability space above and define the sets

$$D_i = \{\omega : X(\omega) = x_i\}.$$

The collection

$$\mathcal{D}_x = \{D_i : i = 1, 2, \ldots, n\}$$

is a finite partition (or a decomposition) of the space Ω and is said to be the decomposition (or partition) **induced by the random variable** X.

Definition 13. Let X be a random variable as in Definition 11 and suppose $\mathcal{D}$ is a finite partition of Ω; we say that X is $\mathcal{D}$-measurable, if and only if $\mathcal{D}$ is finer than $\mathcal{D}_x$, i.e., if X can be represented as

$$X(\omega) = \sum_{j=1}^{r} z_j I_j(\omega),$$

where some of the z_j may be repeated, $\mathcal{D}_x$ is as in Definition 12 and I_j, $j = 1, 2, \ldots, r$, are the characteristic functions of the sets of $\mathcal{D}$.

The following elementary properties of conditional expectations follow almost immediately.

Proposition 18. Let $(\Omega, \mathcal{A}, P)$ be a probability space and X_i, $i = 1, 2$, be discrete (simple) random variables. Define the sets

$$D_{i1} \;=\; \{\omega : X_1(\omega) = x_{i1}, \; i = 1, 2, \ldots, n\},$$

$$D_{j2} \;=\; \{\omega : X_2(\omega) = x_{j2}, \; j = 1, 2, \ldots, m\},$$

and note that the collections, $\mathcal{D}_1 = \{D_{i1} : i = 1, 2, \ldots, n\}$, $\mathcal{D}_2 = \{D_{j2} : j = 1, 2, \ldots, m\}$ are the finite partitions of Ω induced by the variables X_i, $i = 1, 2$, respectively. Suppose, further, that $\mathcal{D}_2$ is a finer partition than $\mathcal{D}_1$, in the sense that every set in $\mathcal{D}_1$ can be expressed as a union of sets in $\mathcal{D}_2$. Then, the following statements are true:

i. $E(X_i \mid X_i) = X_i$, $i = 1, 2$;

ii. $E[E(X_1 \mid X_2)] = E(X_1)$;

iii. if X_3 is another simple random variable with an induced partition $\mathcal{D}_3$, then

$$E(aX_1 + bX_2 \mid X_3) = aE(X_1 \mid X_3) + bE(X_2 \mid X_3);$$

iv. if X_3 is any other random variable, as in iii., i.e., with an induced partition $\mathcal{D}_3$, then, given $\mathcal{D}_2$ is finer than $\mathcal{D}_1$,

$$E[E(X_3 \mid X_2) \mid X_1] = E(X_3 \mid X_1);$$

v. let $\mathcal{D}$ be a decomposition of Ω, and suppose it, $\mathcal{D}$, is finer than $\mathcal{D}_1$; let X_3 be another random variable as in iv., i.e., with an induced partition $\mathcal{D}_3$, then

$$E(X_1 X_3 \mid \mathcal{D}) = X_1 E(X_3 \mid \mathcal{D}).$$

Proof: By definition, $E(X_1 \mid X_1) = \sum_{j=1}^{n} \sum_{i=1}^{n} x_{i1} P(D_{i1} \mid D_{j1}) I_{j1}(\omega)$. Since the constituent sets of a partition are disjoint, $P(D_{i1} \mid D_{j1}) = 0$ if $i \neq j$ and is equal to unity if $i = j$. Thus, we may write

$$E(X_1 \mid X_1) = \sum_{i=1}^{n} x_{i1} I_{i1}(\omega) = X_1.$$

The proof for X_2 is entirely similar.

The proof of ii. is as follows: by definition,

$$E(X_1 \mid X_2) = \sum_{j=1}^{m} E(X_1 \mid D_{j2}) I_{j2}(\omega).$$

Consequently, $E[E(X_1 \mid X_2)] = \sum_{j=1}^{m} E(X_1 \mid D_{j2}) P(D_{j2})$. But,

$$E(X_1 \mid D_{j2}) P(D_{j2}) = \sum_{i=1}^{n} x_{i1} P(D_{i1} \mid D_{j2}) P(D_{j2}).$$

Thus,

$$
\begin{aligned}
E[E(X_1 \mid X_2)] &= \sum_{i=1}^{n} x_{i1} \sum_{j=1}^{m} P(D_{i1} \cap D_{j2}) \\
&= \sum_{i=1}^{n} x_{i1} P(D_{i1}) = E(X_1),
\end{aligned}
$$

which concludes the proof of ii.; the result above may be looked upon as a generalization of the formula for total probability.

The proof of iii. is immediate from the definition of conditional expectation.

To prove iv., we note that by definition

$$E[E(X_3 \mid X_2) \mid X_1] = \sum_{s=1}^{n} E[E(X_3 \mid X_2) \mid D_{i1}]I_{i1}(\omega).$$

In view of the fact that

$$E(X_3 \mid X_2) = \sum_{j=1}^{m} E(X_3 \mid D_{j2})I_{j2}(\omega),$$

we conclude

$$E[E(X_3 \mid X_2) \mid D_{i1}] = \sum_{j=1}^{m} \sum_{s=1}^{k} x_{s3} P(D_{s3} \mid D_{j2}) P(D_{j2} \mid D_{i1}).$$

Since $\mathcal{D}_2$ is finer than $\mathcal{D}_1$, it follows that $P(D_{j2} \cap D_{i1})/P(D_{j2})$ is either 1, when D_{j2} is one of the sets that make up D_{i1}, or else it is zero. Hence, summing over those indices, j, for which $D_{j2} \subset D_{i1}$, we may rewrite the right member of the equation above as

$$\sum_{s=1}^{k} x_{s3} P(D_{s3} \mid D_{i1}) = E(X_3 \mid D_{i1}).$$

Thus,

$$E[E(X_3 \mid X_2) \mid X_1] = \sum_{i=1}^{n} E(X_3 \mid D_{i1})I_{i1}(\omega) = E(X_3 \mid X_1),$$

which proves iv., thus showing that the conditioning over the coarser partition prevails.

The proof for v. is entirely similar; thus, let D_i, $i = 1, 2, \ldots, r$, be the elementary sets of $\mathcal{D}$; since X_1 is $\mathcal{D}$-measurable, it has the representation

$$X_1(\omega) = \sum_{i=1}^{r} y_{i1} I_i(\omega),$$

where some of the y_{i1} may be repeated and I_i, $i = 1, 2, \ldots, r$, are the indicator functions of the elementary sets of $\mathcal{D}$. By definition, then, we have

$$E(X_1 X_3 \mid \mathcal{D}) = \sum_{i=1}^{r} E(X_1 X_3 \mid D_i)I_i(\omega).$$

But,

$$E(X_1 X_3 \mid D_i) = \sum_{m=1}^{r} \sum_{j=1}^{k} y_{m1} x_{j3} P(D_m \cap D_{j3} \mid D_i).$$

In view of the fact that the elementary sets of a partition are disjoint, we must have

$$E(X_1 X_3 \mid D_i) = y_{i1} \sum_{j=1}^{k} P(D_{j3} \mid D_i) = y_{i1} E(X_3 \mid D_i).$$

Thus, we conclude that

$$E(X_1 X_3 \mid \mathcal{D}) = \sum_{i=1}^{r} y_{i1} I_i(\omega) E(X_3 \mid D_i).$$

On the other hand, using again the disjointness of the elementary sets of $\mathcal{D}$, we have that $I_i I_m = 0$, if $m \neq i$, and it is equal to I_i, for $i = m$. Consequently,

$$E(X_1 X_3 \mid \mathcal{D}) = \sum_{i=1}^{r} y_{i1} I_i(\omega) \sum_{m=1}^{r} E(X_3 \mid D_m) I_m(\omega),$$

or that $E(X_1 X_3 \mid \mathcal{D}) = X_2 E(X_3 \mid \mathcal{D})$.

q.e.d.

2.4.2 Conditional Probability in Continuous Models

In this section, we shall extend the notions of conditional probability and conditional expectation to continuous models, or, more precisely, we shall examine the concepts of conditioning with respect to a σ-algebra. We begin with

Definition 14. Let $(\Omega, \mathcal{P}, A)$ be a probability space, let X be a (nonnegative extended) random variable defined thereon, and let $\mathcal{G}$ be a σ-algebra contained in $\mathcal{A}$. The conditional expectation of X with respect to the σ-algebra $\mathcal{G}$, denoted by $E(X \mid \mathcal{G})$, is a (nonnegative extended) random variable such that

    i. $E(X \mid \mathcal{G})$ is $\mathcal{G}$-measurable;

ii. for every set $B \in \mathcal{G}$,

$$\int_B X\, dP = \int_B E(X \mid \mathcal{G})\, dP.$$

Remark 18. When dealing with extended random variables, the question always arises as to when expectations exist. This is true as much in the standard case as it is in the case of conditional expectations. Thus, let X be a random variable in the context of the definition above, except that we do not insist that it is nonnegative. How do we know that conditional expectation, as exhibited above, is well defined? Note that, since we are dealing with nonnegative random variables, the problem is not that some expectation (integral) is unbounded, but rather whether the definition leads to one of the indeterminate forms, such as, e.g., $\infty - \infty$. This is resolved by the convention: The conditional expectation of any random variable X, with respect to the σ-algebra $\mathcal{D}$, which is contained in $\mathcal{A}$, exists if and only if

$$\min[E(X^+ \mid \mathcal{G}),\ E(X^- \mid \mathcal{G})] < \infty.$$

It is evident that the definition of conditional expectation above is not a vacuous one. In particular, note that the Radon-Nikodym (RN) theorem (Proposition 27 of Chapter 1) guarantees that the conditional expectation exists. Thus, recall that setting

$$Q(B) = \int_B X\, dP,$$

where X is a nonnegative random variable and $B \in \mathcal{G}$, we have that Q is a measure that is absolutely continuous with respect to P. The RN theorem asserts the existence of a $\mathcal{G}$-measurable function, $E(X \mid \mathcal{G})$, unique up to sets of P-measure zero such that

$$Q(B) = \int_B E(X \mid \mathcal{G})\, dP,$$

which, therefore, establishes the existence of conditional expectation; its salient properties are given below in

Proposition 19. Let X, X_i, $i = 1, 2$, be random variables defined on the probability space $(\Omega, \mathcal{A}, P)$; let $\mathcal{G}$, $\mathcal{G}_i$, $i = 1, 2$, be σ-(sub)algebras contained in $\mathcal{A}$, and suppose all random variables are extended and that their expectations exist. Then, the following statements [6] are true:

i. if K is a constant and $X_1 = K$ a.c., then $E(X \mid \mathcal{G}) = K$;

ii. if $X_1 \leq X_2$, then $E(X_1 \mid \mathcal{G}) \leq E(X_2 \mid \mathcal{G})$;

iii. for any random variable X, $\mid E(X \mid \mathcal{G}) \mid \leq E(\mid X \mid \mid \mathcal{G})$;

iv. for any scalars, a_i, $i = 1, 2$, such that $\sum_{i=1}^{2} a_i E(X_i)$ is defined,

$$E(a_1 X_1 + a_2 X_2 \mid \mathcal{G}) = a_1 E(X_1 \mid \mathcal{G}) + a_2 E(X_2 \mid \mathcal{G});$$

v. $E(X \mid \mathcal{A}) = X$;

vi. if $\mathcal{G}_0 = (\emptyset, \ \Omega)$, $E(X \mid \mathcal{G}_0) = E(X)$;

vii. if X is a random variable that is independent of the σ-algebra $\mathcal{G}$, then

$$E(X \mid \mathcal{G}) - E(X);$$

viii. if Y is $\mathcal{G}$-measurable, with $E(\mid Y \mid) < \infty$, $E(\mid X \mid) < \infty$, then

$$E(YX \mid \mathcal{G}) = Y E(X \mid \mathcal{G});$$

ix. if $\mathcal{G}_1 \subseteq \mathcal{G}_2$ (i.e., if $\mathcal{G}_2$ is finer), then

$$E[E(X \mid \mathcal{G}_2) \mid \mathcal{G}_1] = E(X \mid \mathcal{G}_1);$$

x. $\mathcal{G}_2 \subseteq \mathcal{G}_1$ (i.e., if $\mathcal{G}_1$ is finer), then

$$E[E(X \mid \mathcal{G}_2) \mid \mathcal{G}_1] = E(X \mid \mathcal{G}_2);$$

xi. $E[E(X \mid \mathcal{G})] = E(X)$.

Proof: To prove i., we note that $X = K$ is both $\mathcal{A}$- and $\mathcal{G}$-measurable since it can be given the trivial representation $X(\omega) = K I(\omega)$, where I is the indicator function of Ω. Hence, for any set $B \in \mathcal{G}$,

$$\int_B X \, dP = \int_B E(X \mid \mathcal{G}) \, dP \quad \text{implies} \quad K P(B) = K P(B),$$

---

[6] These statements are to be understood in the a.c. sense, where appropriate.

which completes the proof of i.

To prove ii., we note that, for any set $A \in \mathcal{G}$,

$$\int_A E(X_1 \mid \mathcal{G}) \, dP = \int_A X_1 \, dP \leq \int_A X_2 \, dP = \int_A E(X_2 \mid \mathcal{G}) \, dP,$$

which implies that

$$E(X_1 \mid \mathcal{G}) \leq E(X_2 \mid \mathcal{G}).$$

To see that, define

$$C = \{\omega : E(X_1 \mid \mathcal{G}) > E(X_2 \mid \mathcal{G})\}.$$

If $P(C) = 0$, then the proof of ii. is complete; if not, consider

$$\int_C [E(X_1 \mid \mathcal{G}) - E(X_2 \mid \mathcal{G})] \, dP,$$

which is unambiguously positive; this is a contradiction, and hence, $P(C) = 0$, which proves ii.

To prove iii., we note that for any random variable, X, $-\mid X \mid \leq X \leq \mid X \mid$; consequently, by ii., we have

$$-E(\mid X \mid \mid \mathcal{G}) \leq E(X \mid \mathcal{G}) \leq E(\mid X \mid \mid \mathcal{G}),$$

which completes the proof of iii.

To prove iv., we note that by definition, for any set $A \in \mathcal{G}$,

$$a_1 \int_A X_1 \, dP = a_1 \int_A E(X_1 \mid \mathcal{G}) \, dP,$$

$$a_2 \int_A X_2 \, dP = a_2 \int_A E(X_2 \mid \mathcal{G}) \, dP.$$

Summing, and using the fundamental properties of the integral, we establish the validity of iv.

The proof of v. is trivial since, evidently, X is $\mathcal{A}$-measurable; consequently, for **every** $A \in \mathcal{A}$,

$$\int_A X \, dP = \int_A E(X \mid \mathcal{A}) \, dP.$$

But, this means that $E(X \mid \mathcal{A}) = X$.

For vi. we note that the integral of any measurable function over the null set is zero, and moreover,

$$\int_\Omega X \, dP = \int_\Omega E(X) \, dP.$$

An argument similar to that used in connection with the proof of ii. will then show the validity of vi.

To prove vii., we note that $E(X)$ is $\mathcal{G}$-measurable, and using the fundamental definition of independence (which will be also be discussed in the next section), we establish, for any $A \in \mathcal{G}$,

$$\int_A X \, dP = \int_\Omega I_A X \, dP = E(I_A)E(X) = P(A)E(X) = \int_A E(X) \, dP.$$

The proof of viii. is as follows: clearly, $Y E(X \mid \mathcal{G})$ is $\mathcal{G}$-measurable; let $B \in \mathcal{G}$, $Y = I_B$, the latter being the indicator function of B, and let A be any set in $\mathcal{G}$. Then,

$$\int_A Y X \, dP = \int_{A \cap B} X \, dP = \int_{A \cap B} E(X \mid \mathcal{G}) \, dP = \int_A I_B E(X \mid \mathcal{G}) \, dP.$$

Hence,

$$E(Y X \mid \mathcal{G}) = Y E(X \mid \mathcal{G})$$

for $Y = I_B$, $B \in \mathcal{G}$; consequently, the result holds for nonnegative simple $\mathcal{G}$-measurable random variables. Thus, by the Lebesgue dominated convergence theorem (Proposition 19 of Chapter 1), if Y is a nonnegative random variable and $\{Y_n : n \geq 1,\ Y_n \leq Y\}$ is a sequence of simple random variables converging to Y, we have that

$$\lim_{n \to \infty} E(Y_n X \mid \mathcal{G}) = E(Y X \mid \mathcal{G}) \text{ a.c.}$$

Moreover, since $E(\mid X \mid) \leq \infty$, it follows that $E(X \mid \mathcal{G})$ is a.c. finite. Consequently,

$$\lim_{n \to \infty} E(Y_n X \mid \mathcal{G}) = \lim_{n \to \infty} Y_n E(X \mid \mathcal{G}) = Y E(X \mid \mathcal{G}),$$

which shows the result to hold for nonnegative Y. The proof for general Y is established by considering $Y = Y^+ - Y^-$.

For the proof of ix., let $Z = E(X \mid \mathcal{G}_2)$; thus, Z is a $\mathcal{G}_2$-measurable random variable, and we wish to show that

$$E(Z \mid \mathcal{G}_1) = E(X \mid \mathcal{G}_1).$$

For any $B \in \mathcal{G}_1$, we have, by definition,

$$\int_B E(Z \mid \mathcal{G}_1) \, dP = \int_B Z \, dP.$$

Since $\mathcal{G}_1 \subseteq \mathcal{G}_2$, $B \in \mathcal{G}_2$ we conclude, bearing in mind the definition of Z, that for all sets, $B \in \mathcal{G}_1$,

$$\int_B E(X \mid \mathcal{G}_2)\, dP = \int_B X\, dP = \int_B E(X \mid \mathcal{G}_1)\, dP.$$

This, in conjunction with the preceding result shows that

$$E[E(X \mid \mathcal{G}_2) \mid \mathcal{G}_1] = E(Z \mid \mathcal{G}_1) = E(X \mid \mathcal{G}_1).$$

To prove x., we must show that $E(Y \mid \mathcal{G}_1) = E(X \mid \mathcal{G}_1)$, where $Y = E(X \mid \mathcal{G}_2)$. Since Y is $\mathcal{G}_2$-measurable and $\mathcal{G}_2 \subseteq \mathcal{G}_1$, Y is also $\mathcal{G}_1$-measurable; moreover, if $B \in \mathcal{G}_2$, then $B \in \mathcal{G}_1$ as well. Consequently, for every $B \in \mathcal{G}_2$,

$$\int_B E(Y \mid \mathcal{G}_1)\, dP = \int_B Y\, dP = \int_B E(X \mid \mathcal{G}_2)\, dP.$$

But, this shows that

$$E[E(X \mid \mathcal{G}_2) \mid \mathcal{G}_1] = E(Y \mid \mathcal{G}_1) = E(X \mid \mathcal{G}_2),$$

which completes the proof of x.

The proof of xi. is a simple consequence of vi. and ix. Thus, let $\mathcal{G}_1 = (\emptyset,\ \Omega)$ and $\mathcal{G}_2 = \mathcal{G}$. Then, clearly, $\mathcal{G}_1 \subseteq \mathcal{G}$, and by ix.,

$$E[E(X \mid \mathcal{G}_2)] = E[E(X \mid \mathcal{G}_2) \mid \mathcal{G}_1] = E(X).$$

q.e.d.

2.4.3 Independence

It is well established in elementary probability theory that two events are "independent" if the probability attached to their intersection, i.e., their joint occurrence, is the product of their individual probabilities. In the preceding sections we have also seen another possible interpretation of independence; this is the, intuitively, very appealing concept that holds that two events, say A and B are independent, if the probability attached to A is the same whether or not we condition on the event B. Another way of expressing this concept is that being told that event B has occurred does not convey any implication regarding the probability of A's occurrence. In this section we shall formalize these notions and apply them to the case of random variables and families of random variables defined on suitable probability spaces. We begin by noting that if A, B are two independent events, i.e.

$$P(A \mid B) = P(A),$$

then, provided that $P(B) > 0$, the condition above, in conjunction with the definition

$$P(A \mid B) = \frac{P(AB)}{P(B)},$$

implies $P(AB) = P(A)P(B)$, which is the operational characterization of independence. In the preceding, the intersection operator ($\cap$) was omitted; we shall follow this practice in this section for notational simplicity, so that the notation AB will always mean $A \cap B$; another notational simplification that will be observed in this section is the following: if $A \supset B$, then

$$A - B = A \cap \bar{B}.$$

These two operations will occur sufficiently frequently in the ensuing discussion so as to make the conventions above quite useful in reducinf notational clutter.

Definition 15. Let $(\Omega,\ \mathcal{A},\ P)$ be a probability space and let $\mathcal{C}_i$, $i = 1, 2$, be two classes of events, contained in $\mathcal{A}$. The two classes are said to be independent classes if and only if any events $C_i \in \mathcal{C}_i$, $i = 1, 2$, are independent, i.e., $P(C_1 C_2) = P(C_1)P(C_2)$.

Definition 16. Let $\mathcal{C}_\pi$, $\mathcal{C}_\lambda$ be two classes of subsets of Ω.

i. $\mathcal{C}_\pi$ is said to be a π-class if and only if $A, B \in \mathcal{C}_\pi$ implies $AB \in \mathcal{C}_\pi$;

ii. $\mathcal{C}_\lambda$ is said to be a λ-class if and only if

    a. $\Omega \in \mathcal{C}_\lambda$;

    b. for $A_i \in \mathcal{C}_\lambda$, $i = 1, 2$, and $A_1 A_2 = \emptyset$, then $A_1 \cup A_2 \in \mathcal{C}_\lambda$;

    c. for $A_i \in \mathcal{C}_\lambda$, $i = 1, 2$, and $A_1 \subset A_2$, then $A_2 - A_1 \in \mathcal{C}_\lambda$;

d. for $A_n \in C_\lambda$, $n \geq 1$, and $A_n \subset A_{n+1}$, then $\lim_{n\to\infty} A_n \in C_\lambda$.

A simple consequence of the definition is

Proposition 20. If a λ-class, C, is also a π-class, then it is a σ-algebra.

Proof: Let $A_i \in C$, $i \geq 1$, and recall that $\Omega \in C$; since the complement of A_i is given by $\Omega - A_i$ and this is in C, due to the fact that the latter is a λ-class, it follows that C is closed under complementation. Next, we show that C is closed under countable unions; thus, consider $A_1 \cup A_2$; if the two sets are distinct, this union lies in C since it is a λ-class; if not distinct, write

$$A_1 \cup A_2 = A = A_1 \cup (A_2 \bar{A}_1).$$

Since C is also a π-class, the second component of the union above is in C; since the two components of the union are disjoint and belong to C, their union also belongs to C because C is a λ-class. Finally, define

$$C_n = \bigcup_{i=1}^{n} A_i.$$

By the preceding discussion, $C_n \subset C_{n+1}$, and $C_n \in C$; since C is a λ-class, $\lim_{n\to\infty} C_n \in C$.

q.e.d.

An interesting consequence of the preceding discussion is

Proposition 21. If a λ-class, C, contains a π-class, D, then it also contains $\sigma(D)$, the σ-algebra generated by D, i.e., the minimal σ-algebra containing D.

Proof: It suffices to show that the minimal λ-class, A, containing D also contains $\sigma(D)$. Define $A_1 = \{A : AD \in A, \text{ for all } D \in D\}$; evidently, A contains D and thus $A_1 \supset A$, since it is a λ-class. From this argument, we conclude that for all $A \in A$ and $D \in D$, $AD \in A$. Next, define $A_2 = \{B : BA \in A, \text{ for all } A \in A\}$; clearly, A_2 is a λ-class, it contains D and thus A. But, this implies that if $A, B \in A$, then $AB \in \mathcal{A}$, so $\mathcal{A}$ is a π-class, as well. By Proposition 20, we conclude that $\mathcal{A}$ is a σ-algebra that contains $\mathcal{D}$; consequently, it contains $\sigma(\mathcal{D})$.

q.e.d.

We may now use these basic concepts to characterize independence among random variables.

Proposition 22. Let $\mathcal{G}_i$, $i = 1, 2$, be independent classes (of subsets of Ω) and suppose further that $\mathcal{G}_2$ is also a π-class. Then, $\mathcal{G}_1$ and $\sigma(\mathcal{G}_2)$ are independent.

Proof: For any $A \in \mathcal{G}_1$, define $\mathcal{A} = \{B : B \in \sigma(\mathcal{G}_2), P(AB) = P(A)P(B)\}$. Clearly, $\mathcal{A} \supset \mathcal{G}_2$; moreover, $\mathcal{A}$ is a λ-class, since

i. if $B_1 B_2 = \emptyset$, then

$$
\begin{aligned}
P[(B_1 \cup B_2)A] &= P(B_1 A) + P(B_2 A) \\
&= P(B_1)P(A) + P(B_2)P(A) \\
&= [P(B_1) + P(B_2)]P(A) = P(B_1 \cup B_2)P(A);
\end{aligned}
$$

ii. if $B_2 \supset B_1$, then $B_2 = B_1 \cup (B_2 - B_1)$, and the two components of the union are disjoint; thus, $P(B_2 A) = P(B_1 A) + P[(B_2 - B_1)A]$; rearranging we have $P[(B_2 - B_1)A] = P(B_2 - B_1)P(A)$;

iii. $\Omega \in \mathcal{A}$, since $\Omega \in \sigma(\mathcal{G}_2)$ and $P(\Omega A) = P(\Omega)P(A)$;

iv. if $B_i \subset B_{i+1}$, $B_i \in \mathcal{A}$, $i \geq 1$, then $P(B_i A) = P(B_i)P(A)$, $\lim_{n \to \infty} B_i = B \in \sigma(\mathcal{G})$, and thus $P(BA) = \lim_{n \to \infty} P(B_i A) = \lim_{n \to \infty} P(B_i)P(A) = P(B)P(A)$.

This concludes the demonstration that $\mathcal{A}$ is a λ-class containing the π-class $\mathcal{G}_2$; hence by Proposition 21, it contains $\sigma(\mathcal{G})$; but, this means that if B is any set in $\sigma(\mathcal{G}_2)$ and A is any set in $\mathcal{G}_1$, then $P(AB) = P(A)P(B)$.

q.e.d.

With these preliminaries aside, we may now turn our attention to the question of independence (of sets) of random variables. We begin with

Definition 17. Let T be a nonempty index set (generally the real line) and let $\{X_t : t \in T\}$ be a family of random variables indexed by the set T. This family of random variables is said to be a **stochastic process**.

The reader no doubt has an intuitive view as to what it means for a **set of random variables to be independent, or to be independent of another set**. No matter what intuitive meaning one ascribes to this concept, the latter would not be very useful unless we can attach to it a specific operational meaning. The question raised here is this: what does it mean, operationally in this context, for random variables to be independent? This is answered in

Definition 18. Let $\{X_i : i = 1, 2, \ldots, n\}$ be a set of random variables defined on the probability space $(\Omega, \mathcal{A}, P)$; they are said to be independent (of one another), or mutually independent, if and only if $\sigma(X_i)$, $i = 1, 2, \ldots, n$, are independent classes.

For stochastic processes, we have the obvious extension.

Definition 19. Let $\{X_t : t \in T\}$ be a stochastic process defined on the probability space $(\Omega, \mathcal{A}, P)$; let T_i, $i \geq 1$, be distinct subsets of the index set T. The (stochastic) subprocesses, $\{X_t : t \in T_i\}$, $i \geq 1$, are said to be independent if and only if $\mathcal{C}_i = \sigma(X_t, \ t \in T_i)$, $i \geq 1$, are independent classes.

Proposition 23. Let $\{X_t : t \in T\}$ be a family of random variables indexed by the nonempty index set T and defined on the probability space $(\Omega, \mathcal{A}, P)$; let T_i, $i = 1, 2$, be disjoint subsets of T and suppose $t_j^{(i)}$, $j = 1, 2, \ldots, m$, are m distinct elements of the the subsets T_i, $i = 1, 2$, respectivcely. Define the sets $D_{im} = \{\omega : X_{ji} \leq x_j, \ j = 1, 2, \ldots, m, \ x_j \in R\}$, for all $x \in R$ and all integers m. Define

$$\mathcal{D}_i = \{D_{im} : m \geq 1\}, \ i = 1, 2.$$

If the $\mathcal{D}_i$, $i = 1, 2$, are independent classes, so are $\sigma(\mathcal{D}_i)$, $i = 1, 2$.

Proof: It is evident that $\mathcal{D}_i$, $i = 1, 2$, are π-classes, since if D_{im} and D_{in} are two sets in $\mathcal{D}_i$, $i = 1, 2$, their intersection is a similar set, i.e., a set that describes the region of the domain over which a group of variables indexed by the set T_i assume values in certain intervals of their range, of the form $(-\infty, \ x]$. By Proposition 22, $\mathcal{D}_1$ is independent of $\sigma(\mathcal{D}_2)$; applying Proposition 22, again, and noting that $\mathcal{D}_1$ is also a π-class, we conclude that the two σ-algebras, $\sigma(\mathcal{D}_i)$, $i = 1, 2$, are independent.

q.e.d.

Corollary 6. Let $\{X_t : t \in T\}$ be a family of random variables as in the proposition above; suppose, further, that the random variables are independent, in the sense that for any indices $j(i) \in T_i$, $i = 1, 2, \ldots, n$, and any integer n, $\sigma(X_{j(i)})$ are independent classes. Let T_1, T_2 be disjoint nonempty subsets of T, then $\sigma(\mathcal{D}_1) = \sigma(X_t, t \in T_1)$ and $\sigma(\mathcal{D}_2) = \sigma(X_t, t \in T_2)$ are independent classes.

Proof: Obvious, since constructing the classes of sets $\mathcal{D}_i$, $i = 1, 2$, of the proposition above, we conclude that they are independent classes; by Proposition 23, so are $\sigma(\mathcal{D}_i)$, $i = 1, 2$; but, it is apparent from the construction of these σ-algebras that $\sigma(\mathcal{D}_i) = \sigma(X_t, t \in T_i)$, $i = 1, 2$, i.e., they amount to the σ-algebras generated by the random variables indexed by the elements of the set T_i.

q.e.d.

We have, finally, the fundamental characterization of independence of sequences of random variables as follows.

Proposition 24. Let $\{X_i : i = 1, 2, \ldots, n\}$ be a sequence of random variables defined on the probability space $(\Omega, \mathcal{A}, P)$; define their (joint) distribution function by

$$F_{(n)}(x_1, \ldots, x_n) = P(A_1 A_2 \cdots A_n),$$

and their individual (marginal) distribution functions by

$$F_i(x_i) = P(A_i), \quad i = 1, 2, \ldots, n,$$

where $A_i = \{\omega : X_i(\omega) \in (-\infty, x_i]\}$. These random variables are independent if and only if

$$F_{(n)}(x_1, \ldots, x_n) = \prod_{i=1}^{n} F_i(x_i).$$

Proof: Necessity is obvious, since if $F_n = \prod_{i=1}^{n} F_i$, then we must have

$$P(A_1 A_2 \cdots A_n) = \prod_{i=1}^{n} P(A_i),$$

which shows the classes $\sigma(X_i)$, $i = 1, 2, \ldots, n$ to be independent. To prove sufficiency note that $A_i \in \sigma(X_i)$ and note, also, that if the random variables are independent then the $\sigma(X_i)$ are independent classes. Hence,

$$P(A_1 A_2 \ldots A_n) = \prod_{i=1}^{n} P(A_i),$$

and the conclusion follows from the definition of distribution functions.

q.e.d.

The following corollaries simply rephrase or articulate more explicitly some of the preceding results.

Corollary 7. Let $\{X_t : t \in T\}$ be a stochastic process; the random variables of the stochastic process are mutually independent if and only if for any finite number of indices $t_i \in T$, $i = 1, 2, \ldots, n$, the joint distribution of the variables X_{t_i}, $i = 1, 2, \ldots, n$, $F_{(n)}$, is equal to the product of their marginal distributions, $\prod_{i=1}^{n} F_{t_i}$.

Corollary 8. Let $\{X_i : i = 1, 2, \ldots, n\}$ and $\{Z_i : i = 1, 2, \ldots, n\}$ be sequences of independent random variables. If X_i and Z_i are **identically distributed**, then the joint distribution of the first sequence is identical to the joint distribution of the second sequence, i.e., if $F_{(n)}$ and $G_{(n)}$ are the joint distributions of the two sequences, respectively, then

$$F_{(n)}(a_1, a_2, \ldots, a_n) = G_{(n)}(a_1, a_2, \ldots, a_n).$$

We close this section with a definition that, in subsequent discussions, will play an important role in examining questions of convergence of sequences of random variables.

Definition 20. Let $\{X_i : i \geq 1\}$ be a sequence of random variables defined on the probability space $(\Omega, \mathcal{A}, P)$; the **tail** σ-algebra of this sequence is given by

$$\bigcap_{n=1}^{\infty} \sigma(X_i, \ i \geq n),$$

where $\sigma(X_i, \ i \geq n)$ is the σ-algebra generated by the semi-algebra

$$\mathcal{J} = \sigma(X_n) \times \sigma(X_{n+1}) \times \sigma(X_{n+2}) \times \cdots.$$

Chapter 3

Convergence of Sequences I

3.1 Convergence a.c. and in Probability

3.1.1 Definitions and Preliminaries

In this chapter, we shall examine issues that relate to the manner in which sequences of random variables approach a limit. When we deal with sequences or series of real numbers, such issues are rather simple in their resolution, i.e., the sequence either has a unique limit or it may have several limit points; and a series may either converge to a finite number or diverge (to $\pm\infty$) or it may have no limit point, as, for example, the series

$$\sum_{i=1}^{\infty}(-1)^i.$$

When dealing with sequences of random variables, the issues are much more varied, and the manner in which convergence may be attained is not unique, in other words, there may be (are) various forms of convergence.

We begin by recalling that, somewhat informally, we say that a sequence of random variables, say $\{X_n : n \geq 1\}$, converges in probability to a random variable, say X, if, as n increases, the probability that X_n deviates from X by a predetermined amount diminishes to zero. On the other hand, we say that it converges with probability one (or almost certainly, a.c., or almost surely, a.s.) if the set of points over which the limit of the sequence deviates from X is "negligible". In what follows, we shall make these statements operationally precise and, thus, more useful.

Definition 1. Let $\{X_n : n \geq 0\}$ be a sequence of random variables defined on the probability space $(\Omega, \mathcal{A}, P)$. Define the sets, for interger r,

$$A_{n,r} = \left\{ \omega : |\, X_n(\omega) - X_0(\omega)\, | > \frac{1}{r} \right\}, \tag{3.1}$$

and let

$$A_r^* = \lim_{n \to \infty} \sup_{k \geq n} A_{k,r}. \tag{3.2}$$

We say that X_n **converges in probability** to X_0 if and only if

$$\lim_{n \to \infty} P(A_{n,r}) = 0 \tag{3.3}$$

for arbitrary integer r, and we denote this by

$$X_n \overset{P}{\to} X_0 \quad \text{or} \quad \operatorname{p} \lim_{n \to \infty} X_n = X_0. \tag{3.4}$$

We say that X_n **converges with probability one** to X_0, or **converges a.c.** (almost certainly), or **converges a.s.** (almost surely), if and only if

$$P(A^*) = 0, \tag{3.5}$$

where

$$A^* = \bigcup_{r=1}^{\infty} A_r^*. \tag{3.6}$$

We denote this by

$$X_n \overset{\text{a.c.}}{\to} X_0.$$

Remark 1. In econometrics, the usual manner in which convergence in probability is stated runs as follows: given any $\epsilon, \delta > 0$, there exists n_0 such that for all $n \geq n_0$, $\Pr(|\, X_n - X_0\, | > \epsilon) < \delta$. While this is perfectly correct, it is rather difficult to render operational instructions like "for all $\epsilon > 0$", since the collection of such entities is uncountable. However, given any $\epsilon > 0$, there exists an integer r such that $\epsilon > (1/r)$; hence, if $\omega \in \{\omega : |\, X_n(\omega) - X_0(\omega)\, | > \epsilon\}$, then $\omega \in A_{n,r}$, and again, if $\delta > 0$ is given, there exists an integer q such that $(1/q) < \delta$. Moreover, by Equation (3.3), given any q, there exists n_0 such that, for all $n \geq n_0$,

$$P(A_{n,r}) < \frac{1}{q}.$$

Thus, the statement in Equation (3.3) is fully sufficient to describe convergence in probability, as the reader is likely to have encountered it in the literature of econometrics.

Turning now to convergence a.c., the intuitive notion may be expressed as follows: if

$$A = \{\omega : \lim_{n\to\infty} |X_n - X_0| \neq 0\}, \tag{3.7}$$

then convergence a.c. would require that $P(A) = 0$. Now, the event

$$\{\omega : \lim_{n\to\infty} |X_n(\omega) - X_0(\omega)| \neq 0\}$$

can be described as the limit

$$A = \lim_{r\to\infty} \{\omega : \lim_{n\to\infty} |X_n(\omega) - X_0(\omega)| > \frac{1}{r}\}.$$

To explore this issue, define

$$B_{n,r} = \{\omega : \sup_{k\geq n} |X_k - X_0| > \frac{1}{r}\}$$

and note that $B_{n,r} \supset B_{n+1,r}$; thus, we deal with a sequence of monotone nonincreasing sets, and the limit of this sequence exists; in particular,

$$\lim_{n\to\infty} B_{n,r} = \bigcap_{n=1}^{\infty} B_{n,r}.$$

Thus, in the intuitive approach, what we require is that for every r

$$P(\lim_{n\to\infty} B_{n,r}) = \lim_{n\to\infty} P(B_{n,r}) = 0.$$

But, it is easy to verify that

$$B_{n,r} = \bigcup_{k\geq n} A_{k,r},$$

so that

$$\lim_{n\to\infty} B_{n,r} = \bigcap_{n=1}^{\infty} B_{n,r} = A_r^* = \lim_{n\to\infty} \sup_{k\geq n} A_{k,r}.$$

Moreover, it is easily seen that $A_r^* \subset A_{r+1}^*$, so that

$$\lim_{r\to\infty} A_r^* = \bigcup_{r=1}^{\infty} A_r^* = A^* = A.$$

The preceding discussion has established that the formal definition we have given fully corresponds to the intuitive understanding of the concept; in addition, it has provided added justification for the use of the rational entities $(1/r)$, instead of ϵ, in measuring the deviation of X_n from the limit, both in the case of convergence in probability as well as convergence a.c.

An immediate consequence of Definition 1 and the remark above is

Proposition 1. Let $\{X_n : n \geq 0\}$ be a sequence of random variables defined on the probability space $(\Omega,\ \mathcal{A},\ P)$. Then,

$$X_n \xrightarrow{\text{a.c.}} X_0 \qquad \text{implies} \qquad X_n \xrightarrow{\text{P}} X_0.$$

Proof: Convergence with probability one, requires that for any integer r,

$$\lim_{n \to \infty} P(B_{n,r}) = 0. \tag{3.8}$$

Since

$$B_{n,r} = \bigcup_{k=n}^{\infty} A_{k,r}, \tag{3.9}$$

we conclude that $\lim_{k \to \infty} P(A_{k,r}) = 0$.

q.e.d.

Remark 2. The converse of this proposition is not valid, i.e., convergence in probability does not imply a.c. convergence. We shall address this issue at a later stage when we examine the relationships among the various forms of convergence, for sequences of random variables.

Proposition 2 (Borel-Cantelli Theorem). Let $\{A_n : n \geq 1\}$ be a sequence of events (see Chapter 2) defined on the probability space $(\Omega,\ \mathcal{A},\ P)$, such that

$$\sum_{i=1}^{\infty} P(A_i) < \infty.$$

Then,

$$P(A_n, i.o.) = 0,$$

where

$$(A_n, i.o.) = \lim_{n \to \infty} \sup_{k \geq n} A_k = A^*.$$

Conversely, if the events are **independent** and

$$\sum_{i=1}^{\infty} P(A_i) = \infty,$$

then

$$P(A_n, i.o.) = 1.$$

Proof: We have that

$$P(A_n, i.o.) = P(\bigcap_{n=1}^{\infty} \bigcup_{k=n}^{\infty} A_k) = \lim_{n \to \infty} P(\bigcup_{k=n}^{\infty} A_k) \le \lim_{n \to \infty} \sum_{k=n}^{\infty} P(A_k).$$

Since $\sum_{i=1}^{\infty} P(A_i) < \infty$, we conclude $P(A_n, i.o.) = 0$. For the second part, note that if the events A_n are independent, then so are their complements $\bar{A}_n$. Hence,

$$P(\bigcap_{k=n}^{\infty} \bar{A}_k) = \prod_{k=n}^{\infty} P(\bar{A}_k) = \prod_{k=n}^{\infty} [1 - P(A_k)].$$

Using the relation that, for $x \in [0, 1]$, $\log(1 - x) \le -x$, we have that

$$\log[1 - P(A_k)] \le -P(A_k).$$

Thus,

$$\log \prod_{k=n}^{\infty} [1 - P(A_k)] = \sum_{k=n}^{\infty} \log[1 - P(A_k)] \le - \sum_{k=n}^{\infty} P(A_k) = -\infty.$$

Hence, for any n,

$$\log \prod_{k=n}^{\infty} P(\bar{A}_k) = -\infty, \quad \text{or} \quad P(\bigcap_{k=n}^{\infty} \bar{A}_k) = 0.$$

But, this implies that

$$P(\liminf_{n \to \infty} \bigcap_{k \ge n} \bar{A}_k) = 0,$$

and consequently, that

$$P(\limsup_{n \to \infty} \bigcup_{k \ge n} A_k) = P(A_k, i.o.) = 1.$$

q.e.d.

Corollary 1. Let $\{X_n : n \geq 0\}$ be a sequence of random variables defined on the probability space $(\Omega, \mathcal{A}, P)$. For integer r define the sets

$$A_{n,r} = \{\omega :| X_n(\omega) - X_0(\omega) | > \frac{1}{r}\}.$$

If, for arbitrary r, $\sum_{n=1}^{\infty} P(A_{n,r}) < \infty$, then

$$X_n \overset{\text{a.c.}}{\to} X_0.$$

Proof: By Proposition 2,

$$\sum_{n=1}^{\infty} P(A_{n,r}) < \infty$$

implies $P(A_{n,r}, i.o.) = 0$. This means that for any r,

$$P(\lim_{n \to \infty} \sup_{k \geq n} A_{k,r}) = 0,$$

which simply states that X_n converges a.c. to X_0.

$$\text{q.e.d.}$$

Corollary 2. Let $\{X_n : n \geq 0\}$ be as in Corollary 1, and let $\{r_n : n \geq 1\}$ be a sequence of integers converging to $+\infty$. For integer r_n, define the sets

$$A_n = \{\omega : | X_n(\omega) - X_0(\omega) | > \frac{1}{r_n}\}.$$

Then, $\sum_{n=1}^{\infty} P(A_n) < \infty$ implies

$$X_n \overset{\text{a.c.}}{\to} X_0.$$

Proof: By Proposition 2, $P(A_n, i.o.) = 0$; thus,

$$P(\limsup_{n \to \infty} A_n) = 0 \quad \text{and consequently,} \quad X_n \overset{\text{a.c.}}{\to} X_0.$$

$$\text{q.e.d.}$$

An extension of this result, due to Kolmogorov, applies to events in a tail σ-algebra. We recall from Chapter 2 that if $\{X_n : n \geq 1\}$ is a sequence of random variables defined on the probability space $(\Omega, \mathcal{A}, P)$, and

$\sigma(X_n)$ denotes the σ-algebra induced by the random variable X_n, then the tail σ-algebra of the sequence is simply $\cap_{n=1}^{\infty}\sigma(X_j, \ j \geq n)$, where the notation $\sigma(X_j, \ j \geq n)$ indicates the σ-algebra induced by the random variables $X_n, X_{n+1}, X_{n+2}, \ldots$ Sets in this algebra are said to be **tail events** and functions measurable in this algebra are said to be **tail functions**. An example of a tail event is the set

$$\{\omega : \sum_{n=1}^{\infty} X_n(\omega) \quad \text{converges}\},$$

since, evidently, whether the series does or does not converge depends only on the "tail" of the sequence. We have

Proposition 3 (Kolmogorov Zero-One Law). Let $\{X_n : n \geq 0\}$ be a sequence of independent random variables defined on the probability space $(\Omega, \ \mathcal{A}, \ P)$; in this sequence, tail events have probability either zero or one.

Proof: The idea of this proof is to show that every event in the tail σ-algebra is independent of itself. Thus, if A is such an event, then

$$P(A) = P(A \cap A) = P(A)P(A) = [P(A)]^2,$$

which would imply that either $P(A) = 0$ or $P(A) = 1$. Thus, define

$$\mathcal{A}_n = \sigma(X_j, \ j = 1, 2, ..., n), \qquad \mathcal{D}_n = \sigma(X_j, \ j > n),$$

and note that, since we are dealing with a sequence of independent random variables, the two classes above are, evidently, independent. Consider

$$\mathcal{A} = \bigcup_{n=1}^{\infty} \mathcal{A}_n, \quad \mathcal{D} = \bigcap_{n=0}^{\infty} \mathcal{D}_n,$$

and note that $\mathcal{A}$ is an algebra, since if $A \in \mathcal{A}$, then $A \in \mathcal{A}_n$, for at least one n; since the latter is a σ-algebra, evidently, the complement of A is in $\mathcal{A}$, i.e., $\bar{A} \in \mathcal{A}$. If $A, B \in \mathcal{A}$, it is also evident that $A \cup B \in \mathcal{A}$. Moreover, since $\mathcal{A}$ is an algebra, it is also a π-class (see Definition 16, of Chapter 2); by Proposition 21 of Chapter 2, $\mathcal{D}$ and $\sigma(\mathcal{A})$ are independent classes. But,

$$\mathcal{D} \subset \mathcal{D}_0 = \sigma(X_j, \ j > 0) = \sigma(\mathcal{A}),$$

thus, concluding that $\mathcal{D} \subset \sigma(\mathcal{A})$ and that $\mathcal{D}$ is independent of $\sigma(\mathcal{A})$. This means that $\mathcal{D}$ is independent of itself, or, in other words, if $A \in \mathcal{D}$, then

$$P(A) = P(A \cap A) = P(A)P(A) = [P(A)]^2,$$

which implies that $P(A) = 0$ or $P(A) = 1$.

q.e.d.

An example of a possible application of the Kolmogorov zero-one law is in the case of a sequence of independent random variables each with mean μ. Defining

$$S_n = \frac{1}{n} \sum_{i=1}^{n} X_i,$$

we note that whether S_n converges or not is a tail event. Since $E(S_n) = \mu$, if S_n converges at all, it will converge to μ a.c. and not merely in probability, or else it will not converge.

3.1.2 Characterization of Convergence a.c. and Convergence in Probability

In this section, we shall explore the properties of the two modes of convergence and the relations between them. We have

Proposition 4. Let $\{X_n : n \geq 0\}$ be a sequence of random variables defined on the probability space $(\Omega, \mathcal{A}, P)$. Then, the following statements are true:

i. $X_n \overset{\text{a.c.}}{\to} X_0$ if and only if

$$\sup_{k>n} | X_k - X_0 | \overset{\text{P}}{\to} 0,$$

i.e., $\lim_{n \to \infty} P(\{\omega : \sup_{k>n} | X_k(\omega) - X_0(\omega) | > \frac{1}{r}\}) = 0$;

ii. $X_n \overset{\text{a.c.}}{\to} X_0$ if and only if, for any integers r, s, there exists an integer n_0 such that for all $n \geq n_0$,

$$P(B_{n,r}) \leq \frac{1}{s},$$

where

$$B_{n,r} = \bigcup_{k=n}^{\infty} A_{k,r}, \quad \text{and} \quad A_{k,r} = \{\omega : |X_k(\omega) - X_0(\omega)| > \frac{1}{r}\};$$

iii. $X_n \overset{\text{a.c.}}{\to} X_0$ if and only if, for arbitrary r,

$$\lim_{n\to\infty} P(D_{n,r}) = 0,$$

where

$$D_{n,r} = \{\omega : \sup_{k\geq n} |X_k(\omega) - X_n(\omega)| > \frac{1}{r}\}.$$

Proof: By definition, $X_n \overset{\text{a.c.}}{\to} X_0$ means $P(A_r^*) = 0$, for all r. Consequently $P(A^*) = 0$, where

$$A_{k,r} = \{\omega : |X_k(\omega) - X_0(\omega)| > \frac{1}{r}\}, \quad A^* = \bigcup_{r=1}^{\infty} A_r^*, \quad A_r^* = \limsup_{n\to\infty} A_{n,r}.$$

Since $A_1^* \subset A_2^* \subset A_3^* \ldots$, it follows that $P(A^*) = \lim_{r\to\infty} P(A_r^*)$ and in order to show that $X_n \overset{\text{a.c.}}{\to} X_0$, it is sufficient to show only that $P(A_r^*) = 0$, for arbitrary r. For integer r, define the sets

$$B_{n,r} = \{\omega : \sup_{k\geq n} |X_n(\omega) - X_0(\omega)| > \frac{1}{r}\};$$

note that they form a monotone nonincreasing sequence and, consequently, that, for given r, the limit, $\lim_{n\to\infty} B_{n,r} = B_r^*$, exists; moreover,

$$B_r^* = \bigcap_{n=1}^{\infty} B_{n,r} \quad \text{and} \quad P(B_r^*) = \lim_{n\to\infty} P(B_{n,r}).$$

A little reflection will show that $B_{n,r} = \bigcup_{k=n}^{\infty} A_{k,r}$ and hence, that

$$B_r^* = \limsup_{n\to\infty} A_{n,r} = A_r^*.$$

Consequently, $P(A_r^*) = 0$ if and only if $P(B_r^*) = 0$, i.e., if and only if

$$P(\{\omega : \sup_{k\geq n} |X_k(\omega) - X_0(\omega)| > \frac{1}{r}\}) \longrightarrow 0,$$

i.e., if and only if, for arbitrary r, $\lim_{n\to\infty} P(B_{n,r}) = 0$. This concludes the proof of part i.

Part ii. of the proposition gives operational meaning to convergence a.c., in finite terms. Clearly, if X_n converges a.c. to X_0, then, by part i., $\lim_{n \to \infty} P(B_{n,r}) = 0$; consequently, given any s, (and r), there exists $n_0(r,s)$ such that for all $n \geq n_0$,

$$P(B_{n,r}) < \frac{1}{s}.$$

Conversely, suppose that the conditions hold, then, given any r, s, there exists $n_0(r,s)$ such that for all $n \geq n_0$

$$P(B_{n,r}) < \frac{1}{s}.$$

But this means

$$P(B_r^*) = \lim_{n \to \infty} P(B_{n,r}) = 0.$$

Since

$$B_r^* = \lim_{n \to \infty} \sup_{k \geq n} A_{k,r} = A_r^*,$$

we conclude that X_n converges a.c. to X_0, which completes the proof of part ii.

To prove iii., we note that

$$\{\omega : \sup_{m \geq n} | X_m(\omega) - X_n(\omega) | > \frac{1}{r}\} = \{\omega : \sup_{s \geq 0} | X_{n+s}(\omega) - X_n(\omega) | > \frac{1}{r}\}.$$

But,

$$\sup_{s \geq 0} | X_{n+s}(\omega) - X_n(\omega) | \leq \sup_{s \geq 0} \sup_{q \geq 0} | X_{n+s}(\omega) - X_{n+q}(\omega) |$$

$$\leq \sup_{s \geq 0} \sup_{q \geq 0} \{| X_{n+s}(\omega) - X_n(\omega) | + | X_{n+q}(\omega) - X_n(\omega) |\}.$$

$$= 2 \sup_{s \geq 0} | X_{n+s}(\omega) - X_n(\omega) |.$$

The first inequality is valid by the definition of the sup operation, and the second is valid in view of the triangle inequality. Let

$$C_{n,r} = \{\omega : \sup_{s \geq 0} | X_{n+s}(\omega) - X_n(\omega) | > \frac{1}{r}\},$$

$$E_{n,r} = \{\omega : 2 \sup_{s \geq n} | X_{n+s}(\omega) - X_n(\omega) | > \frac{1}{r}\},$$

and note that

$$E_{n,r} = C_{n,2r}, \quad C_{n,r} \subset D_{n,r} \subset E_{n,r}.$$

Thus, it will be sufficient to show that $X_n \to X_0$ if and only if, for arbitrary r, $\lim_{n \to \infty} P(C_{n,r}) = 0$. Now, suppose we have convergence a.c.; then, $C_{n,r} \subset B_{n,r}$; by part i. of the proposition

$$X_n \overset{\text{a.c.}}{\to} X_0 \quad \text{implies} \quad \lim_{n \to \infty} P(B_{n,r}) = 0,$$

which, in turn, implies

$$\lim_{n \to \infty} P(C_{n,r}) = 0,$$

thus proving necessity. Next, suppose that $\lim_{n \to \infty} P(B_{n,r}) = 0$. This means that, except possibly on a set of measure zero,

$$\lim_{n \to \infty} \sup_{k \geq n} X_k = \lim_{n \to \infty} \inf_{k \geq n} X_k = \lim_{n \to \infty} X_n = X_0.$$

Consequently, $X_n \longrightarrow X_0$, which completes the proof of part iii.

A more extensive and, perhaps, more transparent alternative proof of sufficiency in part iii. is the following: Let

$$H = \{\omega : \lim_{n \to \infty} \sup_{s \geq 0} \mid X_{n+s}(\omega) - X_n(\omega) \mid \neq 0\},$$

i.e., H is the set over which $\mid X_m - X_n \mid$ fails to converge (to zero); by the condition in part iii., $P(H) = 0$. Hence, over $\Omega \setminus H$ (i.e., over all points in Ω except those in H), the sequence of **real numbers** below obeys

$$\mid X_m(\omega) - X_n(\omega) \mid \longrightarrow 0, \quad \text{for all } \omega \in \Omega \setminus H.$$

By the Cauchy criterion for convergence of sequences of **real numbers**, the sequence $X_n(\omega)$ converges for all $\omega \in \Omega \setminus H$. Denote its *limit* by

$$X_0(\omega) = \lim_{n \to \infty} X_n(\omega), \quad \text{for all } \omega \in \Omega \setminus H.$$

Then, except possibly on a set of measure zero, (H), X_0 is a well defined random variable, and consequently,

$$\mid X_n(\omega) - X_0(\omega) \mid \overset{\text{a.c.}}{\to} 0.$$

q.e.d.

Corollary 3. If X_n converges a.c. to X_0 and g is **any** continuous function, then

$$g(X_n) \overset{\text{a.c.}}{\to} g(X_0).$$

Proof: Let r, s be given and define the sets $A_{k,r}$ as before. Further, define the sets

$$D_{k,s} = \{\omega : |\, g(X_k) - g(X_0)\,| > \frac{1}{s}\}.$$

By the continuity of g, if $\omega \in \bar{A}_{k,r}$ and r is sufficiently large, then

$$|\, g[X_k(\omega)] - g[X_0(\omega)]\,| \le \frac{1}{s},$$

i.e., $\omega \in \bar{D}_{k,s}$. Hence, for given s, there exists r such that

$$\bar{A}_{k,r} \subset \bar{D}_{k,s}, \quad k = 1, 2, 3, \ldots$$

Thus,

$$\bar{A}_{*r} = \lim_{n \to \infty} \inf_{k \ge n} \bar{A}_{k,r} \subset \lim_{n \to \infty} \inf_{k \ge n} \bar{D}_{k,s} = \bar{D}_{*s}. \qquad (3.10)$$

Since $X_n \overset{\text{a.c.}}{\to} X_0$, we must have $P(\bar{A}_{*r}) = 1$; but Equation (3.10) implies

$$P(\bar{D}_{*s}) \ge P(\bar{A}_{*r}).$$

Since the complement of $\bar{D}_{*s}$ is $D_s^* = \lim_{n \to \infty} \sup_{k \ge n} D_{k,s}$, we conclude $P(D_s^*) = 0$, and thus, $g(X_n) \overset{\text{a.c.}}{\to} g(X_0)$.

q.e.d.

This concludes our discussion of the characterization of convergence a.c.; we now turn our attention to the characterization of convergence in probability.

Proposition 5. Let $\{X_n : n \ge 0\}$ be a sequence of random variables defined on the probability space $(\Omega, \mathcal{A}, P)$. Then, the following statements are true:

i. $X_n \overset{P}{\to} X_0$ if and only if, for arbitrary r, $\lim_{n \to \infty} p_n = 0$, where

$$p_n = \sup_{m > n} P(C_{m,n,r}), \quad C_{m,n,r} = \{\omega : |\, X_m(\omega) - X_n(\omega)\,| > \frac{1}{r}\};$$

ii. $X_n \xrightarrow{P} X_0$ if and only if every subsequence of $\{X_n : n \geq 0\}$ contains a further subsequence, say $\{X_k'' : k \geq 1\}$, such that

$$X_k'' \xrightarrow{\text{a.c.}} X_0.$$

Proof: Suppose $X_n \xrightarrow{P} X_0$; then, defining

$$A_{n,r} = \{\omega : |X_n(\omega) - X_0(\omega)| > \frac{1}{r}\},$$

and noting that, by the triangle inequality,

$$|X_m - X_n| \leq |X_m - X_0| + |X_n - X_0|,$$

we conclude that if $\omega \in \left(\bar{A}_{n,2r} \cap \bar{A}_{m,2r}\right)$ then $\omega \in \bar{C}_{m,n,r}$. Consequently,

$$P(C_{m,n,r}) \leq P(A_{m,2r}) + P(A_{n,2r}),$$

and thus,

$$p_n = \sup_{m>n} P(C_{m,n,r}) \leq 2 \sup_{m>n} P(A_{m,2r}).$$

Since $X_n \xrightarrow{P} X_0$, $P(A_{m,2r})$ converges to zero with m; therefore, given arbitrary s, there exists $N(r,s)$, such that for all $n \geq N$, $P(A_{n,2r}) < (1/s)$. Hence, for all $n \geq N$, we have $p_n < (2/s)$; this implies that if $X_n \to X_0$, then

$$\lim_{n \to \infty} p_n = 0. \tag{3.11}$$

Conversely, suppose Equation (3.11) holds; choose a subsequence $\{X_s' : s \geq 1\}$ as follows: Putting

$$X_s' = X_{n(s)},$$

choose $n_0(1) = 1$, and for $s \geq 2$, let $n_s = \max[n_0(s-1) + 1, \ n_0(s)]$, where $n_0(s)$ is the smallest integer such that $P(D_{m,n,s}) < 2^{-s}$, and

$$D_{m,n,s} = \{\omega : |X_m(\omega) - X_n(\omega)| > 2^{-s}, m > n \geq n_0(s)\}.$$

This is always possible since $\lim_{n \to \infty} p_n = 0$. Defining the sets

$$E_s = \{\omega : |X_{s+1}'(\omega) - X_s'(\omega)| > 2^{-s}\}, \quad s = 1, 2, \ldots,$$

we see that

$$\sum_{s=1}^{\infty} P(E_s) < \sum_{s=1}^{\infty} 2^{-s} = 1.$$

By the Borel-Cantelli lemma, we have $P(E_s, i.o.) = 0$, which means that $\{X_s' : s \geq 1\}$ converges a.c., i.e., $\{X_s'(\omega) : s \geq 1\}$, as a sequence of **real numbers**, converges to some limit, except possibly on a set, H, of measure zero. Hence, we may define

$$X_0(\omega) \quad = \quad \lim_{n \to \infty} \inf_{s \geq n} X_s'(\omega), \quad \text{if } \omega \notin H$$

$$= \quad 0, \qquad\qquad \text{if } \omega \in H.$$

By its definition, X_0, is a random variable and, by Proposition 1,

$$X_s' \xrightarrow{\text{P}} X_0.$$

Next, we show that X_n converges to X_0, in probability. Define the sets

$$A_{n,r} \quad = \quad \{\omega : |X_n(\omega) - X_0(\omega)| > \frac{1}{r}\},$$

$$B_{n,n(s),2r} \quad = \quad \{\omega : |X_n(\omega) - X_{n(s)}(\omega)| > \frac{1}{2r}\},$$

$$E_{n(s),2r} \quad = \quad \{\omega : |X_{n(s)}(\omega) - X_0(\omega)| > \frac{1}{2r}\},$$

where, of course, the notation $X_{n(s)}$ simply indicates X_s'. We note that $\bar{A}_{n,r} \supset \left(\bar{B}_{n,n(s),2r} \cap \bar{E}_{n(s),2r}\right)$, or $A_{n,r} \subset \left(B_{n,n(s),2r} \cup E_{n(s),2r}\right)$, and consequently, $P(A_{n,r}) \leq P\left(B_{n,n(s),2r}\right) + P\left(E_{n(s),2r}\right)$. Since $X_{n(s)} \to X_0$, choose, for arbitrary q, s_0 such that, for $s \geq s_0$, we have

$$P(E_{n(s),2r}) < \frac{1}{2q}.$$

Since $\lim_{n \to \infty} p_n = 0$, for q as above, choose s_* such that, for all $s \geq s_*$ and $n \geq n(s)$, $P(B_{n,n(s),2r}) < (1/2q)$. Let $s^* = \max(s_0, s_*)$; then, for $n \geq n(s^*)$, $P(A_{n,r}) < (1/q)$. Since q is arbitrary, $\lim_{n \to \infty} P(A_{n,r}) = 0$; this shows that if

$$\lim_{n \to \infty} p_n = 0,$$

then

$$X_n \xrightarrow{\text{P}} X_0,$$

which completes the proof of i.

As for part ii., suppose that $X_n \xrightarrow{\text{P}} X_0$; then, evidently, **any** subsequence thereof, say $\{X'_s : s \geq 1\}$, also converges to X_0, in probability. By the argument given in part i., such subsequence has a further subsequence that converges a.c. to a random variable, say Z, i.e., there exists a subsequence, $\{X''_k : k \geq 1\}$, of $\{X'_s : s \geq 1\}$, which has the following properties:

$$X''_k \xrightarrow{\text{a.c.}} Z \quad \text{and} \quad X''_k \xrightarrow{\text{P}} X_0. \tag{3.12}$$

Now, Proposition 1 implies, in conjunction with Eq. (3.12), that

$$X''_k \xrightarrow{\text{P}} Z. \tag{3.13}$$

From equations (3.12) and (3.13), we conclude $Z = X_0$ and, consequently, that every subsequence of $\{X_n : n \geq 1\}$ has a further subsequence, say $\{X''_k : k \geq 1\}$ that converges a.c. to X_0. Conversely, suppose that $\{X'_s : s \geq 1\}$ is a (any) subsequence of $\{X_n : n \geq 0\}$; by the conditions of part ii., it has a further subsequence, $\{X''_k : k \geq 1\}$, such that

$$X''_k \xrightarrow{\text{a.c.}} X_0.$$

We shall prove that X_n converges in probability to X_0. Suppose not; then it is possible to choose a (sub)sequence $\{X^*_q : q \geq 1\}$ such that, for any q,

$$P(\{\omega : \mid X^*_q(\omega) - X_0(\omega) \mid > \frac{1}{r}\}) \geq \frac{1}{r}.$$

But, this means that no subsequence of $\{X^*_s : s \geq 1\}$ converges in probability to X_0, and thus, no subsequence converges a.c. to X_0 either. This is a contradiction, since we have found a subsequence of $\{X_n : n \geq 1\}$ none of whose subsequences converge a.c. to X_0, contrary to the assumed conditions. Hence, $X_n \xrightarrow{\text{P}} X_0$.

$$\text{q.e.d.}$$

Corollary 4. Let $\{X_n : n \geq 0\}$ be a sequence of random variables defined on the probability space $(\Omega, \mathcal{A}, P)$ and suppose

$$X_n \xrightarrow{\text{P}} X_0.$$

If g is any continuous function, then

$$g(X_n) \xrightarrow{\text{P}} g(X_0).$$

Proof: Let $Y_n = g(X_n)$. We shall prove that

$$Y_n \xrightarrow{\text{P}} Y_0 \; [= g(X_0)],$$

provided, of course, that this entity is defined. Let $\{Y_{n(s)} : s \geq 1\}$ be any subsequence of $\{Y_n : n \geq 0\}$; this induces a subsequence, $\{X_{n(s)} : s \geq 1\}$, of $\{X_n : n \geq 0\}$, such that

$$Y_{n(s)} = g(X_{n(s)}).$$

Since $X_n \xrightarrow{\text{P}} X_0$, we must also have that $X_{n(s)} \xrightarrow{\text{P}} X_0$; Proposition 5 (part ii.) implies then that there exists a subsequence of $\{X_{n(s)} : s \geq 1\}$, say $\{X'_k : k \geq 1\}$, such that $X'_k \xrightarrow{\text{a.c.}} X_0$. But, this induces the subsequence (of $\{Y_{n(s)} : s \geq 1\}$) $\{Y'_k : k \geq 1\}$ such that $Y'_k = g(X'_k)$. By Corollary 3, $Y_k \xrightarrow{\text{a.c.}} Y_0 \; [= g(X_0)]$ and part ii. of Proposition 5 implies

$$g(X_n) = Y_n \xrightarrow{\text{P}} Y_0 = g(X_0).$$

q.e.d.

Proposition 6. Let X be a random variable, $\{X_n : n \geq 1\}$ be a sequence of random variables, both defined on the probability space (Ω, $\mathcal{A}$, P), and let $\{b_n : n \geq 1\}$ be a (positive) real sequence such that $b_n \to \infty$; then, the following statements are true:

i. if X is an a.c. finite random variable [i.e., for $A = \{\omega :| X(\omega) |= \infty\}$ we have $P(A) = 0$], then

$$(X/b_n) \xrightarrow{\text{a.c.}} 0;$$

ii. if $S_n = \sum_{i=1}^{n} X_i$ and $b_n \geq b_{n-1}$, then

$$\frac{S_n}{b_n} \xrightarrow{\text{P}} 0 \quad \text{or} \quad \frac{S_n}{b_n} \xrightarrow{\text{a.c.}} 0$$

implies

$$\frac{X_n}{b_n} \xrightarrow{\text{P}} 0 \quad \text{or} \quad \frac{X_n}{b_n} \xrightarrow{\text{a.c.}} 0;$$

iii. if the X_i , $i = 1, 2, \ldots,$ are i.i.d. (independent and identically distributed) random variables and

$$\frac{S_n}{b_n} \xrightarrow{P} c \neq 0,$$

then

$$\lim_{n \to \infty} \frac{b_{n-1}}{b_n} = 1.$$

Proof: Let $A_{n,r} = \{\omega : (|X(\omega)| / b_n) > (1/r)\}$; we must prove that $P(A_r^*) = 0$, for all r. Suppose not; then, for any given r, there exists a subsequence, $\{X_{n(s)} : s \geq 1\}$, such that $X_{n(s)} = X/b_{n(s)}$, and $P(A_{n_s, r}) \geq (1/r)$. But, this means that $P(A) \geq (1/r)$, which is a contradiction. Thus, $P(A_r^*) = 0$, and consequently, $P(A^*) = 0$, where $A^* = \bigcup_{r=1}^{\infty} A_r^*$, i.e.,

$$\frac{X}{b_n} \xrightarrow{a.c.} 0.$$

To prove ii., we note that since $\{b_n : n \geq 1\}$ is a monotone nondecreasing positive sequence, $b_{n-1} \leq b_n$, and thus,

$$\frac{|X_n|}{b_n} \leq \frac{|S_{n-1}|}{b_{n-1}} \frac{b_{n-1}}{b_n} + \frac{|S_n|}{b_n}.$$

Since (S_n/b_n), as well as (S_{n-1}/b_{n-1}), converges in probability (or a.c.) to zero, it follows that (X_n/b_n) also converges in probability (or a.c.) to zero.

To prove iii., we note, as before, that

$$\frac{X_n}{b_n} = \frac{S_n}{b_n} - \frac{b_{n-1}}{b_n} \frac{S_{n-1}}{b_{n-1}}.$$

Since (S_n/b_n) converges in probability to $c \neq 0$, a necessary condition is that (X_n/b_n) converge to zero in probability.

Perhaps in this context, a short demonstration of this fact is required. First, we note that since $c \neq 0$, we must have that $E(X_n) \neq 0$, and in fact, $E|X_n| < \infty$. From the generalized Chebyshev inequality, we obtain for arbitrary r,

$$\Pr(\frac{|X_n|}{b_n} > \frac{1}{r}) < \frac{r}{b_n} E|X_n| = \frac{r}{b_n} E|X_1|.$$

The last equality above is valid in view of the fact that the sequence is one of **i.i.d.** random variables. Thus, if we define sets

$$A_{n,r} = \{\omega : \frac{|X_n|}{b_n} > \frac{1}{r}\}$$

we conclude that

$$P(A_{n,r}) < \frac{r}{b_n} E(|X_1|).$$

Since $E|X_1| < \infty$, we conlude that

$$\lim_{n \to \infty} P(A_{n,r}) = 0,$$

which shows that

$$\frac{X_n}{b_n} \xrightarrow{P} 0.$$

Since

$$\frac{X_n}{b_n} = \frac{S_n}{b_n} - \frac{S_{n-1}}{b_{n-1}} \frac{b_{n-1}}{b_n},$$

it therefore follows that

$$\text{p} \lim_{n \to \infty} \frac{X_n}{b_n} = c - \lim_{n \to \infty} \frac{b_{n-1}}{b_n} c = 0. \tag{3.14}$$

But, Eq. (3.14) implies that

$$\lim_{n \to \infty} \frac{b_{n-1}}{b_n} = 1.$$

q.e.d.

Proposition 7 (Uniqueness of Probability Limit). Let $\{X_n : n \geq 0\}$ be a sequence of random variables defined on the probability space (Ω, $\mathcal{A}$, P). If

$$X_n \xrightarrow{P} X_0 \quad \text{and} \quad X_n \xrightarrow{P} X^*,$$

then X_0 and X^* are equivalent, i.e., $P(A) = 0$, where $A = \bigcup_{r=1}^{\infty} A_r$ and $A_r = \{\omega : |X_0(\omega) - X^*(\omega)| > (1/r)\}$.

Proof: We note that $|X_0 - X^*| \leq |X_0 - X_n| + |X^* - X_n|$. Let

$$B_{n,r} = \{\omega : |X_n(\omega) - X_0(\omega)| > \frac{1}{r}\},$$

$$C_{n,r} = \{\omega : |X_n(\omega) - X^*(\omega)| > \frac{1}{r}\},$$

and choose $n_0(r)$ such that, for all $n \geq n_0(r)$,

$$P(B_{n,r}) < \frac{1}{r}, \quad P(C_{n,r}) < \frac{1}{r}.$$

It follows, then, that

$$\bar{A}_{n,r} \supset (\bar{B}_{n,2r} \cap \bar{C}_{n,2r}) \quad \text{or} \quad A_r \subset (B_{n,2r} \cup C_{n,2r}),$$

and $P(A_r) \leq P(B_{n,2r}) + P(C_{n,2r})$. Putting

$$A = \bigcup_{r=1}^{\infty} A_r = \{\omega : |X_0(\omega) - X^*(\omega)| \neq 0\},$$

we note that $A_1 \subset A_2 \subset A_3 \ldots$, and consequently,

$$P(A) = \lim_{r \to \infty} P(A_r) \leq \lim_{r \to \infty} \frac{1}{r} = 0.$$

q.e.d.

We next prove that if two sequences have equivalent probability limits then the sequences must be asymptotically equivalent, in the sense that (the sequence of) their difference is degenerate.

Proposition 8. Let $\{X_n : n \geq 1\}$, $\{Y_n : n \geq 1\}$ be sequences of random variables defined on the probability space $(\Omega, \mathcal{A}, P)$; suppose

$$X_n \xrightarrow{P} X_0, \quad Y_n \xrightarrow{P} Y_0,$$

and further suppose that X_0 and Y_0 are equivalent. Then,

$$|X_n - Y_n| \xrightarrow{P} 0,$$

i.e., if, for arbitrary r, $A_{n,r} = \{\omega : |X_n(\omega) - Y_n(\omega)| > (1/r)\}$, then

$$\lim_{n \to \infty} \sup_{k \geq n} P(A_{k,r}) = 0.$$

Proof: Since X_0, Y_0 are equivalent, then, except possibly on a set of measure zero, $X_0 = Y_0$; moreover,

$$|X_n - Y_n| \leq |X_n - X_0| + |Y_n - Y_0|.$$

As in Proposition 7, define

$$B_{n,r} = \{\omega : \mid X_n(\omega) - X_0(\omega) \mid > \frac{1}{r}\},$$

$$C_{n,r} = \{\omega : \mid Y_n(\omega) - Y_0(\omega) \mid > \frac{1}{r}\},$$

and note that

$$A_{n,r} \subset (B_{n,2r} \cup C_{n,2r}).$$

By the conditions of the proposition, there exists $n_0(r)$ such that, for all $n \geq n_0(r)$,

$$P(B_{n,2r}) < \frac{1}{2r}, \qquad P(C_{n,2r}) < \frac{1}{2r},$$

and thus, $P(A_{n,r}) < (1/r)$. Consequently, for arbitrary r and $n \geq n_0(r)$,

$$\sup_{k \geq n} P(A_{k,r}) < \frac{1}{r},$$

and since r is arbitrary, [1]

$$\lim_{n \to \infty} \sup_{k \geq n} P(A_{k,r}) = 0.$$

q.e.d.

3.2   Laws of Large Numbers

Generally, the notion of convergence in probability, or convergence with probability one (for sequences of random variables), is a broad concept that deals with the convergence of sequences of real valued measurable functions (real variables) to a real valued measurable function. In particular, the limit of the sequence, if it exists in some form of convergence, may be a degenerate random variable, i.e., a constant. The term **law of large numbers** refers exclusively to precisely this case.

Definition 2. Let $\{X_n : n \geq 1\}$ be a sequence of random variables defined on the probability space $(\Omega, \mathcal{A}, P)$ and suppose $E(X_n)$ exists; then

---

[1] The reason we employ the *lim sup* operator below is that we do not wish to inquire as to whether a *lim* exists; employing the *lim sup* operator indicates that of all the limit points that may, possibly, exist we choose the largest.

i. $\{X_n : n \geq 1\}$ is said to obey the **classical stong law of large numbers (SLLN)** if and only if

$$S_n = \frac{1}{n}\sum_{i=1}^{n}[X_i - E(X_i)] \overset{\text{a.c.}}{\rightarrow} 0;$$

ii. $\{X_n : n \geq 1\}$ is said to obey the **classical weak law of large numbers (WLLN)** if and only if

$$S_n = \frac{1}{n}\sum_{i=1}^{n}[X_i - E(X_i)] \overset{\text{P}}{\rightarrow} 0.$$

A more general rendition of the concepts of the SLLN and WLLN is given below.

Definition 3. Let $\{X_n : n > 0\}$ be a sequence of random variables defined on the probability space $(\Omega, \ \mathcal{A}, \ P)$ and let $\{a_n : n \geq 1\}$, $\{b_n : n \geq 1\}$ be two real sequences such that $b_n > 0$ and $b_n \longrightarrow \infty$. Then,

i. $\{X_n : n \geq 1\}$ obeys the SLLN if and only if

$$T_n = \frac{1}{b_n}\sum_{i=1}^{n}(X_i - a_i) \quad \text{obeys} \quad T_n \overset{\text{a.c.}}{\rightarrow} 0;$$

ii. $\{X_n : n \geq 1\}$ obeys the WLLN if and only if

$$T_n \overset{\text{P}}{\rightarrow} 0.$$

Remark 3. The concepts articulated in the definition above are quite useful in econometrics in that they give us a fairly routine way of establishing the convergence of estimators to the parameters they purport to estimate, or the lack of such convergence. As an example, consider the general linear model (GLM) and the least squares estimator of its parameter vector.

Example 1. Let $y = X\beta + u$, where y, X, which are $T \times 1$ and $T \times k$, respectively, denote the data (T observations) on the dependent

and explanatory variables of the problem; β is a k-element vector of un-
known parameters and u is a $T \times 1$ vector consisting of T i.i.d. random
variables, (u_t), which are independent of the explanatory variables and
such that $E(u_t) = 0$, $\mathrm{Var}(u_t) = \sigma^2 > 0$. The least squares estimator of
β, based on T "observations" is given by

$$\hat{\beta}_T = \beta + (X'X)^{-1}X'u,$$

which may also be rendered as

$$\hat{\beta}_T - \beta = \frac{1}{T}\sum_{t=1}^{T}(c_t u_t),$$

where c_t is the tth column of $(X'X/T)^{-1}X'$. Thus, in this context,
$a_i = 0$, $b_T = T$, and the random variables are $c_t u_t$, $t = 1, 2, \ldots$ Hence,

$$(\hat{\beta}_T - \beta) = \frac{1}{T}\sum_{t=1}^{T}(c_t u_t) = \left(\frac{X'X}{T}\right)^{-1}\frac{X'u}{T},$$

and whether

$$(\hat{\beta}_T - \beta) \overset{a.c.}{\to} 0 \quad \text{or} \quad (\hat{\beta}_T - \beta) \overset{P}{\to} 0$$

depends solely on whether $(X'X/T)^{-1}(X'u/T)$ does so or not.

3.3   Convergence in Distribution

It will facilitate the discussion of these modes of convergence if we introduce a few additional concepts.

Definition 4. Let G be a function,

$$G : R \longrightarrow R.$$

The **set of continuity** points of G, denoted by $C(G)$, is defined by

$$C(G) = \{x : x \in R, \ G(x-) = G(x+) = G(x)\},$$

where, for $h > 0$,

$$G(x-) = \lim_{h \to 0} G(x - h), \quad G(x+) = \lim_{h \to 0} G(x + h).$$

Definition 5. Let F be an arbitrary distribution function; then, the **spectrum** or **support** of F is the set

$$S = \{x : x \in R, \ F(x + \epsilon) - F(x - \epsilon) > 0, \ \text{for all} \ \epsilon > 0\}.$$

Remark 4. Note that the set S of Definition 5 is **closed**, i.e., if $x_n \in S$, for $n \geq 1$, then $\lim_{n \to \infty} x_n \in S$. Moreover, $C(F) \cup S = R$.

Definition 6. A sequence of nondecreasing functions, $\{G_n : n \geq 1\}$,

$$G_n : R \longrightarrow R,$$

is said to **converge weakly** to a nondecreasing function, G, denoted by

$$G_n \overset{\text{w}}{\to} G,$$

if and only if

$$\lim_{n \to \infty} G_n(x) = G(x), \quad \text{for all} \ x \in C(G).$$

If, in addition,

$$\lim_{n \to \infty} G_n(\pm\infty) = G(\pm\infty) = \lim_{x \to \pm\infty} G(x),$$

the sequence is said to **converge completely** and this fact is denoted by

$$G_n \overset{\text{c}}{\to} G.$$

We are now in a position to formulate more precisely the notion of convergence in distribution.

Definition 7. Let $\{X_n : n > 0\}$ be a sequence of random variables defined on the probability space $(\Omega, \mathcal{A}, P)$, with respective distribution functions $\{F_n : n \geq 1\}$. Then, X_n is said to **converge in distribution** to a random variable, X, with distribution function, F, if and only if

$$F_n \overset{\text{c}}{\to} F.$$

Remark 5. It is important to realize that convergence in distribution is not necessarily a property of random variables, as such, but rather a property of their associated distribution functions. More precisely, if F_n is the distribution function associated with X_n, then convergence in distribution **is really a property of the sequence** $\{F_n : n \geq 1\}$. In particular, the limit random variable, X, is something we construct from the function F, to which the sequence $\{F_n : n \geq 1\}$ converges. Thus, the limit random variable, X, in the definition above, need not belong to the probability space $(\Omega, \mathcal{A}, P)$. In fact, since the same (type of) distribution may be shared by many random variables, what we really mean when we say that a sequence of random variables converges in distribution to a random variable, X, is that **the sequence in question converges to a member of the class of random variables having the distribution, say** F, **and of which** X **is a representative.**

Contrast this to convergence a.c. and convergence in probability. In such cases, since the entity to which we have convergence is, evidently, defined by a limiting process on a sequence of **random variables**, i.e., measurable functions, the limit itself is defined on the same probability space as the sequence (within the equivalence class of random variables that differ from each other at most on a set of measure zero). It is also evident from the preceeding that if $X_n \overset{a.c.}{\to} X_0$ or $X_n \overset{P}{\to} X_0$, then $X_n \overset{d}{\to} X_0$ a fact we shall formally establish at a later stage.

3.4 Convergence in Mean of Order p

We introduce now another mode of convergence; thus,

Definition 8: Let $\{X_n : n \geq 0\}$ be a sequence of random variables defined on the probability space $(\Omega, \mathcal{A}, P)$ and suppose that the pth order moment is finite, i.e.,

$$E \mid X_n \mid^p < \infty, \quad n \geq 0, \quad p > 0.$$

The sequence is said to converge to X_0, **in mean of order p**, denoted by

$$X_n \overset{L^P}{\to} X_0,$$

if and only if

$$\lim_{n \to \infty} E \mid X_n - X_0 \mid^p = 0.$$

In the case of convergence in distribution, the means by which the properties of the limit entities are established involve essentially **central limit theorems** (CLT), a subject we shall examine in some detail later on. We shall have little occasion to further discuss convergence in distribution in this section. Thus, we turn to the characterization of convergence in mean of order p, which we shall also term, occasionally, L^p convergence.

Proposition 9. Let $\{X_n : n \geq 0\}$ be a sequence of random variables defined on the probability space $(\Omega, \mathcal{A}, P)$ and suppose that for some $p > 0$, $E \mid X_n \mid^p < \infty$, $n \geq 0$. Then,

$$X_n \overset{L^p}{\to} X_0$$

if and only if

$$\lim_{n \to \infty} \sup_{m \geq n} E \mid X_m - X_n \mid^p = 0.$$

Proof: If $X_n \overset{L^p}{\to} X_0$, then, evidently, $\lim_{n \to \infty} E \mid X_n - X_0 \mid^p = 0$. By the triangle inequality,

$$\mid X_m - X_n \mid \leq \mid X_m - X_0 \mid + \mid X_n - X_0 \mid,$$

and consequently, for any $p > 0$,

$$\mid X_m - X_n \mid^p \leq (\mid X_m - X_0 \mid + \mid X_n - X_0 \mid)^p.$$

Since, for nonnegative a_1, a_2 and any $p > 0$, we have $H(a) \leq 0$, where

$$H(a) = (a_1 + a_2)^p - 2^p(a_1^p + a_2^p),$$

we conclude that

$$E \mid X_m - X_n \mid^p \leq 2^p(E \mid X_m - X_0 \mid^p + E \mid X_n - X_0 \mid^p).$$

Thus,

$$\sup_{m \geq n} E \mid X_m - X_n \mid^p \leq 2^p(\sup_{m \geq n} E \mid X_m - X_0 \mid^p + E \mid X_n - X_0 \mid^p).$$

Consequently, since $X_n \overset{L^p}{\to} X_0$, we conlcude that

$$\lim_{n \to \infty} \sup_{m \geq n} E \mid X_m - X_n \mid^p = 0. \tag{3.15}$$

Conversely, suppose that the condition above holds; choose a subsequence of $\{X_n : n \geq 1\}$, say $\{X_{n(s)} : s \geq 1\}$, as follows: set $n(1) = n_0(1) = 1$, and for $s \geq 2$ let $n(s) = \max[n(s-1)+1, \, n_0(s)]$, where $n_0(s)$ is the smallest integer such that

$$E \mid X_{n_0(s)} - X_s \mid \, < 2^{-2ps}.$$

It is easy to see that the sequence, $\{X'_s : s \geq 1, \, X'_s = X_{n(s)}\}$, obeys $E \mid X'_{s+1} - X'_s \mid^p < 2^{-2ps}$. Define now the set

$$A_s = \{\omega : \mid X'_{s+1} - X'_s \mid \, > 2^{-s}\}$$

and note that, by Chebyshev's inequality,

$$E \mid X'_{s+1} - X'_s \mid^p \geq 2^{-ps} P(A_s) \quad \text{or} \quad P(A_s) \leq 2^{-ps}.$$

Since, for finite p,

$$\sum_{s=1}^{\infty} P(A_s) \leq \sum_{s=1}^{\infty} 2^{-ps} = \frac{1}{2^p - 1} < \infty,$$

it follows from the Borel-Cantelli theorem (Proposition 2 of this Chapter) that $P(A_s, \, i.o.) = 0$, i.e., that the sequence $\{X'_s : s \geq 1\}$ converges a.c. to a random variable, say X_0. Next, we observe that by Fatou's lemma (Proposition 18 of Chapter 1)

$$
\begin{aligned}
E \mid X_n - X_0 \mid^p \quad &= \quad E \lim_{s \to \infty} \mid X_n - X_{n(s)} \mid^p \\
&\leq \quad \liminf_{s \to \infty} E \mid X_n - X_{n(s)} \mid^p .
\end{aligned}
\tag{3.16}
$$

But, this implies that, given any arbitrary r, there exists $N(r)$ such that, for all $n > n(s) \geq N(r)$,

$$E \mid X_n - X_{n(s)} \mid^p \, < \frac{1}{r}.$$

Consequently, for all $n > n(s) > N(r)$,

$$E \mid X_n - X_0 \mid^p \, < \frac{1}{r}.$$

q.e.d.

We recall from Chapter 1 that a **Banach space** is a **complete normed linear space.** We shall now show that the L^p-space, i.e., the collection of random variables defined on the probability space $(\Omega, \mathcal{A}, P)$ and having finite p^{th} order moment, i.e., such that, for $p \geq 1$,

$$\int_\Omega |X|^p \, dP < \infty,$$

constitutes[2] a **Banach space.**

It is easy to verify from Definition 36 of Chapter 1 that L^p is a linear space. Define the entity

$$\|X\|_p = (E \, |X|^p)^{1/p}$$

and note that it is a norm; to see that it is a norm we note that given the standard properties of integrals and the Minkowski inequality, see Proposition 16 of Chapter 2, for any random variables, X, X_1, and X_2, the following relations hold:

$$\|X\|_p \;\geq\; 0,$$

$$\|aX\|_p \;=\; |a| \, \|X\|_p \quad \text{for any} \quad a \in R,$$

$$\|X_1 + X_2\|_p \;\leq\; \|X_1\|_p + \|X_2\|_p.$$

To complete the demonstration that $\| \cdot \|_p$ is a norm, we must also show that

$$\|X\|_p = 0 \quad \text{implies} \quad X = 0. \tag{3.17}$$

From Chapter 1, however, we know that for a nonnegative measurable function, f,

$$\int f \, dP = 0 \quad \text{only implies} \quad f = 0 \quad \text{a.e.,} \tag{3.18}$$

so that Eq. (3.17) is not strictly true. To rectify this, **we employ the convention of thinking of random variables in terms of equivalence classes.** Thus, for example, when we speak of the random variable X, we think of it as a representative of the class of random variables defined by

$$\{Y : P(A) = 0, \quad A = \{\omega : |Y(\omega) - X(\omega)| \neq 0\}\}.$$

---

[2] The condition $p \geq 1$ is not required for convergence in *mean of order p*. It is required, however, if, in the discussion below, $\|\cdot\|_p$ is to be a norm; if $p \in (0, 1)$, $\|\cdot\|_p$ does not satisfy the triangle inequality and, hence, cannot be a norm.

Within this framework **the space of random variables having finite p^{th} order moment is a normed linear space, i.e., a Banach space.**
  We now formalize the discussion above in

Proposition 10. Let L^p denote the collection of random variables defined on the probability space (Ω, $\mathcal{A}$, P) and having finite p^{th} order moment, $p \geq 1$. For $X \in L^p$, define the norm

$$\|X\|_p = (E \mid X \mid^p)^{1/p}.$$

Then (L^p, $\| \cdot \|_p$) is a complete normed linear space, i.e., a **Banach space.**

Proof: For notational convenience, we shall denote the Banach space defined above by L^p. To prove the validity of the proposition, we need only show that all Cauchy sequences in this space converge, i.e., if

$$\lim_{n \to \infty} \sup_{m \geq n} \|X_m - X_n\|_p = 0,$$

there exists an element in L^p, say X_0, such that

$$\lim_{n \to \infty} \|X_n - X_0\|_p = 0.$$

Since $(\|X\|_p)^p = E \mid X \mid^p$, we need only show that if $(\|X_m - X_n\|^p)^p$ converges (to zero) then $E \mid X_n - X_0 \mid^p \to 0$. But, this follows immediately from Proposition 9 above.

q.e.d.

Remark 6. The preceding discussion makes clear why, when stating that a sequence $\{X_n : n \geq 0\}$ converges in mean of order p to X_0, we use the notation

$$X_n \overset{L^p}{\to} X_0.$$

3.5   Relations among Convergence Modes

In this section, we shall explore additional implications of the various modes of convergence we have discussed so far and examine the relations among them. We begin with

Proposition 11. Let $\{X_n : n \geq 1\}$, $\{Y_n : n \geq 1\}$ be sequences of random variables defined on the probability space $(\Omega, \mathcal{A}, P)$ and let $\{F_n : n \geq 1\}$, $\{G_n : n \geq 1\}$ be their associated distribution functions (d.f.), respectively. If

$$(X_n - Y_n) \xrightarrow{P} 0, \quad Y_n \xrightarrow{d} Y,$$

then $X_n \xrightarrow{d} Y$.

Proof: Define the sets

$$A_n = \{\omega : |X_n(\omega) - Y_n(\omega)| < \epsilon\}, \quad B_n = \{\omega : X_n(\omega) < x, \ x \in R\},$$

$$C_n = \{\omega : Y_n(\omega) < x + \epsilon\}, \qquad D_n = \{\omega : Y_n \geq x - \epsilon\},$$

and observe that

$$F_n(x) \quad = \quad P(B_n) \quad = \quad P(B_n \cap A_n) + P(B_n \cap \bar{A}_n),$$

$$1 - F_n(x) \quad = \quad P(\bar{B}_n) \quad = \quad P(\bar{B}_n \cap A_n) + P(\bar{B}_n \cap \bar{A}_n),$$

and moreover,

$$B_n \cap A_n \quad = \quad \{\omega : X_n(\omega) < x, \ X_n(\omega) - \epsilon < Y_n(\omega) < X_n(\omega) + \epsilon\}$$

$$\subset \quad C_n \quad = \quad \{\omega : Y_n < x + \epsilon\}$$

$$\bar{B}_n \cap A_n \quad = \quad \{\omega : X_n(\omega) \geq x, \ X_n(\omega) - \epsilon < Y_n(\omega) < X_n(\omega) + \epsilon\}$$

$$\subset \quad D_n \quad = \quad \{\omega : Y_n \geq x - \epsilon\}.$$

Consequently,

$$F_n(x) \quad \leq \quad P(C_n) + P(\bar{A}_n) \quad = \quad G_n(x + \epsilon) + P(\bar{A}_n),$$

$$1 - F_n(x) \quad \leq \quad P(D_n) + P(\bar{A}_n) \quad = \quad 1 - G_n(x - \epsilon) + P(\bar{A}_n),$$

or

$$G_n(x - \epsilon) - P(\bar{A}_n) \leq F_n(x) \leq G_n(x + \epsilon) + P(\bar{A}_n).$$

Because $\lim_{n \to \infty} P(\bar{A}_n) = 0$ and $x \pm \epsilon \in C(F)$, we see that letting $n \to \infty$ we obtain

$$G(x - \epsilon) \leq \liminf_{n \to \infty} F_n(x) \leq \limsup_{n \to \infty} F_n(x) \leq G(x + \epsilon).$$

Since ϵ is arbitrary, we conclude

$$\lim_{n\to\infty} F_n(x) = F(x) = G(x) \ \text{ for } \ x \in C(F).$$

Thus, $X_n \overset{d}{\to} Y$.

q.e.d.

Corollary 5. If $X_n \overset{P}{\to} X$ then $X_n \overset{d}{\to} X$.

Proof: Consider the two sequences $\{X_n : n \geq 1\}$ and $\{Y_n : n \geq 1,\ Y_n = X,$ for all $n\}$. By the assumptions of the corollary $\mid X_n - Y_n \mid \overset{P}{\to} 0$. By Proposition 11 above, $X_n \overset{d}{\to} X$.

q.e.d.

Corollary 6. Let $\{X_n : n \geq 1\}$ be a sequence of random variables such that $X_n \overset{d}{\to} X_0$; let $\{a_n : n \geq 0\}$, $\{b_n : n \geq 0\}$ be sequences of random variables such that $a_n \overset{P}{\to} a_0$ and $b_n \overset{P}{\to} b_0$, where a_0, b_0 are fixed constants. Then,

$$a_n X_n + b_n \overset{d}{\to} a_0 X_0 + b_0.$$

Proof: Let $Y_n = a_n X_n + b_n$, $n \geq 0$, and note that $Y_0 = a_0 X_0 + b_0$ is the limiting random variable. We shall show that $Y_n \overset{d}{\to} Y_0$ by repeated application of Proposition 11.

Since, evidently, $(Y_n - a_n X_n - b_0) \overset{P}{\to} 0$, it will suffice, by Proposition 11, to show that $(a_n X_n + b_0) \overset{d}{\to} Y_0$. In order to do so, we first show that $c_n X_n \overset{P}{\to} 0$, where $c_n = a_n - a_0$. For arbitrary r, define the sets $A_n = \{\omega : \mid c_n(\omega) X_n(\omega) \mid > (1/r)\}$, $B_n = \{\omega : \mid X_n \mid \in (0,\ h]\}$, $n > 0$, and $D_n = \{\omega : \mid c_n(\omega) \mid > (1/rh)\}$, where $\pm h \in C(F)$, F being the distribution function of X_0. If $\omega \in (A_n \cap B_n)$ then it satisfies

$$h \mid c_n(\omega) \mid \ \geq \ \mid X_n(\omega) \mid \mid c_n(\omega) \mid$$

$$\geq \ \mid c_n(\omega) X_n(\omega) \mid > \tfrac{1}{r}.$$

This implies that it also satisfies the condition $\mid c_n(\omega) \mid > (1/rh)$. Thus, we conclude that $(A_n \cap B_n) \subset D_n$. Consequently,

$$
\begin{aligned}
P(A_n) &= P(A_n \cap B_n) + P(A_n \cap \bar{B}_n) \leq P(D_n) + P(\bar{B}_n) \\
&= P(D_n) + P(\bar{B}_0) + [P(B_0) - P(B_n)].
\end{aligned}
$$

Noting that $P(B_0) - P(B_n) = [F(h) - F_n(h)) - (F(-h) - F_n(-h)]$, and moreover, that $X_n \overset{d}{\to} X_0$, take h and n sufficiently large, so that $P(\bar{B}_0) < \delta$ and $|P(B_0) - P(B_n)| < \delta$. Consequently, for h and n as above, we have

$$P(A_n) \leq P(D_n) + 2\delta.$$

By the conditions of the corollary, $P(D_n) \to 0$ with n. Since δ is arbitrary, we conclude that $\lim_{n \to \infty} P(A_n) = 0$, in other words that $c_n X_n \overset{P}{\to} 0$. An immediate consequence of this is that $(a_n X_n + b_0) - (a_0 X_n + b_0) \overset{P}{\to} 0$; hence, by Proposition 11, it will suffice to show that $Z_n = a_0 X_n + b_0 \overset{d}{\to} Y_0$. Without loss of relevance, suppose $a_0 > 0$; we note that if $G_n(x) = P(\{\omega : Z_n(\omega) \in (-\infty, x]\})$, is the distribution function of Z_n then

$$G_n(x) = F_n \left(\frac{x - b_0}{a_0} \right),$$

where $\{F_n : n \geq 1\}$ is the sequence of distribution functions associated with $\{X_n : n \geq 1\}$. Hence,

$$G_n(x) \to F \left(\frac{x - b_0}{a_0} \right) \quad \text{for } x, \quad \frac{x - b_0}{a_0} \in C(F).$$

But, this means that $Z_n \overset{d}{\to} Y_0$.

q.e.d.

Corollary 7. Let $\{X_n : n \geq 1\}$ be a sequence as in Corollary 6 and let $\{\alpha_n : n \geq 0\}$, $\{\beta_n : n \geq 0\}$ be sequences of constants such that

$$\lim_{n \to \infty} \alpha_n = \alpha_0, \quad \lim_{n \to \infty} \beta_n = \beta_0.$$

If $X_n \overset{d}{\to} X_0$ then

$$\alpha_n X_n + \beta_n \overset{d}{\to} \alpha_0 X_0 + \beta_0.$$

Proof: The proof is bascially the same as that for Corollary 6; we repeat it here, *mutatis mutandis*, for pedagogical reasons only. Let $\{Y_n : Y_n = \alpha_n X_n + \beta_n, n \geq 0\}$; we are required to prove that $Y_n \overset{d}{\to} Y_0$. We note that $Y_n - (\alpha_n X_n + \beta_0) \overset{P}{\to} 0$ and hence, by Proposition 11, we need only prove that $\alpha_n X_n + \beta_0 \xrightarrow{d} Y_0$. Moreover, $(\alpha_n X_n + \beta_0) - (\alpha_0 X_n + \beta_0) = (\alpha_n - \alpha_0)X_n \xrightarrow{P} 0$, which follows directly from i. of Proposition 6. Thus, the proof will be completed if we show that $\alpha_0 X_n + \beta_0 \xrightarrow{d} Y_0$. But, this is exactly what was done at the end of the proof of Corollary 6.

q.e.d.

Remark 7. The reader may wonder why, in the proofs of Corollaries 6 and 7, we did not follow what might appear to be a much simpler approach. For example, we could have written $Z_n = Y_n - Y_0 = (a_n - a_0)X_n + a_0(X_n - X_0) + (b_n - b_0)$ and argued as follows: evidently, the last term above converges to zero in probability; the first term converges to zero in probability, as in fact we established in the proof above; finally, we would conclude the proof by arguing that $a_0(X_n - X_0)$ converges *in distribution* to the degenerate random variable zero. The problem with this approach is that the last step in the argument is in error. As we pointed out earlier, convergence in distribution is a property of the sequence of the **associated distribution functions only.** Thus, convergence in distribution **is not convergence to a specific random variable,** but rather to a member of an **equivalence class defined solely by the fact that they have the distribution function to which the sequence of distribution functions converges.** Consequently, when we consider the sequence $\{(X_n - X_0) : n \geq 1\}$, where X_0 is a particular random variable, we cannot infer that this sequence converges, in distribution, to the (particular) degenerate random variable, but only that the distribution function of X_n is increasingly well approximated by the distribution of X_0.

Further results regarding convergence in distribution will be obtained at a later stage, when we have introduced additional concepts, such as characteristic functions and the notion of **uniform integrability (u.i.).** We conclude by summarizing the relation among the four modes of convergence examined in the preceding discussion.

Proposition 12. Let $\{X_n : n \geq 0\}$ be a sequence of random variables defined on the probability space $(\Omega, \mathcal{A}, P)$. Then, the following statements are true:

i. $X_n \overset{a.c.}{\to} X_0$ implies $X_n \overset{P}{\to} X_0$.

ii. $X_n \overset{P}{\to} X_0$ implies $X_n \overset{d}{\to} X_0$.

iii. $X_n \overset{L^p}{\to} X_0$ implies $X_n \overset{P}{\to} X_0$.

iv. $X_n \overset{P}{\to} X_0$ **does not** imply $X_n \overset{L^p}{\to} X_0$.

v. $X_n \overset{P}{\to} X_0$ **does not** imply $X_n \overset{a.c.}{\to} X_0$.

vi. $X_n \overset{L^p}{\to} X_0$ **does not** imply $X_n \overset{a.c.}{\to} X_0$.

Proof: Part i. was proved in Proposition 1; part ii. was proved in Corollary 5.

To prove iii., define the sets $A_{n,r} = \{\omega : |X_n(\omega) - X_0(\omega)| > 2^{-r}\}$, $n \geq 1$, where r is an integer. From Chebyshev's inequality, we conlcude

$$P(A_{n,r}) \leq 2^{pr} E |X_n - X_0|^p .$$

By L^p convergence, to X_0, there exists $N(r)$ such that for all $n \geq N(r)$, $P(A_{n,r}) < 2^{-r}$; this is so since L^p convergence, in this context, implies

$$E |X_n - X_0|^p < 2^{-(p+1)r}.$$

Since r is arbitrary, we conclude $X_n \overset{P}{\to} X_0$.

To prove iv., it is sufficient to produce an example. Thus, take $\Omega = [0, 1]$, $\mathcal{A} =$ the σ-algebra generated by the closed subsets of Ω, $[a, b]$. Moreover, choose P to be Lebesgue measure (length), thus defining the probability space $(\Omega, \mathcal{A}, P)$. In this space, define

$$X_n(\omega) = n^\alpha \quad \text{if } \omega \in [0, \tfrac{1}{n}]$$

$$= 0 \quad \text{if } \omega > \tfrac{1}{n}.$$

Since, for arbitrary r, $P(\{\omega : X_n(\omega) > (1/r)\}) = (1/n)$, it is clear that $X_n \overset{P}{\to} 0$; however, $E |X_n|^p = n^{\alpha p - 1}$, which, as $n \longrightarrow \infty$, converges to zero, only if $\alpha p < 1$; thus, if $\alpha p \geq 1$, the sequence does not converge to zero in L^p mode, but does converge to zero in probability whether $\alpha p < 1$ or not.

To prove v. and vi., consider the probability space defined in the proof of part iv., the sets

$$B_{n,i} = \{\omega : \omega \in [\frac{i-1}{n}, \frac{i}{n}], \ i = 1, 2, \ldots n, \ n = 1, 2, \ldots\},$$

and the random variables

$$\begin{aligned} X_{n,i}(\omega) &= 1 \text{ if } \omega \in B_{n,i} \\ &= 0 \text{ otherwise.} \end{aligned}$$

We note that, for arbitrary r,

$$P(\{\omega : X_{n,i}(\omega) > \frac{1}{r}\}) = P(B_{n,i}) = \frac{1}{n}.$$

Since, evidently,

$$\lim_{n \to \infty} \max_{i \le n} P(B_{n,i}) = 0,$$

we see that $X_{n,i} \overset{P}{\to} 0$. Moreover, since $E \mid X_{n,i} \mid^p = (1/n)$, we see that $X_{n,i} \overset{L^p}{\to} 0$, as well. On the other hand, the sequence does not converge to zero pointwise at any point, say $\omega_0 \in [0,1]$. In particular, given any such ω_0, we can find a subsequence, say $\{X_{n,i_0(n)} : n \ge 1\}$, obeying, for arbitrary r,

$$P(\{\omega : X_{n,i_0(n)}(\omega) > (1/r)\}) = P(B_{n,i_0(n)}) = (1/n),$$

it being understood that $\omega_0 \in B_{n,i_0(n)}$, for every n. Thus, if this subsequence does not converge (a.c.) to zero, the original sequence does not either, and hence, we have produced an example of a sequence that converges in probability and in L^p mode to zero, but does not converge a.c.

q.e.d.

3.6   Uniform Integrability and Convergence

A question frequently arising in the context of an L^p sequence of random variables, say $\{X_n : n \ge 0\}$, is whether $E \mid X_n \mid^p$ converges to $E \mid X_0 \mid^p$, when $X_n \to X_0$ in one mode or another. A variant of the question above that arises frequently, for example in econometrics, is whether

$$\frac{1}{n}\sum_{i=1}^{n}X_i^2$$

obeys the SLLN. In attempting to provide an answer to these questions, the concept of **uniform integrability** is useful.

Definition 9. Let $\{X_n : n \geq 1\}$ be a sequence of random variables defined on the probability space $(\Omega, \mathcal{A}, P)$. The sequence above is said to be **uniformly integrable (u.i.)** if and only if

   i. $\sup_{n\geq 1} E \mid X_n \mid < \infty$, and

   ii. given any integer r, there exists another integer, say q, such that

$$\sup_{n\geq 1} \int_A \mid X_n \mid dP < \frac{1}{r}, \quad \text{whenever} \quad P(A) < \frac{1}{q}.$$

The sequence is said to be **uniformly integrable from above** if and only if $\{X_n^+ : n \geq 1\}$ is **u.i.**; it is said to be **uniformly integrable from below** if and only if $\{X_n^- : n \geq 1\}$ is **u.i.** This suggests the following characterization of u.i.

Proposition 13. Let $\{X_n : n \geq 1\}$ be a sequence of random variables defined on the probability space $(\Omega, \mathcal{A}, P)$. Then, the sequence is u.i. if and only if

$$\lim_{c\to\infty} \sup_{n\geq 1} \int_{A_n} \mid X_n \mid dP = 0,$$

where $c > 0$ and

$$A_n = \{\omega : \mid X_n(\omega) \mid > c\}.$$

Proof: Since the sequence is u.i., there exists a constant $K > 0$, such that $\sup_{n\geq 1} E \mid X_n \mid \leq K < \infty$. Consequently, and with A_n as defined in the statement of the proposition, we have

$$K \geq E \mid X_n \mid = \int_{\Omega} \mid X_n \mid dP \geq \int_{A_n} \mid X_n \mid dP \geq cP(A_n).$$

Moreover, by u.i., given any integer r, we can find a c_0 such that $P(A_n) < (K/c_0) < (1/q)$ and

$$\sup_{n\geq 1} \int_{A_n} \mid X_n \mid dP < \frac{1}{r},$$

where A_n is as in the statement of the proposition, but with $c = c_0$. Since r is arbitrary, $\lim_{c_0 \to \infty} \sup_{n \geq 1} \int_{A_n} |X_n| \, dP = 0$, as required.

Conversely, suppose the conditions of the proposition hold; then, given r, choose c sufficiently large, so that

$$\sup_{n \geq 1} \int_{A_n} |X_n| \, dP < \frac{1}{2r}.$$

Then, for any n, we must have

$$E \, | \, X_n \, | \leq cP(\bar{A}_n) + \frac{1}{2r},$$

and therefore, we conclude that

$$\sup_{n \geq 1} E \, | \, X_n \, | \leq K \quad \text{where} \quad K = cP(\bar{A}_n) + \frac{1}{2r}.$$

In addition, for $P(A) < (1/q)$, note that

$$
\int_A |X_n| \, dP \;=\; \int_{A \cap \bar{A}_n} |X_n| \, dP + \int_{A \cap A_n} |X_n| \, dP
$$

$$
\leq \quad cP(A) + \int_{A_n} |X_n| \, dP
$$

$$
\leq \quad cP(A) + \frac{1}{2r}.
$$

Choosing q such that $(c/q) < (1/2r)$, we find that, given any r, there exists q such that, for any n,

$$\int_A |X_n| \, dP < \frac{1}{r} \quad \text{for} \quad P(A) < \frac{1}{q}.$$

Thus, $\sup_{n \geq 1} \int_A |X_n| \, dP < (1/r)$ for $P(A) < (1/q)$.

q.e.d.

A few additional properties of u.i. are given in

Proposition 14. Let $\{X_n : n \geq 1\}$, $\{Y_n : n \geq 1\}$ be sequences of random variables defined on the probability space $(\Omega, \mathcal{A}, P)$. Then, the following statements are true:

    i. if $\{X_n : n \geq 1\}$ and $\{Y_n : n \geq 1\}$ are u.i., then so is $\{X_n + Y_n : n \geq 1\}$;

ii. $\{X_n : n > 1\}$ is u.i. if and only if it is u.i. from above and from below;

iii. $\{X_n : n \geq 1\}$ is u.i. if and only if $\{|X_n| : n \geq 1\}$ is;

iv. if $\{X_n : n \geq 1\}$ is u.i., then so is every subsequence thereof;

v. if $|X_n| \leq Y$, $E(Y) < \infty$, then $\{X_n : n \geq 1\}$ is u.i.

Proof: By uniform integrability, let r be given and choose c_1, c_2 such that

$$\sup_{n \geq 1} \int_{A_n} |X_n| \, dP < \frac{1}{2r}, \quad \sup_{n \geq 1} \int_{B_n} |Y_n| \, dP < \frac{1}{2r},$$

where $A_n = \{\omega : |X_n| > c_1\}$, $B_n = \{\omega : |Y_n| > c_2\}$, and $P(A_n) < (1/q)$, $P(B_n) < (1/q)$. With these definitions, note that for **any** n **and** $Z_n = Y_n + X_n$, $A = A_n \cap B_n$, we find

$$\int_A |Z_n| \, dP \leq \int_A |X_n| \, dP + \int_A |Y_n| \, dP$$

$$\leq \int_{A_n} |X_n| \, dP + \int_{B_n} |Y_n| \, dP < \frac{1}{r}$$

where $P(A) < (1/q)$, thus proving i.

To prove ii., we note that if $\{X_n : n \geq 1\}$ is u.i. from above and from below, then $\{X_n^+ : n \geq 1\}$ and $\{X_n^- : n \geq 1\}$ are u.i.; by i., we conlcude that $X_n = X_n^+ - X_n^-$ is also u.i.; conversely, since

$$\int_A X_n^+ \, dP \leq \int_A |X_n| \, dP, \quad \int_A X_n^- \, dP \leq \int_A |X_n| \, dP$$

it follows immediately that if $\{X_n : n \geq 1\}$ is u.i. , then it is u.i. from above as well as from below.

Part iii. is obvious since if $\{X_n : n \geq 1\}$ is u.i. then $\{|X_n| : n \geq 1\}$ is also u.i., due to the fact that the absolute value of X_n is exactly the same as the absolute value of $|X_n|$. Conversely, if $\{|X_n| : n \geq 1\}$ is u.i., the conclusion that $\{X_n : n \geq 1\}$ is u.i. follows instantly since all the conditions for this to be so are stated in terms of $|X_n|$.

Part iv. is also self evident since

$$\sup_{n \geq 1} \int_A |X_n| \, dP \geq \sup_{k \geq 1} \int_A |X_{n(k)}| \, dP,$$

where $P(A) < (1/q)$ and $\{X_{n(k)}\}$ is a subsequence of $\{X_n\}$. Moreover, since $\sup_{k \geq 1} E \mid X_{n(k)} \mid \leq \sup_{n \geq 1} E \mid X_n \mid < \infty$, the u.i. property follows immediately.

As for v., let $A = \{\omega : Y(\omega) > c\}$, for some real c; choose c such that $P(A) < (1/q)$, $\int_A Y \, dP < (1/r)$. Since, for any n, $\mid X_n \mid < Y$, we have

$$\int_A \mid X_n \mid \, dP < \int_A Y \, dP, \quad E \mid X_n \mid < E(Y).$$

Consequently,

$$\sup_{n \geq 1} \int_A \mid X_n \mid \, dP \leq \int_A Y \, dP < \frac{1}{r}, \quad \sup_{n \geq 1} E \mid X_n \mid \leq EY < \infty.$$

q.e.d.

A useful restatement of the conditions that must be satisfied by sequences possessing the u.i. property is given below.

Proposition 15. Let $\{X_n : n \geq 1\}$ be a sequence of random variables defined on the probability space $(\Omega, \mathcal{A}, P)$; the sequence has the u.i. property if and only if

i. (uniform boundedness of the first moment) $\sup_{n \geq 1} E \mid X_n \mid < \infty$;

ii. the set function $d_n(A)$ is **uniformly absolutely continuous** with respect to P, where $A \in \mathcal{A}$ and $d_n(A) = \int_A \mid X_n \mid \, dP$;[3]

Proof: If $\{X_n : n \geq 1\}$ is a sequence (of random variables) having the u.i. property, then i. and ii. would hold by Definition 9; conversely, if i. and ii. hold then putting

$$d(A) = \sup_{n \geq 1} d_n(A) = \sup_{n \geq 1} \int_A \mid X_n \mid \, dP,$$

we conclude that

$$d(A) < \frac{1}{r} \quad \text{whenever} \quad P(A) < \frac{1}{q}.$$

q.e.d.

---

[3] Uniform absolute continuity here means that, given any integer r, there exists an integer q such that, for all n, $d_n(A) < (1/r)$ whenever $P(A) < (1/q)$.

Remark 8. An alternative way of characterizing the u.i. property is as follows: a sequence $\{X_n : n \geq 1\}$ is said to have the u.i. property if (a) its first moment is uniformly bounded, i.e., if there exists $K < \infty$ such that $E \mid X_n \mid \leq K < \infty$, for all n, or otherwise put, if $\sup_{n \geq 1} E \mid X_n \mid < \infty$ and (b) if the measure

$$d(A_n) = \int_{A_n} \mid X_n \mid \, dP$$

is **uniformly absolutely continuous**. This means that if

$$A_n = \{\omega : \mid X_n \mid > c_n\}$$

then we can find a number c such that $c_n = c$, for all n, and moreover, if $P(A_n) < (1/q)$ then $d(A_n) < (1/r)$. In the preceding, r is arbitrary, and q may depend on r but not on n.

The significance and utility of the concept of u.i. is, perhaps, made evident in the Proposition below.

Proposition 16. Let $\{X_n : n \geq 1\}$ be a sequence of random variables defined on the probability space $(\Omega, \mathcal{A}, P)$. Then, the following statements are true:

i. if the sequence has the u.i. property, then

$$E(\liminf_{n \to \infty} X_n) \leq \liminf_{n \to \infty} E(X_n) \leq \limsup_{n \to \infty} E(X_n) \leq E(\limsup_{n \to \infty} X_n);$$

ii. if the sequence has the u.i. property and $X_n \overset{a.c.}{\to} X$ then X is integrable, i.e., $E \mid X \mid < \infty$; moreover,

$$\lim_{n \to \infty} E(X_n) = E(X), \text{ and } \lim_{n \to \infty} E \mid X_n - X \mid = 0;$$

iii. if $\{\mid X_n \mid^p : n \geq 1\}$ is u.i. for some $p > 0$ and $X_n \overset{P}{\to} X$ then

$$X \in L^p, \quad \text{and} \quad X_n \overset{L^p}{\to} X;$$

iv. if

$$X_n \overset{L^p}{\to} X, \quad X_n \in L^p,$$

then

$$X_n \overset{P}{\to} X, \quad X \in L^p,$$

and $\{\mid X_n \mid^p : n \geq 1\}$ is u.i. ;

v. if for all n, $X_n \geq 0$, $EX_n < \infty$, and $X_n \overset{\text{a.c.}}{\to} X$, then $EX_n \longrightarrow$ EX if and only if $\{X_n : n \geq 1\}$ is u.i.

Proof: To prove i., define $A_{n1} = \{\omega : X_n < -c\}$, $n \geq 1$, $A_{n2} = \bar{A}_{n1}$, and let I_{ni} be the characteristic functions of the sets A_{ni}, $i = 1, 2$, respectively. Moreover, by the u.i. property of the sequence, take $c > 0$ sufficiently large, so that, for arbitrary integer r, $\sup_{n \geq 1} | EX_n I_{n1} | <$ $(1/r)$, and note, in addition, that

$$X_n = X_n I_{n1} + X_n I_{n2}, \quad X_n \leq X_n I_{n2}. \tag{3.19}$$

It follows from Eq. (3.19) that $\liminf_{n \to \infty} X_n \leq \liminf_{n \to \infty} X_n I_{n2}$; using, in addition, Fatou's theorem (Proposition 18 of Chapter 1), we conlcude

$$E(\liminf_{n \to \infty} X_n) \leq E(\liminf_{n \to \infty} X_n I_{n2}) \leq \liminf_{n \to \infty} E(X_n I_{n2}).$$

Using, again, Eq. (3.19), we find $E(X_n I_{n2}) = E(X_n) - E(X_n I_{n1})$, from which we conclude

$$\liminf_{n \to \infty} E(X_n I_{n2}) \leq \liminf_{n \to \infty} E(X_n) + \sup_{n \geq 1} | E(X_n I_{n1}) | \leq \liminf_{n \to \infty} E(X_n) + \frac{1}{r}.$$

In conjunction with an earlier result, we therefore conclude that

$$E(\liminf_{n \to \infty} X_n) \leq \liminf_{n \to \infty} E(X_n I_{n2}) \leq \liminf_{n \to \infty} E(X_n) + \frac{1}{r};$$

because r is arbitrary, we obtain

$$E(\liminf_{n \to \infty} X_n) \leq \liminf_{n \to \infty} E(X_n). \tag{3.20}$$

Moreover, since $\liminf_{n \to \infty} E(X_n) \leq \limsup_{n \to \infty} E(X_n)$, using again Eq. (3.19) and Fatou's theorem we have

$$\limsup_{n \to \infty} E(X_n) \leq \limsup_{n \to \infty} E(X_n I_{n2}) \leq E(\limsup_{n \to \infty} X_n I_{n2}).$$

Using the first relation in Eq.(3.19), we obtain

$$E[\limsup_{n \to \infty} E(X_n I_{n2})] \leq E(\limsup_{n \to \infty} X_n) + (1/r),$$

and since r is arbitrary, we conlcude

$$E(\liminf_{n \to \infty} X_n) \leq \liminf_{n \to \infty} E(X_n) \leq \limsup_{n \to \infty} E(X_n) \leq E(\limsup_{n \to \infty} X_n),$$

thus completing the proof of i.

To prove ii., we note that if $X_n \overset{\text{a.c.}}{\to} X$, then $\limsup_{n\to\infty} X_n = \liminf_{n\to\infty} = X$, and consequently, we find from part i. $E(X) \le \liminf_{n\to\infty} E(X_n) \le \limsup_{n\to\infty} E(X_n) \le E(X)$, which establishes the integrability of X. Now, put $Y_n = X_n - X$ and note that by hypothesis $Y_n \overset{\text{a.c.}}{\to} 0$ and that, moreover, $|Y_n| \le |X_n - X|$; hence, it is integrable. Define $A_{nr} = \{\omega : |Y_n| > (1/r)\}$ and note that

$$E|Y_n| = \int_{\bar{A}_{nr}} |Y_n| \, dP + \nu(A_{nr}),$$

where $\nu(A_{nr}) = \int_{A_{nr}} |Y_n| \, dP$, is a measure that is absolutely continuous with respect to P. Since, for any r, $\lim_{n\to\infty} P(A_{nr}) = 0$, we conclude that given any integers r, q, however large, there eixsts n_0 such that, for all $n \ge n_0$, $E|Y_n| < (1/r) + (1/q)$, in other words that

$$\lim_{n\to\infty} E|X_n - X| = 0,$$

which concludes the proof of ii.

To prove iii., we note that by Proposition 5, there exists a subsequence, say $\{X_{n(k)} : k \ge 1\}$, such that $X_{n(k)} \overset{\text{a.c.}}{\to} X$. Since $|X_{n(k)}|^p$ is integrable, we have, by Fatou's theorem

$$E|X|^p = E\liminf_{n\to\infty} |X_{n(k)}|^p \le \liminf_{n\to\infty} E|X_{n(k)}|^p \le \sup_{n\ge 1} E|X_n|^p < \infty.$$

The next to the last inequality is self evident, and the last is a consequence of the u.i. property of the sequence. Thus, $X \in L^p$. To complete the proof, we must show that $E|X_n - X|^p \longrightarrow 0$. The condition $X_n \overset{P}{\to} X$ means that, given any r, there exists n_0 such that, for all $n \ge n_0$, we have [4]

$$P(|X_n - X| > \frac{1}{r}) < \frac{1}{r}.$$

Define now the sets $A_{n1} = \{\omega : |X_n(\omega)| > c\}$, $A_{n2} = \bar{A}_{n1}$. By the u.i. property, given any r, it is possible to choose c large enough so that

---

[4] The expression $P(|X_n - X| > 1/r)$ is shorthand for $P(C_n)$, where

$$C_n = \{\omega : |X_n(\omega) - X(\omega)| > (1/r)\}.$$

We shall frequently use this notation when the meaning is clear and no confusion is likely to arise.

$\sup_{n\geq 1} E(\mid X_n \mid^p I_{n1}) < (1/r)$, where I_{ni} are the characteristic functions of the sets A_{ni}, $i = 1, 2$, respectively. Consequently,

$$
\begin{aligned}
E \mid X_n - X \mid^p &= E(\mid X_n - X \mid^p I_{n1}) + E(\mid X_n - X \mid^p I_{n2}) \\
&\leq r^{-p} + 2^p [E(\mid X_n \mid^p I_{n2}) + E(\mid X \mid^p I_{n2})] \\
&\leq r^{-p} + 2^{p+1} r^{-1} < 2^{p+1}(\frac{1}{r^p} + \frac{1}{r}).
\end{aligned}
$$

Since r is arbitrary, $E \mid X_n - X \mid^p \longrightarrow 0$, and thus, $X_n \overset{LP}{\to} X$, which completes the proof of part iii.

To prove iv., note that in Proposition 12 we have shown that $X_n \overset{LP}{\to} X$ implies $X_n \overset{P}{\to} X$; that $X \in L^p$ is readily established by Proposition 10; thus, we need only show that the sequence $\{\mid X_n \mid^p: n \geq 1\}$ is u.i.. But, $X_n \in L^p$ means that for every n, $E \mid X_n \mid^p < \infty$. Hence, there exists K such that for all n, $E \mid X_n \mid^p \leq K$ and, consequently,

$$\sup_{n\geq 1} E \mid X_n \mid^p < \infty. \tag{3.21}$$

With these conditions we can establish the u.i. property as follows: define $A_n^* = \{\omega : \mid X_n \mid^p > c_n\}$, such that

$$d(A_n^*) = \int_{A_n^*} \mid X_n \mid^p \, dP < \frac{1}{r},$$

choose $c = \sup_{n\geq 1} c_n$, and note that $c < \infty$. Now, define

$$A_n = \{\omega : \mid X_n(\omega) \mid^p > c\}.$$

Since $\mid X_n \mid^p > 0$ and $A_n \subset A_n^*$ we have that $d(A_n) \leq d(A_n^*) \leq (1/r)$. Moreover, if q is any integer there exists a number c, sufficiently large, so that for $P(A_n) \leq (1/q)$, we have $\sup_{n\geq 1} d(A_n) < (1/r)$, which establishes the u.i. property of the sequence and, thus, completes the proof of iv.

To prove v., we note first that the sufficiency part follows from the proof of part ii. The necessity proof can be inferred from the fact that, since $X_n > 0$ and it converges to X, a.c., then for sufficiently large n, we must have, say, $X_n \leq X + (2/r)$. Define now $A_n = \{\omega : X_n > c_n\}$,

$A_c = \{\omega : X(\omega) + (2/r) > c\}$, and note that for sufficiently large n, i.e., for $n \geq n_0$ and $c_n = c$, $A_n \subset A_c$; consequently,

$$\int_{A_c} X_n \, dP \leq \int_{A_c} X \, dP + \frac{2}{r} P(A_c).$$

Since X is integrable, we conclude that the sequence is u.i..

q.e.d.

Corollary 8. Let $\{X_n : n \geq 0\}$ be a sequence of random variables defined on the probability space $(\Omega, \mathcal{A}, P)$ and suppose $X_n \overset{\text{a.c.}}{\to} X_0$. If $\{X_n : n \geq 1\}$ is u.i. , then

$$E \mid X_n \mid^p \longrightarrow E \mid X_0 \mid^p .$$

Moreover, if $q \leq p$, then $\{\mid X_n \mid^p\}$ is u.i., and

$$E \mid X_n \mid^q \longrightarrow E \mid X_0 \mid^q .$$

Proof: The first part of the corollary is an immediate consequence of part i. of Proposition 16. As for the second part, for all $\omega \in \Omega$ and $\mid X_n \mid \geq 1$, we have $\mid X_n \mid^q \leq \mid X_n \mid^p$. Hence, for all $\omega \in \Omega$, $\mid X_n \mid^q \leq 1 + \mid X_n \mid^p$ and thus, $E \mid X_n \mid^q \leq 1 + E \mid X_n \mid^p$. By the u.i. property of $\{\mid X_n \mid^p : n \geq 1\}$, it follows that

$$\sup_{n \geq 1} E \mid X_n \mid^q < \infty, \quad q \leq p.$$

Next, define the sets $A_n = \{\omega : \mid X_n \mid > c\}$ and obtain

$$s(A_n) = \int_{A_n} \mid X_n \mid^q \, dP \leq P(A_n) + \int_{A_n} \mid X_n \mid^p \, dP = P(A_n) + d(A_n).$$

By the u.i. property of $\{\mid X_n \mid^p : n \geq 1\}$, there exists c such that $d(A_n) < (1/2r)$ for $P(A_n) < (1/2r)$. But, for such c and $P(A_n) < (1/2r)$, we have $s(A_n) < (1/r)$, i.e., that $\sup_{n \geq 1} s(A_n) < (1/r)$, for $P(A_n) < (1/2r)$, $n \geq 1$. Thus, $\{\mid X_n \mid^q : n \geq 1\}$ is a u.i. sequence, and since $\mid X_n \mid^q \overset{\text{a.c.}}{\to} \mid X_0 \mid^q$ and $E \mid X_n \mid^q < \infty$, it follows from Proposition 16 that $E \mid X_n \mid^q \longrightarrow E \mid X_0 \mid^q$ for $q \leq p$.

q.e.d.

A related result is

Corollary 9. Let $\{X_n : n \geq 0\}$ be a sequence of random variables defined on the probability space $(\Omega, \mathcal{A}, P)$; if $X_n \in L^p$, $n \geq 1$, and $X_n \overset{L^p}{\to} X_0$ then $X_0 \in L^p$ and $E \mid X_n \mid^p \longrightarrow E \mid X_0 \mid^p$.

Proof: Since for $X_n \in L^p$, we have that, for all n, $E \mid X_n \mid^p < K$, and $\sup_{n \geq 1} E \mid X_n \mid^p < \infty$. Consequently, by part iii. of Proposition 16, $\{\mid X_n \mid^p : n \geq 1\}$ is u.i. Let $\{Z_n = \mid X_n \mid^p - \mid X_0 \mid^p, \ n \geq 1\}$ and note that it is a sequence possessing the u.i. property, owing to the fact that $X_0 \in L^p$; the latter follows easily by noting that $\mid X_0 \mid \leq \mid X_n - X_0 \mid + \mid X_n \mid$. Since L^p convergence implies convergence in probability, we also have that $Z_n \overset{P}{\to} 0$. By part ii. of Proposition 16, $Z_n \overset{L^p}{\to} 0$, for $p = 1$. But, this means that $E \mid X_n \mid^p \longrightarrow E \mid X_0 \mid^p$.

q.e.d.

Remark 9. For econometrics, the relevance of Corollary 8 is to demonstrate that if a sequence of random variables converges to a limit random variable **it does not follow**, without additional conditions, that the moments of the random variables of the sequence converge to the corresponding moments of the limit random variable. The additional restriction required is **uniform integrability**. Thus, if $X_n \overset{a.c.}{\to} X$ and $\{X_n : n \geq 1\}$ is u.i., then $EX_n \longrightarrow EX$; if, in addition, $\{\mid X_n \mid^p : n \geq 1\}$ is u.i., then it is a simple consequence of the preceding that $E \mid X_n \mid^p \longrightarrow E \mid X \mid^p$.

The relevance of Corollary 9 is to demonstrate that if a sequence of random variables has finite p^{th} order moments and **if it converges in mean of order p** then the pth moments of the (random variables of the) sequence converge to the corresponding moments of the limit random variable. Moreover, if the statement above holds for p, then it also holds for all $q \leq p$. Note that $p > 0$ **and** $q > 0$. The perceptive reader would, no doubt, have noted that if $X_n \in L^p$ and $X_n \overset{L^p}{\to} X$ then the sequence $\{\mid X_n \mid^p : n \geq 1\}$ is u.i. Thus, the reader will do well to remember that convergence in distribution **does not imply convergence of moments**.

3.7 Criteria for the SLLN

3.7.1 Sequences of Independent Random Variables

In this section, we shall discuss the conditions under which a sequence or a series (of independnet random variables) may be amenable to the application of the strong law of large numbers . Before we do so, however, a number of preliminary results are useful.

Lemma 1. Let $\{a_n : n \geq 0\}$, $\{b_n : n \geq 0\}$ be sequences of real numbers and define

$$A_n = \sum_{j=0}^{n} a_j, \quad A_n^* = \sum_{j=n+1}^{\infty} a_j, \quad n = 0, 1, 2, \ldots$$

Suppose further that $b_0 = 0$; then, the following statements are true:

i. $\sum_{j=0}^{n} a_j b_j = A_n b_n - A_0 b_1 - \sum_{i=1}^{n-1} A_i (b_{i+1} - b_i)$;

ii. if $\sum_{j=0}^{\infty} a_j < \infty$, and thus, $A_n^* < \infty$, for all n, then

$$\sum_{j=0}^{n} a_j b_j = A_0^* b_1 - A_n^* b_n + \sum_{i=1}^{n-1} A_i^* (b_{i+1} - b_i);$$

iii. if, in addition, $a_n \geq 0$, $b_{n+1} \geq b_n \geq 0$, then

$$\sum_{j=0}^{\infty} a_j b_j = A_0^* b_1 + \sum_{i=1}^{\infty} A_i^* (b_{i+1} - b_i).$$

Proof: Part i. follows immediately if we note that $a_n = A_n - A_{n-1}$. Similarly, part ii. follows quite easily if we note that $a_n = A_{n-1}^* - A_n^*$. As for part iii., we note that by part ii. we can write

$$\sum_{j=0}^{n} a_j b_j = A_0^* b_1 - A_n^* b_n + \sum_{i=1}^{n-1} A_i^* (b_{i+1} - b_i).$$

Since $\sum_{j=0}^{\infty} a_j < \infty$, it follows that

$$\lim_{n \to \infty} A_n^* = 0.$$

Consequently, if $\lim_{n \to \infty} A_n^* b_n = 0$, the proof is conlcuded. This is so since, if we take limits in the representation above, we find

$$\sum_{j=0}^{\infty} a_j b_j = A_0^* b_1 + \sum_{i=1}^{\infty} A_i^* (b_{i+1} - b_i).$$

If $\lim_{n\to\infty} A_n^* b_n > 0$, we conclude that $\sum_{j=0}^{\infty} a_j b_j = \infty$, due to the fact that $\sum_{j=n+1}^{\infty} a_j b_j \geq A_n^* b_n$. Thus,

$$\sum_{j=0}^{n} a_j b_j \leq A_0^* b_1 + \sum_{i=1}^{n-1} A_i^*(b_{i+1} - b_i),$$

and taking limits, we conclude

$$\infty = \sum_{j=0}^{\infty} a_j b_j \leq A_0^* b_1 + \sum_{i=1}^{\infty} A_i^*(b_{i+1} - b_i),$$

which shows that the right member of the inequality above is also un-bounded.

q.e.d.

Lemma 2 (Toeplitz). Let $\{a_n : a_n \geq 0 \ , \ n \geq 1\}$, put $b_n = \sum_{j=1}^{n} a_j$, and suppose that $b_n \longrightarrow \infty$. Futher, let $\{\xi_n : n \geq 1\}$ be a seqence of real numbers converging to ξ. Then,

$$\lim_{n\to\infty} \frac{1}{n} \sum_{j=1}^{b_n} a_j \xi_j = \xi.$$

Proof: In view of the fact that $\xi_n \longrightarrow \xi$, there exists n_0 such that, for all $n \geq n_0$, $| \xi_n - \xi | < (1/2r)$. Since $b_n \longrightarrow \infty$, choose $n_1 \geq n_0$ such that, for $n \geq n_1$,

$$\left| \frac{1}{b_n} \sum_{j=1}^{n} a_j(\xi_j - \xi) \right| < \frac{1}{2r}.$$

Thus, for $n \geq n_1 \geq n_0$, we must have

$$\left| \frac{1}{b_n} \sum_{j=1}^{n} a_j(\xi_j - \xi) \right| \leq \left| \frac{1}{b_n} \sum_{j=1}^{n_1} a_j(\xi_j - \xi) \right| + \frac{1}{b_n} \sum_{j=n_1+1}^{n} a_j \, | \xi_j - \xi |$$

$$< \frac{1}{2r} + \frac{b_n - b_{n_1}}{b_n} \frac{1}{2r} < \frac{1}{r}.$$

q.e.d.

Lemma 3. (Kronecker) Let $\{b_n : b_n > 0 \ , \ n \geq 0\}$ be a sequence of real numbers such that $b_n \longrightarrow \infty$; let $\{\xi_n : n \geq 0\}$ be a sequence, also of real numbers, such that $\sum_{j=1}^{\infty} \xi_j = \xi < \infty$, and suppose that $b_0 = \xi_0 = 0$. Then,

$$\lim_{n \to \infty} \frac{1}{b_n} \sum_{j=1}^{n} b_j \xi_j = 0.$$

Proof: From Lemma 1 we can write

$$\frac{1}{b_n} \sum_{j=1}^{n} b_j \xi_j = A_n - \frac{1}{b_n} \sum_{i=1}^{n-1} A_i a_{i+1} \quad \text{where} \quad A_n = \sum_{j=0}^{n} \xi_j, \quad a_n = b_n - b_{n-1}.$$

Since $A_i = \sum_{j=0}^{i} \xi_j \longrightarrow \xi$, $a_{i+1} \geq 0$, $b_n = \sum_{i=0}^{n} a_i$, it follows by Lemma 2, that

$$\frac{1}{b_n} \sum_{i=1}^{n-1} A_i a_{i+1} \longrightarrow \xi,$$

and consequently,

$$\lim_{n \to \infty} \frac{1}{b_n} \sum_{j=1}^{n} b_j \xi_j = \xi - \xi = 0.$$

q.e.d.

We now introduce

Definition 12. Let $\{X_n : n \geq 1\}$ be a sequence of random variables defined on the probability space $(\Omega, \mathcal{A}, P)$. The sequence is said to be **uniformly bounded** (u.b.) if and only if there exists a constant $c > 0$ such that, for all n, $P(A_n) = 0$, where $A_n = \{\omega : | X_n(\omega) | > c\}$.

Remark 10. Without loss of generality, we may take $c = 1$, since if the sequence $\{X_n : n \geq 1\}$ is u.b., as in Definition 12, then the sequence $\{Y_n : n \geq 1\}$ is u.b., with $c = 1$, where $Y_n = (1/c)X_n$. We shall adhere to this convention in the discussion below.

Proposition 17 (Kolmogorov's Inequality). Let $\{X_n : n \geq 1\}$ be a sequence of independent, L^2 random variables with $EX_n = 0$. Then, given any integer r,

i. $P(A_n) \leq r^2 E S_n^2$, where

$$S_n = \sum_{i=1}^{n} X_i, \quad A_n = \{\omega : \max_{1 \leq k \leq n} | S_k | \geq \frac{1}{r}\};$$

ii. if, in addition, the sequence is u.b., then

$$P(A_n) \geq 1 - \frac{(1+r)^2}{r^2 E S_n^2}.$$

Proof: Put

$$B_k = \{\omega : | S_i(\omega) | < \frac{1}{r}, \quad i = 1, 2, \ldots, k-1 \quad \text{and} \quad | S_k(\omega) | \geq \frac{1}{r}\}$$

and note that the B_k are **disjoint sets**, with $A_n = \cup_{k=1}^n B_k$. Denote by I_k the characteristic functions of B_k, by I_{ni}, $i = 1, 2$, the charactertistic functions of A_n, $\bar{A}_n$, respectively, and note that they obey, respectively, $I_{n2} = 1 - I_{n1}$, $I_{n1} = \sum_{k=1}^n I_k$. Since $S_n^2 = S_n^2 I_{n1} + S_n^2 I_{n2}$, we have that $E S_n^2 \geq E(S_n^2 I_{n1}) = \sum_{k=1}^n E(S_n^2 I_k)$. Moreover, since $S_n = S_k + S_k^*$, with $S_k^* = \sum_{j=k+1}^n X_j$, we obtain

$$\begin{aligned} E(S_n^2 I_k) &= E(S_k^2 I_k) + 2 E(S_k S_k^* I_k) + E(S_k^{*2} I_k) \\ &= E(S_k^2 I_k) + P(B_k) E S_k^{*2} \geq E(S_k^2 I_k), \end{aligned}$$

where the second equality holds by virtue of the fact that the sequence is one of **independent** random variables. In addition, since for all $\omega \in B_k$, $| S_k |^2 \geq (1/r^2)$, we have

$$E S_n^2 \geq \sum_{k=1}^n E(S_k^2 I_k) \geq \frac{1}{r^2} \sum_{k=1}^n P(B_k) = \frac{1}{r^2} P(A_n),$$

which is equivalent to $P(A_n) \leq r^2 E S_n^2$, which completes the proof of part i.

To prove part ii., we note that if $\omega \in \bar{A}_n$ then $S_n^2(\omega) \leq (1/r^2)$. Consequently, $E(S_n^2 I_{n2}) \leq (1/r^2)[1 - P(A_n)]$, and thus,

$$E(S_n^2 I_{n1}) = E S_n^2 - E(S_n^2 I_{n2}) \geq E S_n^2 - \frac{1}{r^2}[1 - P(A_n)]. \quad (3.22)$$

Next, note that $E(S_n^2 I_{n1}) = \sum_{k=1}^n E(S_n^2 I_k) = \sum_{k=1}^n E[(S_k^2 + S_k^{*2}) I_k]$; the last equality is true because we deal with a sequence of independent random variables, and consequently, the expectation of the cross product, $E S_k S_k^* I_k$, vanishes. Moreover, for $\omega \in B_k$, we have, by the definition of B_k and the u.b. property of the sequence,

$$| S_k | \leq | S_{k-1} | + | X_k | \leq \frac{1}{r} + 1 \quad \text{or} \quad S_k^2 \leq \frac{(1+r)^2}{r^2}.$$

Consequently, $E(S_k^2 I_k) \le (1+r)^2/r^2$, and thus,

$$E(S_n^2 I_{n1}) \le \sum_{k=1}^{n} [\frac{(1+r)^2}{r^2} + ES_k^{*2}] P(B_k)$$

$$\le \sum_{k=1}^{n} [\frac{(1+r)^2}{r^2} + ES_n^2] P(B_k) \qquad (3.23)$$

$$= [\frac{(1+r)^2}{r^2} + ES_n^2] P(A_n).$$

Combining Eqs. (3.22) and (3.23), we conclude that

$$P(A_n) \ge 1 - \frac{(1+r)^2}{(1+r)^2 - 1 + r^2 ES_n^2} \ge 1 - \frac{(1+r)^2}{r^2 ES_n^2}.$$

q.e.d.

Remark 11. In plain language, Kolmogorov's inequality states that for zero mean u.b. sequences of independent random variables having finite second order moments

$$1 - \frac{(1+r)^2}{r^2 ES_n^2} \le P(\max_{1 \le k \le n} |S_k| > \frac{1}{r}) \le r^2 ES_n^2,$$

and moreover, that the u.b. condition is not required for the right inequality.

An important consequence of Kolmogorov's inequality is

Proposition 18 (Kolmogorov Khinchine Convergence Criterion). Let $\{X_n : n \ge 1\}$ be a sequence of independent L^2 random variables, with $EX_n = 0$, for all n, defined on the probability space $(\Omega, \mathcal{A}, P)$. The following statements are true:

i. if $\sum_{i=1}^{\infty} EX_n^2 < \infty$, then S_n converges a.c. (to a finite quantity), where $S_n = \sum_{i=1}^{n} X_i$;

ii. if, in addition, the random variables are u.b. , then the converse is also true, i.e., if S_n converges a.c., then $\sum_{i=1}^{\infty} EX_i^2 < \infty$.

Proof: By Proposition 4 of this chapter, S_n converges a.c. if and only if, for any integer r, $P(A_{m,r})$ converges to zero with m, where

$$A_{m,r} = \{\omega : \sup_{k \ge 1} |S_{m+k}(\omega) - S_m(\omega)| > \frac{1}{r}\}.$$

Now, if we put

$$B_{N,r} = \{\omega : \max_{1 \leq k \leq N} |S_{m+k}(\omega) - S_m(\omega)| > \frac{1}{r}\},$$

we see that

$$B_{N,r} \subset B_{(N+1),r}, \qquad A_{m,r} = \cup_{N=1}^{\infty} B_{N,r} = \lim_{N \to \infty} B_{N,r}.$$

By Kolmogorov's inequality,

$$P(A_{m,r}) = \lim_{N \to \infty} P(B_{N,r}) \leq r^2 \lim_{N \to \infty} \sum_{i=m+1}^{m+N} EX_i^2 = r^2 \sum_{i=m+1}^{\infty} EX_i^2. \quad (3.24)$$

Consequently, if

$$\sum_{i=1}^{\infty} EX_i^2 < \infty, \quad \text{then} \quad \lim_{m \to \infty} \sum_{i=m+1}^{\infty} EX_i^2 = 0,$$

and thus, S_n converges, a.c. Conversely, suppose S_n converges a.c.; then, by Proposition 4 and m sufficiently large, we obtain, say, $P(A_{m,r}) < (1/2)$. We shall now show that if $\sum_{i=1}^{\infty} EX_i^2 = \infty$, then we are led to a contradiction. Thus, suppose the series is unbounded as above; by part ii. of Kolmogorov's inequality,

$$P(A_{m,r}) = \lim_{N \to \infty} P(B_{N,r}) \geq \lim_{N \to \infty} [1 - \frac{(1+r)^2}{r^2 \sum_{i=m+1}^{m+N} EX_i^2}]$$

$$= 1 - \frac{(1+r)^2}{r^2 \sum_{i=m+1}^{\infty} EX_i^2} = 1.$$

But, this is a contradiction; hence, $\sum_{i=1}^{\infty} EX_i^2 < \infty$.

q.e.d.

We have two further elaborations of this result.

Proposition 19. Let $\{X_n : n \geq 1\}$ be a sequence of **independent** random variables defined on the probability space $(\Omega, \mathcal{A}, P)$ and define $S_n = \sum_{i=1}^{n} X_i$.

   i. If, $\sum_{i=1}^{\infty} EX_i$ converges, and $\sum_{i=1}^{\infty} \text{Var}(X_i) < \infty$, then S_n converges a.c.;

ii. if, in addition, the sequence is u.b. and S_n converges a.c., then

$$\sum_{i=1}^{\infty} EX_i \quad \text{converges and} \quad \sum_{i=1}^{\infty} \text{Var}(X_i) < \infty.$$

Proof: By Proposition 18, $S_n^* = \sum_{i=1}^{n}(X_i - EX_i)$ converges a.c.; since by hypothesis $\sum_{i=1}^{\infty} EX_i < \infty$, it follows immediately that S_n converges a.c. To prove part ii., we employ the following heuristics, in order to keep the argument at an elementary level. Let $\{Y_n : n \geq 1\}$ be a sequence of independent random variables having the same distribution(s) as those of the original sequence $\{X_n : n \geq 1\}$. Clearly, if S_n converges a.c., then the same must be true of $S_n^* = \sum_{i=1}^{n} Y_i$ and $S_n^{**} = \sum_{i=1}^{n} Z_i$, where $Z_i = X_i - Y_i$. But, $EZ_i = 0$ and, since both sequences are u.b.,

$$|Z_i| \leq |X_i| + |Y_i| \leq 2.$$

Since S_n^{**} converges a.c., Proposition 18 implies that $\sum_{i=1}^{\infty} \text{Var}(Z_i) < \infty$. Since the two processes are mutually independent and have the same distribution functions, we conclude that $\text{Var}(X_i) = (1/2)\text{Var}(Z_i)$; consequently,

$$\sum_{i=1}^{\infty} \text{Var}(X_i) = \frac{1}{2} \sum_{i=1}^{\infty} \text{Var}(Z_i) < \infty.$$

q.e.d.

Proposition 20 (Kolmogorov's Three Series Theorem). Let $\{X_n : n \geq 1\}$ be a sequence of independent random variables defined on the probability space $(\Omega, \mathcal{A}, P)$. Then, $S_n = \sum_{i=1}^{n} X_i$ converges a.c. if and only if the following three conditions hold:

i. $\sum_{n=1}^{\infty} P(A_n) < \infty$, where $A_n = \{\omega : |X_n(\omega)| > 1\}$;

ii. $\sum_{n=1}^{\infty} EY_n$ converges, where $Y_n = X_n I_{n2}$ and I_{n2} is the characteristic function of $\bar{A}_n$;

iii. $\sum_{n=1}^{\infty} \text{Var}(Y_n) < \infty$.

Proof: (Sufficiency) In view of ii. and iii., Proposition 19 implies the convergence a.c. of $S_n^* = \sum_{i=1}^{n} Y_i$. In view of i. and Proposition 2

(Borel-Cantelli), $P(A_n, i.o.) = 0$. Hence, X_n and Y_n are equivalent, and consequently, S_n converges a.c. as well. As for necessity, suppose S_n converges a.c.; then, evidently, $X_n \overset{\text{a.c.}}{\to} 0$. A consequence of this, however, is that the "event" $|X_n(\omega)| > 1$ occurs, at most, only finitely many times, i.e.,

$$P(A_n, i.o.) = P(\limsup_{n \to \infty} A_n) = 0.$$

Consequently, $\sum_{n=1}^{\infty} P(A_n) < \infty$. We demonstrate this by contradiction. Suppose not; then, since we are dealing with independent random variables, Proposition 2 (Borel-Cantelli) implies $P(A_n, i.o.) = 1$, which is a contradiction. Thus, condition i. holds. As for conditions ii. and iii., consider $Y_n = X_n I_{n2}$ and note that the set $\{\omega : |X_n - Y_n| > 0\}$, is exacly the set A_n. Hence, the sequences $\{X_n : n \geq 1\}$ and $\{Y_n : n \geq 1\}$ are equivalent and since, by hypothesis, S_n converges a.c., the same is true of S_n^*. Moreover, $\{Y_n : n \geq 1\}$ is u.b.; consequently, conditions ii. and iii. hold, by Proposition 19.

q.e.d.

An almost immediate implication of the Kolmogorov three series theorem is

Proposition 21. Let $\{X_n : n \geq 1\}$ be a sequence of independent random variables defined on the probability space $(\Omega, \mathcal{A}, P)$ and define $S_n = \sum_{k=1}^{n} X_k$. The following statements are true:

i. If $EX_n = 0$, for all n, and $\sum_{k=1}^{\infty} E[X_k^2 I_{k2} + |X_k| I_{k1}] < \infty$, then S_n converges a.c., where I_{n1}, I_{n2} are, respectively, the characteristic functions of A_n and $\bar{A}_n$, and as before,

$$A_n : \{\omega : |X_n| > 1\} ;$$

ii. S_n converges a.c. if $\sum_{n=1}^{\infty} |X_n|^{\alpha_n} < \infty$ for $\alpha_n \in (0, 2]$, provided $EX_n = 0$, whenever $\alpha_n \in [1, 2]$.

Proof: To prove i., we note that since $EX_n = 0$ and $X_n = X_n I_{n1} + X_n I_{n2}$, it follows that $E(X_n I_{n2}) = -E(X_n I_{n1})$. Consequently,

$$\left| \sum_{n=1}^{\infty} E(X_n I_{n2}) \right| = \left| \sum_{n=1}^{\infty} E(X_n I_{n1}) \right| \leq \sum_{n=1}^{\infty} E(|X_n| I_{n1}) < \infty.$$

Moreover,

$$E(|\,X_n\,|\,I_{n1}) = \int_{A_n} |\,X_n\,|\ dP \ge \int_{A_n} dP = P(A_n),$$

and thus, $\sum_{n=1}^{\infty} P(A_n) \le \sum_{n=1}^{\infty} E(|\,X_n\,|\,I_{n1}) < \infty$, which satisfies condition i. of Proposition 20. Define now $Y_n = X_n I_{n2}$ and note that $\{Y_n : n \ge 1\}$ is u.b. sequence of independent random variables. In addition, it is evident that

   a. $\sum_{n=1}^{\infty} EY_n \le \sum_{n=1}^{\infty} |\,E(X_n I_{n2})\,| < \infty\,;$

   b. $\sum_{n=1}^{\infty} \mathrm{Var}(Y_n) \le \sum_{n=1}^{\infty} EY_n^2 < \infty.$

Consequently, conditions ii. and iii. of Proposition 20 are satisfied as well and S_n converges a.c.

To prove part ii., consider first the case $\alpha_n \in [1,2]$ and $EX_n = 0$. In this context,

$$X_n^2 I_{n2} + |\,X_n\,|\,I_{n1} \le |\,X_n\,|^{a_n}\,.$$

This is so since if $\omega \in \bar{A}_n$ then $|\,X_n(\omega)\,|^2 \le |\,X_n(\omega)\,|^{\alpha_n}$, while, if $\omega \in A_n$, $|\,X_n(\omega)\,| \le |\,X_n(\omega)\,|^{\alpha_n}$. Hence, by part i. of this proposition, S_n converges a.c.

Consider now the case $\alpha_n \in (0,1)$. In this case, evidently,

$$
\begin{aligned}
E\,|\,X_n\,|^{\alpha_n} &= E(|\,X_n\,|^{\alpha_n}\,I_{n1}) + E(|\,X_n\,|^{\alpha_n}\,I_{n2})\\
&\ge E(|\,X_n\,|^{\alpha_n}\,I_{n1}) \ge P(A_n).
\end{aligned}
$$

Thus, $\sum_{n=1}^{\infty} P(A_n) \le \sum_{n=1}^{\infty} E\,|\,X_n\,|^{\alpha_n} < \infty$. Next, define $Y_n = X_n I_{n2}$ and note that

$$
\begin{aligned}
EY_n &\le E(|\,X_n\,|\,I_{n2}) \le E\,|\,X_n\,|^{\alpha_2}\\
\mathrm{Var}(Y_n) &\le EY_n^2 = E(X_n^2 I_{n2}) \le E\,|\,X_n\,|^{\alpha_n}.
\end{aligned}
$$

This implies that

$$\sum_{n=1}^{\infty} EY_n < \infty, \quad \sum_{n=1}^{\infty} \mathrm{Var}(Y_n) < \infty.$$

Consequently, by Proposition 20, we conclude that S_n converges a.c.

q.e.d.

Of more immediate applicability in econometrics are the following results.

Proposition 22 (Kolmogorov's Criterion). Let $\{X_n : n \geq 1\}$ be a sequence of independent and L^2 random variables defined on the probability space $(\Omega, \mathcal{A}, P)$; put $S_n = \sum_{i=1}^n X_i$, and let $\{b_n : n \geq 1\}$ be a nondecreasing sequence of positive numbers such that $b_n \longrightarrow \infty$. If

$$\sum_{n=1}^{\infty} \frac{\mathrm{Var}(X_n)}{b_n} < \infty,$$

then

$$\frac{S_n - ES_n}{b_n} \xrightarrow{\text{a.c.}} 0.$$

Proof: We may rewrite the expression above as

$$\frac{S_n - ES_n}{b_n} = Q_n = \frac{1}{b_n} \sum_{k=1}^n b_k \xi_k,$$

where

$$\xi_k = \frac{X_k - EX_k}{b_k}, \quad E\xi_k = 0, \quad E(\xi_k^2) = \frac{\mathrm{Var}(X_k)}{b_k^2}.$$

We note that for $\omega \in \Omega$, $\{Q_n(\omega) : n \geq 1\}$ is a sequence of **real numbers**. From Lemma 3 (Kronecker's lemma), this sequence will converge if $\sum_{k=1}^{\infty} \xi_k(\omega)$ converges. Now think of $\sum_{k=1}^n \xi_k$ as a sequence of random variables and observe that

$$E\xi_k = 0, \quad \sum_{k=1}^{\infty} \mathrm{Var}(\xi_k) = \sum_{k=1}^{\infty} \frac{\mathrm{Var}(X_k)}{b_k^2}.$$

By Proposition 18, we conclude that $\sum_{k=1}^{\infty} \xi_k$ converges a.c.; hence, for all $\omega \in \Omega$, except possibly for a set of measure zero, the sequence (of real numbers) $\{Q_n(\omega) : n \geq 1\}$ converges to zero, in virtue of Lemma 3 (Kronecker's lemma). Consequently,

$$Q_n = \frac{S_n - ES_n}{b_n} \xrightarrow{\text{a.c.}} 0.$$

$$\text{q.e.d.}$$

Corollary 10. Let $\{X_n : n \geq 1\}$ be a sequence of random variables such that, $EX_n = \mu_n$ and $E \mid X_n \mid^{\alpha_n} < \infty$, for $\{\alpha_n : n \geq 1, \alpha_n \in (0, 1]\}$. If

$$\sum_{n=1}^{\infty} \frac{\mid X_n - \mu_n \mid^{\alpha_n}}{b_n^{\alpha_n}} < \infty,$$

then,

$$Z_n = \frac{S_n - ES_n}{b_n} \xrightarrow{\text{a.c.}} 0.$$

Proof: As above, rewrite

$$Z_n = \frac{1}{b_n} \sum_{k=1}^{n} b_k \xi_k, \quad EX_k = \mu_k, \quad \xi_k = \frac{X_k - \mu_k}{b_k},$$

and note that $E\xi_k = 0$, $\sum_{k=1}^{\infty} | \xi_k |^{\alpha_k} < \infty$. By part ii. of Proposition 21, $\sum_{k=1}^{\infty} \xi_k$ converges a.c.; thus, for all $\omega \in \Omega$, except possibly for a set of measure zero, $Z_n(\omega) \longrightarrow 0$, by Lemma 3. Consequently,

$$\frac{S_n - ES_n}{b_n} \xrightarrow{\text{a.c.}} 0.$$

q.e.d.

Remark 11. In the special case, $b_n = n$, Kolmogorov's criterion reduces to

$$\sum_{n=1}^{\infty} \frac{\mathrm{Var}(X_n)}{n^2} < \infty$$

and the criterion of the corollary reduces to

$$\sum_{n=1}^{\infty} \frac{| X_n |^{\alpha_n}}{n^{\alpha_n}} < \infty \quad \text{or} \quad \sum_{n=1}^{\infty} \frac{| X_n - \mu_n |^{\alpha_n}}{n^{\alpha_n}} < \infty,$$

depending on the specification.

In the proof of the next proposition, the following auxiliary result is required.

Lemma 4. Let X be a nonnegative random variable defined on the probability space $(\Omega, \mathcal{A}, P)$. Then

$$\sum_{n=1}^{\infty} P(X \geq n) \leq EX \leq 1 + \sum_{n=1}^{\infty} P(X \geq n).$$

Proof: Put

$$A_n = \{\omega : X(\omega) \geq n\}, \quad B_k = \{\omega : k \leq X(\omega) \leq (k+1)\},$$

and note that $P(A_n) = P(X \geq n)$. Moreover,

a. the sets $\{B_k : k \geq 0\}$ form a countable partition of Ω, i.e., the sets are disjoint and $\bigcup_{k=0}^{\infty} B_k = \Omega$;

b. $A_n = \bigcup_{k \geq n} B_k$.

Let I_k, $k \geq 0$, be the characteristic functions of the sets B_k, $k \geq 0$, respectively, and let I_{n1}, I_{n2} be the characteristic functions of the sets A_n, $\bar{A}_n$, respectively. We also note that

$$\sum_{n=0}^{\infty} P(A_n) = \sum_{n=0}^{\infty} \sum_{k=n}^{\infty} P(B_k) = \sum_{k=0}^{\infty} kP(B_k),$$

and moreover,

$$EX = \int_{\Omega} X(\omega)\, dP = \sum_{k=0}^{\infty} \int_{B_k} X(\omega)\, dP.$$

Consequently,

$$\sum_{k=0}^{\infty} kP(B_k) \leq EX \leq \sum_{k=0}^{\infty}(k+1)P(B_k)$$

or

$$\sum_{n=1}^{\infty} P(X \geq n) \leq EX \leq 1 + \sum_{n=1}^{\infty} P(X \geq n).$$

q.e.d.

Proposition 23 (Kolmogorov). Let $\{X_n : n \geq 1\}$ be a sequence of independent, identically distributed (i.i.d.) random variables defined on the probability space $(\Omega,\ \mathcal{A},\ P)$ and suppose $E \mid X_1 \mid < \infty$. Let $EX_1 = \mu$, and $S_n = \sum_{k=1}^{n} X_i$. Then,

$$\frac{S_n}{n} \overset{\text{a.c.}}{\to} \mu.$$

Proof: This proof has three essential steps; first, we simplify the problem by subtracting out the mean; second, we trim the sequence so that it becomes bounded, although not u.b.; and third, we apply Lemmata 2 and 3 (Toeplitz and Kronecker) in order to get the desired conclusions. We begin by noting that $(S_n/n) - \mu = (1/n)\sum_{i=1}^{n}(X_i - \mu)$. Consequently, putting $Y_n = X_n - \mu$, we transform the problem to: given that $\{Y_n : n \geq 1\}$ is a **zero mean** sequence of i.i.d. random variables, show that

$$\frac{S_n^*}{n} \overset{\text{a.c.}}{\to} 0, \quad \text{where} \quad S_n^* = \sum_{i=1}^{n} Y_i.$$

Define now, relative to the Y-sequence, the sets A_n, $\bar{A}_n$, B_k and their respective characteristic functions I_{n1}, I_{n2}, I_k, as in Lemma 4, except that now

$$B_k = \{\omega : (k-1) \leq |Y_n| \leq k \ , \ k = 1, 2, 3, \ldots\}.$$

Put $Z_n = Y_n I_{n2}$, consider the sets $\{\omega : |Y_n - Z_n| > 0\} = \{\omega : |Y_n(\omega)| \geq n\} = A_n$, and note that we are dealing here with a sequence of i.i.d. random variables. Thus, $P(A_n) = P(|Y_1| \geq n)$, for all n. Furthermore, since $E|Y_1| < \infty$, we conclude, by Lemma 4,

$$\sum_{n=1}^{\infty} P(A_n) < \infty.$$

It follows then, by Proposition 2 (Borel-Cantelli), that $P(A_n \ , \ i.o.) = 0$, which means that the two sequences $\{Y_n : n \geq 1\}$, $\{Z_n : n \geq 1\}$ are equivalent. Thus, it will be sufficient to show that

$$\frac{S_n^{**}}{n} \overset{\text{a.c.}}{\to} 0, \quad \text{where} \quad S_n^{**} = \sum_{k=1}^{n} Z_k.$$

Note that $EZ_k \neq 0$, but that $EZ_k \longrightarrow 0$. Employing Lemma 2 (Toeplitz), we therefore conclude that

$$\frac{1}{n} \sum_{k=1}^{n} EZ_k \longrightarrow 0;$$

therefore instead of dealing with the convergence properties of (S_n^{**}/n), we may, equivalently, deal with those of

$$Q_n = \frac{S_n^{**}}{n} - \frac{\sum_{k=1}^{n} EZ_k}{n} = \frac{\sum_{k=1}^{n} kW_k}{n} \quad \text{where} \quad W_k = \frac{Z_k - EZ_k}{k}.$$

We note that, by Lemma 3 (Kronecker), if we can show that, as a sequence of **real numbers**, $\sum_{k=1}^{n} W_k(\omega)$ converges then we can conclude that $Q_n(\omega)$ converges to zero. But $\{W_k : k \geq 1\}$ is a zero mean sequence of independent random variables; by part i. of Proposition 18, if we can show that $\sum_{k=1}^{\infty} EW_k^2 < \infty$ then we can conclude that $\sum_{k=1}^{n} W_k$ converges a.c. Now, $EW_k^2 \leq (1/k^2)EZ_k^2$, and moreover [5]

$$
\begin{aligned}
EZ_n^2 &= \int_{\bar{A}_n} |Y_n(\omega)|^2 \ dP = \int_{\bar{A}_n} |Y_1(\omega)|^2 \ dP \\
&= \int_{\cup_{k=1}^n B_k} |Y_1|^2 \ dP = \sum_{k=1}^n \int_{B_k} |Y_1(\omega)|^2 \ dP \\
&\leq \sum_{k=1}^n k \int_{B_k} |Y_1| \ dP = \sum_{k=1}^n kE(|Y_1| \ I_k)
\end{aligned}
$$

Consequently [6]

$$
\begin{aligned}
\sum_{n=1}^{\infty} EW_n^2 &\leq \sum_{n=1}^{\infty} \frac{EZ_n^2}{n^2} \\
&\leq \sum_{n=1}^{\infty} \frac{\sum_{k=1}^n kE(|Y_1| \ I_k)}{n^2} \\
&= \sum_{k=1}^{\infty} kE(|Y_1| \ I_k) \sum_{n=k}^{\infty} \frac{1}{n^2} \\
&\leq 2 \sum_{k=1}^{\infty} E(|Y_n| \ I_k) \leq 2E |Y_1| < \infty,
\end{aligned}
$$

and thus, $\sum_{k=1}^n W_k$ converges a.c. This means that for all $\omega \in \Omega$, except possibly for a set of measure zero, $\{Q_n(\omega) : n \geq 1\}$, as a sequence of **real numbers**, converges to zero by Lemma 3. Thus, $Q_n \overset{a.c.}{\to} 0$; since $Q_n = (S_n^{**}/n) - (\sum_{k=1}^n EZ_k/n)$ and $(\sum_{k=1}^n EZ_k/n) \longrightarrow 0$, we conlcude that

$$
\frac{S_n^{**}}{n} \overset{a.c.}{\to} 0.
$$

Since the Z- and Y-processes are equivalent, we also conclude that $(S_n^*/n) \overset{a.c.}{\to} 0$. Finally, since $(S_n^*/n) = (S_n/n) - \mu$, we conclude that

$$
\frac{S_n}{n} \overset{a.c.}{\to} \mu.
$$

q.e.d.

---

[5] The second equality below follows from the i.i.d. property of the sequence; the third equality follows from the fact that $\bar{A}_n = \cup_{k=1}^n B_k$; the first inequality is valid since within the set B_k, $|Y_1| \leq k$.

[6] The third inequality below follows from the fact that $\sum_{n=k}^{\infty}(1/n^2) \leq (2/k)$, bearing in mind that $\sum_{n=1}^{\infty}(1/n^2) = (\pi^2/6)$.

3.7.2 Sequences of Uncorrelated Random Variables

We are often faced, in econometrics, with the problem of evaluating the limits of sums of uncorrelated random variables. We shall close the chapter with a few results pertinent to such cases.

Definition 13. Let $\{X_n : n \geq 1\}$ be a sequence of random variables defined on the probability space $(\Omega, \mathcal{A}, P)$. The sequence is said to be an **orthogonal** sequence if and only if for every pair, X_n, X_m, $m \neq n$, $E(X_n X_m) = 0$.

Definition 14. Let $\{X_n : n \geq 1\}$ be a sequence of random variables defined on the probability space $(\Omega, \mathcal{A}, P)$. The sequence is said to be an **uncorrelated** sequence if and only if for every pair, X_n, X_m, $m \neq n$, $E(X_n X_m) - E(X_n)E(X_m) = 0$.

Remark 13. Evidently, a zero mean orthogonal sequence is also uncorrelated and every uncorrelated zero mean sequence is also orthogonal. This result does not hold, however, if the sequence does not have zero means.

Remark 14. We remind the reader that the **covariance** between any two members of the sequence above is given by

$$\text{Cov}(X_n, X_m) = E[(X_n - E(X_n))][(X_m - E(X_m))],$$

and their **correlation** is defined as the their covariance divided by the square root of the product of their variances.

Proposition 24. Let $\{X_n : n \geq 1\}$ be an uncorrelated sequence of random variables defined on the probability space $(\Omega, \mathcal{A}, P)$; suppose further that there exists a constant, K, such that $\text{Var}(X_n) = E(X_n - \mu_n)^2 < K$, for all n, where $E(X_n) = \mu_n$. Then,

$$\frac{S_n}{n} \xrightarrow{\text{P}} 0,$$

where $S_n = \sum_{k=1}^{n}(X_k - \mu_k)$.

Proof: Define the sets, for arbitrary integer r,

$$A_{nr} = \{\omega : \frac{|S_n|}{n} > \frac{1}{r}\},$$

and note that by Chebyshev's inequality,

$$P(A_{nr}) < \frac{E(S_n^2)r^2}{n^2}.$$

Since the variance sequence is bounded by K and the sequence is uncorrelated, we easily find $E(S_n^2) \leq nK$. We thus conclude that for arbitrary r, $\lim_{n \to \infty} P(A_{nr}) = 0$.

q.e.d.

Proposition 25. Under the same conditions as in Proposition 24,

$$\frac{S_n}{n} \overset{\text{a.c.}}{\to} 0.$$

Proof: This proposition is stated mainly in order to introduce a particular method of proof. We shall first show that the conclusion of the proposition holds for a particular subsequence of S_n/n and then extend the result. Without loss of generality, assume that we are dealing with a zero mean sequence, consider the subsequence S_{n^2}, and define the sets

$$B_{n^2 r} = \{\omega : \frac{|S_{n^2}|}{n^2} > \frac{1}{r}\}.$$

By Chebyshev's inequality, we easily establish

$$P(B_{n^2 r}) < \frac{Kr^2}{n^2},$$

and since $\sum_{n=1}^{\infty}(1/n^2) < \infty$, we conclude, by the Borel-Cantelli theorem (Chapter 1), $P(B_{n^2 r}, i.o.) = 0$, in other words, that $(S_{n^2}/n^2) \overset{\text{a.c.}}{\to} 0$. To complete the proof of the proposition, we must show that this can be extended to S_k/k. To this effect, define

$$C_n = \max_{n^2 \leq k \leq (n+1)^2} |S_k - S_{n^2}|$$

and note that

$$C_n \leq 2n \, |S_{(n+1)^2} - S_{n^2}| = 2n \, |\sum_{j=n^2+1}^{(n+1)^2} X_j|.$$

An easy calculation yields $E(C_n^2) \leq 4n^2 K$. Define, for arbitrary integer r, the sets

$$D_{nr} = \{\omega : \frac{C_n}{n^2} > \frac{1}{r}\}$$

and note that, by Chebyshev's inequality, $P(D_{nr}) < (4r^2/n^2)$. We therefore conclude by the Borel-Cantelli theorem that

$$\frac{C_n}{n^2} \xrightarrow{\text{a.c.}} 0.$$

Next, we observe that for $n^2 \leq k \leq (n+1)^2$,

$$\frac{S_k}{k} \leq \frac{S_{n^2} + C_n}{n^2}.$$

Since the right members converge to zero a.c., we conclude that

$$\frac{S_k}{k} \xrightarrow{\text{a.c.}} 0.$$

q.e.d.

This result can be strengthened considerably as evidenced by the proposition below.

Proposition 26. Let $\{X_n : n \geq 1\}$ be an uncorrelated sequence of random variables defined on the probability space $(\Omega, \mathcal{A}, P)$; suppose further that the sequence $\{\text{Var}(X_n) : n \geq 1\}$ obeys $\text{Var}(X_n) \leq cn^\alpha$, $\alpha \in [0, \frac{1}{2})$, where $\text{Var}(X_n) = E(X_n - \mu_n)^2$, and $E(X_n) = \mu_n$. Then,

$$\frac{S_n}{n} \xrightarrow{P} 0,$$

where $S_n = \sum_{k=1}^{n}(X_k - \mu_k)$.

Proof: Proceed, exactly as in the proof of Proposition 25, to construct *mutatis mutandis* the entity C_n and the sets B_{n^2r}, $D_{n,r}$. In this case, we obtain

$$\sum_{n=1}^{\infty} P(B_{n^2r}) \leq c \sum_{n=1}^{\infty} \frac{1}{n^{1+\gamma}}, \qquad \gamma = 1 - \alpha \in [\tfrac{1}{2}, 1).$$

Similarly,

$$\sum_{n=1}^{\infty} P(D_{nr}) \leq c \sum_{n=1}^{\infty} \frac{1}{n^{1+\delta}}, \qquad 1 - 2\alpha = \delta > 0.$$

Since the two series above converge, it follows from the Borel-Cantelli theorem that $(S_n/n) \xrightarrow{\text{a.c.}} 0$.

q.e.d.

Chapter 4

Convergence of Sequences II

4.1 Introduction

In the previous chapter, we examined abstractly, four modes of convergence: **convergence a.c., convergence in probability, L^p convergence and Convergence in distribution**; in addition, we had also explored the manner in which they are related to each other, and we had given conditions under which we may obtain convergence a.c., convergence in probability, or L^p convergence for sequences of random variables. These last results, however, had been obtained on the assertion that the sequence(s) to which they were applied consisted of **independent random variables**. Moreover, the implicit framework of that discussion was one of **scalar** random variables. While many of the proofs easily generalize or, more appropriately, are applicable without modification, to sequences of **random vectors**, for some this is not the case. Specifically, in the proof of Proposition 11 and its related corollaries (in Chapter 3), we made explicit use of the natural order of the number system, and this does not lend itself, easily, to generalization in cases where we deal with entities more complicated than scalar random variables.

Thus, there are two aspects in which our earlier discussion is deficient. First, it is not clear that such results apply to **random vectors** or other more complicated entities, such as **random functions** and second, it is not clear what the situation is with respect to sequences of **dependent random variables**. We take up first the question of which, if any, of the results above apply to more complicated entities than random variables. This is important, since in econometrics we seldom deal with (scalar) random variables.

In order to deal with the extension of the results of the previous chapter to random vectors or matrices or random sequences or random functions or, in general, to entities more complex than **scalar** random variables, we must broaden the framework of our analysis. Up to now, our discussion dealt with measurable functions, defined on a probability space, $(\Omega, \mathcal{A}, P)$, whose range is the Borel space $(R, \mathcal{B})$. Now, we need to deal with **random elements**, see, e.g., Chapter 2, Section 3.2; in particular, if $(\Omega, \mathcal{A}, P)$ and $(\Psi, \mathcal{G})$ are, respectively, probability and measurable spaces, we shall deal with functions

$$X : \Omega \longrightarrow \Psi,$$

which are $\mathcal{A} \mid \mathcal{G}$-measurable. This means that for every set $G \in \mathcal{G}$, we have that $\{\omega : X(\omega) \in G\} \in \mathcal{A}$ or that $X^{-1}(G) \in \mathcal{A}$. We then say that X **is a random element with values in** Ψ.

In contemplating the various convergence definitions and criteria discussed earlier, we note that central in these considerations was some notion of "distance". Thus, for example, if

$$S_n = \frac{1}{n} \sum_{i=1}^{n} X_i,$$

and the X_i, $i = 1, 2, \ldots, n$, are independent random variables, with mean μ, one of the issues examined may be rephrased as follows: under what conditions would the "distance between S_n and μ" approach zero in probability or with probability one? Thus, any extension of the results of the previous chapter to a more general context would require us to operate with spaces in which some measure of distance or magnitude is defined.

Example 1. Let $\Psi = R^k$, $\mathcal{G} = \mathcal{B}^k$ and note that the random element here is simply a k-dimensional random vector. Moreover, if we introduce the usual Euclidean norm, namely, $\| x \| = (\sum_{i=1}^{k} x_i^2)^{1/2}$, the space $(R^k, \mathcal{B}^k)$ is both complete and separable. In fact, it is interesting to observe, as we shall examine in some detail below, that random $m \times n$ matrices are also random elements in this space!

Example 2. Let $\mathcal{M}$ be the collection of all $m \times n$ matrices with real elements; provided some convention has been agreed upon regarding reference to the elements of the matrix and putting $k = nm$, then

$$X : \Omega \longrightarrow \mathcal{M},$$

represents a random element in $(R^k, \mathcal{B}^k)$.

Example 3. Let $\Psi = R^\infty$ with the σ-algebra generated by the finite dimensional cylinders. A random element in this space, then, would be an infinite sequence of random variables.

As the examples above make clear, once we leave the simplicity of scalar random variables, the entities we deal with exhibit manifold forms, and it is really not convenient to study each one of them separately. Rather what is called for is the development of a flexible general framework in which such types of random entities may be studied satisfactorily. It turns out that such issues may be studied quite adequately, from the point of view we have in mind, in the context of linear topological spaces, or metric or normed linear spaces.

We recall from Chapter 1 (Section 5) that a linear space is one in which the operations of (vector) addition and scalar multiplication are defined as continuous operations; that a topological space is simply a space on which a topology (a collection of "open" sets with certain properties) is defined. Hence the meaning of a linear topological space is apparent. A metric space is a space on which a metric is defined, a normed space is a space on which a norm is defined, and so on.

4.2   Properties of Random Elements

As was pointed out in this and the preceding chapter, if $(\Omega, \mathcal{A}, P)$, $(\Psi, \mathcal{G}, \rho)$ are a probability and metric space, respectively, the mapping

$$X : \Omega \longrightarrow \Psi,$$

is said to be a random element, if X is $\mathcal{A} \mid \mathcal{G}$-measurable, i.e., if for any $G \in \mathcal{G}$, $X^{-1}(G) \in \mathcal{A}$.

In this section, we shall always take note explicitly of the (Borel) σ-algebra containing the open sets of the space Ψ. Moreover, since the term "random element(s)" occurs very frequently, we shall use the abbreviated expression r.e.

We begin by showing that measurable transformations of r.e. are r.e.

Proposition 1. Let $(\Omega, \mathcal{A}, P)$, $(\Psi_i, \mathcal{G}_i, \rho_i)$, $i = 1, 2$, be a probability and metric space, respectively, and suppose X is a random element with values in Ψ_1, while

$$Y : \Psi_1 \longrightarrow \Psi_2$$

is a $\mathcal{G}_1$-measurable function from Ψ_1 to the metric space $(\Psi_2, \mathcal{G}_2, \rho_2)$. Then, the composite function

$$Z = Y \circ X : \Omega \longrightarrow \Psi_2$$

is a random element with values in Ψ_2.

Proof: Let $B_2 \in \mathcal{G}_2$; then, since Y is $\mathcal{G}_1$-measurable, $B_1 = Y^{-1}(B_2) \in \mathcal{G}_1$. In addition, since X is $\mathcal{A}$-measurable, $X^{-1}(B_1) \in \mathcal{A}$. Thus, for any $B_2 \in \mathcal{G}_2$, $Z^{-1}(B_2) = X^{-1} \circ Y^{-1}(B_2) \in \mathcal{A}$.

q.e.d.

Proposition 2. Let $(\Omega, \mathcal{A}, P)$, $(\Psi, \mathcal{G}, \rho)$ be a probability and metric space, respectively, and suppose that $\{\Omega_n : n \geq 1, \Omega_n \in \mathcal{A}\}$ is a countable (and possibly finite) partition of Ω.[1] If $\psi = \{\psi_n : \psi_n \in \Psi, n \geq 1\}$ is a sequence of elements of Ψ, and X is a mapping,

$$X : \Omega \longrightarrow \Psi,$$

such that, for $\forall \omega \in \Omega_n$, $X(\omega) = \psi_n$, then X is a r.e. with values in Ψ.

---

[1] We remind the reader that if $\{A_n : n \geq 1\}$ is a countable partition of a space, Ω, this means that the sets, A_n, are disjoint, and moreover, $\bigcup_{n=1}^{\infty} A_n = \Omega$.

Proof: Let $G \subset \Psi$ be any subset of Ψ. Since X assumes only countably many values in Ψ, we need only inquire how many of these values are in G. These values are given by $\psi \cap G = \{\psi_{n_j} : j \in J\}$, where J is a countable set and possibly finite. Consequently,

$$X^{-1}(G \cap \psi) = \bigcup_{j \in J} \Omega_j \in \mathcal{A}.$$

q.e.d.

Remark 1. The burden of the proposition above is to define, for r.e., the class of "simple (or elementary) functions". We recall that in the case of **random variables**, a r.v. was said to be simple if there existed a countable partition of the space, Ω, such that the r.v. was "constant" over the sets of the partition. This result implies that every r.v. can be approximated by "simple" r.v., and generally, the approximation becomes increasingly accurate as one utilizes more terms or, in other words, as the partition becomes finer.

Proposition 3. Let $(\Omega, \mathcal{A}, P)$, $(\Psi, \mathcal{G}, \rho)$ be a probability and metric space, respectively, and

$$X_n : \Omega \longrightarrow \Psi, \ n \geq 1,$$

a sequence of r.e. with values in Ψ. If $X_n \longrightarrow X$, pointwise, i.e., if

$$\lim_{n \to \infty} X_n(\omega) = X(\omega), \quad \text{for any } \omega \in \Omega,$$

then X is a random element.

Proof: It will suffice to show that for every closed subset of Ψ, say B, $X^{-1}(B) \in \mathcal{A}$. This is so since, if E is an open set, its complement, $\bar{E}$, is a closed set; if $X^{-1}(\bar{E}) \in \mathcal{A}$, then $\overline{X^{-1}(\bar{E})} \in \mathcal{A}$. But this implies $\overline{X^{-1}(\bar{E})} = X^{-1}(E) \in \mathcal{A}$. Thus, suppose $B \subset \Psi$ is a closed set. For each $x \in B$, construct the spheres

$$S_{x,r} = \{\psi : \rho(x, \psi) < \frac{1}{r}\},$$

where r is an integer, and note that they are open sets. Consider now

$$S_r = \bigcup_{x \in B} S_{x,r}, \quad r \geq 1.$$

The sets, $\{S_r : r \geq 1\}$, form a countable collection of open sets each containing B; moreover, it is clear that

$$B = \bigcap_{r=1}^{\infty} S_r.$$

Consequently,

$$X^{-1}(B) = \bigcap_{r=1}^{\infty} X^{-1}(S_r),$$

and we need only show that $A_r = X^{-1}(S_r) \in \mathcal{A}$ in order to complete the proof. Consider the sequence $\{A_{r,m} : m \geq 1\}$, where $A_{r,m} = \{\omega : X_m(\omega) \in S_r\}$. By construction, however, this is a sequence converging to A_r, i.e.,

$$A_r = \bigcup_{n=1}^{\infty} \bigcap_{m=n}^{\infty} A_{r,m} \in \mathcal{A}.$$

q.e.d.

We now give an important characterization of r.e.

Proposition 4. Let $(\Omega, \mathcal{A}, P)$, $(\Psi, \mathcal{G}, \rho)$ be a probability and metric space, respectively. The mapping

$$X : \Omega \longrightarrow \Psi$$

is a random element if and only if there exists a countably valued sequence of r.e., say $\{X_n : n \geq 1\}$, converging uniformly to X.

Proof: The sufficiency part follows immediately by Proposition 3. As for the necessity part, suppose X is a random element, let

$$f_n : \Psi \longrightarrow \Psi, \quad n \geq 1$$

be measurable functions obeying the condition that for every $\psi \in \Psi$, $\rho(f_n(\psi), \psi) < (1/n)$, and define

$$f_n \circ X = X_n : \Omega \longrightarrow \Psi.$$

Evidently, the X_n are random elements with values in Ψ, since, given any set $B \in \mathcal{G}$, we obtain

$$X_n^{-1}(B) = X^{-1}[f_n^{-1}(B)] \in \mathcal{A},$$

in view of the fact that f_n is $\mathcal{G}$-measurable, while X is $\mathcal{A}$-measurable. Moreover, for any $\omega \in \Omega$, $\rho[X_n(\omega), X(\omega)] = \rho[f_n(\psi), \psi] < (1/n)$, which shows the sequence to converge uniformly to X.

q.e.d.

In order to proceed with our discussion of properties of random elements, it is necessary to introduce a few facts regarding **separable** linear spaces; the concept of separable space was discussed in Chapter 1, Section 8, Definition 43 and Proposition 29.

4.3   Base and Separability

When dealing with random variables, we take it as almost "self evident" that the sum of random variables is itself a random variable. When dealing with r.e. taking values in an arbitrary metric space, such relations are not only **not self evident, but need not be true.** Generally, more structure is required, and it is for this reason that the digression of this section is necessary. Most of the results we shall obtain in our discussion of r.e. will require the separability of the underlying (linear) space.

Proposition 5. Let $(\Psi,\ \rho)$ be a **separable** metric space. Then, the following conditions are equivalent:

  i. Ψ is separable;

  ii. Ψ has a countable base;

  iii. every open cover of a subset of Ψ has a countable subcover.

Proof: [2] Suppose Ψ is separable; then, it has a countable dense subset, say D, whose closure is Ψ. Define the class of spheres (open sets)

$$\mathcal{V} = \{S_{x_i,k} : x_i \in D,\ k \text{ rational},\ i = 1, 2, \ldots\}.$$

By construction, $\mathcal{V}$ is a countable class of open subsets of Ψ, consisting of spheres with centers in D and rational radii. These sets may be

---

[2] Part of this proof was given in the proof of Proposition 29 of Chapter 1.

put into one-one correspondence with the set of integers as follows: first put the rational index set into a one-one correspondence with the set of integers; having done so, put the two resulting integer index sets into one-one correspondence with the set of integers, by taking, for example, the first element of the first set, then the first element of the second set, then the second element of the first set, then the second element of the second set, and so on. In the context of the resulting index set, we can write

$$\mathcal{V} = \{V_r : r = 1, 2, \ldots\}.$$

Let G be an open subset of Ψ and consider the set

$$G_1 = \bigcup_{r=1}^{\infty} (G \cap V_r).$$

Evidently $G_1 \subset G$. To prove $G \subset G_1$, consider any $x \in G$. Since x is in the closure of D, there exists an element of $\mathcal{V}$, say $V_r = S_{x_i,k}$, such that $x \in V_r$. This is so since, G being an open set, it totally contains the sphere $S_{x,\delta}$, for $\delta > 0$. Choosing $k < \delta$, k rational, completes the justification. We have thus shown that if x is any element of G, then there exists an element of $\mathcal{V}$ say V_r, such that $x \in G \cap V_r$. Consequently, $G \subset G_1$, which proves that i. implies ii.

Next, we prove that ii. implies iii. Let $\mathcal{V}$ be the countable base and suppose $\{A_\gamma : \gamma \in \Gamma\}$, where Γ is an arbitrary index set, is an open cover for an open set $A \subset \Psi$. Since $\mathcal{V}$ is a countable base, we can put $A \subset \bigcup_{k=1}^{\infty} V_k$; moreover, since $A \subset \bigcup_{\gamma \in \Gamma} A_\gamma = A^*$, define $V_k^* = A^* \cap V_k$, $k = 1, 2, \ldots$ and note that V_k^*, $k = 1, 2, \ldots$ is a countable collection of open sets such that $\bigcup_{k=1}^{\infty} V_k^* = A^* \cap (\bigcup_{k=1}^{\infty} V_k) \supset A$. Consequently, $A \subset \bigcup_{k=1}^{\infty} V_k^*$, thus proving that ii. implies iii.

To prove that iii. implies i., define $S_{x,r} = \{\psi : \rho(x, \psi) < (1/r)\}$, for integer r. The collection of spheres,

$$\mathcal{C}^* = \{S_{x,r} : x \in \Psi, \ r \text{ integer}\},$$

is, evidently, an open cover for Ψ. By iii., there exists a countable open cover, say

$$\mathcal{C} = \{S_{x_i,r} : x_i \in \Psi, \ i = 1, 2, \ldots\}.$$

One can now prove that the set

$$D = \{x_i : S_{x_i,r} \in C\}$$

is a countable dense set in Ψ. That it is a countable subset of Ψ is obvious; thus, we need only show that it is dense, i.e., that its closure is Ψ. Let ψ be any point in Ψ and consider the sphere $S_{\psi,(1/r)}$. Since C is an open cover for Ψ, there exists at least one element, say $S_{x_i,(1/r)} \in C$, such that $\psi \in S_{x_i,(1/r)}$. But, this shows that every neighborhood of **an arbitrary point** in Ψ contains a point in D, which, in turn, implies that D is dense in Ψ and, hence, that the latter is separable.

q.e.d.

Remark 2. Given a metric space, $(\Psi,\ \rho)$, we can always obtain the σ-algebra generated by the open sets of the space as follows: given the metric, generate the spheres $S_{x,\delta} = \{\psi : \rho(x,\ \psi) < \delta,\ \delta > 0\}$. Define $\mathcal{G}$ to be the intersection of all σ-algebras containing the spheres. When we say that $(\Psi,\ \rho)$ is a metric space, we also have in mind that it is a measurable space as well, namely, $(\Psi,\ \mathcal{G})$. Whether this is explicitly stated or not, this is to be understood in all subsequent discussion.

Proposition 6. Let $(\Psi_i,\ \mathcal{G}_i)$ be measurable spaces on which we have defined, respectively, the metrics ρ_i, $i = 1, 2$. Let $(\Psi,\ \mathcal{G})$ be the product measurable space, where $\Psi = \Psi_1 \times \Psi_2$, and $\mathcal{G} = \sigma(\mathcal{C})$, i.e., it is the σ-algebra generated by the class

$$\mathcal{C} = \{A : A \subset \Psi,\ A \text{ open}\}.$$

The product space is separable if and only if the individual spaces are separable. Moreover, if Ψ is separable, then $\sigma(\mathcal{C}) = \sigma(\mathcal{E})$, where

$$\mathcal{E} = \{A : A = A_1 \times A_2,\quad A_i \in \mathcal{G}_i,\quad \text{and } A_i \text{ open},\ i = 1, 2\}.$$

Proof: We first note that we may define, on Ψ, the metric

$$\rho(x,\ y) = [\rho_1(x_1,\ y_1) + \rho_2(x_2,\ y_2)]^{1/2},$$

which, thus, defines the open sets on Ψ. If Ψ_i, $i = 1, 2$, are separable, let $\mathcal{V}_i$ be their respective bases. It is easy to see that

$$\mathcal{V} = \{V : V = V_1 \times V_2,\ V_1 \in \mathcal{V}_1,\ V_2 \in \mathcal{V}_2\}$$

is a base for Ψ. This is so since if $\psi \in \Psi$, $\psi = (\psi_1,\ \psi_2)$, with $\psi_1 \in \Psi_1$ and $\psi_2 \in \Psi_2$. Consequently, there exist elements of the bases such that $\psi_i \in V_{1i} \in \mathcal{V}_i$, $i = 1, 2$, respectively. Thus, $\psi \in V_{11} \times V_{12} \in \mathcal{V}$. Next, suppose that ψ is in two base elements of $\mathcal{V}$, say $\psi \in V_1 \cap V_2$. Let $V_i = V_{i1} \times V_{i2}$, $i = 1, 2$, and note that $V_1 \cap V_2 = (V_{11} \cap V_{21}) \times (V_{12} \cap V_{22})$. Since, the collections $\mathcal{V}_i$, $i = 1, 2$ are bases, there exist base sets V_{3i}, $i = 1, 2$, such that $\psi_i \in V_{3i} \subset (V_{1i} \cap V_{2i})$, $i = 1, 2$, respectively. But $V_3 = V_{31} \times V_{32} \in \mathcal{V}$, and $\psi \in V_3 \subset (V_1 \cap V_2)$, which completes the demonstration that $\mathcal{V}$ is a base for the (product) topology of the space $\Psi = \Psi_1 \times \Psi_2$. Since, by construction, it is also countable, we have shown that Ψ is separable. Next, suppose that Ψ is separable, so that it has a countable base, $\mathcal{V} = \{V : V = A \times B,\ A \text{ open in } \Psi_1 \text{ and } B \text{ open in } \Psi_2\}$. Define now the functions

$$\pi_i : \Psi \longrightarrow \Psi_i, \quad i = 1, 2,$$

such that if $V_{j1} \times V_{j2} = V_j \in \mathcal{V}$, then $\pi_1(V_j) = V_{j1}$, $\pi_2(V_j) = V_{j2}$. The reader may easily verify that the entities

$$\mathcal{V}_i = \{V_{ji} : V_{ji} = \pi_i(V_j),\ V_j \in \mathcal{V},\ i = 1, 2\}$$

are countable bases, respectively, for the spaces Ψ_i, $i = 1, 2$.

For the last part of the proposition, let $A \in \mathcal{E}$ and suppose Ψ to be **separable**. Then, $A = A_1 \times A_2$, where $A_i \in \mathcal{G}_i$, $i = 1, 2$, are open. Consider now the sets $\pi_i^{-1}(A_i) \in \Psi$. Since the functions π_i are continuous, it follows that the sets $\pi_i^{-1}(A_i)$ are open. In fact,

$$\pi_1^{-1}(A_1) = A_1 \times \Psi_2, \quad \pi_2^{-1}(A_2) = \Psi_1 \times A_2.$$

Consequently, since $\pi_1^{-1}(A_1) \cap \pi_2^{-1}(A_2) = A_1 \times A_2 = A$, we conclude that $A \in \mathcal{C}$. This is so because the left member of the equation above is, evidently, an open set and, hence, in $\mathcal{C}$. This shows that $\mathcal{E} \subset \mathcal{C}$ and, consequently, that $\sigma(\mathcal{E}) \subset \sigma(\mathcal{C})$. To show that $\sigma(\mathcal{C}) \subset \sigma(\mathcal{E})$, let $A \in \mathcal{C}$

be any open set in Ψ; thus, there exist open sets G_γ, $\gamma \in \Gamma$, where Γ is an arbitrary index set, such that

$$A = \bigcup_{G_\gamma \subseteq A} G_\gamma.$$

Since Ψ is **separable**, this can be reduced to a countable open cover, and by the previous result we have

$$A = \bigcup_{r=1}^{\infty} G_r, \quad G_r = G_{r1} \times G_{r2}, \quad G_{ri} \in \mathcal{G}_i, \quad i = 1, 2.$$

Thus, $A = A_1 \times A_2$, with A_i open; consequently, $A \in \mathcal{E}$, which implies $\mathcal{C} \subset \mathcal{E}$. We conclude, therefore, that $\sigma(\mathcal{C}) = \sigma(\mathcal{E})$.

q.e.d.

For linear spaces, the existence of a certain type of base allows greater simplicity and scope in arguments involving properties of random elements. We have

Definition 1. Let Ψ be a linear topological space. The sequence $v = \{v_\gamma : v_\gamma \in \Psi, \gamma \in \Gamma\}$ is said to be a **Schauder base** or an S-base, if for every element $X \in \Psi$ there exists a unique sequence $a = \{a_\gamma : a_\gamma \in R, \gamma \in \Gamma\}$ such that

$$X = \sum_{\gamma=1}^{\infty} a_\gamma v_\gamma.$$

Definition 2. Suppose that the space, Ψ, of Definition 1, is also a metric space with metric ρ. Define the collection of linear functionals, π_γ, by the condition

$$\pi_\gamma(X) = a_\gamma, \quad \gamma \in \Gamma, \quad \text{for any } X \in \Psi.$$

The elements of this collection are said to be the **coordinate functionals** corresponding to the base v.

Remark 3. The coordinate functionals are linear, i.e., for any $X_i \in \Psi$, $i = 1, 2$, $\pi_\gamma(X_1 + X_2) = \pi_\gamma(X_1) + \pi_\gamma(X_2)$, and they are continuous for Banach (and Hilbert) spaces; they need not, however, be continuous for all spaces. We also note that if the underlying (linear) space is separable then the sum of two r.e. is also a r.e., and we have no difficulty in defining sums or linear combinations of r.e., a fact that will become quite transparent as the discussion unfolds.

An interesting class of random elements, in the context of the ensuing discussion, is given below.

Definition 3. Let $(\Omega,\ \mathcal{A},\ P)$, $(\Psi,\ \mathcal{G},\ \|\cdot\|)$ be a probability and normed space, respectively. A mapping,

$$X : \Omega \longrightarrow \Psi,$$

is said to be **strongly ($\mathcal{A}$)-measurable** if there exists a sequence, say, $\{X_n : X_n \in \Psi,\ n \geq 1\}$, of **countably valued** $\mathcal{A}$-measurable functions such that the sequence

$$\{a_n(\omega) : a_n(\omega) = \|\, X_n(\omega) - X(\omega)\,\|,\ n \geq 1\}$$

converges to zero pointwise, or a.s. (almost surely).

Remark 4. Note that if the normed space above is a **separable Banach space**, then all r.e. therein are **strongly measurable**. We conclude this section with

Proposition 7. Let $(\Omega,\ \mathcal{A},\ P)$, $(\Psi,\ \mathcal{G},\ \rho)$ be a probability and **separable** metric space, respectively, and let X, Y be r.e. with values in Ψ. Then, the real valued function, ζ, defined by $\zeta = \rho(X,\ Y)$, is a random variable.

Proof: Let Ψ_i, $i = 1, 2$, be copies of the space Ψ and consider the pair $(X,\ Y)$ as a random element (from Ω to the product space $\Psi_1 \times \Psi_2$). Thus, we have

$$Z = (X,\ Y) : \Omega \longrightarrow \Psi_1 \times \Psi_2.$$

Interpret now ρ to be the metric on this product space and note that since the metric is a continuous function, we can interpret ζ as the composition $\zeta = \rho \circ Z$ and conclude, by Proposition 1, that

$$\zeta = \rho(Z) : \Omega \longrightarrow R$$

is a random element in R, i.e., a random variable.

q.e.d.

An alternative characterization of a r.e. in a separable space is given by

Proposition 8. Let $(\Omega,\ \mathcal{A},\ P)$, $(\ \Psi,\ \mathcal{G}\ )$ be a probability and separable (linear metric) space, respectively. Then, a mapping

$$X : \Omega \longrightarrow \Psi$$

is a random element if and only if for every [3] $f \in \Psi^*$, $f(X)$ is a random variable.

Proof: If X is a r.e. then, by Proposition 1, $f(X)$ is a random variable (since f is a bounded continuous linear function), so that we need only prove the sufficiency part. Thus, suppose for very $f \in \Psi^*$, $f(X)$ is a random variable; consider now the class

$$\mathcal{C} = \{C : C = f^{-1}(B),\ f \in \Psi^*,\ B \in \mathcal{B}\}.$$

We note that $\mathcal{C}$ contains the inverse images of all **open** sets in $\mathcal{B}$. Let $\sigma(\mathcal{C})$ be the σ-algebra generated by the class $\mathcal{C}$. We shall first show that $\mathcal{G} = \sigma(\mathcal{C})$. It is evident that $\sigma(\mathcal{C}) \subset \mathcal{G}$, since if $f \in \Psi^*$ then f is $\mathcal{G}$-measurable; thus, we need only show that $\mathcal{G} \subset \sigma(\mathcal{C})$. Since Ψ is a separable normed space, we can define a metric on it by $\rho(\psi_1,\ \psi_2) = \|\ \psi_1 - \psi_2\ \|$. By Proposition 29 of Chapter 1, the resulting metric space has a countable base, say

$$S = \{S_r : S_r \subset \Psi,\ \text{and}\ S_r\ \text{is open},\ r \geq 1\}.$$

Let A be an open set in $\mathcal{G}$; by the definition of a base, there exists an index set, say I, which is at most countable, such that $A = \bigcup_{m \in I} S_m$. Since every $f \in \Psi^*$ is continuous, it follows that $f(S_m)$ is open, and consequently, for some $f_m \in \Psi^*$, $f_m(S_m) = B_m \in \mathcal{B}$. Thus, given any $A \in \mathcal{G}$, we can write

$$A = \bigcup_{m \in I} f_m^{-1}(B_m) \in \sigma(\mathcal{C}).$$

---

[3] We remind the reader that the dual space to Ψ is the collection of all linear bounded (continuous) functionals defined thereon and that it is denoted by Ψ^*.

Since a closed set can be expressed as the limit (intersection) of open sets containing it, the preceding shows that $\mathcal{G} \subset \sigma(\mathcal{C})$, and consequently, that $\mathcal{G} = \sigma(\mathcal{C})$. To complete the proof, we must now show that for any $C \in \Psi$, $X^{-1}(C) \in \mathcal{A}$. To that end, we may, without loss of generality and for simplicity of exposition, assume that there exist a set $B \in \mathcal{B}$ and a function $f \in \Psi^*$, such that $C = f^{-1}(B)$. Thus,

$$X^{-1}(C) = X^{-1}[f^{-1}(B)] = X^{-1} \circ f^{-1}(B) \in \mathcal{A},$$

due to the fact that $f(X)$ is a random variable and $B \in \mathcal{B}$.

q.e.d.

It is not always easy to determine whether a space is separable and, if it is, whether it has an S-base. In the case of **Hilbert** spaces, the existence of the **inner product** function affords us an opportunity to demonstrate how an S-base may be constructed. First, we have

Definition 4. Let (Ψ, $\mathcal{G}$) be a Hilbert space; a collection, $\mathcal{S} \subset \Psi$, is said to be **orthogonal**, if for every pair $s_i \in \mathcal{S}$, $i = 1, 2$, $< s_1, s_2 > = 0$.[4] If, in addition, for all $s \in \mathcal{S}$, $\| s \| = 1$, then the set is said to be **orthonormal**. The orthonormal set $\mathcal{S}$ is said to be **maximal**, if the only element $\psi \in \Psi$ that satisfies $< \psi, s > = 0$, for all $s \in \mathcal{S}$, is the zero element of the space.

An immediate consequence of the preceding is

Proposition 9. Let (Ψ, $\mathcal{G}$) be a Hilbert space; if $\mathcal{S}$ is a maximal orthonormal set, then it is an orthonormal base for the space. Moreover, if $\mathcal{S}$ is countable, then it is an S-base for the space.

Proof: By the linearity of the space, given any $\psi \in \Psi$,

$$\psi_0 = \sum_{s \in \mathcal{S}} < \psi, s > s \in \Psi.$$

---

[4] In chapter 1, when we first defined the inner product function, we employed the common notation $(\cdot, \cdot)$. Unfortunately, in the context of the present discussion this common usage will lead to confusion and thus we shall employ the alternative notation $< \cdot, \cdot >$.

The element $\psi - \psi_0$, is orthogonal to the set $\mathcal{S}$. Since $\mathcal{S}$ is maximal, we conclude that $\psi = \psi_0$, i.e., that for any $\psi \in \Psi$, $\psi = \sum_{s \in \mathcal{S}} < \psi,\, s > s$. But, this shows that $\mathcal{S}$ is a base for the space. If the space is separable, then without loss of generality we can take the maximal orthonormal set $\mathcal{S}$ to be countable, which completes the proof.

q.e.d.

Remark 4. When an S-base exists, as in the case above, it is easy to demonstrate that the sum of two r.e. is also a random element. Thus, if X_i, $i = 1, 2$, are two random elements in that space then each has the representation, respectively, $X_i = \sum_{\gamma=1}^{\infty} < X_i,\, s_\gamma > s_\gamma$. Hence, $X_1 + X_2 = \sum_{\gamma=1}^{\infty} < X_1 + X_2,\, s_\gamma > s_\gamma$. If $f \in \Psi^*$, then $f(X_1 + X_2) = \sum_{\gamma=1}^{\infty} < X_1 + X_2,\, s_\gamma > f(s_\gamma)$, which is evidently a random variable. Hence, by Proposition 8, $X_1 + X_2$ is a r.e.

4.4   Distributional Aspects of R.E.

In this and the next section, we make clear the meaning of independence for random elements as well the sense in which the distributions or distribution functions of random elements are to be understood.

Definition 5. Let $(\Omega,\, \mathcal{A},\, P)$, $(\Psi,\, \mathcal{G},\, \rho)$ be a probability and metric space, respectively, and let X, Y be random elements with values in Ψ. For any $G \in \mathcal{G}$, consider the sets

$$A_x = \{\omega : X(\omega) \in G\},\ A_y = \{\omega : Y(\omega) \in G\}.$$

The two random elements are said **to have the same distribution,** or **to be identically distributed,** if and only if $P(A_x) = P(A_y)$. A collection of random elements is said to be **identically distributed,** if and only if every pair is identically distributed.

4.4.1   Independence for Random Elements

Definition 6. Let $(\Omega,\, \mathcal{A},\, P)$, $(\Psi,\, \mathcal{G},\, \rho)$ be a probability and metric space, respectively; let $\{X_i : i = 1, 2, ..., n\}$ be a **finite** collection of r.e.

with values in Ψ; moreover, define the sets $\{G_i : G_i \in \mathcal{G}, \ i = 1, 2, ..., n\}$ and $\{A_i : X_i(\omega) \in G_i, \ i = 1, 2, ..., n\}$. The r.e. are said to be **mutually independent**, or simply **independent**, if and only if

$$P\left(\bigcap_{i=1}^{n} A_i\right) = \prod_{i=1}^{n} P(A_i).$$

A collection of r.e. (not necessarily countable) is said to be independent if and only if every finite set of such r.e. is independent.

In general, measurable transformations of random elements preserve the independent or identical distribution properties of the original set. Thus, we have,

Proposition 10. Let $(\Omega, \mathcal{A}, P)$, $(\Psi_i, \mathcal{G}_i, \rho_i)$, $i = 1, 2$, be a probability and metric space, respectively, and let $\{X_\gamma : \gamma \in \Gamma\}$, Γ not necessarily countable, be a collection of r.e. with values in Ψ_1. The following statements are true:

 i. if

$$U : \Psi_1 \longrightarrow \Psi_2$$

 is $\mathcal{G}_1$-measurable and the elements of the collection $\{X_\gamma : \gamma \in \Gamma\}$ are identically distributed, then so are the elements of $\{Y_\gamma : Y_\gamma = U \circ X_\gamma, \ \gamma \in \Gamma\}$;

 ii. if the collection $\{X_\gamma : \gamma \in \Gamma\}$ is one of independent elements and

$$T_\gamma : \Psi_1 \longrightarrow \Psi_2, \ \gamma \in \Gamma$$

 is a set of $\mathcal{G}_1$-measurable transformations, then the set

$$\{Z_\gamma : Z_\gamma = T_\gamma \circ X_\gamma, \ \gamma \in \Gamma\}$$

 is also one of independent r.e., with values in Ψ_2.

Proof: By Proposition 1, the entities Y_γ, $\gamma \in \Gamma$, are r.e. Thus, to prove part i., we need only show that they are identically distributed.

Let $C_2 \in \mathcal{G}_2$; since $Y_\gamma = U \circ X_\gamma$, we note that $Y_\gamma^{-1} = X_\gamma^{-1} \circ U^{-1}$. Consequently, with $C_1 = U^{-1}(C_2)$, we find, for $\gamma \neq \gamma'$,

$$Y_\gamma^{-1}(C_2) \;=\; X_\gamma^{-1} \circ U^{-1}(C_2) \;=\; X_\gamma^{-1}(C_1) \;=\; A_\gamma,$$

$$Y_{\gamma'}^{-1}(C_2) \;=\; X_{\gamma'}^{-1} \circ U^{-1}(C_1) \;=\; X_{\gamma'}^{-1}(C_1) \;=\; A_{\gamma'}.$$

The collection $\{X_\gamma : \gamma \in \Gamma\}$ is one of identically distributed r.e.; it follows, then, that $P(A_\gamma) = P(A_{\gamma'})$. But, this implies that, for any $C_2 \in \mathcal{G}_2$,

$$P[Y_\gamma^{-1}(C_2)] = P[Y_{\gamma'}^{-1}(C_2)],$$

thus completing the proof of i.

As for part ii., we note that to show independence we need do so only for a finite set. Thus, consider the r.e. Z_{γ_i}, $i = 1, 2, ..., n$, and let $C_{2i} \in \mathcal{G}_2$, $i = 1, 2, ..., n$. Since the transformations T_γ are measurable, $C_{1i} = T_{\gamma_i}^{-1}(C_{2i}) \in \mathcal{G}_1$, $i = 1, 2, ..., n$. Consequently [and putting, for notational ease, $A_i = Z_{\gamma_i}^{-1}(C_{2i}) = X_{\gamma_i}^{-1}(C_{1i})$], we note that $A_i \in \mathcal{A}$, so that the Z_{γ_i} are, indeed, r.e., as is also indicated by Proposition 1; moreover,

$$P\left(\bigcap_{i=1}^{n} A_i\right) = P\left(\bigcap_{i=1}^{n} X_{\gamma_i}^{-1}(C_{1i})\right) = \prod_{i=1}^{n} P\left(X_{\gamma_i}^{-1}(C_{1i})\right) = \prod_{i=1}^{n} P(A_i),$$

owing to the independence of the set $\{X_\gamma : \gamma \in \Gamma\}$.

q.e.d.

4.4.2   Distributions of Random Elements

In dealing with issues of convergence of sequences of r.e., we note that the concepts of convergence in probability or convergence *a.c.* need not be redefined, since the definitions we have given in Chapter 3 are fully applicable in the context of r.e., as well. This is also true about the characterization of these two modes of convergence and their relationship with each other. Basically, the same may be said about L^p-convergence, except that for random elements we shall have to explore the issues of integrability relating to them. However, in considering issues relating to covergence in distribution, it is desirable to depart from the practice we followed in the case of random variables, where we relied entirely on **distribution functions**. While in that case we also introduced the concept of the **distribution**, as distinct from the **distribution function**, we had made no use of the former. We remind the reader that if X is a **random variable**, then

$$X : \Omega \longrightarrow R.$$

Moreover, if $\mathcal{B}$ is the usual Borel σ-algebra on R, we may define a probability measure on R, as follows: for any $B \in \mathcal{B}$, let $A = X^{-1}(B) \in \mathcal{A}$; put $\mathcal{P}(B) = P(A)$. It may be verified that $\mathcal{P}$ is a countably additive measure defined on $\mathcal{B}$ and such that $\mathcal{P}(R) = 1$; hence, it is a probability measure. The reader should also note that this probability measure **is induced, on R, by the random variable** X. In addition, one may also verify that if F is the **distribution function** of X and if $B = (-\infty, x]$, then $F(x) = \mathcal{P}(B)$. The concepts of **distribution** and **distribution function** are completely equivalent but, in the context of measure theoretic arguments, it is immensely more convenient to deal with **distributions**, rather than **distribution functions**.

Definition 7. Let $(\Omega, \mathcal{A}, P)$, $(\Psi, \mathcal{G}, \rho)$ be a probability and metric space, respectively, and suppose X is a random element with values in Ψ. The **distribution** of X is the probability measure, $\mathcal{P}$, induced on $\mathcal{G}$ by X, as follows: for any $G \in \mathcal{G}$, $\mathcal{P}(G) = P[X^{-1}(G)]$.

In this chapter, we shall discuss issues of convergence (of sequences of r.e.) almost exclusively in terms of **distributions**. In this connection, the following concept is quite useful.

Definition 8. Let $\mathcal{P}$ be a probability measure induced on the metric space above, by a random element, X. A set $A \in \mathcal{G}$ is said to be a **continuity set**, or a $\mathcal{P}$-continuity set, if and only if $\mathcal{P}(\partial A) = 0$.

4.4.3   Moments of Random Elements

Definition 9. Let $(\Omega, \mathcal{A}, P)$, $(\Psi, \mathcal{G})$ be a probability and linear measurable space, respectively. If

$$X : \Omega \longrightarrow \Psi$$

is a r.e. with values in Ψ, we say that it has expected value, denoted by $E(X)$, if $E(X) \in \Psi$ and if

$$E[f(X)] = f[E(X)],$$

for every $f \in \Psi^*$.

Note that, in the **displayed** relation above, the first operator, $E(f(X))$ is to be understood as the ordinary expected value operator for random variables, since f is a real valued function. The second operator, however, is to be understood in the sense of the definition. The definition of the **variance** of a r.e. entails no novelty, in that it involves only the expected value operator for random variables. We have

Definition 10. Let $(\Omega, \mathcal{A}, P)$, $(\Psi, \mathcal{G}, \| \cdot \|)$ be a probability and normed linear space, respectively. Suppose X is a r.e. as above whose expectation, $E(X)$, exists. The **variance** of X, denoted by Var(X), is defined by

$$\mathrm{Var}(X) = \int_\Omega \| X - E(X) \|^2 \, dP.$$

Remark 5. Note that, since $\| X - E(X) \|$ is **nonnegative**, the integral above will always exist, although it may well be unbounded. While unboundedness of moments is permitted by the definition, in our discussion it will be implicitly assumed that all moments are bounded. Thus, if we deal with a moment of a r.v or a r.e., the reader should that moment to be finite, unless otherwise indicated. We also note that Definition 9 implies the linearity of the expected value operator.

Proposition 12. Let $(\Omega, \mathcal{A}, P)$, $(\Psi, \mathcal{G}, \| \cdot \|)$ be a probability and normed linear space, respectively. The following statements are true, where X, X_1, and X_2 are r.e. with values in Ψ:

i. if $E(X_i)$, $i = 1, 2$, exist and if $X_1 + X_2$ is a r.e., then $E(X_1 + X_2) = E(X_1) + E(X_2)$;

ii. if $E(X)$ exists and $b \in R$, then $E(bX) = bE(X)$;

iii. if Ψ_1 is a linear topological space and

$$g : \Psi \longrightarrow \Psi_1$$

is a continuous linear function then for any $X \in \Psi$, such that $E(X)$ exists, $E[g(X)] = g[E(X)]$;

iv. if $E(X)$ exists, then

$$\| E(X) \| \leq E(\| X \|).$$

Proof: It is evident that parts i., ii., and iii. do not require that Ψ be normed, only that it be a linear measurable space. The existence of a norm is solely required for part iv.

Now, to prove i., we note that by the linearity of the space $E(X_1) + E(X_2) \in \Psi$. Thus, consider, for any $f \in \Psi^*$,

$$
\begin{aligned}
f[E(X_1) + E(X_2)] &= f[E(X_1)] + f[E(X_2)] \\
&= E[f(X_1)] + E[f(X_2)] = E[f(X_1) + f(X_2)] \\
&= E[f(X_1 + X_2)].
\end{aligned}
$$

The first equality above follows from the linearity of f; the second, by the definition of $E(X_i)$, $i = 1, 2$; the third, by the linearity of the expected value operator for random variables; and the last by the linearity of f.

To prove ii., we note that by the linearity of Ψ, $bX \in \Psi$; moreover, $E[f(bX)] = E[bf(X)] = bE[f(X)] = bf[E(X)] = f[bE(X)]$, which means that $E(bX) = bE(X)$. The justification of the set of equalities above is the same as in part i.

To prove iii., we note that since g is a continuous linear function defined on Ψ, then $g \in \Psi^*$; hence, for any $f \in \Psi^*$, we also have that $f \circ g \in \Psi^*$. Consequently, $E\{f[g(X)]\} = f\{E[g(X)]\} = f \circ g[E(X)] = f\{g[E(X)]\}$. The first equality follows from the linearity of f, the second from the linearity of g, and the third is the result of simply rewriting the preceding expression. Note that if we put $Y = g(X)$ then what we have shown is that, for any $f \in \Psi^*$, $E[f(Y)] = f[E(Y)]$, which is what is required.

To prove iv., we note that if $E(X) = 0$, there is nothing to prove. Thus, suppose $E(X) \neq 0$; by a result of functional analysis, there exists a function, say $h \in \Psi^*$, such that, for any element $X \in \Psi$, $\| h \| = 1$, and $h(X) = \| X \|$. Consequently,

$$\| E(X) \| = | h[E(X)] | = | E[h(X)] | \leq E(\| h \| \| X \|) = E \| X \| .$$

The first equality follows from the result from functional analysis just cited, applied to $E(X) \in \Psi$; the second follows from the linearity of h; the next inequality follows from the properties of integrals of random variables; and the last equality is due to the fact that $\| h \| = 1$.

q.e.d.

The preceding discussion invites the question of whether there exist operational ways in which the expected value of r.e. may be determined, and if so, for what class of r.e. is this possible? We have

Definition 11. Let $(\Omega, \mathcal{A}, P)$, $(\Psi, \mathcal{G}, \| \cdot \|)$ be a probability and normed linear space, respectively, and let X be a **countably valued** r.e., with values in Ψ. The **Bochner** integral, or B-integral of X, denoted by $\int_\Omega X \, dP$, is defined as

$$\int_\Omega X \, dP = \sum_{r=1}^{\infty} x_r P(A_r),$$

where $A_r = \{\omega : X(\omega) = x_r, \ x_r \in \Psi\}$, provided $\sum_{r=1}^{\infty} \| x_r \| P(A_r) < \infty$.

Remark 6. We may rephrase the definition by noting, first, that the series whose convergence is required for the existence of the B-integral is simply $\int_\Omega \| X \| \, dP$. Consequently, we may state that, in the context of Definition 9, the B-integral of the countably valued random element is defined as

$$\int_\Omega X \, dP = \sum_{r=1}^{\infty} x_r P(A_r), \quad \text{provided} \quad \int_\Omega \| X \| \, dP < \infty.$$

This definition immediately leads to the following characterization of the existence of the expectation of a certain class of r.e.

Proposition 13. Let $(\Omega, \mathcal{A}, P)$, $(\Psi, \mathcal{G}, \| \cdot \|)$ be a probability and Banach space, respectively, and let X be a **strongly measurable** r.e. with values in Ψ. If $E(\| X \|) < \infty$, then $E(X)$ exists.

Proof: If X is countably valued, then by the preceding definition

$$E(X) = \sum_{r=1}^{\infty} x_r P(A_r)$$

is well defined by the conditions of the proposition. To show that $E(X) \in \Psi$ we note that a Banach space is complete; to show that it is, indeed, the expected value of X, consider any $f \in \Psi^*$ and observe that

$$
\begin{aligned}
f[E(X)] &= f[\lim_{n \to \infty} \sum_{r=1}^{n} x_r P(A_r)] \\
&= \lim_{n \to \infty} \sum_{r=1}^{n} f(x_r) P(A_r) \\
&= \sum_{r=1}^{\infty} f(x_r) P(A_r) = E[f(X)],
\end{aligned}
$$

which shows that $E(X)$ is, indeed, the expected value of X. Next, suppose that X is **any** strongly measurable r.e.; then, by Definition 1 and Proposition 4, there exists a sequence, say $\{X_n : n \geq 1\}$, of countably valued r.e. converging uniformly to X. By the argument above, $E(X_n)$ exists for all n. We note that $X_n - X_m$ is a random element and, by Proposition 12 (parts i. and ii.), $E(X_n - X_m) = E(X_n) - E(X_m)$. Consequently, we have

$$\| E(X_n) - E(X_m) \| = \| E(X_n - X_m) \| \leq E(\| X_n - X_m \|).$$

Given any $\epsilon > 0$ there exists, by the uniform convergence of the sequence $\{X_n : n \geq 1\}$, an N such that, for all $n, m > N$, and $\omega \in \Omega$ we have $\| X_n(\omega) - X_m(\omega) \| < \epsilon$. It follows, therefore, that $E(\| X_n - X_m \|) < \epsilon$ and, consequently, that $\{E(X_n) : n \geq 1\}$ is a Cauchy sequence. Since the space is complete, the sequence converges to, say $E(X) \in \Psi$. To show that this is, indeed, the expected value of X, we note that, for any $f \in \Psi^*$,

$$
\begin{aligned}
f[E(X)] &= f[\lim_{n \to \infty} E(X_n)] = \lim_{n \to \infty} f[E(X_n)] \\
&= \lim_{n \to \infty} E[f(X_n)] = E[\lim_{n \to \infty} f[X_n]] \\
&= E[f(X)].
\end{aligned}
$$

The first equality follows by the definition of $E(X)$ as the limit of the sequence $\{E(X_n) : n \geq 1\}$; the second follows from the continuity of f; the third by the properties of $E(X_n)$; the fourth by the Lebesgue convergence theorem (Proposition 18 of Chapter 1); the fifth by the continuity of f, and the fact that $\| X_n - X \|$, converges to zero uniformly.

q.e.d.

Remark 7. We note that if the Banach space of the proposition above is **separable** then all random elements therein are **strongly measurable,** and consequently, in a **separable Banach space** the criterion for the existence of the expected value of a r.e. is simply

$$
E(X) \quad \text{exists if} \quad E(\| X \|) < \infty.
$$

4.4.4   Uncorrelated Random Elements

Although, in the context of Banach spaces, it is possible to define (and we have, in fact, defined) the mean and variance of a r.e., we have really no instrument by which to define what we might wish to mean by "lack of correlation" between two r.e., or what we might want to mean by the variance of a sum of two r.e.

For the first problem, we note that if we operate with **Hilbert** spaces we may use the inner product as a means to that end; for the second problem, we need to define the circumstances under which the sum of two r.e. is also a r.e. In the latter case, we have

Proposition 14. Let $(\Omega, \mathcal{A}, P)$, $(\Psi, \mathcal{G}, \rho)$ be a probability and a separable metric (linear) space, respectively. If $X_i \in \Psi$ are r.e. with values in Ψ and $a_i \in R$, $i = 1, 2$, then $a_1 X_1 + a_2 X_2$ is a r.e. with values in Ψ.

Proof: That the $a_i X_i$, $i = 1, 2$, are r.e. is evident by Proposition 1. Next, note that for any $f \in \Psi^*$, $f(a_1 X_1 + a_2 X_2) = f(a_1 X_1) + f(a_2 X_2)$, by the linearity of f. Since, by Proposition 1, the $a_i X_i$, $i = 1, 2$, are r.e., it follows by Proposition 8 that the $f(a_i X_i)$, $i = 1, 2$, are random variables; consequently, their sum is also a random variable and, again by Proposition 8, we conclude that $a_1 X_1 + a_2 X_2$ is a r.e.

q.e.d.

Definition 12. Let $(\Omega, \mathcal{A}, P)$ be a probability space and $(\Psi, \mathcal{G})$ a separable Hilbert space. Then, the covariance of (any) two r.e., $X_i \in \Psi$, $i = 1, 2$, is defined by

$$\mathrm{Cov}(X_1, X_2) = E(< X_1 - E(X_1), X_2 - E(X_2) >).$$

Proposition 15. Let X_i, $i = 1, 2$, be two r.e., as in Definition 11, and suppose further that $E \parallel X_i \parallel^2 < \infty$, $i = 1, 2$. Then,

$$\mathrm{Cov}(X_1, X_2) = 0$$

if and only if $E(< X_1, X_2 >) = < E(X_1), E(X_2) >$.

Proof: From the definition of an inner product we note that by fixing one of its arguments it (the inner product) becomes a continuous linear function of the other (argument); i.e., if we put $h(y) = < x, y >$ then, for fixed $x \in \Psi$, $h(\cdot)$ is a continuous function at all $y \in \Psi$. Since, by the conditions of the proposition, $E(X_i) \in \Psi$, $i = 1, 2$, it follows, by Proposition 10, that $X_i - E(X_i) \in \Psi$, $i = 1, 2$. An easy computation, then, yields $\mathrm{Cov}(X_1, X_2) = E(< X_1, X_2 >) - < E(X_1), E(X_2) >$.

q.e.d.

Definition 13. Two r.e., X, Y, are said to be **uncorrelated** if and only if their covariance vanishes; they are said to be **orthogonal** if they obey $E(< X, Y >) = 0$. A collection of r.e. is said to be **uncorrelated**, if its elements are pairwise uncorrelated and it is said to be **orthogonal** if its elements are pairwise orthogonal.

Remark 8. Notice that, although not explicitly stated, the discussion above provides a means of defining, in appropriate spaces, the variance of sums of r.e. in terms of the variances and covariances of their components. Moreover, notice further that a pair of uncorrelated r.e. is **also orthogonal** if at least one of the r.e. has mean zero.

4.5   Laws of Large Numbers for R.E.

4.5.1   Preliminaries

In the case of random variables, various laws of large numbers (LLN) involve the use, in one form or another, of the variance of the constituent random variables. Since, for r.e., we have defined variance in terms of the norm of the space, we might expect that our discussion would be carried out, at least, in the context of normed spaces. Unfortunately, the normed space does not provide sufficient structure since, to be assured that sums of r.e. are also r.e., we require separability as well. Thus, if we are discussing sequences of **independent random variables**, a separable Banach space would be adequate structure for establishing LLN. Proofs in Banach space, however, are rather complex. This is so since, in the context of a Banach space, we have no definition for the multiplication of one element of the space by another (vector multiplication). Thus, we have no simple way of expressing the variance of a sum in terms of the variances of the constituent r.e. For this reason, our discussion of LLN for r.e. will take place in the context of a **separable Hilbert** space with norm defined by

$$< \psi, \ \psi > \ = \ \| \psi \|^2, \quad \text{for all} \quad \psi \in \Psi.$$

If ψ is a r.e., then we would mean by the inner product the entity $E(< \psi_1, \ \psi_2 >)$. Since from the properties of the inner product we find

$$< \psi_1 + \psi_2, \ \psi_1 + \psi_2 > \ = \ < \psi_1, \ \psi_1 > + < \psi_2, \ \psi_2 > + 2 < \psi_1, \ \psi_2 >,$$

it follows that

$$< \psi_1, \ \psi_2 > \ = \frac{1}{4}[\| \ \psi_1 + \psi_2 \ \| - \| \ \psi_1 - \psi_2 \ \|]. \tag{4.1}$$

We see, therefore, that a sufficient condition for the definition of the inner product of two random elements is that their variance exists. Now, for their variance to exist, we must require that the norm, say $\| \ \psi_i \ \|$, be a random variable. This will be so since the space is separable; the proof of this fact follows closely the lines of the proof of Proposition 7. Thus, in order to deal effectively with LLN for r.e., we must have that if X is a r.e. in a separable Hilbert space then $E \| \ X \ \| < \infty$; this is also a sufficient condition for the B-integral of X to exist, and thus for the expectation, $E(X)$, to exist. The existence of the variance further requires that $E \| \ X \ \|^2 < \infty$. These conditions will constitute a part of the context in discussing LLN, whether the fact is explictly stated or not.

4.5.2   WLLN and SLLN for R.E.

Perhaps the prototypical LLN relates to sequences of independent, identically distributed random variables. We prove this result for r.e., carefully pointing out the manner in which the proof is nearly identical to that for random variables.

Proposition 16. Let $(\Omega, \ \mathcal{A}, \ P)$, $(\Psi, \ \mathcal{G})$ be a probability and separable Hilbert space, respectively. Let $\{X_n : n \geq 1\}$ be a sequence of i.i.d. r.e. with values in Ψ, and suppose that $E \| \ X_1 - E(X_1) \ \|^2 < \infty$. Then,

$$\frac{S_n}{n} \xrightarrow{P} 0, \quad \text{where} \quad S_n = \sum_{k=1}^{n}[X_k - E(X_k)].$$

Proof: We shall prove that $\| \ S_n \ \| /n \longrightarrow 0$. By the properties of the norm, this will, in turn, imply that $S_n/n \longrightarrow 0$, as required. We note that, by the separability of the space, S_n is a r.e.; consequently, $\| \ S_n \ \|$, is a random variable. Evidently, the expectation of S_n is zero, and thus, its variance is $E \| \ S_n \ \|^2 = n\sigma^2$. To evaluate this expression consider

$$E < S_n, \ S_n > \ = \sum_{k=1}^{n} E < X_k - E(X_k), \ X_k - E(X_k) > \ = n\sigma^2,$$

where $\sigma^2 = \text{Var}(X_1)$. We remind the reader that all cross products vanish, owing to the independence[5] property of the sequence. Let r, an integer, be given and define

$$A_{n,r} = \left\{ \omega : \frac{1}{n} \parallel S_n \parallel \geq \frac{1}{r} \right\}.$$

By Chebyshev's inequality,

$$P(A_{n,r}) \leq \frac{\sigma^2}{nr^2}.$$

Consequently, since for **any** r, $\lim_{n \to \infty} P(A_{n,r}) = 0$, we conclude that $(S_n/n) \overset{P}{\to} 0$.

q.e.d.

Corollary 1. The same result holds if the sequence is merely one of independent r.e. with (uniformly) bounded variance.

Proof: Let the bound be K and use it in the same way that σ^2 was used in the proof of the proposition.

q.e.d.

Corollary 2. The same result, as in Corollary 1, holds if the sequence were one of **uncorrelated** rather than independent r.e. with (uniformly) bounded variance.

Proof: Notice that the computation of the variance of S_n remains identical whether the sequence is one of independent or merely one of uncorrelated r.e.

q.e.d.

Remark 10. It should be apparent to the reader that there is little difference in the manner of proofs of WLLN as between the case of random

---

[5] We should remark here that while this fact is quite evident in the case of random variables, it does require proof in the case of r.e., since the multiplication involved here is quite complex and deeply hidden. Nonetheless, one could show that the coordinate functionals of independent r.e. are independent random variables. Consequently, for r.e. as well, it is true that independence implies lack of correlation.

variables and r.e.; the main additional work in the latter is simply the computation of the variance of the partial sums. The same is also true for SLLN. We give here the generalization to r.e. of the SLLN given (as Proposition 25) at the end of Chapter 3; in particular, we are dealing with the case of a sequence of uncorrelated random variables with (uniformly) bounded variance. Again, the reader should note the identity of the arguments involved, *mutatis mutandis*. This is actually a more general phenomenon, in that most LLN for scalar random variables hold for r.e., in (separable) Hilbert space.

Proposition 17. Let $(\Omega, \mathcal{A}, P)$, $(\Psi, \mathcal{G})$ be a probability and separable Hilbert space, respectively. Let $\{X_n : n \geq 1\}$ be a sequence of uncorrelated r.e. with values in Ψ, and suppose, in addition, that $E \parallel X_n - E(X_n) \parallel^2 < K$, for all n. Then,

$$\frac{S_n}{n} \xrightarrow{\text{a.c.}} 0, \quad \text{where} \quad S_n = \sum_{k=1}^{n} [X_k - E(X_k)].$$

Proof: Consider, first, the subsequence S_{n^2} and note that it has mean zero. Consequently, its variance is given by

$$E < \frac{S_{n^2}}{n^2}, \frac{S_{n^2}}{n^2} > = \frac{1}{n^4} \sum_{k=1}^{n^2} \text{Var}(X_k) \leq \frac{K}{n^2}.$$

Since, for any integer r and

$$A_{n,r} = \left\{ \omega : \frac{\parallel S_{n^2} \parallel}{n^2} \geq \frac{1}{r} \right\},$$

we have $P(A_{n,r}) \leq (K/n^2 r^2)$ it follows, by the Borel-Cantelli result, that

$$P(A_{n,r}, \, i.o.) = 0, \quad \text{or that} \quad \frac{S_{n^2}}{n^2} \xrightarrow{\text{a.c.}} 0.$$

Next, define

$$D_k = \max_{n^2 \leq k < (n+1)^2} \parallel S_k - S_{n^2} \parallel$$

and note that it easily obeys $D_k \leq (2n) \parallel \sum_{s=n^2+1}^{(n+1)^2} X_s \parallel$. Consequently, defining

$$B_{k,r} = \left\{ \omega : \frac{D_k}{n^2} \geq \frac{1}{r} \right\}, \quad n^2 \leq k < (n+1)^2,$$

we find that $P(B_{k,r}) \leq (4K/n^2r^2)$; it follows, by the Borel-Cantelli result, that

$$P(B_{k,r},\ i.o.) = 0, \text{ or that } \quad \frac{D_k}{n^2} \overset{\text{a.c.}}{\to} 0.$$

Since

$$\frac{S_k}{k} \leq \frac{S_{n^2} + D_k}{n^2}$$

and the right member above converges to zero a.c., we conclude that the left member also converges to zero a.c.

q.e.d.

4.6   Convergence in Probability for R.E.

As we have remarked earlier, issues of convergence in probability entail, in general, the definition of some measure of "distance". More specifically, suppose $\{X_n : n \geq 1\}$ is a sequence of r.e., and we wish to show that it converges in probability to some constant element, say X_0, all in some appropriate space. To attain this end, we need to define some measure of the extent to which the elements of the sequence are "close" to X_0. If the underlying space is separable, we can accomplish that through the metric and the fact that, by Proposition 7 above, the resulting entity is a random variable. We are thus led to

Definition 14. Let $(\Omega,\ \mathcal{A},\ P)$, $(\Psi,\ \mathcal{G},\ \rho)$ be a probability and metric space, respectively, and let $\{X_n : n \geq 1\}$ be a sequence of r.e. with values in Ψ. The sequence is said to converge in probability to the constant element $X_0 \in \Psi$ if and only if, given any integer r,

$$\lim_{n \to \infty} P(A_{nr}) = 0,$$

where $A_{nr} = \{\omega : \rho(X_n(\omega), X_0) \geq \frac{1}{r}\}$.

Remark 12. A little reflection will show that the definition above corresponds exactly to that given for random variables, since the metric merely expresses the distance (or deviation) between X_n and X_0. The definition thus simply states that a sequence **converges in probability** to a constant element if and only if the probability of large deviations from the constant limit declines as we move farther out into the sequence.

Remark 13. Evidently, the definition above makes sense only when the metric, $\rho(\cdot, \cdot)$, is a random variable. But, if Ψ is separable then by Proposition 6 $\Psi_1 \times \Psi_2$ is also separable, where the Ψ_i, $i = 1, 2$, are copies of Ψ, and ρ is reinterpreted as the metric on the product space. It also follows from Proposition 1 of this chapter, that the function $\zeta(\omega) = \rho[X_n(\omega), X_m(\omega)]$ is a random variable. But, this means that, in the case of r.e. assuming values in a metric space, all the discussion of the previous chapter regarding the **properties of convergence in probability and convergence with probability one, as well as the connection between the two modes of convergence, is fully applicable.**

4.7   Weak Convergence

4.7.1   Preliminaries

In dealing with issues of convergence in distribution, we shall employ the concept of weak convergence, i.e., the convergence of the **sequence of probability measures induced, on the range space, by the (sequence of) random elements.** It should be emphasized that weak convergence of the sequence of probability measures is perfectly equivalent to convergence in distribution of the corresponding sequence of random elements. Whether one states the results in the form of weak convergence or convergence in distribution is immaterial and depends solely on the nature of emphasis one wishes to impart on the results. For example, suppose we are dealing with the metric space $(\Psi, \mathcal{G}, \rho)$ and we have defined on it the (distribution) measure, P, such that $P(\Psi) = 1$. Define on Ψ the function

$$Z(\psi) = \psi$$

and note that $(\Psi, \mathcal{G}, P)$ is a probability space and, consequently, that Z is a r.e. that assumes values in Ψ and has P as its distribution. Shifting the focus of discussion from **distribution functions** to **distributions** greatly facilitates the discussion in the case of r.e., and the discussion is fully applicable to the case of random variables, as well. However, the approach we have followed in that case, i.e., reliance on properties of convergence of the **distribution functions** of the random variables in question, involves procedures that are too closely tied to the properties of the number system that do not easily generalize. A consequence of this strategy is that a few additional mathematical concepts will be required.

Definition 15. Let $\{P, P_n : n = 1, 2, \ldots\}$ be a sequence of measures defined on the metric space $(\Psi, \mathcal{G})$. We say that the sequence **converges weakly** to P, denoted by

$$P_n \xrightarrow{w} P$$

if and only if, for every function f in the dual space,[6] Ψ^*,

$$\lim_{n \to \infty} \int_\Psi f \, dP_n = \int_\Psi f \, dP.$$

In order that we may use the concept of weak convergence effectively in our discussion, we require a thorough understanding of its implications and a fuller grasp of the properties of measures. Since we had not addressed these issues in Chapter 1, a digression is now in order.

Definition 16. Let $(\Psi, \mathcal{G})$ be a general topological space. A set, $A \subset \Psi$, is said to be **compact** if and only if every (open) cover of A contains a finite subcover, i.e., if and only if every open cover can be reduced to a finite open cover.

Definition 17. Let $(\Psi, \mathcal{G})$ be a metric space. A collection of points, $\psi = \{\psi_k : k \geq 1\}$, is said to be an ϵ-net for a set $A \subset \Psi$ if and only if, given any $a \in A$, there exists an element, say $\psi_r \in \psi$, such that $\rho(a, \psi_r) < \epsilon$.

Definition 18. A set A, as in Definition 17, is said to be **totally bounded** if and only if, given any $\epsilon > 0$, **it has a finite** ϵ**-net**, i.e., the collection ψ, of Definition 17, has a finite number of elements.

Definition 19. Let $(\Psi, \mathcal{G})$ be a metric space. A set $A \subset \Psi$ is said to be σ-compact if and only if it is the countable union of compact sets.

The implications of set compactness are made clear in

---

[6] When dealing with issues of weak convergence, the dual space will consist of all **bounded uniformly continuous real functions** defined on Ψ. We recall that in the discussion of the preceding sections we required the elements of the dual space to be **linear** as well.

Proposition 18. Let $(\Psi, \mathcal{G})$ be a metric space. The following conditions are equivalent for any set $A \subset \Psi$:

   i. the closure of A, A^c, is compact;

   ii. every countable open cover of A^c contains a finite subcover;

   iii. every sequence in A has at least one limit point, i.e., it contains at least one subsequence that converges (to an element in A^c);

   iv. A is totally bounded and A^c is complete, i.e., all Cauchy sequences in A converge.

Proof: That i. implies ii. is quite evident from the definition of compactness.

To prove that ii. implies iii., let $\{a_n : n \geq 1,\ a_n \in A\}$ and define $B_n = $ closure of the set $\{a_s : s \geq n\}$. Note that if $\bigcap_{n=1}^\infty B_n$ is nonempty then the sequence has at least one limit point, and consequently, the implication is proved. Thus, suppose that $\bigcap_{n=1}^\infty B_n = \emptyset$. It follows, then, that $\{\bar{B}_n : n \geq 1\}$ is a countable open cover for A; by ii., there exists a finite collection, say $\{\bar{B}_s : s \leq m\}$, that is a cover for A. This leads to the conclusion that $A \cap B_n = \emptyset$, for $n > m$, which is a contradiction. Thus, ii. implies iii.

To prove that iii. implies iv., suppose that iii. holds, but that A is **not** totally bounded. This means that, given any $\epsilon > 0$, there exists a sequence $\{b_r : r \geq 1\}$ such that, for $m \neq n$, $\rho(b_n, b_m) \geq \epsilon$. This, means, however, that the sequence has no limit point, which is a contradiction establishing the fact that A is totally bounded. Moreover, if $\{b_r : r \geq 1\}$ is any sequence in A, then iii. asserts that it has at least one limit point, say b; if, in addition, it is Cauchy, i.e., $\rho(b_n, b_m) \longrightarrow 0$, then b can be shown to be the limit of the sequence using the relation

$$\rho(b_n,\ b) \leq \rho(b_n,\ b_m) + \rho(b_m,\ b).$$

This establishes the fact that A is complete.

The proof that iv. implies i. is established by contradiction but, in the interest of brevity, we omit the argument involved since it is rather inessential to our purposes.

q.e.d.

4.7.2   Properties of Measures

Regular and Compact Measures

We now turn our attention to the the meaning of compactness and other properties of families of probability measures.

Definition 20. Let $(\Psi, \mathcal{G})$ be a metric space and P a measure defined on $\mathcal{G}$. The measure P is said to be **regular** if and only if for every set $B \in \mathcal{G}$ there exist a closed set A_1 and an open set A_2 such that $A_1 \subset B \subset A_2$ and

$$P(A_2 - A_1) = P(A_2 \cap \bar{A}_1) = 0.$$

Remark 14. It may be shown that every probability measure on a metric space is regular. The definition thus suggests that the properties of probability measures are determined by their behavior on closed sets.

Definition 21. Let $(\Psi, \mathcal{G})$ be a metric space. A family, $\mathcal{F}$, of probability measures on $\mathcal{G}$ is said to be **relatively compact**, if and only if every sequence with elements in $\mathcal{F}$ contains a weakly converging subsequence.

Definition 22. Let $(\Psi, \mathcal{G})$ be a metric space and let P be a probability measure defined on $\mathcal{G}$. A set $A \in \mathcal{G}$ is said to be a **support** for P if and only if $P(A) = 1$.

Definition 23. Let $(\Psi, \mathcal{G})$ be a metric space. A probability measure, P, defined on $\mathcal{G}$ is said to be **tight** if and only if, given any integer r, there exists a compact set $M \in \mathcal{G}$ such that $P(M) < 1 - \frac{1}{r}$.

An immediate consequence of the preceding is

Proposition 19. Let $(\Psi, \mathcal{G})$ be a metric space and suppose, in addition, that it is **separable and complete**. If P is **any** probability measure defined on $\mathcal{G}$, then P is tight.

Proof: We shall show that given any integer q, we can find a compact set, say A^c, such that $P(A^c) > 1 - \frac{1}{q}$. Let q be any integer and define the spheres of radius $(1/r)$, $\{S_{rj} : j \geq 1\}$. Since Ψ is separable, we can write, for each r, $\Psi = \bigcup_{j=1}^{\infty} S_{rj}$. Choose j_r such that the set

$A_r = \bigcup_{j \leq j_r} S_{rj}$ obeys $P(A_r) > 1 - \frac{1}{q}2^{-r}$ and define $A = \bigcap_{r=1}^{\infty} A_r$. We note that A is totally bounded. This is so since, if $\epsilon > 0$ is given then for **any** $\psi \in A$, we have $\psi \in A_r$, for every r; moreover, choose r_0, such that $(1/r_0) < \epsilon$, and note that $\psi \in S_{r_0 j_0}$. Consequently, there is $\psi_{r_0} \in S_{r_0 j_0}$ such that $\rho(\psi, \psi_{r_0}) < (1/r_0) < \epsilon$. This establishes that A is totally bounded. Since Ψ is complete, the closure of A, A^c, is complete. By iv. of Proposition 18, it follows that A^c is compact. Since $P(A^c) > 1/q$, the proof is complete.

q.e.d.

We had earlier defined what was meant when two random variables (and by implication two r.e.) were said to be equivalent. The definition entails looking at their difference, assuming the latter is defined, and obtaining the **inverse image of the set over which the difference does not vanish.** If the inverse image has measure zero, the two entities are said to be equivalent; if the measure is not zero, the two elements are not equivalent. What is the analogous concept for probability measures defined on metric spaces? We have

Proposition 20. Let $(\Psi, \mathcal{G})$ be a metric space and let P_i, $i = 1, 2$, be two measures defined on $\mathcal{G}$. If

$$\int_{\Psi} f \, dP_1 = \int_{\Psi} f \, dP_2, \quad \text{for all} \quad f \in \Psi^*,$$

then $P_1 = P_2$.

Proof: Let $A \in \mathcal{G}$ be any **closed** set, define the real valued function

$$g(t) = \quad 1 \quad \text{if} \quad t \leq 0$$
$$= \quad 1 - t \quad \text{if} \quad 0 \leq t \leq 1$$
$$= \quad 0 \quad \text{if} \quad t \geq 1,$$

put $g_n(t) = g(nt)$, and consider the sequence $\{f_n : n \geq 1\}$, where $f_n(\psi) = g_n[r\rho(\psi, A)]$.[7] We note that $\{f_n : n \geq 1\}$ is a sequence of continuous bounded real valued functions on Ψ, and thus, $f_n \in \Psi^*$ for

---

[7] We remind the reader that the distance of a point, ψ, from a set, A, in a metric space is defined by $\rho(\psi, A) = \inf_{x \in A} \rho(\psi, x)$.

all n. Since $f_n \longrightarrow I_A$, where the latter is the indicator function of the set A, the bounded convergence theorem (Proposition 16 of Chapter 1) implies

$$\lim_{n\to\infty} \int_\Psi f_n \, dP_1 = P_1(A), \quad \lim_{n\to\infty} \int_\Psi f_n \, dP_2 = P_2(A).$$

By the conditions of the proposition, we thus conclude that $P_1(A) = P_2(A)$, for all closed sets. Definition 20 and Remark 14, then, suggest that $P_1 = P_2$.

q.e.d.

We close this section by offering a characterization of weak convergence of measures in a metric space.

Proposition 21. Let $\{P, P_n : n \geq 1\}$ be a sequence of measures defined on the metric space above. Then, the following conditions are equivalent:

i. $P_n \overset{w}{\to} P$;

ii. $\lim_{n\to\infty} \int_\Psi f \, dP_n = \int_\Psi f \, dP$, for all real, bounded, (uniformly) continuous functions f;

iii. $\lim \sup_{n\to\infty} P_n(B) \leq P(B)$, for all closed sets $B \in \mathcal{G}$;

iv. $\lim \inf_{n\to\infty} P_n(A) \geq P(A)$, for all open sets $A \in \mathcal{G}$;

v. $\lim_{n\to\infty} P_n(C) = P(C)$, for all P-continuity sets $C \in \mathcal{G}$.

Proof: That i. implies ii. is, of course, quite evident from Definition 15.

To prove that ii. implies iii., suppose ii. holds and let B be a closed set in $\mathcal{G}$; given an arbitrary integer q, define the sets $\{A_r : r \geq 1\}$ such that $A_r = \{\psi : \rho(\psi, B) < (1/r)\}$ and $P(A_r) < P(B) + (1/q)$, for all $r \geq r_0$. By construction, $P_n(B) = \int_B f \, dP_n \leq \int_\Psi f \, dP_n$, where

$$
\begin{aligned}
f(\psi) &= 1 & &\text{if } \psi \in B \\
&= 1 - r\rho(\psi, B) & &\text{if } \rho(\psi, B) \leq \tfrac{1}{r} \\
&= 0 & &\text{if } \rho(\psi, B) \geq \tfrac{1}{r},
\end{aligned}
$$

and we note that for $\psi \in \bar{A}_r$, $f(\psi) = 0$, while for all other ψ, $0 \leq f(\psi) \leq 1$. Combining this with the previous result, we have

$$\limsup_{n \to \infty} P_n(B) \leq \lim_{n \to \infty} \int_\Psi f dP_n = \int_\Psi f dP = \int_{A_r} f dP \leq P(A_r) < P(B) + \frac{1}{q}.$$

Since q is arbitrary, this shows that $\limsup_{n \to \infty} P_n(B) \leq P(B)$, for all closed sets.

We next show that iii. is equivalent to iv.; this is so since if C is any open set then $\bar{C}$ is a closed set. Assuming iii. holds, we have

$$\limsup_{n \to \infty} P_n(\bar{C}) \leq P(\bar{C}).$$

Since $\limsup_{n \to \infty} P_n(\bar{C}) = 1 - \liminf_{n \to \infty} P_n(C)$, the conlcusion follows immediately.

To show the equivalence of iii. and v., let A by any P-continuity set and let A°, A^c be its interior and closure, respectively. Since iii. and thus iv. hold, we have

$$P(A^c) \geq \limsup_{n \to \infty} P_n(A^c) \geq \limsup_{n \to \infty} P_n(A)$$
$$\geq \liminf_{n \to \infty} P_n(A) \geq \liminf_{n \to \infty} P_n(A^\circ)$$
$$\geq P(A^\circ).$$

Since $P(\partial A) = 0$, comparing the first and last members of the relation above we conclude that iii. implies v.; to prove the converse, let A be a closed set. We note that there exists a sequence of P-continuity sets, say $\{A_r : r \geq 1\}$, such that $A_r = \{\psi : \rho(\psi, A) \leq (1/r)\}$. Since, evidently $A \subset A_r$, for all r, it follows by v. that

$$\limsup_{n \to \infty} P_n(A) \leq \lim_{n \to \infty} P_n(A_r) = P(A_r), \quad r \geq 1.$$

Moreover, $\{A_r : r \geq 1\}$ is a monotone decreasing sequence of closed sets converging to A, and the conlcusion follows.

It only remains now to show that iii. implies i. Take any $f \in \Psi^*$; since we are dealing with real continuous **bounded** functions, it involves no loss of generality to assume that $0 \leq f(\psi) < 1$, for any $\psi \in \Psi$. Partition the range of f at the points $(i/m) : i = 0, 1, \ldots, m$, and let

$A_i : i = 0, 1, \ldots, m$, be the sets $A_i = \{\psi : f(\psi) \geq (i/m)\}$. From the definition of the intergral, we immediately conclude

$$\int_\Psi f \, dP_n \; < \; \sum_{i=1}^m \frac{i}{m} [P_n(A_{i-1}) - P_n(A_i)],$$

or, upon rearranging (since $P_n(A_m) = 0, \; P_n(A_0) = 1$),

$$\int_\Psi f \, dP_n < \frac{1}{m} + \frac{i}{m} \sum_{i=1}^m P_n(A_i).$$

From iii., we thus conclude

$$\limsup_{n \to \infty} \int_\Psi f \, dP_n \leq \frac{1}{m} + \frac{1}{m} \sum_{i=1}^m P(A_i) \leq \frac{1}{m} + \int_\Psi f \, dP.$$

A similar argument relative to $-f$ will complete the proof.

q.e.d.

In connection with Proposition 21 a few other aspects of weak convergence are useful; the proof we give follows the lines of similar proofs for sequences of real numbers.

Proposition 22. Let $\{P, P_n : n \geq 1\}$ be a sequence of measures defined as in Proposition 21. Then, the following statements are true:

i. if $P_n \xrightarrow{w} P$, then every subsequence thereof obeys $P_{n_k} \xrightarrow{w} P$;

ii. $P_n \xrightarrow{w} P$ if and only if every subsequence thereof contains a further subsequence that converges weakly to P.

Proof: To prove part i., we note that from Proposition 21, part ii., we need only prove that if $\{P_{n_k} : k \geq 1\}$ is any subsequence then, for any real, bounded, continuous function f,

$$\lim_{k \to \infty} \int_\Psi f \, dP_n = \int_\Psi f \, dP.$$

Fix f and consider the sequence of real numbers $\{\alpha_n : n \geq 1\}$, where $\alpha_n = \int_\Psi f \, dP_n$ and $\alpha = \int_\Psi f \, dP$. Since the sequence converges, given any r, there exists n_0 such that for all $n \geq n_0$, $| \alpha_n - \alpha | < (1/r)$, where evidently $\alpha = \int_\Psi f \, dP$. Since $\lim_{k \to \infty} n_k = \infty$ and $n_{k_2} \geq n_{k_1}$, for

$k_2 \geq k_1$, it follows that there exists a smallest index, say k_0, such that $n_{k_0} \geq n_0$. Consequently, given any r, $\mid a_{n_k} - \alpha \mid < (1/r)$, for $k \geq k_0$. This concludes the proof of part i.

As for part ii., let us show necessity first. From part i., and using the same construction, we note $\mid \alpha_n - \alpha_m \mid \leq \mid \alpha_n - \alpha \mid + \mid \alpha_m - \alpha \mid \leq (1/r)$; therefore, $\mid \alpha_n - \alpha_m \mid \longrightarrow 0$, with m and n. Let $\{\alpha_{n'} : n' \geq 1\}$ be any subsequence; we must show that that it contains a (further) subsequence that converges. Let $\{P_{n'} : n' \geq 1\}$ be the subsequence in question. By part i., it converges to α. Again, by part i., there exists a (further) subsequence, say $\{\alpha_{n'_k} : k \geq 1\}$, that converges to α. This concludes the proof of necessity.

As for sufficiency, suppose every subsequence of $\{\alpha_n : n \geq 1\}$ has a (further) subsequence converging to α; we must show that the original sequence converges to α. Suppose not; then, given any r, we can find a subsequence, say $\{\alpha_{n_k} : k \geq 1\}$, such that for every k $\mid \alpha_{n_k} - \alpha \mid > (1/r)$. But, then, no subsequence of this subsequence can possibly converge. This is a contradiction.

q.e.d.

It should be noted that the same sort of consideration will be applied to the case where we are dealing with the familiy of distributions $\{P_t : t \in T\}$, where T is a linear index set, not necessarily countable. In such a case, issues of convergence are to be examined in the context of **sequences of the form** $\{P_{t_n} : n = 1, 2, \ldots, t_n \in T\}$.

4.7.3   Determining Classes

Often, in attempting to prove that a certain property holds (over the elements of a σ-algebra), it turns out that we can accomplish the same by proving that the property holds over a narrower class. For example, in Proposition 21 (part v.), we have seen that if we can prove that a sequence of probability measures, say $P, P_n : n \geq 1$, converges over the class of P-continuity sets then it converges weakly. Rendered more extensively, we have the following situation: If $\{P, P_n : n \geq 1\}$ is a sequence of measures defined on the metric space $(\Psi, \mathcal{G})$ then showing that $P_n(C) \longrightarrow P(C)$, for $C \in \mathcal{C}$, is equivalent to showing that $P_n(G) \longrightarrow P(G)$, **for any**

$G \in \mathcal{G}$, where $\mathcal{C}$ is a certain class of subsets of Ψ, say the class of P-continuity sets. Evidently, this is a very convenient property and leads us to the concept of determining classes.

Definition 24. Let $(\Psi, \mathcal{G})$ be a metric space and let P_i, $i = 1, 2$, be two measures defined on $\mathcal{G}$; a collection of sets, $\mathcal{D} \subset \mathcal{G}$, is said to be a **determining class** if and only if $P_1(A) = P_2(A)$, for **every** $A \in \mathcal{D}$, implies $P_1 = P_2$.

Definition 25. Let $(\Psi, \mathcal{G})$ be a metric space; a collection of sets, $\mathcal{C} \subset \mathcal{G}$, is said to be a **convergence determining class** if and only if, given any sequence of probability measures $\{P, P_n : n \geq 1\}$, the condition

$$P_n(A) \longrightarrow P(A), \quad \text{for all} \quad A \in \mathcal{C}$$

implies $P_n \overset{w}{\to} P$.

Proposition 23. Let $(\Psi, \mathcal{G})$ be a metric space and $\mathcal{C} \subset \mathcal{G}$ a collection of sets such that

i. if $C_i \in \mathcal{C}$, $i = 1, 2$, then $C_1 \cap C_2 \in \mathcal{C}$;

ii. if $G \in \mathcal{G}$ is **any** open set, then $G = \bigcup_{i \in J} C_i$, where J is a finite or countable index set and $C_i \in \mathcal{C}$, for all $i \in J$.

Then, the collection $\mathcal{C}$ is a convergence determining class.

Proof: We need to show that if for a sequence of probability measures, $P, P_n : n \geq 1$, $P_n(C) \longrightarrow P(C)$, for any $C \in \mathcal{C}$, then $P_n \overset{w}{\to} P$. Let $C_i \in \mathcal{C} : i = 1, 2, ..., q$, and consider their union $C = \bigcup_{i=1}^{q} C_i$. We have, by the usual rules,

$$P_n(C) = \sum_{i=1}^{q} P_n(C_i) - \sum_{i \neq j} P(C_i C_j) + \sum_{i \neq j \neq k} P(C_i C_j C_k) - \cdots .$$

Since $\mathcal{C}$ is closed under finite intersections, it follows that

$$P_n(C) \longrightarrow \sum_{i=1}^{q} P(C_i) - \sum_{i \neq j} P(C_i C_j) + \sum_{i \neq j \neq k} P(C_i C_j C_k) - \cdots = P(C).$$

Let $G \in \mathcal{G}$ be **any** open set and note that, by the properties of $\mathcal{C}$, the latter contains sets C_γ such that $G = \bigcup_{\gamma \in \Gamma} C_\gamma$, where Γ is at most a countable index set. Now, given any integer r, there exists m_0, such that $P(G) - (1/r) < P(\bigcup_{i=1}^{m_0} C_i)$. Moreover, for any n, we must also have $P_n(G) \geq P_n(\bigcup_{i=1}^{m_0} C_i)$. Consequently,

$$\liminf_{n\to\infty} P_n(G) \geq \lim_{n\to\infty} P_n(\bigcup_{i=1}^{m_0} C_i) = P(\bigcup_{i=1}^{m_0} C_i) \geq P(G),$$

and it follows immediately, from part iv. of Proposition 21, that $P_n \xrightarrow{w} P$.

q.e.d.

Another interesting result is

Proposition 24. Let $(\Psi, \mathcal{G})$ be a **separable** metric space, and $\mathcal{D} \subset \mathcal{G}$ a collection of sets, satisfying the conditions

   i. $\mathcal{D}$ is closed under finite intersections, i.e., if $D_i \in \mathcal{D}$, $i = 1, 2$, then $D_1 \cap D_2 \in \mathcal{D}$.

   ii. Let $S_{\psi,r} \subset \Psi$ be an open sphere of radius $(1/r)$ and center ψ; if $x \in \Psi$ is **any point** in Ψ then there exists a set $D \in \mathcal{D}$, such that $x \in D^\circ \subset D \subset S_{x,r}$.

Then, $\mathcal{D}$ is a convergence determining class.

Proof: Under the premises of the proposition, $\mathcal{D}$ satisfies condition i. of Proposition 23 since it is closed under finite interesections. Thus, it will suffice to prove that property ii. of this proposition implies the property stated in part ii. of Proposition 23. Let G be any open set and $x \in G$ be any point. Since the space is separable then, by Proposition 5, there exists a countable collection of spheres, say with rational radii, such that

$$G \subset \bigcup_{i \in J} S_{x,r_i},$$

where J is a countable index set. By the properties of $\mathcal{D}$, for every $x \in G$, there exists $D \in \mathcal{D}$ such that $x \in D^\circ \subset D \subset S_{x,r_i} \subset G$. Consequently, there exists a countable collection of elements of $\mathcal{D}$ such that $G \subset \bigcup_{i \in J} D_i^\circ$. But, this shows that $\mathcal{D}$ has the properties of $\mathcal{C}$, stated in part ii. of Proposition 23 (when the space is separable).

q.e.d.

4.7.4   Weak Convergence in Product Space

Suppose we are dealing with two sequences of r.e., $\{X_{ni} : n \geq 1\}$, defined, perhaps, on the same probability space, but assuming values in the metric spaces $(\Psi_i,\ \mathcal{G}_i,\ \rho_i)$. If $\{P_{ni} : n \geq 1\}$, $i = 1, 2$, are the corresponding sequences of their distributions, does weak convergence, $P_{ni} \xrightarrow{w} P_i$, $i = 1, 2$, imply the weak convergence, $P_n \xrightarrow{w} P$? In the preceding argument, $\{P_n : n \geq 1\}$ is the sequence of distributions of $\{Z_n : n \geq 1,\ Z_n = (X_{n1},\ X_{n2})\}$ and, evidently, P_n is defined on the σ-algebra of the product space, $\Psi = \Psi_1 \times \Psi_2$.

The general answer to the question we have posed is **negative**, unless the underlying spaces are **separable**. [8]

Remark 15. When dealing with product spaces, we recall from Chapter 2, that the Kolmogorov consistency condition requires that the marginal probability distributions satisfy, in the context of the particular product space of this discussion and for the set $G = G_1 \times G_2$, $G_i \in \mathcal{G}_i$, $i = 1, 2$,

$$P_1(G_1) = P(G_1 \times \Psi_2), \quad P_2(G_2) = P(\Psi_1 \times G_2).$$

The major result for product spaces is given in [9]

Proposition 25. Let $\{X_{ni} : n \geq 1\}$ be sequences of r.e. defined on the probability space $(\Omega,\ \mathcal{A},\ \mathcal{P})$ and assuming values in the metric spaces $(\Psi_i,\ \mathcal{G}_i,\ \rho_i)$, $i = 1, 2$, respectively; let $(\Psi,\ \mathcal{G},\ \rho)$ be the induced product space, where $\Psi = \Psi_1 \times \Psi_2$, and suppose that the product space is

---

[8] The problem lies in the fact that unless the underlying spaces are separable, the σ-algebra generated by the collection $\mathcal{G}_1 \times \mathcal{G}_2 = \{G : G = G_1 \times G_2,\ G_i \in \mathcal{G}_i,\ i = 1, 2\}$ will not necessarily coincide with the σ-algebra generated by the open sets of the product space $\Psi_1 \times \Psi_2$. This would invalidate the method of proof employed in establishing such results.

[9] In the remainder of this chapter we shall denote the *probability measure*, in the context of the probability space, by $\mathcal{P}$ instead of the usual P. By the latter notation we shall denote *probability distributions*. The reason for this notational aberration is that, in the remainder of the chapter, we shall have far less need for the notation $(\Omega,\ \mathcal{A},\ \mathcal{P})$ than for the notation pertaining to probability distributions. We remind the reader that if X is a r.e. (or a r.v.) defined on the probability space $(\Omega,\ \mathcal{A},\ \mathcal{P})$ and assuming values in the metric space $(\Psi,\ \mathcal{G},\ \rho)$, the probability distribution of X is the probability measure, say P, defined on $\mathcal{G}$ as follows. For any set $G \in \mathcal{G}$ obtain its inverse image under X, say $X^{-1}(G) = A$, and put $P(G) = \mathcal{P}(A)$.

separable. Consider, further, the sequence $\{Z_n : Z_n = (X_{n1}, X_{n2})\}$ and the associated distributions $\{P_n : n \geq 1\}$ defined on $\mathcal{G}$. The following statements are true:

i. $P_n \overset{w}{\to} P$, i.e., the sequence converges weakly to the distribution P if and only if $P_n(G) \longrightarrow P(G)$, for every set $G = C_1 \times C_2$, such that C_i is a P_i-continuity set and P_i, $i = 1, 2$, are the marginal distributions of P;

ii. if $\{P_{ni} : n \geq 1\}$ and P_i, $i = 1, 2$, are probability measures defined, respectively, on $\mathcal{G}_i$, then $P_{n1} \times P_{n2} \overset{w}{\to} P_1 \times P_2$ if and only if $P_{ni} \overset{w}{\to} P_i$, $i = 1, 2$. [10]

Proof: To prove necessity (for part i.), we need to prove that if $P_n \overset{w}{\to} P$ then $P_n(G) \longrightarrow P(G)$, where $G = C_1 \times C_2$ and the C_i are P_i-continuity sets, $i = 1, 2$. Now, if Ψ is separable, then so are Ψ_1 and Ψ_2, and moreover, if $G = C_1 \times C_2$, then $G \in \mathcal{G}$. In addition,

$$\partial G \subset (\partial C_1 \times \Psi_2) \cup (\Psi_1 \times \partial C_2).$$

Consequently,

$$P(\partial G) \leq P(\partial C_1 \times \Psi_2) + P(\Psi_1 \times \partial C_2) = P_1(\partial C_1) + P_2(\partial C_2) = 0,$$

which, by part v. of Proposition 20, concludes the proof of necessity.

To prove sufficiency (for part i.), we shall use the results of Proposition 23; thus, define

$$\mathcal{C} = \{G : G = C_1 \times C_2\},$$

where $C_i \in \mathcal{G}_i$, $i = 1, 2$, and the C_i are P_i-continuity sets. If $G_1, G_2 \in \mathcal{C}$, then clearly $G_1 \cap G_2 = (C_{11} \cap C_{21}) \times (C_{12} \cap C_{22}) \in \mathcal{C}$, so that $\mathcal{C}$ is closed under finite intersections. Moreover, by hypothesis,

$$\lim_{n \to \infty} P_n(G) = P(G),$$

for any (all) $G \in \mathcal{C}$. To complete the proof, we need only demonstrate that given any point $\psi \in \Psi$ there is a set, say $G \in \mathcal{C}$, such that $\psi \in G^\circ \subset G \subset S_{\psi q}$, where $S_{\psi q}$ is a sphere with center ψ and radius

---

[10] Evidently, $P_{n1} \times P_{n2}$ and $P_1 \times P_2$ are defined on $\mathcal{G}$.

$(1/q)$. Given $\psi = (\psi_1, \psi_2)$ and q, choose $r > q$ and define the sets $G_r = C_{1r} \times C_{2r}$ by the condition $C_{ir} = \{x_i : \rho_i(\psi_i, x_i)\}$, i=1,2. We note that, for distinct r, the sets ∂C_{ir} are disjoint, and moreover, that $P_i(\partial C_{ir}) = 0$, $i = 1, 2$; thus, for any (integer) r, $G_r \in \mathcal{C}$. Moreover, if we choose the metric on Ψ by

$$\rho(\psi_1, \psi_2) = \max[\rho_1(\psi_{11}, \psi_{21}), \ \rho_2(\psi_{12}, \psi_{22})],$$

the set G_r is simply a sphere with center ψ and radius $1/r$. Consequently, the conditions of Proposition 23 are fulfilled and the proof of part i. is completed.

As for part ii., we note that, by the separability of the space, $\mathcal{G}$ is exactly the σ-algebra generated by the collection $\mathcal{C} = \{G : G = G_1 \times G_2, \ G_i \in \mathcal{G}_i\}$. Thus, $P_n = P_{n1} \times P_{n2}$ is a sequence of distributions defined on $\mathcal{G}$, and the P_{ni}, $i = 1, 2$, are, evidently, the marginal distributions of P_n. The conclusion then follows immediately from part i.

q.e.d.

4.8   Convergence in Distribution for R.E.

Here, we give a number of very basic results for convergence in distribution for r.e.

Proposition 26. Let $(\Omega, \mathcal{A}, \mathcal{P})$, $(\Psi, \mathcal{G}, \rho)$ be, respectively, a probability and separable metric space, and $\{X, X_n : n \geq 1\}$, $\{Y_n : n \geq 1\}$ two sequences of r.e. (with values in Ψ). If

    i. $X_n \overset{d}{\to} X$, and

    ii. $\rho(X_n(\omega), Y_n(\omega)) \overset{P}{\to} 0$,[11]

---

[11] This notion of distance between sequences is not to be confused with the **Levy distance**, $\lambda(F, G)$, between (the cumulative distribution functions of) two random variables, which is defined as the *supremum* of r such that $F(x - \frac{1}{r}) - \frac{1}{r} \leq G(x) \leq F(x + \frac{1}{r}) + \frac{1}{r}$.

then

$$Y_n \xrightarrow{d} X.$$

Proof: The first sequence of r.e. above induces a sequence of probability measures (distributions) on $\mathcal{G}$, viz., $\{P, P_n : n \geq 1\}$, such that, if $G \in \mathcal{G}$,

$$P_n(G) = \mathcal{P} \circ X_n^{-1}(G) = \mathcal{P}(C), \quad C = X_n^{-1}(G).$$

Since $P_n \xrightarrow{w} P$ is equivalent to the statement $X_n \xrightarrow{d} X$, we conclude, by Proposition 21, that we can show $Y_n \xrightarrow{d} X$, if we can show that, for every closed set $G \in \mathcal{G}$,

$$\limsup_{n \to \infty} Q_n(G) \leq P(G),$$

where $\{Q_n : n \geq 1\}$ is the sequence of distributions induced on $\mathcal{G}$, by the second sequence of r.e. ($\{Y_n : n \geq 1\}$).

Now, given any closed set $G \in \mathcal{G}$, define, for arbitrary r,

$$G_r = \left\{\psi : \rho(\psi, G) \leq \frac{1}{r}\right\}.$$

Define, also,

$$A_n = \{\omega : Y_n(\omega) \in G\}, \quad B_n = \{\omega : \rho(X_n, Y_n) \geq \frac{1}{r}\},$$

$$C_{nr} = \{\omega : X_n(\omega) \in G_r\},$$

and note that G_r is a closed set and that $A_n \subset B_n \cup C_{nr}$.[12] This immediately implies $\mathcal{P}(A_n) \leq \mathcal{P}(B_n) + \mathcal{P}(C_{nr})$. Since, by construction, $\mathcal{P}(A_n) = Q_n(G)$ and by the premise of the proposition $\lim_{n \to \infty} \mathcal{P}(B_n) = 0$, we conlcude that

$$\limsup_{n \to \infty} Q_n(G) \leq P(G_r).$$

Since both G and G_r are closed and since, as $r \to \infty$, $G_r \downarrow G$, we have $\lim_{r \to \infty} \limsup_{n \to \infty} Q_n(G) = \limsup_{n \to \infty} Q_n(G) \leq P(G)$, thus concluding the proof.

q.e.d.

---

[12] This is so since if $\omega \in \bar{B}_n \cap \bar{C}_{nr}$, this implies that $\omega \in \bar{A}_n$, and consequently $A_n \subset B_n \cup C_{nr}$, as claimed.

A slight extension of the result above, applying to double arrays of r.e. is:

Proposition 27. Let $(\Omega,\ \mathcal{A},\ \mathcal{P})$, $(\Psi,\ \mathcal{G},\ \rho)$ be, respectively, a probability and separable metric space and $\{X, X_m, X_{mn} : m, n \geq 1\}$, $\{Y_n : n \geq 1\}$ be sequences of r.e. (with values in Ψ). If, for each m,

   i. $X_{mn} \overset{d}{\to} X_m$;

   ii. $X_m \overset{d}{\to} X$;

   iii. for any integer r, $\lim_{m\to\infty} \limsup_{n\to\infty} \mathcal{P}(B_{mn}) = 0$, where $B_{mn} = \{\omega : \rho(X_{mn}(\omega), Y_m(\omega)) \geq \frac{1}{r}\}$,

then $Y_n \overset{d}{\to} X$.

Proof: Repeating, *mutatis mutandis*, the construction of the proof of Proposition 26, we have that $\mathcal{P}(A_m) \leq \mathcal{P}(C_{mnr}) + \mathcal{P}(B_{mn})$. Using again the relation $Q_n(G) = \mathcal{P}(A_n)$ and the fact that $X_{mn} \overset{d}{\to} X_m$, we obtain, for any closed set $G \in \mathcal{G}$,

$$Q_m(G) \leq \mathcal{P}(C_{mr}) + \limsup_{n\to\infty} \mathcal{P}(B_{mn}).$$

Moreover, using the second condition of the proposition, we find

$$\limsup_{m\to\infty} Q_m(G) \leq \mathcal{P}(C_r) = P(G_r),$$

where P is the distribution (probability measure) induced by X on $\mathcal{G}$.

q.e.d.

Corollary 3. Let $(\Omega,\ \mathcal{A},\ \mathcal{P})$, $(\Psi,\ \mathcal{G},\ \rho)$ be, respectively, a probability and separable metric space and $\{X, X_n : n \geq 1\}$ be a sequence of r.e. (with values in Ψ). If $X_n \overset{P}{\to} X$, i.e., if $\rho(X_n(\omega), X(\omega)) \overset{P}{\to} 0$, then $X_n \overset{d}{\to} X$.

Proof: Define the sequence $\{Y_n : Y_n = X,\ n \geq 1\}$ and note that, by construction, $Y_n \overset{P}{\to} X$. Moreover, $\rho(Y_n(\omega), X_n(\omega)) \overset{P}{\to} 0$, by the conditions of the corollary. The result then follows immediately from Proposition 26.

q.e.d.

Corollary 4. Under the conditions of Corollary 3, let $\Psi = R^k$ and $\{X, X_n : n \geq 1\}$, $\{Y_n : n \geq 1\}$ be two sequences of r.e. with values in Ψ, i.e., k-dimensional random vectors, satisfying the conditions

i. $X_n \overset{d}{\to} X$,

ii. $|X_n - Y_n| \leq \zeta_n |Y_n|$, where $|\cdot|$ indicates the ordinary Euclidean metric,

iii. $\zeta_n \overset{P}{\to} 0$,

then $Y_n \overset{d}{\to} X$.

Proof: Since $|Y_n|$, $n \geq 1$ are a.c. finite random variables, it follows by the conditions of the corollary that $\rho(X_n, Y_n) \overset{P}{\to} 0$. Consequently, by Proposition 26, we conclude that $Y_n \overset{d}{\to} X$.

q.e.d.

4.8.1 Convergence of Transformed Sequences of R.E.

The question often arises as to the convergence of certain transformations of sequences of r.e. For example, suppose it is known that $X_n \overset{d}{\to} X$, for some sequence of r.e., $\{X, X_n : n \geq 1\}$. What can we say about the convergence properties of the sequence $\{Y_n : n \geq 1, Y_n = g(X_n)\}$, where g is some appropriate transformation? We know from Proposition 21 that $X_n \overset{d}{\to} X$ if and only if $\lim_{n\to\infty} \int_\Psi f dP_n = \int_\Psi f dP$, for all real, bounded, continuous functions f, where $\{P, P_n : n \geq 1\}$ is the sequence of distributions induced, on the range space, by the sequence of r.e. If we were to consider the sequence $\{Y_n : n \geq 1\}$, we might attempt to investigate issues of convergence by treating them as a simple case of change in variable. Using a more convenient notation, we note that $J_n = \int_\Psi f dP_n = \int_\Psi f(\psi) P_n(d\psi)$; if we change variable, in the integrals above, we may consider a transformation, g,

$$g : \Psi \longrightarrow \Psi_1,$$

so that J_n is transformed to

$$J_n = \int_{\Psi_1} f[g^{-1}(\psi_1)] P_n[g^{-1}(d\psi_1)].$$

Note that

$$f[g^{-1}(\psi_1)] = f \circ g^{-1}(\psi_1) = h(\psi_1),$$

so that if g is continuous then h will be a real, bounded, continuous function whenever f has these properties. Thus, if $\lim_{n\to\infty} J_n = \int_\Psi f dP$ holds for every real, bounded, continuous function f, one would conjecture that

$$\lim_{n\to\infty} \int_{\Psi_1} f \circ g^{-1}(\psi_1) P_n \circ g^{-1}(d\psi_1) = \int_{\Psi_1} f \circ g^{-1}(\psi_1) P \circ g^{-1}(d\psi_1),$$

which would imply that

$$P_n \circ g^{-1} \xrightarrow{w} P \circ g^{-1}, \quad \text{or that} \quad g(X_n) \xrightarrow{d} g(X),$$

provided, of course, that the latter is well defined.

It turns out that continuity for g is not quite required. Before we continue with that aspect of the problem, however, it is well to clear up a possible difficulty with the notation we have just employed above.

Remark 16. Perhaps a discussion of the notation we have employed above will help in making clear the essential simplicity of the proofs of the propositions we are about to discuss. If f is a real valued function and P is a probability measure defined on the measurable space $(\Psi, \mathcal{G})$, we had, earlier, consistently employed the notation $\int_\Psi f dP$ to denote the integral of f over Ψ relative to the measure P. What this means, reverting to first principles, is that we partition the range of f, which is the real line or a subset thereof, into a set of, say, half open intervals, I_i, $i = 1, 2, \ldots, n$. Within each interval, we find the maximum and minimum of the function, $f_i^{\max}$, $f_i^{\min}$, respectively. We then form the upper and lower sums,

$$S_L = \sum_{i=1}^n f_i^{\max} P(f^{-1}(I_i)), \qquad s_L = \sum_{i=1}^n f_i^{\min} P(f^{-1}(I_i)).$$

If, as $n \to \infty$, these sums approach a common limit, this common limit is the integral in question, which we had consistently denoted by $\int_\Psi f dP$

above. Expanding on this, we note that if f is at least measurable then $A_i = f^{-1}(I_i) \in \mathcal{G}$, so that the operation, $P[f^{-1}(I_i)] = P(A_i)$, in the upper and lower sums makes sense.

In light of this exposition, the integral could equally well be denoted by $\int_\Psi f(\psi)P(d\psi)$, since as $n \to \infty$ the intervals I_i shrink and, consequently, the sets A_i also "degenerate". Thus, the notation $P(d\psi)$ is appropriately suggestive.

In this context, the question we posed earlier can be readily cast within the framework of "change in variable" topics.

Remark 17. Just to illuminate the issues, consider the integral $J = \int_\psi f \, dP$ and let us employ the transformation

$$g : \Psi \longrightarrow \Psi_1 .$$

The problem now is to express J as an **integral over Ψ_1 rather than over Ψ**. Implementing the transformation we have

$$f[g^{-1}(\psi_1)] = f \circ g^{-1}(\psi_1) \equiv h(\psi_1),$$

so that

$$h : \Psi_1 \longrightarrow R .$$

Evidently, the range space of h is exactly that of f so that, proceeding in exactly the same manner as above, the intervals of partition, I_i, give rise to the upper and lower sums,

$$S_L = \sum_{i=1}^{n} h_i^{\max} P_1[h_i^{-1}(I_i)], \quad s_L = \sum_{i=1}^{n} h_i^{\min} P_1[h_i^{-1}(I_i)].$$

The problem now is how to define the probability measure P_1 on the σ-algebra of the space Ψ_1. If we put $h^{-1}(I_i) = B_i$, we see that the problem is how to assign a measure to the set $B_i \in \mathcal{G}_1$. By definition, $B_i = h^{-1}(I_i) = g[f^{-1}(I_i)] = g(A_i)$, or alternatively, $A_i = g^{-1}(B_i)$. Thus, the probability measure, P, defined on the space Ψ, induces, through the transformation g, the probability meassure P_1, defined on the space Ψ_1, such that [13]

---

[13] The composition notation $P \circ g^{-1}$, although not standard is highly suggestive in this context.

$$P_1(B_i) = P[g^{-1}(B_i)] = P \circ g^{-1}(B_i).$$

Thus, the measure to be assigned to B_i is $P(A_i)$, and consequently, we have the natural definition $P_1 = P \circ g^{-1}$. That P_1 is, indeed, a measure is easily verified; in particular, since g is $\mathcal{G}$-measurable, Proposition 4 of Chapter 1 implies that $g^{-1}(\mathcal{G}_1) \subset \mathcal{G}$, which confirms the propriety of the definition $P_1 = P \circ g^{-1}$.

The point of the preceding discussion is to introduce the following problem: if $\{X, X_n : n \geq 1\}$ is a sequence of r.e., with associated distributions $\{P, P_n : n \geq 1\}$, and if it is given that $X_n \xrightarrow{d} X$, does it follow that $Y_n \xrightarrow{d} g(X)$, where g is a continuous (minimally, at least a measurable) function and $Y_n = g(X_n)$? The point of the last two remarks was to make it evident that the question just posed is equivalent to: if $P_n \xrightarrow{w} P$ and g is a continuous function, does it follow that $P_n \circ g^{-1} \xrightarrow{w} P \circ g^{-1}$? The answer is, in general, yes, and it is not necessary that g be continuous.

In this context, we recall that if g is $\mathcal{G}$-measurable then D_g is also measurable, where D_g is the set of discontinuities of g in Ψ, i.e., the set of points at which g fails to be continuous.

Proposition 28. Let $(\Psi, \mathcal{G}, \rho)$, $(\Psi_1, \mathcal{G}_1, \rho_1)$ be two metric spaces and $\{P, P_n : n \geq 1\}$ a sequence of distributions defined on $\mathcal{G}$. Suppose, further, that

$$g : \Psi \longrightarrow \Psi_1$$

is a measurable function, and D_g is its set of discontinuities. If

   i. $P_n \xrightarrow{d} P$ and

  ii. $P(D_g) = 0$,

then $P_n \circ g^{-1} \xrightarrow{d} P \circ g^{-1}$.

Proof: By Proposition 21, we need only show that

$$\limsup_{n \to \infty} P_n[g^{-1}(G_1)] \leq P[g^{-1}(G_1)],$$

for any closed set $G_1 \in \mathcal{G}_1$. Define $G = g^{-1}(G_1)$ and note that by the measurability of g, $G \in \mathcal{G}$. Consider its closure, say G^c, and note that

$P_n[g^{-1}(G_1)] \leq P_n(G^c)$, for any closed set $G_1 \in \mathcal{G}_1$. Thus, by condition i. of the proposition,

$$\limsup_{n \to \infty} P_n[g^{-1}(G_1)] \leq P(G^c).$$

On the other hand, since $G^c \subset g^{-1}(G_1 \cup D_g)$, we conclude, by condition ii. of the proposition, that $P(G^c) = P[g^{-1}(G_1)]$. Consequently, we have established that, for every closed set $G_1 \in \mathcal{G}_1$, $\limsup_{n \to \infty} P_n \circ g_{-1}(G_1) \leq P \circ g^{-1}(G_1)$, which, by Proposition 21, implies

$$P_n \circ g^{-1} \xrightarrow{w} P \circ g^{-1}.$$

q.e.d.

Corollary 5. Let $(\Omega, \mathcal{A}, \mathcal{P})$, $(\Psi, \mathcal{G}, \rho)$ be a probability and metric space, respectively, $\{X, X_n : n \geq 1\}$ a sequence of r.e. with values in Ψ, and P the distribution induced by X on Ψ. Let

$$g : \Psi \longrightarrow \Psi_1$$

be a measurable function, where $(\Psi_1, \mathcal{G}_1)$ is a measurable space and D_g is the set of discontinuities of g. If

    i. $X_n \xrightarrow{d} X$ and

    ii. $P(D_g) = 0$,

then

$$g(X_n) \xrightarrow{d} g(X).$$

Proof: Let $\{P, P_n : n \geq 1\}$ be the sequence of distributions induced by the sequence of r.e. By Proposition 28, $P_n \circ g^{-1} \xrightarrow{d} P \circ g^{-1}$. But, $P_n \circ g^{-1}$ and $P \circ g^{-1}$ are the distributions of $g(X_n)$ and $g(X)$, respectively. Hence, $g(X_n) \xrightarrow{d} g(X)$.

q.e.d.

Corollary 6. Let $(\Omega, \mathcal{A}, \mathcal{P})$, $(\Psi, \mathcal{G}, \rho)$ be a probability and metric space, respectively, and suppose further that $\Psi = R^m$, $\rho = |\cdot|$, i.e., that $(\Psi, \mathcal{G}, \rho)$ represents the usual Euclidean metric. If $\{\xi, \xi_n : n \geq 1\}$, $\{b, b_n : n \geq 1\}$ are sequences of (m- and k-element) random vectors, respectively, and $\{A_n : n \geq 1\}$ is a sequence of $k \times m$ random matrices such that

   i. $\xi_n \overset{d}{\to} \xi$,

   ii. $b_n \overset{P}{\to} b$,

  iii. $A_n \overset{P}{\to} A$, and

  iv. A, b are **a nonrandom matrix and vector**, respectively, with rank$(A) = k$, $k \le m$,

then

$$A_n \xi_n + b_n \overset{d}{\to} A\xi + b.$$

Proof: Evidently, A_n, ξ_n, b_n, etc. are r.e. in appropriate metric spaces, as is also $A_n \xi_n + b_n$. Since $A_n \xi_n + b_n - (A_n \xi_n + b) \overset{P}{\to} 0$, we conclude, by Corollary 3, that the former converges to the same distribution as $A_n \xi_n + b$. Since $\mid A_n \xi_n + b - (A \xi_n + b) \mid \le \|A_n - A\| \mid \xi_n \mid$ and, by condition iii. of this proposition, $\|A_n - A\| \overset{P}{\to} 0$, we conclude, by Corollary 4, that $A_n \xi_n + b_n$ and $A \xi_n + b$ converge in distribution to the same entity. Thus, it would suffice to examine the convergence aspects of $A \xi_n + b$. Since A, b are nonrandom, this is simply a continuous (and thus measurable) transformation from R^m, to R^k. Specifically,

$$g(\xi_n) = A \xi_n + b.$$

By condition i. of this corollary and Corollary 5, we thus conclude that

$$A_n \xi_n + b_n \overset{P}{\to} A\xi + b.$$

q.e.d.

In an earlier section of this chapter we have introduced the concepts of relative compactness and tightness; these play a role in obtaining convergence results for infinite dimensional spaces, as in the case of the space $\mathcal{C}$ – the space of continuous functions over some interval, say $[a, b]$. We close this section with a fundamental result, due to Prohorov.

Proposition 29. Let $(\Psi, \mathcal{G}, \rho)$ be a complete, separable, metric space and $\mathcal{P}$ **a family** of probability measures, defined on $\mathcal{G}$. Then, $\mathcal{P}$ is relatively compact if and only if it is tight. [14],

---

[14] We shall prove this result only in the case where $\Psi = R$. A somewhat more general form, in which it is shown that tightness implies relative compactness without

Proof: Necessity: Suppose $\mathcal{P}$ is a family of distributions that is relatively compact, but it is not tight. Then, given any integer r and for any compact set $K \subset R$,

$$\sup_{P_\gamma \in \mathcal{P}} P(R - K) > \frac{1}{r},$$

where $\gamma \in \Gamma$ and Γ is countable. In particular, for intervals, say $D_n = (-n, n)$, we can select an index, say γ_n, such that

$$P_{\gamma_n}(R - D_n) > \frac{1}{r}.$$

Since $\mathcal{P}$ is relatively compact, by Definition 21, the countable sequence thus selceted, viz., $\{P_{\gamma_n} : n \geq 1\}$, contains a converging subsequence, say $\{P_{\gamma_{n_k}} : k \geq 1\}$, such that $P_{\gamma_{n_k}} \overset{w}{\to} Q$, for some probability measure Q. Since $R - D_n$ is closed (because it is the complement of an open set in R), it follows by part iii. of Proposition 21 that

$$\limsup_{k \to \infty} P_{\gamma_{n_k}}(R - D_n) \leq Q(R - D_n),$$

for every $n \geq 1$. By the continuity of probability measures, we have that $Q(R - D_n) \downarrow 0$. This implies that $\lim_{n \to \infty} \limsup_{k \to \infty} P_{\gamma_{n_k}}(R - D_n) \leq 0$, which is a contradiction.

Sufficiency: Let $\{P_s : s \geq 1\}$ be a sequence in the tight family $\mathcal{P}$ and let $\{F_s : s \geq 1\}$ be the corresponding sequence of (cumulative) distribution functions. By a theorem of analysis, [15] we can choose a subsequence, say $\{F_{s_k} : k \geq 1\}$, such that it converges to a generalized distribution function, F. If F is a proper distribution function then there exists a distribution, say Q, corresponding to it. This would mean that the corresponding subsequence $\{P_{s_k} : k \geq 1\}$ converges to an element $Q \in \mathcal{P}$. We shall now show that since $\mathcal{P}$ is tight, F must be a proper distribution function. To show that this is so, given any r, consider the half open

---

the requirement of completeness and separability, as well as a general proof, may be found in Billingsley (1968, p. 37ff and p. 239ff.)

[15] The theorem in question is referred to as Helly's theorem and may be stated as follows: Let $\mathcal{G}$ be the class of generalized distribution functions, i.e., of functions that have all properties of distribution functions, except that they only obey $F(-\infty) \geq 0$, $F(\infty) \leq 1$. Then, $\mathcal{G}$ is **sequentially compact**, i.e., every sequence $\{F_n : n \geq 1\}$ in $\mathcal{G}$ contains a subsequence, say $\{F_{n_k} : k \geq 1\}$, which converges to a function $F \in \mathcal{G}$, for every point of its continuity set.

interval $D_n = (a_n, b_n]$ such that $a_{n_2} < a_{n_1}$ and $b_{n_1} < b_{n_2}$, for $n_1 < n_2$. By the tightness property of the family, there exists n_0 such that

$$\sup_{s \geq 1} P_s(R - D_{n_0}) < \frac{1}{r},$$

or, conversely, that for every member of the sequence, i.e., for all $s \geq 1$,

$$P_s(D_{n_0}) \geq \frac{1}{r}.$$

Since this holds for all members of the sequence, it holds *a fortiori* for all members of the subsequence corresponding to $\{F_{s_k} : k \geq 1\}$, which converges to F. Thus, we have

$$\frac{1}{r} \leq P_{s_k}(D_{n_0}) \leq P_{s_k}(D_{n_1}) = F_{s_k}(b_{n_1}) - F_{s_k}(a_{n_1}) \longrightarrow F(b_{n_1}) - F(a_{n_1}),$$

where $n_1 \geq n_0$, and b_{n_1}, a_{n_1} are continuity points for F. It follows, therefore, that $F(+\infty) = 1$, $F(-\infty) = 0$, which show that if $\mathcal{P}$ is tight then it is relatively compact.

q.e.d.

4.9   Characteristic Functions

In this section, we shall examine some of the salient properties of characteristic functions. We have no intrinsic interest in this topic beyond the extent to which the method of characteristic functions (CF) is employed in the the discussion of central limit theorems (CLT). For this reason, proofs will not always be given and we shall confine our attention to the the special metric space (R^m, $\mathcal{B}(R^m)$, ρ). We begin with

Definition 26. Let $(\Omega, \mathcal{A}, \mathcal{P})$, $(\Psi, \mathcal{G}, \rho)$ be a probability and metric space, respectively, and suppose that $\Psi = R^m$ and $\mathcal{G} = \mathcal{B}(R^m)$. Let

$$X : \Omega \longrightarrow R^m$$

be a r.e., and P its associated distribution — defined on $\mathcal{B}(R^m)$. The **characteristic function** of the r.e. (random vector) X or, equivalently, the characteristic function of P, is defined by

$$\phi(t) = \int_{R^m} e^{it'\xi} P(d\xi), \quad t \in R^m,$$

where i is the imaginary unit obeying $i^2 = -1$.

Remark 19. It is useful for the reader to note that for the case $m = 1$ the CF is simply the Fourier transform of advanced calculus as follows: Let F be the distribution function corresponding to the distribution P and suppose the former is differentiable; let f be the density corresponding to F. Then, looking upon a variant of the integral of Definition 26 as a **Riemann** integral, we see that

$$\phi(t) = \int_{-\infty}^{\infty} e^{it\xi} f(\xi) d\xi, \quad t \in R,$$

which shows that ϕ is, indeed, the Fourier transform of the density function f. From the theory of Fourier transforms, we also know that ϕ may be "inverted" to give us back the density. Thus,

$$f(\xi) = \frac{1}{2\pi} \int_{R^m} e^{-it\xi} \phi(t) \, dt,$$

so that f and ϕ are a pair of Fourier transforms!

Some of the elementary properties of CF are given below.

Proposition 30. Let P be a probability distribution as in Definition 28 and let ϕ be its associated CF. The following statements are true:

  i. $| \phi(t) | \leq \phi(0) = 1$;

 ii. $\phi(t)$ is uniformly continuous;

iii. $\overline{\phi(t)} = \phi(-t)$;

 iv. ϕ is real valued if and only if P is a symmetric distribution;[16]

  v. if $E(| X_i |^n) < \infty$, $i = 1, 2, \ldots, m$, for some $n \geq 1$, then the derivative

$$\frac{\partial^s}{\partial t_1^{s_1} \cdots \partial t_m^{s_m}} \phi(t) = \int_{R^m} \prod_{j=1}^{m} (i\xi_j)^{s_j} e^{it'\xi} P(d\xi), \quad s = \sum_{i=1}^{m} s_i, \quad s \leq n,$$

---

[16] Symmetry here means **symmetry about the origin**; this is, perhaps, made clearest in the case of random variables, i.e., when $m = 1$. In such a case, the space is $(R, \mathcal{B})$ and symmetry means $P(A) = P(B)$, where $B = \{x : -x \in A\}$.

exists; denoting this derivative, evaluated at $t = 0$, by $\phi_{s_1 \ldots s_m}(0)$, we also have

$$\mu_{s_1, s_2, \cdots, s_m} = E(X_1^{s_1} X_2^{s_2} \ldots X_m^{s_m}) = \frac{\phi_{s_1 \ldots s_m}(0)}{i^s};\ _{17}$$

vi. when the nth order moment exists as, in v. above, then we can write the characteristic function as

$$\phi(t) = \sum_{s=0}^{n} \frac{i^s}{s_1! s_2!, \ldots, s_m!} \mu_{s_1, s_2, \ldots, s_m} t_1^{s_1} t_2^{s_2} \cdots t_m^{s_m} + o(|\ t\ |^n),$$

where the notation $o(r^p)$ means that $\lim_{r \to 0} [o(r^p)/r^p] = 0$.

Under the same conditions as above, but in the special case $m = 1$, i.e., when dealing with random variables rather than random vectors we obtain the result

$$\phi(t) = \sum_{s=0}^{n} \frac{(it)^s}{s!} E(X^s) + \frac{(it)^n}{n!} r_n(t),$$

$$|\ r_n(t)\ | \leq 3E\ |\ X\ |^n \quad \text{and such that}$$

$$\lim_{t \to 0} r_n(t) = 0.$$

Proof: The proof of i. is immediate since $|\ e^{it'\xi}\ | = 1$.

The proof of ii. is as follows. Note that

$$|\ \phi(t_1) - \phi(t_0)\ | \leq \int_{R^m} |\ e^{it_1\xi}(1 - e^{i(t^0 - t_1)'\xi})\ |\ P(d\xi)$$

$$\leq \int_{R^m} |\ 1 - e^{i(t_0 - t_1)'\xi}\ |\ P(d\xi),$$

holds for **any** $t_0, t_1 \in R^m$. Since $|\ e^{it_1'\xi}\ | = 1$ and

$$|\ 1 - e^{i(t_0 - t_1)'\xi}\ |^2 = 2(1 - cos(t_0 - t_1)'\xi)$$

the uniform continuity of ϕ becomes quite evident.

The validity of iii. is apparent from the definition of ϕ since P is a real valued function.

The validity of iv. is evident since $e^{it'\xi} = \cos t'\xi + i \sin t'\xi$, and the cosine is an even function while the sine is an odd function.

---

[17] Occasionally this is called the mixed moment of order s.

The validity of v. follows from the definition of derivatives and the fact that the integrand is uniformly bounded. Just to see what the argument involves, consider the case $m = 1$ and the fundamental definition of derivatives, viz.,

$$\phi'(t) = \lim_{h \to 0} \frac{\phi(t+h) - \phi(t)}{h}.$$

But,

$$\phi(t+h) - \phi(t) = \int_R e^{it\xi}(e^{ih\xi} - 1)P(d\xi).$$

Since

$$\left| \frac{e^{ih\xi} - 1}{h} \right| \le |\xi|,$$

the fact that $E \mid X \mid < \infty$ ensures the existence of the first derivative, by the dominated convergence theorem, Proposition 19 of Chapter 1. Moreover,

$$\frac{e^{ih\xi} - 1}{h} = \frac{\cos h\xi - 1}{h} + i \frac{\sin h\xi}{h}$$

results in an indeterminate form as $h \to 0$. Employing L'Hôpital's rule, we consider the limit

$$\lim_{h \to 0} \left[\frac{-\xi \sin h\xi}{1} + i\xi \frac{\cos h\xi}{1} \right] = i\xi,$$

which gives the apppropriate form for the derivative.

As for vi., we have already proved nearly all its claims through the discussion in the proof of part v. The only remaining aspect is the bound on the remainder, whose proof we shall omit since it is rather more trouble than the benefits to be derived therefrom. We only note for the record that in the case $m = 1$ the remainder obeys $\mid r_n(t) \mid \le 3E \mid X \mid^n$.

q.e.d.

The natural question to ask now is if a characterisitc function, say ϕ, is given, is there more than one distribution that corresponds to it? The answer, in the negative, is given by

Proposition 31. Let $(\Psi, \mathcal{G}, \rho)$ be a metric space [18] and P, ϕ be, respectively, a probability distribution and its associated characteristic

---

[18] It is generally understood in this section that $\Psi = R^m$, $\mathcal{G} = \mathcal{B}(R^m)$.

function. If there exists another distribution function, say Q, such that

$$\int_\Psi e^{it'\xi} P(d\xi) = \phi(t) = \int_\Psi e^{it'\xi} Q(d\xi),$$

then $P = Q$.

Proof: Let $\mathcal{K} = \{f : \int_\Psi f P(d\xi) = \int_\Psi f Q(d\xi)\}$. It follows from the premises of the proposition that $\mathcal{K}$ contains all functions of the form

$$S(\xi) = \sum_{r=1}^q b_r e^{it'_r \xi}.$$

Evidently, $\mathcal{K}$ is closed relative to the operation of taking limits of uniformly bounded everywhere converging sequences of functions. More precisely, if $\{f_n : n \geq 1\}$ is a sequence of uniformly bounded functions such that

$$\lim_{n\to\infty} f_n(\xi) = f(\xi), \quad \xi \in R^m,$$

then, by the dominated convergence theorem (Proposition 19 of Chapter 1),

$$\lim_{n\to\infty} \int_\Psi f_n(\xi) P(d\xi) = \int_\Psi \lim_{n\to\infty} f_n(\xi) P(d\xi) = \int_\Psi f(\xi) P(d\xi),$$

whence we conclude that $f \in \mathcal{K}$. In analysis, it is shown (Weierstrass appproximation theorem) that any continuous function over a compact set (or a bounded function over R^m) can be approximated by a sequence of uniformly bounded functions converging to it pointwise. Given any $A \in \mathcal{B}(R^m)$, define its indicator function,

$$
\begin{aligned}
I_A(\xi) &= 1 \quad \text{if } \xi \in A \\
&= 0 \quad \text{otherwise.}
\end{aligned}
$$

Evidently, $I_A \in \mathcal{K}$, for every $A \in \mathcal{B}(R^m)$. Thus, for every $A \in \mathcal{B}(R^m)$ we have

$$P(A) = \int_{R^m} I_A(\xi) P(d\xi) = \int_{R^m} I_A(\xi) Q(d\xi) = Q(A).$$

It follows, therefore, that $P = Q$.

$$\text{q.e.d.}$$

The result above raises the question: suppose we have a sequence of probability distributions and their associated characteristic functions; is it true that if the characteristic functions converge then the same is true of distribution functions? The answer to this question is yes, provided certain conditions hold. We have

Proposition 32. Let $(\Psi, \mathcal{G}, \rho)$ be a metric space and $\{P_n : n \geq 1\}$, $\{\phi_n : n \geq 1\}$ be, respectively, sequences of probability distributions (defined on $\mathcal{G}$) and their associated characteristic functions. If $\phi_n \to \phi$ **and ϕ is continuous at $t = 0$**, then there exists a distribution, P, such that ϕ is its characteristic function and $P_n \overset{\text{w}}{\to} P$.

Proof: We shall use the results of Proposition 28, which indicate that in the case of a **separable and complete space**, as R^m is with the usual Euclidean metric, tightness implies relative compactness. Thus, our first task is to show that given the premises the sequence of distributions is tight. Define the sets

$$A = [-a, a] \times [-a, a] \times \cdots \times [-a, a], \qquad (4.2)$$

$$B = [-\frac{2}{a}, \frac{2}{a}] \times \cdots \times [-\frac{2}{a}, \frac{2}{a}], \qquad (4.3)$$

where $a > 0$, and set

$$J_n = \frac{1}{(2a)^m} \int_A [1 - \phi_n(t)] \, dt = \frac{1}{(2a)^m} \int_A \left[\int_{R^m} (1 - e^{it'\xi}) P_n(d\xi) \right] dt$$

$$= \frac{1}{(2a)^m} \int_{R^m} \left[\int_A (1 - e^{it'\xi}) \, dt \right] P_n(d\xi). \qquad (4.4)$$

The last equality above is valid in view of the uniform boundedness of the integrand and Fubini's theorem, Proposition 8, Chapter 2. Noting that

$$\int_A (1 - e^{it'\xi}) \, dt = \int_A dt - \prod_{j=1}^m \int_{-a}^a e^{it_j \xi_j} \, dt_j$$

$$= (2a)^m \left[1 - \prod_{j=1}^m \left(\frac{\sin a\xi_j}{a\xi_j} \right) \right],$$

we find that

$$J_n = \int_{R^m} \left[1 - \prod_{j=1}^m \left(\frac{\sin a\xi_j}{a\xi_j} \right) \right] P_n(d\xi). \qquad (4.5)$$

To evaluate the integral of Eq. (4.5) we note that for $|\xi_j| > (2/a)$, we have $|(\sin a\xi_j/a\xi_j)| \leq \frac{1}{2}$. We conclude, therefore, that

$$J_n \geq \frac{1}{2} \int_B P_n(d\xi) = \frac{1}{2} P_n(\bar{B}). \qquad (4.6)$$

Since ϕ_n is, for every n, a characteristic function, it is continuous at zero. Thus, given any r, we may take a sufficiently small so that $J_n \leq (1/2r)$. From Eq. (4.6), we see that $P_n(B) = 1 - P_n(\bar{B}) \geq 1 - 2J_n > 1 - (1/r)$. This construction implies that if we choose a finite index n_0, then we can show that for all $n \leq n_0$ the distributions P_n are tight. Now, since ϕ [19] is **continuous** at zero and since $\phi_n \to \phi$, then, given any r, we can find m_0 such that for all $n \geq m_0$, $J_n < J + (1/kr)$, where k is a suitable integer. Take now a small enough so that $J \leq (1/sr)$, where s is another suitable integer. Hence, for any index n (and a sufficiently small), we can state

$$P_n(B) \geq 1 - 2J_n \geq 1 - 2\left(J + \frac{1}{kr}\right) \geq 1 - 2\left(\frac{1}{kr} + \frac{1}{sr}\right).$$

We may thus conclude that, for the choice $s, k \geq 4$, given any r, there exists a set B such that $P_n(B) > 1 - (1/r)$, which shows that the sequence is relatively compact. Thus, there is a subsequence, say $\{P_{n_k} : k \geq 1\}$, that converges weakly to some distribution, say P. But, this means that the limit of the corresponding subsequence, $\{\phi_{n_k} : k \geq 1\}$, of characteristic functions, is ϕ; this is so since the **original sequence converges** to ϕ. We must thus conclude that ϕ is the characteristic function corresponding to P; it follows immediately that the sequence $\{P_n : n \geq 1\}$ also converges to P. For, suppose not; then, we must be able to find another subsequence, say $\{P_{n_{k'}} : k' \geq 1\}$, such that it converges to, say P'. Again, working through the sequence of (the correspodning) characteristic functions, we must conclude that the characteristic function of P' is ϕ, since the original sequence of charcteristic functions converges to ϕ. By the uniqueness of charcteristic functions, we have that $P = P'$ and, thus, that $P_n \xrightarrow{w} P$.

q.e.d.

---

[19] Note that ϕ is not assumed to be a characteristic function; only that it is **continuous** at zero and that it is the pointwise limit of a sequence of characteristic functions.

We now give a result that states the essential equivalence between weak convergence of distributions and pointwise convergence of characteristic functions.

Proposition 33. Let $(\Psi, \mathcal{G}, \rho)$ be a metric space and $\{P, P_n : n \geq 1\}$, $\{\phi, \phi_n : n \geq 1\}$ be, respectively, sequences of probability distributions (defined on $\mathcal{G}$) and their associated characteristic functions. Then,

$$P_n \overset{w}{\to} P$$

if and only if

$$\lim_{n \to \infty} \phi_n(t) = \phi(t).$$

Proof: Necessity: Suppose $P_n \overset{w}{\to} P$. Since $e^{it'X_n}$ is a uniformly bounded function, the very definition of weak convergence implies the pointwise convergence of the associated characteristic functions.

   Sufficiency: Suppose that $\phi_n \to \phi$; then, since ϕ is a characteristic function, it is continuous at zero and hence, by Proposition 32 above, $P_n \overset{w}{\to} P$.

q.e.d.

Remark 20. The major attraction of characteristic functions, introduced into this literature by Liapounov, is that they simplify issues of convergence for sequences of random variables or vectors. Of course, random variables are much simpler to handle than random vectors. It is thus felicitous that the following result, due to H. Cramer and H. Wold, reduces issues involving the convergence of random vectors to issues involving the convergence of random variables! In presenting this result, it is more convenient to deal with the r.e. (random vectors) and random variables themselves, rather than their associated distributions. Thus, the reader should bear in mind that if $\{X, X_n : n \geq 1\}$ is a sequence of random vectors (or variables) and $\{P, P_n : n \geq 1\}$ the sequence of their respective distributions then the statement $P_n \overset{w}{\to} P$ has exactly the same meaning, in this context, as $X_n \overset{d}{\to} X$.

Proposition 34. Let $(\Psi, \mathcal{G}, \rho)$ be a metric space and $\{X_n : n \geq 1\}$ a sequence of r.e. (random vectors) with values in Ψ. Then, $X_n \overset{d}{\to} X$

if and only if, for every vector $t \in R^m$,

$$t'X_n \overset{d}{\to} t'X.$$

Proof: Let $y_n = t'X_n$ and note that the premises of the proposition state that, for any $u \in R$,

$$\phi_{y_n}(u) = E(e^{iut'X_n}) \to E(e^{iut'X}).$$

By the continuity of characteristic functions, it therefore follows that, for $u = 1$,

$$\phi_{y_n}(1) = E(e^{it'X_n}) \to E(e^{it'X}).$$

But, by Proposition 31, this implies that $X_n \overset{d}{\to} X$.

q.e.d.

The results above establish the uniqueness of the correspondence between probability distributions (or cumulative probability distribution functions) and characteristic functions. On the other hand, if we are given the form of the charctcristic function, they do not provide us with a means of establishing the particular form of the distribution function.

A particular example of how this may be done in the special case where $\Psi = R$ is given below.

Proposition 35 (Inversion Formula). Let $(R, \mathcal{B}, \rho)$ be a metric space, P a distribution function defined on $\mathcal{B}$, F the corresponding cumulative (or probability) distribution function, and ϕ the characteristic function associated with them. If $a (\leq) b \in C(F)$, i.e., if a, b are points of continuity for F, then

$$F(b) - F(a) = \lim_{d \to \infty} \frac{1}{2\pi} \int_{-d}^{d} \frac{e^{-ita} - e^{-itb}}{it} \phi(t)\, dt.$$

Proof: We have

$$\frac{1}{2\pi} \int_{-d}^{d} \frac{e^{-ita} - e^{-itb}}{it} \phi(t)\, dt = \frac{1}{2\pi} \int_{-d}^{d} \frac{e^{-ita} - e^{-itb}}{it} \left[\int_{-\infty}^{\infty} e^{it\xi} dF(\xi) \right] dt$$

$$= \frac{1}{2\pi} \int_{-\infty}^{\infty} \left[\int_{-d}^{d} \frac{e^{it(\xi-a)} - e^{it(\xi-b)}}{it} dt \right] dF(\xi)$$

$$= \frac{1}{2\pi} \int_{-\infty}^{\infty} J_d(\xi)\, dF(\xi), \qquad (4.7)$$

where, evidently,

$$J_d(\xi) = \frac{1}{2\pi} \int_{-d}^{d} \frac{e^{it(\xi-a)} - e^{it(\xi-b)}}{it} \, dt. \qquad (4.8)$$

The first equality in Eq. (4.7), follows by the definition of characteristic functions; the second, by Fubini's theorem, Proposition 9, of Chapter 2. Moreover, note that the integrand in Eq. (4.8) can be rewritten as

$$\frac{\cos t(\xi - a) - \cos t(\xi - b)}{it} + \frac{\sin t(\xi - a) - \sin t(\xi - b)}{t}.$$

The first fraction above is an **odd function**, i.e., $g(-t) = -g(t)$, while the second fraction is an **even function**, i.e., $g(-t) = g(t)$. Consequently, upon integrating over $(-d, d)$, the first term vanishes and, after the change in variable $u = \xi - a$, $v = \xi - b$, we are left with

$$J_d(\xi) = \frac{1}{2\pi} \int_{-d(\xi-a)}^{d(\xi-a)} \frac{\sin u}{u} \, du - \frac{1}{2\pi} \int_{-d(\xi-b)}^{d(\xi-b)} \frac{\sin v}{v} \, dv. \qquad (4.9)$$

We now evaluate the limit of the integrals in Eq. (4.9), as $d \to \infty$. For the case $\xi < a$ (and hence $\xi < b$), we find [20]

$$\lim_{d \to \infty} J_d = 0 \ \text{ for } \xi < a < b$$

$$= 0 \ \text{ for } \xi > b > a$$

$$= \frac{1}{2} \ \text{ for } \xi = a, \ \text{ and, hence, } \xi < b$$

$$= \frac{1}{2} \ \text{ for } \xi = b, \ \text{ and hence } \xi > a$$

$$= 1 \ \text{ for } \xi \in (a, b). \qquad (4.10)$$

Since $a, b \in C(F)$, we conclude that

$$\lim_{d \to \infty} \int_{-\infty}^{\infty} J_d(\xi) \, dF(\xi) = F(b) - F(a).$$

q.e.d.

---

[20] The relations exhibited here follow quite easily if the reader bears in mind that

$$\int_{s}^{q} \frac{\sin u}{u} \, du \longrightarrow \pi,$$

as $s \to -\infty$ and $q \to \infty$.

We close this section by presenting, without proof, a number of useful properties of characteristic functions for (scalar) random variables.

Proposition 36. Let ϕ be a function,

$$\phi : R \longrightarrow C,$$

where C is the set of complex numbers. Then, the following statements are true:

    i. if ϕ is an even, [21] nonnegative, continuous function that is convex on $[0, \infty)$, and in addition, $\lim_{t \to \infty} \phi(t) = 0$, then ϕ is a characteristic function;

    ii. if ϕ is continuous, then it is a characteristic function if and only if it is positive semidefinite, i.e., for any collection $\{t_j : t_j \in R, j = 1, 2 \ldots, n\}$ and **complex** $\{\beta_j : j = 1, 2, \ldots, n\}$, $\beta' \Phi \bar{\beta} \geq 0$, where

$$\Phi = \begin{bmatrix} \phi(t_1 - t_1) & \phi(t_1 - t_2) & \cdots & \phi(t_1 - t_n) \\ \phi(t_2 - t_1) & \phi(t_2 - t_2) & \cdots & \phi(t_n - t_2) \\ \vdots & & & \\ \phi(t_n - t_1) & \phi(t_n - t_2) & \cdots & \phi(t_n - t_n) \end{bmatrix} ;$$

    iii. if ϕ is a characteristic function of the form

$$\phi(t) = e^{\pi(t)}$$

and $\pi(t)$ is a **polynomial**, then it is a **polynomial of degree at most** 2;

    iv. if $| \phi(t_0) | = 1$, for some $t_0 \neq 0$, then there exists a random variable, say X, constructed from the cumulative (probability) distribution function F, corresponding to ϕ, such that the sequence of sets $A_n = \{\omega : X(\omega) = a + nh\}$ obeys

$$\sum_{n=-\infty}^{\infty} P(A_n) = 1,$$

    i.e., X is a **discrete** random variable;

---

[21] Note that, in view of part iii. of Proposition 30, if ϕ is even then it is a real valued function!

v. if $\mid \phi(t) \mid = \mid \phi(\gamma t) \mid = 1$, for any two distinct points t and γt such that γ is irrational, then there exists a random variable, X, and a scalar, $a \in R$, such that if $A = \{\omega : X(\omega) = a\}$ then $\mathcal{P}(A) = 1$, i.e., X is a **scalar constant**, i.e., it is a **degenerate random variable**;

vi. if $\mid \phi(t) \mid = 1$, for all $t \in R$, then, as in v., there exists a random variable, X, and a constant, a, such that $X = a$, as in v., i.e., the random variable X is **degenerate**;

vii. if $\phi(t) = 1$, for all $t \in R$, then the constant a of vi. obeys $a = 0$.

4.10 CLT for Independent Random Variables

4.10.1 Preliminaries

In the previous sections, we examined in considerable detail the concept of weak convergence and its logical ramifications. We have seen that the concepts of convergence (in distribution) of sequences of r.e. (random variables), weak convergence of sequences of probability distributions, pointwise convergence (on the continuity set of the limit function) for sequences of cumulative (probability) distribution functions, and convergence of sequences of characteristic functions are all essentially variants of the same central concept. On the other hand, the discussion of the previous sections did not supply us with the tools for determining the particular form of the distribution to which some sequence might converge.

This task is undertaken in this section. Specifically, the issue to be addressed is when does a sequence of random variables converge, and can we determine the form of the distribution of the limit to which it converges. It turns out that under a very wide set of circumstances the limiting distribution is the unit normal, and for this reason, such theorems are typically referred to as **Central Limit Theorems** (CLT).

Before we embark on this discussion, we present a useful mathematical result.

Proposition 37. Let $(\Omega, \mathcal{A}, \mathcal{P})$ be a probability space and

$$X : \Omega \longrightarrow R$$

be a random variable such that $E(X) = 0$, $E \mid X \mid^n < \infty$, for some integer $n \geq 1$, and let F be the cumulative distribution function associated with it. Then,

$$J = \int_{-\infty}^{\infty} |\xi|^n \, dF(\xi) = n \int_0^\infty \xi^{n-1}[1 - F(\xi) + F(-\xi)] \, d\xi.$$

Proof: Note that the left integral above obeys

$$J = \int_0^\infty \xi^n \, dF(\xi) + \int_{-\infty}^0 |\xi|^n \, dF(-\xi). \tag{4.11}$$

In the second integral of the right hand member of Eq. (4.11) make the change in variable from ξ to ξ and slightly rewite the first integral of the right hand member so that

$$J = -\int_0^\infty \xi^n \, d[1 - F(\xi)] + \int_0^\infty \xi^n \, dF(-\xi). \tag{4.12}$$

Interpret the integral $\int_0^\infty$ as the limit, $\lim_{c \to \infty} \int_0^c$, and use integration by parts to obtain

$$-\int_0^c \xi^n \, d[1 - F(\xi)] = -\xi^n[1 - F(\xi)] \mid_0^c + n \int_0^c \xi^{n-1}[1 - F(\xi)] \, d\xi$$

$$= -c^n[1 - F(c)] + n \int_0^c \xi^{n-1}[1 - F(\xi)] \, d\xi, \tag{4.13}$$

and, moreover, again using integration by parts,

$$\int_0^c \xi^n \, dF(-\xi) = -\xi^n F(-\xi) \mid_0^c + n \int_0^c \xi^{n-1} F(-\xi) \, d\xi$$

$$= -c^n F(-c) + n \int_0^c \xi^n F(-\xi) \, d\xi. \tag{4.14}$$

Combining Eqs. (4.13) and (4.14), we find

$$J = -\lim_{c \to \infty} c^n[1 - F(c) + F(-c)] + n \int_0^\infty \xi^{n-1}[1 - F(\xi) + F(-\xi)] \, d\xi. \tag{4.15}$$

Thus, the proof will be complete if we can show that the first term in the right member of Eq. (4.15) vanishes. We note that since

$$E \mid X \mid^n = \lim_{c \to \infty} \int_{-c}^{c} \mid \xi \mid^n dF(\xi) < \infty,$$

we must have that

$$\lim_{c \to \infty} \int_{c}^{\infty} \mid \xi \mid^n dF(\xi) = \lim_{c \to \infty} \int_{-\infty}^{-c} \mid \xi \mid^n dF(\xi) = 0. \qquad (4.16)$$

Put $A_c = \{\omega : \mid X(\omega) \mid > c\}$ and observe that

$$c^n [1 - F(c) + F(-c)] = c^n \mathcal{P}(A_c).$$

The conclusion then follows immediately by Eq. (4.16), since

$$\int_{c}^{\infty} \mid \xi \mid^n dF(\xi) + \int_{-\infty}^{-c} \mid \xi \mid^n dF(\xi) \geq c^n \mathcal{P}(A_c).$$

q.e.d.

4.10.2   Characteristic Functions
for Normal Variables

Since, as we have noted above, the central limit theorems we shall deal with involve convergence to the normal distribution, it is convenient at this junction to obtain its associated characteristic function. The notation

$$X \sim N(\mu, \Sigma)$$

is to be read: the (m-element) random vector, X, has the multivariate normal distribution with mean μ and covariance matrix Σ.[22]

Proposition 38. Let

$$X : \Omega \longrightarrow R^m$$

---

[22] Note that the density of the multivariate normal distribution is given by

$$(2\pi)^{-\frac{m}{2}} \mid \Sigma \mid^{-\frac{1}{2}} e^{-\frac{1}{2}(X-\mu)'\Sigma^{-1}(X-\mu)}.$$

Unless otherwise specified, the covariance matrix, Σ, is always assumed to be a **positive definite matrix**, notation $\Sigma > 0$.

be a random vector having the multivariate normal distribution with mean μ and covariance matrix $\Sigma > 0$. The associated characteristic function is given by

$$\phi(t) = E(e^{it'X}) = e^{it'\mu - \frac{1}{2}t'\Sigma t}.$$

Proof: By definition, the characteristic function is

$$\phi(t) = E(e^{it'X}) = (2\pi)^{-\frac{m}{2}} \mid \Sigma \mid^{-\frac{1}{2}} \int_{R^m} e^{it'\xi} e^{-\frac{1}{2}(\xi - \mu)'\Sigma^{-1}(\xi - \mu)} \, d\xi. \quad (4.17)$$

Collecting terms and completing the square, the exponent becomes

$$-\frac{1}{2}(\xi - \nu)'\Sigma^{-1}(\xi - \nu) + it'\mu - \frac{1}{2}t'\Sigma t,$$

where, $\nu = \mu + i\Sigma t$. Consequently, Eq. (4.17) may be rewritten as

$$\phi(t) = e^{it'\mu - \frac{1}{2}t'\Sigma t} \left[(2\pi)^{-\frac{m}{2}} \mid \Sigma \mid^{-\frac{1}{2}} \int_{R^m} e^{-\frac{1}{2}(\xi - \nu)'\Sigma^{-1}(\xi - \nu)} \, d\xi \right]. \quad (4.18)$$

The bracketed expression in the rightmost member of Eq. (4.18) is re-congnized as the integral of a multivariate normal density, and hence, it is equal to unity.

q.e.d.

Corollary 7. The characteristic function of the univariate normal with mean μ and variance σ^2 is given by

$$\phi(t) = e^{it'\mu - \frac{1}{2}t^2\sigma^2}.$$

Proof: Obvious by taking t to be a **scalar** and setting $\Sigma = \sigma^2$.

The following result is quite useful in reducing consideration of issues of convergence for random vectors to consideration of the the same issues for random variables.

Proposition 39. Let

$$X : \Omega \longrightarrow R^m$$

be a random vector with $E(X) = \mu$ and $\text{Cov}(X) = \Sigma$. If, for arbitrary (conformable) vectors, λ,

$$\lambda'X \sim N(\lambda'\mu, \lambda'\Sigma\lambda),$$

then

$$X \sim N(\mu, \Sigma).$$

Proof: Let $y_\lambda = \lambda'X$ and note that by the premises of the proposition and Corollary 7

$$\phi_{y_\lambda}(s) = e^{is\lambda'\mu - \frac{1}{2}s^2\lambda'\Sigma\lambda}. \tag{4.19}$$

Putting $t = s\lambda$, in Eq. (4.19), we have

$$\phi_{y_\lambda}(s) = E(e^{it'X}) = e^{it'\mu - \frac{1}{2}t'\Sigma t},$$

which, by Proposition 38, is the characteristic function of the $N(\mu, \Sigma)$ distribution function.

q.e.d.

Remark 21. The manner in which the proposition above reduces the case of random vectors to the case of **random variables** can be stated as follows: By Proposition 34, a sequence of random vectors $\{X, X_n : n \geq 1\}$

$$X_n \xrightarrow{d} X$$

if and only if, for arbitrary conformable vectors, λ,

$$\lambda'X \xrightarrow{d} \lambda'X.$$

Proposition 39 tells us that if, for arbitrary conformable vectors, λ, $\lambda'X$ is normal with mean $\lambda'\mu$ and variance $\lambda'\Sigma\lambda$ then $X \sim N(\mu, \Sigma)$. The consequence of these results is that we need only consider CLT for **univariate random variables**.

4.10.3   Convergence in Probability and Characteristic Functions

In earlier discussion, we had established that if a sequence of r.e., say $\{X_n : n \geq 1\}$, obeyed $X_n \xrightarrow{P} X$ then this fact implied that $X_n \xrightarrow{d} X$, but that the converse was not, in general, true. Here, we shall show that in a particular case this implication holds. We have

Proposition 40. Let $(\Omega, \mathcal{A}, \mathcal{P})$, $(R^m, \mathcal{B}(R^m), \rho)$ be a probability and metric space, respectively, and let

$$X_n : \Omega \longrightarrow R^m, \ n \geq 1$$

be a sequence of random vectors obeying

$$X_n \xrightarrow{\text{d}} X,$$

and suppose further that $X = K$, i.e., it is a constant. Then,

$$X_n \xrightarrow{\text{P}} K.$$

Proof: For arbitrary integer r, define the set $C_r = \{x : \rho(K, x) < (1/r)\}$ and let $\{P, P_n \cdot n \geq 1\}$ be the sequence of distributions induced by $\{X, X_n : n \geq 1\}$. Notice that for every r, $C_r \in \mathcal{B}(R^m)$ and that the induced sequence of distributions is also defined on $\mathcal{B}(R^m)$. Since C_r is a P-continuity set, the premise of the proposition implies that $\lim_{n \to \infty} P_n(C_r) = P(C_r) = 1$. On the other hand, define

$$A_{n,r} = \{\omega : X_n(\omega) \in C_r\}, \quad A_r = \{\omega : X(\omega) \in C_r\}$$

and note, for example, that we can also write, equivalently, $A_{n,r} = \{\omega : \rho(K, X(\omega)) < (1/r)\}$; note, also, that $A_{n,r} = X_n^{-1}(C_r)$, $P_n(C_r) = \mathcal{P}(A_{n,r})$, and $P(C_r) = \mathcal{P}(A_r)$. Consequently,

$$\lim_{n \to \infty} \mathcal{P}(A_{n,r}) = \lim_{n \to \infty} P_n(C_r) = P(C_r) = \mathcal{P}(A_r).$$

This means that, given any r, there exists n_0 such that, for all $n \geq n_0$,

$$\mathcal{P}(A_{n,r}) \geq \mathcal{P}(A_r) - \frac{1}{r} = 1 - \frac{1}{r},$$

or, since r is arbitrary, $\lim_{n \to \infty} \mathcal{P}(A_{n,r}) = 1$.

q.e.d.

An application of the result above may be made in the context of the following proposition.

Proposition 41. Let $\{X_n : n \geq 1\}$ be a sequence of **independent, identically distributed** random variables with mean μ. Then,

$$\frac{S_n}{n} \xrightarrow{d} \mu, \quad S_n = \sum_{j=1}^{n} X_j.$$

Proof: Put $z_n = (S_n/n)$ and note that its chracteristic function is given by

$$\phi_{z_n}(s) = E(e^{isz_n}) = \prod_{j=1}^{n} E\left(e^{i\frac{s}{n}X_j}\right) = \left[\phi\left(\frac{s}{n}\right)\right]^n,$$

where ϕ is the characteristic function of X_j. By part vi. of Proposition 30, we can write

$$\phi\left(\frac{s}{n}\right) = 1 + i\frac{s}{n}\mu + o\left(\frac{s}{n}\right).$$

It follows, therefore, from the definition of the irrational number, e, that

$$\lim_{n \to \infty} \phi_{z_n}(s) = \lim_{n \to \infty} \left[1 + i\frac{s}{n}\mu + o\left(\frac{s}{n}\right)\right]^n = e^{is\mu}.$$

By part vi. of Proposition 36, we conclude that z_n converges to a degenerate random variable; in fact, this variable is simply μ.

q.e.d.

Corollary 8. Under the conditions of Proposition 41,

$$\frac{S_n}{n} \xrightarrow{P} \mu.$$

Proof: This is obvious, by Propositions 40 and 41.

4.10.4 CLT for i.i.d. Random Variables

The method of chracteristic functions makes the proof of CLT for i.i.d. random variables rather simple. We have seen this in the proof of Proposition 41. Suppose, however, that in context of Proposition 41 we wished to determine not how (S_n/n) behaves but, rather, how $(S_n/\sqrt{n})$ does. If we retrace the steps of that proof, we shall see that the approach will fail, since replacing n by $\sqrt{n}$ in the last limit of the proof **will not yield** the irrational number e. Another, and more intuitive, way of capturing the nature of the problem is to note that the variance of $(S_n/\sqrt{n})$ is simply $\sqrt{n}\sigma^2$, which will diverge to $+\infty$ with n. Thus, we would require stronger conditions. This is quite evident in the following proposition.

Proposition 42. Let $\{X_n : n \geq 1\}$ be a sequence of i.i.d. random variables such that $E(X_1) = \mu$ and $\mathrm{Var}(X_1) = \sigma^2 < \infty$. Then,

$$\frac{S_n - E(S_n)}{\sqrt{n}} \xrightarrow{\text{d}} X, \quad X \sim N(0, \sigma^2).$$

Proof: Define $\zeta_n = [(S_n - n\mu)/\sqrt{n}]$ and note that

$$\phi_{\zeta_n}(s) = \left[\phi\left(\frac{s}{\sqrt{n}}\right)\right]^n,$$

where ϕ is the characteristic function of $X_j - \mu$. Again, by part vi. of Proposition 30, we can write

$$\phi\left(\frac{s}{\sqrt{n}}\right) = 1 - \frac{s^2}{2n}\sigma^2 + o\left(\frac{s^2}{n}\right).$$

It follows, threfore, that

$$\lim_{n \to \infty} \phi_{\zeta_n}(s) = e^{-\frac{1}{2}s^2\sigma^2},$$

which, by Corollary 7, is recognized as the characteristic function of a normal distribution with mean zero and variance σ^2.

$$\text{q.e.d.}$$

Remark 22. In the next section, where we shall take up the CLT related to the **Lindeberg** condition, we shall alter our notation somewhat to conform with the standard notation in the econometrics literature. Thus, instead of the index of the summand r.v. being i or j and the upper limit being n, we shall typically use t for the index and T for the upper limit.

4.10.5   CLT and the Lindeberg Condition

Preliminaries

As we have seen, CLT involve the examination of the limiting distribution of **normalized** sequences. For example, if $\{Y_t : t \geq 1\}$ is a sequence of random variables, the question answered by a CLT involves not that sequence precisely but rather the sequence $\{S_T : T \geq 1\}$, where $S_T = \sum_{t=1}^{T} Y_t$ or $S_T = \sum_{t=1}^{T}(Y_t - EY_t)$. Often, however, such sequences will not be well behaved, owing to the fact that their variance may grow without limit as $T \to \infty$, thus requiring a normalization. A normalization often used is $T^{-(1/2)}$, which implicitly assumes that

$$\lim_{T \to \infty} \frac{1}{T} \sum_{t=1}^{T} \text{Var}(Y_t) < \infty.$$

This sort of normalization is very common in econometrics due, chiefly, to the fact that in many areas of economics it is assumed that second moments of economic variables are bounded. However, it is not necessary to adhere to that convention; another normalization, which also has the advantage of simplifying notation, is $(1/\sigma_T)$, where $\sigma_T^2 = \sum_{t=1}^{T} \text{Var}(Y_t)$. When this normalization is employed, the entity about whose limiting behavior we are inquiring is

$$z_T = \frac{S_T}{\sigma_T} = \sum_{t=1}^{T} X_{tT} \tag{4.20}$$

where

$$S_T = \sum_{t=1}^{T}(Y_t - EY_t),$$

$$X_{tT} = \frac{Y_t - EY_t}{\sigma_T},$$

$$\sigma_T^2 = \sum_{t=1}^{T} \sigma_{tt}^2, \quad \sigma_{tt}^2 = \text{Var}(Y_t),$$

$$\text{Var}(X_{tT}) = \frac{\sigma_{tt}^2}{\sigma_T^2} = \sigma_{tT}^2. \tag{4.21}$$

An interesting consequence of the notational scheme in Eq. (4.21) is that for each T, $\sum_{t=1}^{T} \sigma_{tT}^2 = 1$.

In the discussion below, we shall employ the notation of Eqs. (4.20) and (4.21) in stating and proving CLT, but we will later "translate" the conditions entailed by this notational scheme. Thus, the main discussion will be in terms of the synthetic variables, X_{tT}, while the translations will be in terms of the more "natural" variables, $Y_t - EY_t$.

Remark 23. To facilitate the transition between these two notational frameworks, we remind the reader of the following useful fact: if F is the distribution function of a random variable X, then $F(\xi) = Pr\{X \leq \xi\}$, to be read as the probability that X will assume a value in $(-\infty, \xi]$. If $Y = aX + b$ then, provided $a > 0$, we have $Pr\{Y \leq \zeta\} = Pr\{X \leq (\zeta - b)/a\} = F[(\zeta - b)/a]$.

The Lindeberg Condition

Define, for arbitrary given r,

$$W_T = \sum_{t=1}^{T} \int_{|\xi| > \frac{1}{r}} \xi^2 \, dF_{tT}(\xi). \tag{4.22}$$

The Lindeberg condition is given by

$$\lim_{T \to \infty} W_T = 0. \tag{4.23}$$

We begin by proving a slightly more general CLT than that implied by the **Lindeberg condition** and shall return to explore the connection between the two.

Proposition 43. Let $\{Y_t : t \geq 1\}$ be a sequence of r.v. defined on the probability space $(\Omega, \mathcal{A}, \mathcal{P})$, obeying $E(Y_t) = \mu_t < \infty$, $E(Y_t - \mu_t)^2 = \sigma_{tt}^2 < \infty$. Define, now, as in Eqs. (4.20) and (4.21), the r.v. X_{tT}, S_T, and z_T. A sufficient condition for

$$z_T \xrightarrow{\text{d}} z \sim N(0,1)$$

is that, given any integer r,

$$\lim_{T \to \infty} \sum_{t=1}^{T} \int_{|\xi| > (1/r)} |\xi| \, |F_{tT}(\xi) - \Phi_{tT}(\xi)| \, d\xi = 0, \tag{4.24}$$

where F_{tT} is the distribution function of X_{tT}, and Φ_{tT} is the distribution function of a random variable that is the product of σ_{tT} and

ξ, **the latter being a** $N(0,1)$ **random variable,** [23] i.e., $\Phi_{tT}(\xi) = \Phi(\xi/\sigma_{tT})$, where Φ is the (cumulative) distribution function of the standard unit normal variable.

Proof: Define

$$g_{tT}(s) = E(e^{isX_{tT}}), \qquad g_{T}(s) = E(e^{is\frac{S_T}{\sigma_T}}) \qquad (4.25)$$

$$\psi_{tT}(s) = \int_{R} e^{is\xi}\, d\Phi_{tT}(\xi), \qquad \psi(s) = \int_{R} e^{is\xi}\, d\Phi(\xi). \qquad (4.26)$$

It is easy to verify that

$$\psi_{tT}(s) = e^{-\frac{1}{2}s^2\sigma_{tT}^2}, \qquad \psi(s) = e^{-\frac{1}{2}s^2}, \qquad \psi(s) = \prod_{t=1}^{T} \psi_{tT}(s). \qquad (4.27)$$

By Proposition 33, we shall complete the proof of this proposition if we show that

$$\lim_{T\to\infty} g_T(s) = \psi(s). \qquad (4.28)$$

Consider the difference

$$V_T^*(s) = \prod_{t=1}^{T} g_{tT}(s) - \prod_{t=1}^{T} \psi_{tT}(s). \qquad (4.29)$$

Since $\mid g_{tT}(s)\mid \,\leq 1$, $\mid \psi_{tT}(s)\mid \,\leq 1$, [24] we can obtain a bound on V_T, viz.,

$$V_T(s) = \mid V_T^*(s)\mid \,\leq \sum_{t=1}^{T} \mid g_{tT}(s) - \psi_{tT}(s)\mid \, = \sum_{t=1}^{T} \left|\int_{R} e^{is\xi} dG_{tT}(\xi)\right|, \qquad (4.30)$$

---

[23] Note that as a consequence of the definitions above

$$\int_{R} \xi\, dF_{tT}(\xi) = \int_{R} \xi\, d\Phi_{tT}(\xi) = 0$$

and

$$\int_{R} \xi^2\, dF_{tT}(\xi) = \int_{R} \xi^2\, d\Phi_{tT}(\xi) = \sigma_{tT}^2.$$

[24] By way of illustration, if $\mid a_i\mid \,\leq 1$, $\mid b_i\mid \,\leq 1$, $i = 1,2$, then we have

$$
\begin{aligned}
\mid a_1 a_2 - b_1 b_2\mid \; &= \; \mid b_2(a_1 - b_1) + a_1(a_2 - b_2)\mid \\
&\leq \; \mid b_2\mid \mid a_1 - b_1\mid + \mid a_1\mid \mid a_2 - b_2\mid \\
&\leq \; \mid a_1 - b_1\mid + \mid a_2 - b_2\mid.
\end{aligned}
$$

where

$$G_{tT}(\xi) = F_{tT}(\xi) - \Phi_{tT}(\xi). \tag{4.31}$$

In view of Footnote 23, we can also write the bound above as

$$V_T(s) \le \sum_{t=1}^{T} \left| \int_R e^{is\xi} \, dG_{tT}(\xi) \right| = \sum_{t=1}^{T} \left| \int_R [e^{is\xi} - is\xi + \frac{1}{2}s^2\xi^2] \, dG_{tT}(\xi) \right|. \tag{4.32}$$

Integrating by parts in Eq. (4.32) yields

$$V_T(s) \le \sum_{t=1}^{T} \left| is \int_R [e^{is\xi} - 1 - is\xi] G_{tT}(\xi) \, d\xi \right|. \tag{4.33}$$

This is so since

$$\lim_{c \to \infty} \left(e^{is\xi} - is + \frac{1}{2}s^2\xi^2 \right) [F_{tT}(\xi) - \Phi_{tT}(\xi)] \, |_{-c}^{c} = 0.\ [25]$$

Consequently, we need to deal only with

$$V_T(s) \le \sum_{t=1}^{T} |s| \int_R |e^{is\xi} - 1 - is\xi| |G_{tT}(\xi)| \, d\xi = \sum_{t=1}^{T} |s| J_{tT}. \tag{4.34}$$

For arbitrary integer, r, we may write the integral J_{tT}, implicitly defined in Eq. (4.32), as

$$J_{tT1} = \int_{|\xi| \le \frac{1}{r}} |e^{is\xi} - 1 - is\xi| |G_{tT}(\xi)| \, d\xi, \tag{4.35}$$

$$J_{tT2} = \int_{|\xi| > \frac{1}{r}} |e^{is\xi} - 1 - is\xi| |G_{tT}(\xi)| \, d\xi, \tag{4.36}$$

$$J_{tT} = J_{tT1} + J_{tT2}. \tag{4.37}$$

The proof will be completed if we can show that the contribution made by the J_{tT} to V_T vanishes as $T \to \infty$. Now, from the series expansion of $e^{is\xi}$, we obtain the three inequalities below:

$$|e^{is\xi} - 1 - is\xi| \le \frac{1}{2} |s|^2 |\xi|^2 \tag{4.38}$$

$$\le |e^{is\xi} - 1| + |is\xi|$$

$$\le 2 |s| |\xi|. \tag{4.39}$$

---

[25] As an example consider the middle term, which may be expressed as

$$-is\{c[1 - \Phi_{tT}(c)] - c[1 - F_{tT}(c)] - cF_{tT}(-c) + c\Phi_{tT}(-c)\},$$

and, evidently, converges to zero as $c \to \infty$.

Using the bound of Eq. (4.38) in the integral J_{tT1} and that of Eq. (4.39) in the integral J_{tT2}, we find

$$J_{tT} \le \frac{1}{2r}s^2 \int_{\xi \le \frac{1}{r}} |\, \xi \,| \,|\, G_{tT}(\xi) \,| \, d\xi + 2 \,|\, s \,| \int_{\xi > \frac{1}{r}} |\, \xi \,| \,|\, G_{tT}(\xi) \,| \, d\xi, \quad (4.40)$$

or, for notational economy,

$$J_{tT} \le \frac{1}{2r}s^2 K_{tT} + 2 \,|\, s \,| \, L_{tT}. \quad (4.41)$$

Now,

$$K_{tT} \;=\; \int_{|\xi| \le \frac{1}{r}} |\, \xi \,| \,|\, G_{tT}(\xi) \,| \, d\xi \quad (4.42)$$

$$=\; \int_0^\infty |\, \xi \,| \,|\, G_{tT}(\xi) \,| \, d\xi + \int_{-\infty}^0 |\, \xi \,| \,|\, G_{tT}(\xi) \,| \, d\xi \quad (4.43)$$

$$=\; \int_0^\infty |\, \xi \,| \,|\, G_{tT}(\xi) \,| \, d\xi + \int_0^\infty |\, \xi \,| \,|\, G_{tT}(-\xi) \,| \, d\xi \quad (4.44)$$

$$\le\; \int_0^\infty \xi[1 - \Phi_{tT}(\xi) + \Phi_{tT}(-\xi)] \, d\xi + \int_0^\infty \xi \, H_{tT}(\xi) \, d\xi \quad (4.45)$$

$$\le\; 4\sigma_{tT}^2, \quad (4.46)$$

where $H_{tT}(\xi) = 1 - F_{tT}(\xi) + F_{tT}(-\xi)$. In Eq. (4.42) we simply have the definition of K_{tT}; the transition from Eq. (4.42) to (4.43), is quite evident; the transition from Eq. (4.43) to (4.44) involves only the change in variable $\xi \to -\xi$, in the second integral. The transition from Eq. (4.44) to (4.45) involves simply rewriting, in the first integral only, G_{tT} of (4.31) as $G_{tT} = (1 - \Phi_{tT}) - (1 - F_{tT})$ and applying the triangle inequality; finally the transition from Eq. (4.45) to (4.46) is valid by Proposition 37 and Footnote 23. Collecting the results in Eqs. (4.34), (4.40), (4.41) and (4.46), we find that

$$V_T(s) \le \frac{2}{r} \,|\, s \,|^3 + 2s^2 \sum_{t=1}^T \int_{|\xi| > \frac{1}{r}} |\, \xi \,| \,|\, F_{tT}(\xi) - \Phi_{tT}(\xi) \,| \, d\xi. \quad (4.47)$$

In view of the fact that r is arbitrary, we conclude that $\lim_{T \to \infty} V_T(s) = \lim_{T \to \infty} |\, g_T(s) - \psi(s) \,| = 0$.

q.e.d.

We consider now the **Lindeberg condition** in Eq. (4.23), and its relation to the condition of Proposition 43 – Eq. (4.24).

Proposition 44. The Lindeberg condition, in Eq. (4.23), implies

   i. $\lim_{T \to \infty} \alpha_T^2 = 0$, where

$$\alpha_T^2 = \max_{1 \leq t \leq T} \sigma_{tT}^2 = \max_{1 \leq t \leq T} \mathrm{Var}(X_{tT});$$

   ii. the r.v. X_{tT} are **asymptotically negligible**, i.e., for given r and $A_{tT} = \{\omega : | X_{tT}(\omega) |> \frac{1}{r}\}$, we have

$$\lim_{T \to \infty} \max_{1 \leq t \leq T} P(A_{tT}) = 0.$$

Proof: To prove i., let r be given, define the indicator functions

$$
\begin{aligned}
I_{tT1}(\omega) &= 1 \quad \text{if } | X_{tT} | \leq \frac{1}{r} \\
&= 0 \quad \text{otherwise,} \\
I_{tT2}(\omega) &= 1 - I_{tT1}(\omega),
\end{aligned}
$$

and note that

$$X_{tT}^2 = X_{tT}^2 I_{tT1} + X_{tT}^2 I_{tT2} \leq \frac{1}{r^2} + X_{tT}^2 I_{tT2}. \qquad (4.48)$$

Consequently,

$$\sigma_{tT}^2 = \mathrm{Var}(X_{tT}) \leq \frac{1}{r^2} + \int_{|\xi|>\frac{1}{r}} \xi^2 \, dF_{tT}(\xi). \qquad (4.49)$$

It follows immediately from Eq. (4.49) that

$$\alpha_T^2 = \max_{1 \leq t \leq T} \sigma_{tT}^2 \leq \frac{1}{r^2} + \sum_{t=1}^{T} \int_{|\xi|>\frac{1}{r}} \xi^2 dF_{tT}(\xi), \qquad (4.50)$$

which proves part i., since r is arbitrary.

As for part ii., we note that by Chebyshev's inequality we have, for **any** t, $P(A_{tT}) \leq r^2 \sigma_{tT}^2 \leq r^2 \alpha_T^2$. Consequently, $\max_{1 \leq t \leq T} P(A_{tT}) \leq r^2 \alpha_T^2$, and the conclusion follows from part i.

q.e.d.

Remark 24. The results of Proposition 44 suggest that the Lindeberg condition governs the behavior of CLT in the case of asymptotically
negligible random variables, i.e., the condition in Eq. (4.23) ensures
that the X_{tT} are asymptotically negligible random variables, as well as
$\sum_{t=1}^{T} X_{tT} = z_T \sim N(0,1)$, a fact to be proved below.

Proposition 45 (Lindeberg). Let $\{Y_t : t \geq 1\}$ be a sequence of r.v.
defined on the probability space $(\Omega, \mathcal{A}, \mathcal{P})$, obeying $E(Y_t) = \mu_t < \infty$,
$E(Y_t - \mu_t)^2 = \sigma_{tt}^2 < \infty$. Define, now, as in Eqs. (4.20) and (4.21) the r.v.
X_{tT}, S_T and z_T. If Eq. (4.23) – the **Lindeberg condition** – holds,
then

$$z_T \xrightarrow{\text{d}} z \sim N(0,1).$$

Proof: We shall prove that the Lindeberg condition implies Eq. (4.24);
the conclusion of the proposition would follow, then, directly from Proposition 43.

We first show that, for arbitrary r,

$$\lim_{T \to \infty} Q_T^* = 0, \quad Q_T^* = \sum_{t=1}^{T} \int_{|\xi| > \frac{1}{r}} \xi^2 \, d\Phi_{tT}(\xi).$$

Using the results of Proposition 44 and making the change in variable
$\zeta = (\xi / \sigma_{tT})$, we find

$$
\begin{aligned}
Q_T^* &= \sum_{t=1}^{T} \sigma_{tT}^2 \int_{|\zeta| > \frac{1}{r\sigma_{tT}}} \zeta^2 \, d\Phi(\zeta) \\
&\leq \sum_{t=1}^{T} \sigma_{tT}^2 \int_{|\zeta| > \frac{1}{r\alpha_T}} \zeta^2 \, d\Phi(\zeta) \\
&= \int_{|\zeta| > \frac{1}{r\alpha_T}} \zeta^2 \, d\Phi(\zeta). \quad (4.51)
\end{aligned}
$$

By Proposition 44 (and since $\sigma_{tT}^2 < \infty$), it follows that $\lim_{T \to \infty} Q_T^* = 0$
or that, in conjunction with Eq. (4.23),

$$\lim_{T \to \infty} Q_T = 0, \quad Q_T = \int_{|\xi| > \frac{1}{r}} \xi^2 \, d[F_{tT}(\xi) + \Phi_{tT}(\xi)]. \quad (4.52)$$

We next show that Eq. (4.52) implies the condition in Eq. (4.24), which
will conclude the proof of the proposition. Now, let r be given, define

the function

$$
\begin{aligned}
h(x) &= & 0 & \quad \text{for } |x| \in \left[0, \tfrac{1}{2r}\right] \\
&= & -\tfrac{1}{3r^2} + \tfrac{4}{3}x^2 & \quad \text{for } |x| \in \left(\tfrac{1}{2r}, \tfrac{1}{r}\right] \\
&= & x^2 & \quad \text{for } |x| > \tfrac{1}{r},
\end{aligned}
$$

and note that h is an **even function**; in addition, it may be verified that it is also continuous. Moreover, note that

$$
\begin{aligned}
|h'(x)| &= & 0 & \quad \text{for } |x| \in \left(0, \tfrac{1}{2r}\right) \\
&= & \tfrac{8}{3}|x| & \quad \text{for } |x| \in \left(\tfrac{1}{2r}, \tfrac{1}{r}\right) \\
&= & 2|x| & \quad \text{for } |x| > \tfrac{1}{r},
\end{aligned}
$$

so that $h'(x)$ has discontinuities only at $\tfrac{1}{2r}$ and $\tfrac{1}{r}$. Finally, note that for $|x| > \tfrac{1}{2r}$, we have

$$
|x| \le \frac{1}{2} |h'(x)|. \tag{4.53}
$$

Putting

$$
\begin{aligned}
V_T &= \sum_{t=1}^{T} \int_{|\xi| > \frac{1}{r}} |\xi| \, | F_{tT}(\xi) - \Phi_{tT}(\xi) | \, d\xi \\
&\le \sum_{t=1}^{T} \int_{|\xi| > \frac{1}{2r}} |\xi| \, | F_{tT}(\xi) - \Phi_{tT}(\xi) | \, d\xi \\
&\le \sum_{t=1}^{T} \int_{|\xi| > \frac{1}{2r}} |h'(\xi)| \, | F_{tT}(\xi) - \Phi_{tT}(\xi) | \, d\xi \tag{4.54} \\
&= \sum_{t=1}^{T} J_{tT}, \tag{4.55}
\end{aligned}
$$

where Eq. (4.55) serves as an implicit definition of J_{tT}, we obtain

$$
J_{tT} = \int_{\xi > \frac{1}{2r}} h'(\xi) \, | G_{tT}(\xi) | \, d\xi + \int_{\xi < -\frac{1}{2r}} |h'(\xi)| \, | G_{tT}(\xi) | \, d\xi = K_{tT} + L_{tT}. \tag{4.56}
$$

The rightmost member of Eq. (4.56) serves to define K_{tT} and L_{tT}, and for notational simplicity, we have again used the notation $G_{tT} =$

$F_{tT} - \Phi_{tT}$. Make the change in variable $\zeta = -\xi$ and note that

$$
\begin{aligned}
L_{tT} &= -\int_{\infty}^{\frac{1}{2r}} |h'(-\zeta)| \, |G_{tT}(-\zeta)| \, d\zeta \\
&= \int_{\frac{1}{2r}}^{\infty} |h'(\zeta)| \, |G_{tT}(-\zeta)| \, d\zeta \\
&\leq \int_{\frac{1}{2r}}^{\infty} h'(\zeta) F_{tT}(-\zeta) \, d\zeta + \int_{\frac{1}{2r}}^{\infty} h'(\zeta) \Phi_{tT}(-\zeta) \, d\zeta. \quad (4.57)
\end{aligned}
$$

In Eq. (4.57), integrate by parts to obtain

$$
\begin{aligned}
L_{tT} &\leq h(\zeta)[F_{tT}(-\zeta) + \Phi_{tT}(-\zeta)] \Big|_{\frac{1}{2r}}^{\infty} + \int_{\frac{1}{2r}}^{\infty} h(\zeta) \, d[F_{tT}(\zeta) + \Phi_{tT}(\zeta)] \\
&= \int_{\frac{1}{2r}}^{\infty} h(\zeta) \, d[F_{tT}(-\zeta) + \Phi_{tT}(-\zeta)], \quad (4.58)
\end{aligned}
$$

in view of the fact that $\lim_{x \to (1/2r)} h(x) = 0$. Finally, make the change in variable $\zeta \to -\zeta$ and rewrite Eq. (4.58) as

$$
L_{tT} \leq \int_{-\infty}^{-\frac{1}{2r}} h(\zeta) \, d[F_{tT}(\zeta) + \Phi_{tT}(\zeta)]. \quad (4.59)
$$

Next, using the triangle inequality, we have from the definition of K_{tT} in Eq. (4.56)

$$
\begin{aligned}
K_{tT} &= \int_{\frac{1}{2r}}^{\infty} h'(\zeta) \, |[1 - \Phi_{tT}(\zeta)] - [1 - F_{tT}(\zeta)]| \, d\zeta \\
&\leq \int_{\frac{1}{2r}}^{\infty} h'(\zeta)[1 - \Phi_{tT}(\zeta)] d\zeta + \int_{\frac{1}{2r}}^{\infty} h'(\zeta)[1 - F_{tT}(\zeta)] d\zeta. \quad (4.60)
\end{aligned}
$$

Again, integrating by parts yields

$$
K_{tT} \leq \int_{\frac{1}{2r}}^{\infty} h(\zeta) \, d[F_{tT}(\zeta) + \Phi_{tT}(\zeta)]. \quad (4.61)
$$

Combining Eqs. (4.56), (4.59) and (4.61) we obtain

$$
\begin{aligned}
J_{tT} = K_{tT} + L_{tT} &\leq \int_{\frac{1}{2r}}^{\infty} h(\zeta) \, d[F_{tT}(\zeta) + \Phi_{tT}(\zeta)] \\
&\quad + \int_{-\infty}^{-\frac{1}{2r}} h(\zeta) \, d[F_{tT}(\zeta) + \Phi_{tT}(\zeta)] \\
&= \int_{|\zeta| > \frac{1}{2r}} h(\zeta) \, d[F_{tT}(\zeta) + \Phi_{tT}(\zeta)]. \quad (4.62)
\end{aligned}
$$

The last member of Eq. (4.62) above is valid because h is an **even function**. In addition, since for $\mid x \mid > \frac{1}{2r}$, $\mid h(x) \mid \leq x^2$, we have

$$V_T \leq \sum_{t=1}^{T} J_{tT} \leq \sum_{t=1}^{T} \int_{|\zeta|>\frac{1}{2r}} \zeta^2 \, d[F_{tT}(\zeta) + \Phi_{tT}(\zeta)]. \qquad (4.63)$$

Consequently, since r is arbitrary, we conclude, by Eq. (4.52),

$$\lim_{T \to \infty} V_T = 0.$$

q.e.d.

Remark 25. As indicated at the begining of this discussion, we now offer a translation of the conditions in Proposition 45 [Eqs. (4.22), (4.23)] and Proposition 43 [Eq. (4.24)]. Since in economics it is customary to work not with $z_T = (S_T/\sigma_T)$, but rather with $w_T = (S_T/\sqrt{T})$, we wish to restate the conditions of Eqs. (4.22), (4.23) and (4.24) in terms of the variables $Y_t - \mu_t$, rather than X_{tT}. We first note, however, that since

$$w_T = \frac{\sigma_T}{\sqrt{T}} z_T,$$

and, by the conditions of Propositions 42 and 44,

$$z_T \xrightarrow{\text{d}} z \sim N(0,1),$$

it follows that $(\sigma_T/\sqrt{T})$ must be well behaved as $T \to \infty$. Thus, before we proceed, **we must add to the conditions of Propositions 43 and 45**, the requirement that

$$\lim_{T \to \infty} \frac{\sigma_T^2}{T} = \lim_{T \to \infty} \frac{1}{T} \sum_{t=1}^{T} \sigma_{tt}^2 = \sigma^2 < \infty. \qquad (4.64)$$

With this proviso, the entities in Eqs. (4.22) and (4.24) may be modified as follows: make the change in variable $\zeta = \sigma_T \xi$, denote the distribution of $Y_t - \mu_t$ by F_t and by Φ_t denote the distribution function of the product of σ_{tt} and a unit normal random variable; note that **subject to these changes** Eqs. (4.23) and (4.24) are rendered, respectively, as

$$\lim_{T \to \infty} W_T = \lim_{T \to \infty} \frac{1}{\sigma_T^2} \sum_{t=1}^{T} \int_{|\zeta|>\frac{\sigma_T}{r}} \zeta^2 \, dF_t(\zeta) = 0,$$

$$\lim_{T \to \infty} \frac{1}{\sigma_T^2} \sum_{t=1}^{T} \int_{|\zeta|>\frac{\sigma_T}{r}} \mid \zeta \mid \mid F_t(\zeta) - \Phi_t(\zeta) \mid d\zeta = 0.$$

Remark 26. We see that the proof of Proposition 45 consists of showing that the **Lindeberg condition** implies the condition of Proposition 43. On the other hand, from Proposition 44, we have that **it also implies** $\max_{1 \leq t \leq T} \sigma_{tT}^2 \to 0$, as well as the validity of Eq. (4.52). Consequently, if $\lim_{T \to \infty} a_T^2 = 0$ **and** $V_T(s)$ **of Eq. (4.30) converges to zero with** T, i.e., $z_T \xrightarrow{d} z \sim N(0,1)$, then it follows from Eq. (4.63) that the **Lindeberg condition is also necessary.** This modified converse (of Proposition 45) is often lumped together with the proposition and referred to as the Lindeberg-Feller CLT.

When moments higher than the second are known to exist, it is possible to employ another condition for convergence; this is embodied in the CLT due to Liapounov.

Proposition 46. Let $\{Y_t : t \geq 1\}$ be a sequence of r.v. defined on the probability space $(\Omega, \mathcal{A}, \mathcal{P})$, obeying $E(Y_t) = \mu_t < \infty$, $E(Y_t - \mu_t)^2 = \sigma_{tt}^2 < \infty$,[26] and for some constant $\delta > 0$, $E \mid Y_t - \mu_t \mid^{2+\delta} = \rho_{tt}^{2+\delta} < \infty$. Define, now, as in Eqs. (4.20) and (4.21) the entities z_T, S_T, σ_T^2, and in addition,

$$\rho_T^{2+\delta} = \sum_{t=1}^{T} \rho_{tt}^{2+\delta}. \tag{4.65}$$

Suppose further that σ_T^2 diverges to $+\infty$ with T. A sufficient condition for

$$z_T \xrightarrow{d} z \sim N(0,1)$$

is that

$$\lim_{T \to \infty} \frac{\rho_T^{2+\delta}}{\sigma_T^{2+\delta}} = 0. \tag{4.66}$$

Proof: We shall show that the premise of this proposition implies the **Lindeberg** condition. We have

$$E \mid Y_t - \mu_t \mid^{2+\delta} = \int_R \mid \zeta \mid^{2+\delta} dF_t(\zeta)$$

$$\geq \int_{\mid \zeta \mid \frac{\sigma_T}{r}} \mid \zeta \mid^{2+\delta} dF_t(\zeta)$$

$$\geq (\frac{\sigma_T}{r})^{\delta} \int\!\!\int_{\mid \zeta \mid > \frac{\sigma_T}{r}} \zeta^2 dF_t(\zeta). \tag{4.67}$$

---

[26] Strictly speaking, this and the preceding condition are implied by the following, which states that the sequence of r.v. in question possesses finite $(2+\delta)^{th}$ moments.

It follows immediately that

$$\frac{1}{\sigma_T^2}\sum_{t=1}^{T}\int_{|\zeta|>\frac{\sigma_T}{r}}\zeta^2 d\zeta \le r^\delta \frac{\rho_T^{2+\delta}}{\sigma_T^{2+\delta}},\qquad(4.68)$$

which, by the premise of this proposition, implies that the **Lindeberg condition** is satisfied. The result then follows by Proposition 43.

q.e.d.

Remark 27. The CLT we have examined in this section assert that for a certain sequence of r.v. (such as, for example, z_T of Propositions 43, 45, or 46), the limiting distribution is the unit normal. The practical significance of such results is to enable us to approximate the distribution of $\sigma_T z_T$, or of $\sqrt{T}w_T$, by $N(0,\sigma_T^2)$. The results of the propositions, however, do not indicate anything about the magnitude of the error entailed by such approximations. We present, without proof, the Berry–Esseen theorem which attempts to provide such an answer.

Proposition 47 (Berry–Esseen). Let $\{Y_t : t \ge 1\}$ be a sequence of r.v. defined on the probability space $(\Omega,\ \mathcal{A},\ \mathcal{P})$, obeying $E(Y_t) = \mu_t <$ $\infty,$ [27] $E(Y_t)^2 = \sigma_{tt}^2 < \infty$, and for some constant $\delta > 0$, $E\mid Y_t\mid^{2+\delta}=$ $\rho_{tt}^{2+\delta} < \infty$. Define, now, as in Eqs. (4.20) and (4.21), the entities z_T, S_T, σ_T^2, and in addition,

$$\rho_T^{2+\delta} = \sum_{t=1}^{T}\rho_{tt}^{2+\delta}.\qquad(4.69)$$

Then, for $\delta \in (0,1]$,

$$\sup_{x\in R}\mid D_T(x) - \Phi(x)\mid \le C\left(\frac{\rho_T}{\sigma_T}\right)^{2+\delta},$$

where D_T is the distribution function of z_T, Φ is the (cumulative) distribution function of the unit normal and C **depends only on** δ.

Proof: See Chow and Teicher (1988, p. 299).

---

[27] For simplicity of exposition we shall assume that $\mu_t = 0$, for all t.

Chapter 5

Dependent Sequences

5.1 Preliminaries

When dealing with convergence properties of sequences in the previous two chapters, we had obtained specific results, generally, only for the case where the elements of the sequence in question were **independent** or minimally **uncorrelated** random variables or random elements. In this chapter, we shall examine some of the same problems as before, especially laws of large numbers and CLT in the case where the constituent elements are **dependent random variables, or random elements**. We shall examine two general classes of dependence, **martingale** and **stationary** sequences.

In so far as martingale processes involve extensive use of conditional expectations, we shall find it convenient in several applications to translate the definitions of Chapter 2 in terms of the concepts of distribution functions, or densities. We recall from Section 4 of Chapter 2 that, if X is a r.v. (or random element where appropriate) defined on the probability space $(\Omega, \mathcal{A}, \mathcal{P})$ and if $\mathcal{G}$ is a σ-algebra contained in $\mathcal{A}$, the conditional expectation of X, relative to the σ-algebra $\mathcal{G}$, is a $\mathcal{G}$-**measurable function**, say $E(X \mid \mathcal{G})$, such that, for all sets $A \in \mathcal{G}$,

$$\int_A X \, d\mathcal{P} = \int_A E(X \mid \mathcal{G}) \, d\mathcal{P}. \tag{5.1}$$

The context in which conditional expectations would be useful when discussing martingales is the following: we have an entity, say $S_n = \sum_{i=1}^n X_i$, and we wish to determine the conditional expectation of S_n, given S_{n-1}. To adapt to the present context, let

$$\mathcal{A}_n = \sigma(X_1, X_2, \ldots, X_n). \tag{5.2}$$

It is easy to see that

$$\mathcal{A}_{n-1} \subset \mathcal{A}_n \subset \mathcal{A}. \tag{5.3}$$

Thus, to deal with S_n it would suffice to operate with the space $(\Omega, \mathcal{A}_n, \mathcal{P})$. The spaces induced by

$$X_{(n)} \doteq (X_1, X_2, \ldots, X_n), \qquad X_{(n-1)} = (X_1, X_2, \ldots, X_{n-1}) \tag{5.4}$$

are, respectively, $(R^n, \mathcal{B}(R^n), P^{(n)})$ and $(R^{n-1}, \mathcal{B}(R^{n-1}), P^{(n-1)})$. Now, if $A \in \mathcal{A}_{n-1}$, and thus, say $X_{(n-1)}(A) = B_1 \times B_2 \times \cdots \times B_{n-1} = B \in \mathcal{B}(R^{n-1})$, then we must have that $X_{(n)}(A) = B \times R$. Consequently, defining

$$P^{(n)}(B \times R) = \mathcal{P}(A), \qquad P^{(n-1)}(B) = \mathcal{P}(A) \tag{5.5}$$

respects the consistency requirement for product spaces.

In this context, how are we to define the conditional expectation of $g(X_{(n)})$, relative to $\mathcal{A}_{n-1}$ or, equivalently, **given** $X_{(n-1)}$, where g is an arbitrary measurable function? When the distributions $P^{(n)}$ and $P^{(n-1)}$ have densities, respectively, f_n, f_{n-1}, then

$$P^{(n)}(B_n) = \int_{B_n} f_n(\xi_{(n)}) \, d\xi_{(n)}, \quad P^{(n-1)}(B_{n-1}) = \int_{B_{n-1}} f_{n-1}(\xi_{(n-1)}) \, d\xi_{(n-1)}, \tag{5.6}$$

and the translation is quite transparent, yielding

$$\begin{aligned}
J_1 &= \int_A g(X_{(n)}) \, d\mathcal{P} = \int_{B_1 \times \cdots \times B_{n-1} \times R} g(\xi_1, \ldots, \xi_n) \, dP^{(n)} \\[2mm]
&= \int_{B_1 \times \cdots \times B_{n-1} \times R} g(\xi_{(n)}) f_n(\xi_{(n)}) \, d\xi_{(n)} \\[2mm]
&= \int_{B_1} \int_{B_2} \cdots \int_{B_{n-1}} \int_R g(\xi_1, \ldots, \xi_n) f_n(\xi_1, \ldots, \xi_n) \, d\xi_n \cdots d\xi_1 \quad (5.7)
\end{aligned}$$

and

$$J_2 = \int_A E[g(X_{(n)}) \mid X_{(n-1)}] \, d\mathcal{P} = \int_{B_1 \times \cdots \times B_{n-1}} \zeta \, dP^{(n-1)}$$

$$= \int_{B_1 \times \cdots \times B_{n-1}} \zeta f_{n-1}(\xi_1, \ldots, \xi_{n-1}) \, d\xi_{n-1} \ldots d\xi_1$$

$$= \int_{B_1} \int_{B_2} \cdots \int_{B_{n-1}} \zeta f_{n-1}(\xi_1, \ldots, \xi_{n-1}) \, d\xi_{n-1} \ldots d\xi_1. \tag{5.8}$$

The problem now is how to reconcile Eqs. (5.7) and (5.8), i.e., how to define the function ζ. Return to Eq. (5.7) and rewrite the integrand as

$$g(\xi_{(n)}) f_n(\xi_{(n)}) = f_{n-1}(\xi_{(n-1)}) g(\xi_{(n)}) h(\xi_n \mid \xi_{(n-1)}), \tag{5.9}$$

$$h(\xi_n \mid \xi_{(n-1)}) = \frac{f_n(\xi_{(n)})}{f_{n-1}(\xi_{(n-1)})}. \tag{5.10}$$

Equation (5.7) may, as a consequence, be rewritten as

$$J_1 = \int_{B_1} \int_{B_2} \cdots \int_{B_{n-1}} f_{n-1}(\xi_{(n-1)}) \left[\int_R g(\xi_{(n-1)}, \xi_n) h(\xi_n \mid \xi_{(n-1)}) \, d\xi_n \right] d\xi_{(n-1)}. \tag{5.11}$$

Comparing with Eq. (5.8) we conclude that if we define

$$\zeta(\xi_{(n-1)}) = \int_R g(\xi_{(n-1)}, \xi_n) h(\xi_n \mid \xi_{(n-1)}) \, d\xi_n \tag{5.12}$$

then $J_1 = J_2$, and thus, we should have a set of equations – Eqs. (5.7) and (5.8) – consistent with the requirement of conditional expectations given in Eq. (1). Hence, in the case where the random variables (or random elements) have distributions possessing densities, **we define conditional expectation by**

$$E(g(X_{(n)}) \mid X_{(n-1)}) = \int_R g(X_{(n-1)}, \xi_n) h(\xi_n \mid X_{(n-1)}) \, d\xi_n, \tag{5.13}$$

which is, evidently, $\mathcal{A}_{n-1}$-measurable and obeys Eq. (5.1) as well.

5.2 Definition of Martingale Sequences

Martingale theory, like so much of (early) probability theory, owes its origins to gambling problems. Many of the concepts we shall define below are essentially the mathematical idealization and abstraction of basic issues in games of chance. This will, perhaps, become self evident as we set forth the definitions. The origins of the theory notwithstanding, applications of its theorems are quite extensive and occur at very basic theoretical as well as applied levels. Our interest in this topic is motivated by its relevance to issues of convergence, as they arise in the case of laws of large numbers and CLT for **dependent stochastic sequences**.

Definition 1. Let $(\Omega, \mathcal{A}, \mathcal{P})$ be a probability space and consider the sequence of (sub) σ-algebras

$$\mathcal{A}_{n-1} \subset \mathcal{A}_n(\subset \mathcal{A}), \quad n \in N,$$

where N is a subset of the integers in $(-\infty, \infty)$. The collection $\{\mathcal{A}_n : n \in N\}$ is said to be a **stochastic basis**.

If $\{X_n : n \in N\}$ is a sequence of random variables defined on the probability space above such that X_n is $\mathcal{A}_n$-measurable and $\{\mathcal{A}_n : n \in N\}$ is a stochastic basis, then the sequence of pairs $\{(X_n, \mathcal{A}_n) : n \in N\}$ is said to be a **stochastic sequence**. [1]

If $E \mid X_n \mid^p < \infty$, $n \in N$, $p > 0$, the sequence is said to be an L^p-**sequence**, while if $\sup_{n \in N} E \mid X_n \mid^p < \infty$, the sequence is said to be an L^p-**bounded stochastic sequence**.

Remark 1. Although the terms "stochastic basis" and "stochastic sequence" were defined in terms of a bilateral sequence, in the remainder of our discussion, we shall take the set N to consist of zero and the **positive integers** only, i.e., we shall take N to be a subset of $\{0, 1, 2, 3, ...\}$.

Definition 2. In the context of Definition 1, suppose the the stochastic sequence therein obeys $E \mid X_n \mid < \infty$, for all $n \geq 0$. The sequence is said to be

   i. a **martingale** [2] if $E(X_{n+1} \mid \mathcal{A}_n) = X_n$;

   ii. a **submartingale** if $E(X_{n+1} \mid \mathcal{A}_n) \geq X_n$;

   iii. a **supermartingale** if $E(X_{n+1} \mid \mathcal{A}_n) \leq X_n$;

   iv. a **martingale difference** if $E(X_{n+1} \mid \mathcal{A}_n) = 0$.

---

[1] If the set N were not discreet but rather continuous, the sequence of pairs would have been termed a **stochastic process**.

[2] The term *martingale* seems to have originated in gambling practice where the strategy of doubling the bet after each loss and terminating the game after the first win is called a *martingale*.

Example 1. Let $(\Omega, \mathcal{A}, \mathcal{P})$ be a probability space, $\{\mathcal{A}_n : n \geq 0\}$ be a sequence of (sub) σ-algebras such that $\mathcal{A}_{n-1} \subset \mathcal{A}_n$ and ξ be a random variable defined on the probability space. Put $X_n = E(\xi \mid \mathcal{A}_n)$, $n \geq 0$. Clearly, by the discussion of Chapter 2, X_n is a sequence of $\mathcal{A}_n$-measurable functions (random variables), and $\{\mathcal{A}_n : n \geq 0\}$ is a stochastic basis. If $\xi \in L^1$, then $\{(X_n, \mathcal{A}_n) : n \geq 0\}$ is a martingale, since

$$E(X_{n+1} \mid \mathcal{A}_n) = E[E(\xi \mid \mathcal{A}_{n+1}) \mid \mathcal{A}_n] = E(\xi \mid \mathcal{A}_n) = X_n.$$

In the preceding, the first and last equalities follow from the definition of the process and the second from part ix., Proposition 19 of Chapter 2.

Example 2. Let $(\Omega, \mathcal{A}, \mathcal{P})$ be a probability space, $\{\xi_n : n \geq 0\}$ be a sequence of r.v. (with $\xi_0 = 0$), and define $\sigma(\xi_0) = (\emptyset, \Omega)$, $\mathcal{A}_n = \sigma(\xi_1, \ldots, \xi_n)$, $S_n = \sum_{i=0}^{n} \xi_i$. Two facts are immediately recognized: (a) S_n is $\mathcal{A}_n$-measurable, and (b) $\{(S_n, \mathcal{A}_n) : n \geq 0\}$ is a stochastic sequence, where S_0, or perhaps S_{-1}, is defined to be a **fixed constant**. Is it a martingale? Well, putting $S_n = S_{n-1} + \xi_n$, $n \geq 1$, we see that we have a martingale only if $E(\xi_n \mid \mathcal{A}_{n-1}) = 0$. But, if the initial sequence is one of zero mean independent elements, then clearly, $E(S_n \mid \mathcal{A}_{n-1}) = S_{n-1}$, which shows the stochastic sequence to be a **martingale**.

Notice, further, that $\{(\xi_n, \mathcal{A}_n) : n \geq 0\}$ is also a stochastic sequence, which is, in fact, a **martingale difference**.

Remark 2. Note that Example 2 depicts the typical gambler's wealth (or gambler's ruin) problem. If a gambler enters a game with initial wealth S_0, his wealth after n games is S_n, provided ξ_i represents his winnings (losses, if negative) at game i.

Many of the concepts we shall presently introduce have been motivated by gambling. For example, the gambler's ruin problem can be posed as: will a gambler, whatever his initial wealth, be ruined in finite time with probability one? In precise terms, this question asks is it true that, for **any given** S_0, there exists $N_0 < \infty$, such that $\mathcal{P}(A) = 1$, where $A = \{\omega : S_{N_0} = 0, S_n > 0, n < N_0\}$?[3] It is such concerns that

---

[3] It is understood, in this context, that once the gambler loses his initial wealth, i.e., $S_n = 0$, the game ceases.

have been responsible for the formulation of the problems that led to the martingale convergence theorem as well as various notions of stopping rules.

5.3   Basic Properties of Martingales

We now establish a few simple properties for martingales, submartingales, and supermartingales.

Proposition 1. Let $(\Omega, \mathcal{A}, \mathcal{P})$ be a probability space, $\{\mathcal{A}_n : n \geq 0\}$ be a sequence of (sub) σ-algebras such that $\mathcal{A}_{n-1} \subset \mathcal{A}_n$, and $\{X_n : n \geq 0\}$ a sequence of random variables defined on the probability space. Put $X = \{(X_n, \mathcal{A}_n) : n \geq 0\}$; the following statements are true:

    i. if $\alpha \in R$ and X is a sub- or sup- or (plain) martingale, then $X^* = \{(X_n - \alpha, \mathcal{A}_n) : n \geq 0\}$ is a sub- or sup- or a plain martingale;

    ii. if X is a martingale, then $X^+ = \{(X_n^+, \mathcal{A}_n) : n \geq 0\}$ and $X^- = \{(X_n^-, \mathcal{A}_n) : n \geq 0\}$ are submartingales;

    iii. if X is a submartingale, then X^+ is also a submartingale;

    iii. if X is a supermartingale, then X^- is a submartingale.

Proof: To prove i., we need only show that $X_n - \alpha$ is an L^1, $\mathcal{A}_n$-measurable function, provided X_n shares these properties. The L^1 property is evident; moreover, for any $c \in R$, the $\mathcal{A}_n$-measurability of X_n implies $A = \{\omega : X_n(\omega) < c\} \in \mathcal{A}_n$. But, then,

$$A_\alpha = \{\omega : X_n(\omega) - \alpha < c\} = \{\omega : X_n(\omega) < c + \alpha\},$$

which establishes the validity of part i.

The proof for ii., iii., and iv. is as follows: suppose X is either a martingale or a submartingale; then,

$$\begin{aligned} X_n^+ &= \max(0, X_n) \leq \max\left[0, E(X_{n+1} \mid \mathcal{A}_n)\right] \\ &\leq E(X_{n+1}^+ \mid \mathcal{A}_n), \end{aligned} \tag{5.14}$$

which establishes that X^+ is a submartingale. The validity of the last inequality in Eq. (5.14) may be justified as follows: by the definition of conditional expectation, put

$$E(X_{n+1} \mid A_n) = E(X_{n+1}^+ \mid A_n) - E(X_{n+1}^- \mid A_n), \qquad (5.15)$$

and observe that

$$
\begin{aligned}
\max\left[0,\ E(X_{n+1} \mid A_n)\right] &= \max\left[0,\ E(X_{n+1}^+ \mid A_n) - E(X_{n+1}^- \mid A_n)\right] \\
&\leq E(X_{n+1}^+ \mid A_n). \qquad (5.16)
\end{aligned}
$$

Next, suppose X is either a martingale or a supermartingale. Then,

$$
\begin{aligned}
X_n^- &= \max(0,\ -X_n) \leq \max\left[0,\ -E(X_{n+1} \mid A_n)\right] \\
&= \max\left[0,\ E(X_{n+1}^- \mid A_n) - E(X_{n+1}^+ \mid A_n)\right] \\
&\leq E(X_{n+1}^- \mid A_n), \qquad (5.17)
\end{aligned}
$$

which establishes X^- to be a submartingale.

q.e.d.

Proposition 2. Let $(\Omega,\ A,\ P)$ be a probability space, $\{A_n : n \geq 0\}$ be a sequence of (sub) σ-algebras such that $A_{n-1} \subset A_n$, $\{X_n : n \geq 0\}$ a sequence of random variables defined on the probability space and put $X = \{(X_n, A_n) : n \geq 0\}$. The following statements are true:

i. if X is a **martingale**, then EX_n is a **constant**;

ii. if X is a **submartingale**, then $EX_n \geq EX_{n-1}$, i.e., it is a monotonic nondecreasing function of n;

iii. if X is a **martingale**, then $E \mid X_n \mid \geq E \mid X_{n-1} \mid$, $n \geq 1$;

iv. if X is an L^p-sequence, $p \geq 1$, and a **martingale**, then

$$\{(\mid X \mid^p, A_n) : n \geq 1\}$$

is a **submartingale**;

v. if X is a **submartingale** and

$$f : R \longrightarrow R$$

is a monotone nondecreasing convex function, then $Y = \{(Y_n, \mathcal{A}_n) : n \geq 1\}$ is also a **submartingale**, where $Y_n = f(X_n)$.

Proof: To prove i., we note that, both by the definition of a martingale and the properties of conditional expectations, we have

$$\int_\Omega X_{n+1} \, d\mathcal{P} = \int_\Omega E(X_{n+1} \mid \mathcal{A}_n) \, d\mathcal{P} = \int_\Omega X_n \, d\mathcal{P}. \tag{5.18}$$

But, Eq. (5.18) simply states that $EX_{n+1} = EX_n$.

To prove ii., we similarly note that

$$\int_\Omega X_{n+1} \, d\mathcal{P} = \int_\Omega E(X_{n+1} \mid \mathcal{A}_n) \, d\mathcal{P} \geq \int_\Omega X_n \, d\mathcal{P}. \tag{5.19}$$

For iii., we note that since $\mid X_n \mid - X_n^+ + X_n^-$, the result follows directly from part ii. of Proposition 1.

For iv., we note that by part ii. of Proposition 1 we obtain $E(\mid X_{n+1} \mid \mid \mathcal{A}_n) \geq \mid X_n \mid$. Moreover, from the Liapounov inequality (Proposition 14 of Chapter 2), we have for $p \geq 1$,

$$[E(\mid X_{n+1} \mid^p \mid \mathcal{A}_n)]^{\frac{1}{p}} \geq E(\mid X_{n+1} \mid \mid \mathcal{A}_n) \geq \mid X_n \mid, \tag{5.20}$$

or $E(\mid X_{n+1} \mid^p \mid \mathcal{A}_n) \geq \mid X_n \mid^p$.

Finally, for v., we have

$$E(Y_{n+1} \mid \mathcal{A}_n) = E[f(X_{n+1}) \mid \mathcal{A}_n] \geq f(E[X_{n+1} \mid \mathcal{A}_n])$$

$$\geq f(X_n) = Y_n.$$

The first and last equality reflect the definition of Y_n ; the first **inequality** follows by the convexity of the function f; the second inequality reflects the monotone (nondecreasing) property of f and the fact that X is a **submartingale**.

q.e.d.

5.4 Square Integrable Sequences

When we take up the discussion of CLT for martingale processes, we will deal with L^2-sequences, or **square integrable** sub- or super- or just plain martingales. Thus, it is desirable to introduce at this stage a few additional concepts.

Definition 3. Let $(\Omega, \mathcal{A}, \mathcal{P})$ be a probability space, $\{\mathcal{A}_n : n \geq 0\}$ be a stochastic basis, i.e., a sequence of (sub) σ-algebras such that $\mathcal{A}_{n-1} \subset \mathcal{A}_n$, and $\{X_n : n \geq 0\}$ a sequence of random variables defined on the probability space above. Suppose further that X_n is $\mathcal{A}_{n-1}$-measurable, and $\mathcal{A}_0 = \mathcal{A}_{-1}$. The stochastic sequence $X = \{(X_n, \mathcal{A}_{n-1}) : n \geq 0\}$ is said to be **predictable**. If, in addition, $X_0 = 0$, $\mathcal{A}_{-1} = \mathcal{A}_0 = (\emptyset, \Omega)$, and $X_n \leq X_{n+1}$, $n \geq 0$, then X is said to be an **increasing predictable sequence**.

Proposition 3 (Doob Decomposition). Let $(\Omega, \mathcal{A}, \mathcal{P})$ be a probability space, $\{\mathcal{A}_n : n \geq 0\}$ be a stochastic basis, [i.e., a sequence of (sub) σ-algebras such that $\mathcal{A}_{n-1} \subset \mathcal{A}_n$,] $\{X_n : n \geq 0\}$ be a sequence of random variables such that X_n is $\mathcal{A}$-measurable, and put $X = \{(X_n, \mathcal{A}_n) : n \geq 0\}$. If X is a **submartingale**, then there exist a **martingale** $m = (m_n, \mathcal{A}_n)$, $n \geq 0$, and an **increasing predictable sequence**, $a = (a_n, \mathcal{A}_{n-1})$, $n \geq 0$, such that

$$X_n = m_n + a_n,$$

and moreover, this decomposition is **unique**.

Proof: Putting $m_0 = X_0$, $a_0 = 0$, we have, after adding and substracting various entities,

$$X_n = m_n + a_n, \tag{5.21}$$

where

$$m_n = m_0 + \sum_{j=0}^{n-1}[X_{j+1} - E(X_{j+1} \mid \mathcal{A}_j)], \tag{5.22}$$

$$a_n = \sum_{j=0}^{n-1}[E(X_{j+1} \mid \mathcal{A}_j) - X_j]. \tag{5.23}$$

We need only establish the uniqueness of the decomposition and the properties of the decomposing processes. Clearly, m is an L^1-sequence; evidently, m_n is $\mathcal{A}_n$-measurable, by construction. Moreover, since

$$m_{n+1} = m_n + X_{n+1} - E(X_{n+1} \mid \mathcal{A}_n), \qquad (5.24)$$

it follows that m is a martingale. Next, note that, by construction, a_n is $\mathcal{A}_{n-1}$-measurable, and in addition,

$$a_{n+1} = a_n + E(X_{n+1} \mid \mathcal{A}_n) - X_n \geq a_n. \qquad (5.25)$$

Thus, we have established that a is an increasing predictable sequence. To show uniqueness, suppose there exists another decomposition, say $X_n = m_n^* + a_n^*$, with the same properties as above. Subtracting, we have

$$a_{n+1} - a_n + m_{n+1} - m_n = a_{n+1}^* - a_n^* + m_{n+1}^* - m_n^*. \qquad (5.26)$$

Taking, in Eq. (5.26), conditional expectations relative to $\mathcal{A}_n$ yields

$$a_{n+1} - a_n = a_{n+1}^* - a_n^*, \quad n \geq 0. \qquad (5.27)$$

Since $a_0 = a_0^* = 0$, we conlcude that $a_n = a_n^*$, for all n; this implies, from Eq. (5.26), that $m_{n+1} - m_n = m_{n+1}^* - m_n^*$. Since, however, we have set $m_0 = m_0^* = X_0$, we conclude that $m_n = m_n^*$, for all n.

q.e.d.

Example 3. Suppose $X = \{(X_n, \mathcal{A}_n) : n \geq 0\}$ is a square integrable martingale. Consider now its square sequence, $Y = \{(Y_n, \mathcal{A}_n) : n \geq 0\}$, where $Y_n = X_n^2$. From part iv. of Proposition 2, we have that Y is a **submartingale**. Hence, by Proposition 3, it has the decomposition $Y_n = m_n + a_n$, where

$$a_n = \sum_{j=0}^{n-1} [E(Y_{j+1} \mid \mathcal{A}_j) - Y_j]. \qquad (5.28)$$

But, Eq. (28) may also be rendered as

$$a_n = \sum_{j=0}^{n-1} E[(\Delta X_{j+1})^2 \mid \mathcal{A}_j], \qquad (5.29)$$

owing to the fact that

$$
\begin{aligned}
E[(\Delta X_{j+1})^2 \mid A_j] &= E[(X_{j+1}^2 - 2X_{j+1}X_j + X_j^2) \mid A_j] \\
&= E(X_{j+1}^2 \mid A_j) - X_j^2 \\
&= E(Y_{j+1} \mid A_j) - Y_j.
\end{aligned}
\tag{5.30}
$$

It is also interesting to observe that

$$
E(a_n) = \sum_{j=0}^{n-1} E[E(X_{j+1}^2 \mid A_j) - X_j^2] = E(X_n^2) - E(X_0^2).
\tag{5.31}
$$

Evidently, if $X_0 = 0$ then $E a_n = E(X_n^2)$. In addition, noting the definition of conditional expectations and the fact that $\Omega \in A_n$, we have

$$
\int_\Omega X_{n+1} \, d\mathcal{P} = \int_\Omega E(X_{n+1} \mid A_n) \, d\mathcal{P}.
\tag{5.32}
$$

Noting that $m_0 = 0$, we have that Eq. (5.32), in conjuction with Eq. (5.22), implies

$$
E(m_n) = \int_\Omega m_n \, d\mathcal{P} = \sum_{j=0}^{n-1} [\int_\Omega X_{j+1} \, d\mathcal{P} - \int_\Omega E(X_{j+1} \mid A_j) \, d\mathcal{P}] = 0.
\tag{5.33}
$$

The discussion in Example 3 suggests another useful definition.

Definition 4. Let $(\Omega, A, \mathcal{P})$ be a probability space, $\{A_n : n \geq 0\}$ be a stochastic basis, i.e., a sequence of (sub) σ-algebras such that $A_{n-1} \subset A_n$. Moreover, let $\{X_n : n \geq 0\}$, $\{Y_n : n \geq 0\}$ be two sequences of random variables defined on the probability space above and such that X_n, Y_n are A-measurable. If $X = \{(X_n, A_n) : n \geq 0\}$, $Y = \{(Y_n, A_n) : n \geq 0\}$ are two **square integrable** martingales, their **conditional variation**[4] is given, respectively, by the sequences

$$
\begin{aligned}
CV_n(X) &= \sum_{j=1}^{n} E\left[(\Delta X_j)^2 \mid A_{j-1}\right], \quad n \geq 1, \\
CV_n(Y) &= \sum_{j=1}^{n} E\left[(\Delta Y_j)^2 \mid A_{j-1}\right], \quad n \geq 1.
\end{aligned}
\tag{5.34}
$$

---

[4] There does not appear to be a standard terminology for this concept. Perhaps a better term might be **mean** or **expected conditional quadratic variation**. We shall reserve the term **quadratic variation** for another concept to be defined presently.

Their **conditional covariation** is defined by

$$CV_n(X,Y) = \frac{1}{4}[CV_n(X+Y,\ X+Y) - CV_n(X-Y,\ X-Y)]. \quad (5.35)$$

The **quadratic variation** of the two sequences above is given by

$$\begin{aligned} QV_n(X) &= \sum_{j=1}^{n}(\Delta X_j)^2, \\ QV_n(Y) &= \sum_{j=1}^{n}(\Delta Y_j)^2, \end{aligned} \quad (5.36)$$

and their **quadratic covariation** is defined by

$$QV_n(X,Y) = \frac{1}{4}[QV_n(X+Y,\ X+Y) - QV_n(X-Y,\ X-Y)].$$

As a matter of convention, we shall omit the subscript for the limit, i.e., we shall write, for example,

$$CV(X) = \sum_{j=1}^{\infty} E[(\Delta X_j)^2 \mid \mathcal{A}_{j-1}] \quad \text{or} \quad QV(X) = \sum_{j=1}^{\infty}(\Delta X_j)^2.$$

Remark 3. It is worth pointing out, from Example 3, that the conditional variation of a square integrable martingale is simply **the increasing predictable sequence corresponing of the Doob decomposition of its square.** More precisely, if $Y_n = X_n^2$ and $Y_n = m_n + a_n$ then

$$CV_n(X) = a_n. \quad (5.37)$$

From Eq. (31), we also see that

$$CV_n(X) = a_n = \sum_{j=1}^{n} E[(\Delta X_j)^2 \mid \mathcal{A}_{j-1}] = \sum_{j=1}^{n} E(\xi_j^2),$$

where it was assumed that $X_n = \sum_{j=1}^{n}\xi_j$, and the $\xi's$ are **independent** random variables with finite second moments. If the $\xi's$ have mean zero, then the relation above would read

$$CV_n(X) = a_n = \sum_{j=1}^{n} \text{Var}(\xi_j).$$

If it is also assumed that $Y_n = \sum_{j=1}^n \zeta_j$ and that the $\zeta's$ are zero mean square integrable independent random variables, then the conditional covariation between the two martingales, X and Y, is given by

$$CV_n(X,Y) = \sum_{j=1}^n \mathrm{Cov}(\xi_j, \zeta_j).$$

This is easily verified if one notes that

$$4(\Delta X_j \Delta Y_j) = (\Delta X_j + \Delta Y_j)^2 - (\Delta X_j + \Delta Y_j)^2,$$

and $E[(\Delta X_j \Delta Y_j) \mid \mathcal{A}_{j-1}] = \mathrm{Cov}(\xi_j, \zeta_j)$.

5.5 Stopping Times

Earlier in the discussion, we mentioned the martingale strategy, in which a gambler doubles his bet so long as he is losing and quits when he wins for the first time. This is an example of a stopping time, i.e., the time at which the process is "stopped" pursuant to some rule. In other words, given the outcomes of the process over the times $\{1, 2, 3, \ldots, n\}$, the rule picks the time n to terminate the process. Evidently, this time of termination is a random variable, since it depends on the outcomes generated by the process. These ideas are formalized in

Definition 5. Let $(\Omega, \mathcal{A}, \mathcal{P})$ be a probability space and $\{\mathcal{A}_n : n \in N\}$, where $N = \{0, 1, 2, 3, \ldots, \infty\}$, be a stochastic basis. The measurable function

$$\tau : \Omega \longrightarrow N$$

is said to be a **Markov time** if it is $\mathcal{A}_n$-measurable. If $\mathcal{P}(A) = 1$, for $A = \{\omega : \tau(\omega) < \infty\}$, then it is said to be a **stopping time**.[5]

---

[5] The usage here varies; some authors call "stopping time" what has been termed here Markov time. They call "finite stopping time" what has been termed here stopping time. The usage chosen appears to be slightly preferable since it would be rather odd to call someting a stopping time if the event $\{\omega : \tau(\omega) = \infty\}$, is assigned positive probability.

If we define

$$B_n \;=\; \{\omega : \tau(\omega) = n\}, \quad n \geq 0 \qquad (5.38)$$

$$I_n(\omega) \;=\; 1, \quad \text{if } \omega \in B_n$$

$$\;=\; 0, \quad \text{otherwise}, \qquad (5.39)$$

$$X_\tau \;=\; \sum_{n=0}^{\infty} X_n I_n, \qquad (5.40)$$

how are we to interpret X_τ? This will be clarified somewhat if we consider the set $A \in \mathcal{B}(R)$ and ask ourselves what is the probability that X_τ will assume a value in A? A little thought will convince us that

$$\mathcal{P}(A_\tau) = \sum_{n=0}^{\infty} \mathcal{P}(A_n \cap B_n), \qquad (5.41)$$

where

$$A_\tau \;=\; \{\omega : X_\tau \in A\},$$

$$A_n \;=\; \{\omega : X_n(\omega) \in A\}, \quad n \geq 0$$

$$B_n \;=\; \{\omega : \tau(\omega) = n\}, \qquad n \geq 0.$$

This is so since a value in A may be assumed at time 0, which means $X_0 \in A$ and $\tau = 0$; or at time 1, which would mean $X_1 \in A$ and $\tau = 1$, etc. Evidently, $A_n, B_n \in \mathcal{A}_n \subset \mathcal{A}$, so that $A_\tau \in \mathcal{A}$, which shows that X_τ is $\mathcal{A}$-measurable, and hence, a random variable.

Remark 4. It should be noted that since any Markov time, τ, is a random variable on $\mathcal{A}$ it induces a σ-algebra, say $\mathcal{A}_\tau \subset \mathcal{A}$. Specifically, put

$$\mathcal{A}_\tau = \{A : A \in \mathcal{A}, A \cap B_n \in \mathcal{A}_n, \ n \geq 0\}. \qquad (5.42)$$

To see that this is, indeed, a σ-algebra, note that if $A_1, A_2 \in \mathcal{A}_\tau$ then $A_1 \cup A_2 \in \mathcal{A}$ and $(A_1 \cup A_2) \cap B_n \in \mathcal{A}_n$, for all n. Moreover, $\bar{A}_1 \in \mathcal{A}$ and

$$\bar{A}_1 \cap B_n = (\Omega - A_1) \cap B_n = B_n \cap \overline{(A_1 \cap B_n)}.$$

Since $B_n, A_1 \cap B_n \in \mathcal{A}_n$, it follows that $\bar{A}_1 \in \mathcal{A}_\tau$. Finally, one can show that if a sequence of sets belongs to $\mathcal{A}_\tau$ then so does its limit, thus completing the demonstration that $\mathcal{A}_\tau$ is, indeed, a σ-algebra.

Example 4. As an example of the use to which the process X_τ can be put, consider the martingale strategy alluded to above. Precisely, let $\{X_n : n \geq 1\}$ be a sequence of i.i.d. random variables assuming the value 1 with probability p and the value -1 with probability $q = 1 - p$. The betting strategy involves a sequence $d_n : n \geq 1$, such that $d_1 = 1$ and for $i > 1$,

$$
\begin{aligned}
d_i &= 2^{i-1}, \quad \text{if } X_1 = X_2 = \cdots = X_{i-1} = -1 \\
&= 0, \quad \text{otherwise.}
\end{aligned}
$$

The gambler's worth after n trials is [6]

$$
W_n = \sum_{i=1}^{n-1} X_i d_i.
$$

What is the stopping time with this strategy, i.e., when is the first win? To be precise, define the Markov time as $\tau = \inf\{n \geq 1 : X_n = 1\}$. If $p = q = \frac{1}{2}$, then the probability that $\tau = t$ is given by $(\frac{1}{2})^t$, and the probability of the event $B_N = \{w : \tau(w) < N\}$ is given by

$$
\mathcal{P}(B) = \sum_{t=1}^{N-1} \left(\frac{1}{2}\right)^t.
$$

Since $B_N \subset B_{N+1}$ and the event $B = \{w : \tau(w) < \infty\}$ is simply the limit of B_N, we conclude that

$$
\mathcal{P}(B) = \lim_{N \to \infty} \mathcal{P}(B_N) = 1.
$$

This means that τ is a stopping time. In fact, a simple calculation shows that if the process has stopped at time n then the gambler's gain up to the nth game would be [7]

$$
-\sum_{j=1}^{n-1} 2^{(j-1)} = -(2^{n-1} - 1).
$$

On the nth game, the martingale strategy requires a bet of 2^{n-1}; for gambling to stop at the end of n games, we must have that $X_n = 1$, in

---

[6] This mathematical formulation assumes the gambler has some "outside" wealth, say W_0, that finances his bets.

[7] A minus sign indicates losses. The reader may also verify the result of the summation by simply computing $(2 - 1)\sum_{j=0}^{n-2} 2^j$.

which case the gambler's wealth would be $W_\tau = 2^{n-1} - (2^{n-1} - 1) = 1$.
Since the probability that the game will terminate in finite time is one,
it follows that $W_\tau = 1$ with probability one, and moreover, $E(W_\tau) = 1$.
This is so since $E(W_\tau \mid \tau = n) = 1$, while the probability that $\tau = n$ is
given by $(\frac{1}{2})^n$. Thus,

$$E(W_\tau) = E\left[E(W_\tau \mid \mathcal{A}_n)\right] = \sum_{n=1}^{\infty} \left(\frac{1}{2}\right)^n = 1.$$

Finally, in this connection, we wish to introduce the notion of the "stopped
process" in finite time. Specifically, [8]

$$X_{\tau \wedge n} = \sum_{k=0}^{n-1} X_k I_k + X_n I_{\tau \geq n}, \tag{5.43}$$

where I_k is as defined in Eq. (5.39) and $I_{\tau \geq n}$ is the indicator function
of the event $\tau \geq n$. Noting that

$$X_{\tau \wedge n+1} - X_{\tau \wedge n} = I_{\tau > n}(X_{n+1} - X_n), \tag{5.44}$$

we conclude that if the original sequence is a martingale (or a submartingale) the stopped sequence, relative to any Markov time, will also be a
martingale (or a submartingale, respectively).

We shall now present a number of results that follow quite easily from
the definition and properties of Markov times.

Proposition 4. Let $(\Omega,\ \mathcal{A},\ \mathcal{P})$ be a probability space, $\{\mathcal{A}_n : n \in N\}$
be a stochastic basis, [i.e., a sequence of (sub) σ-algebras such that
$\mathcal{A}_{n-1} \subset \mathcal{A}_n \subset \mathcal{A}$,] and $\tau_i,\ i = 1, 2$ be Markov times. Then, the following
statements are true:

    i. if ϕ is a Borel function,

        $\phi : N \longrightarrow N$,

        and τ is a Markov time then $\phi(\tau)$ is a Markov time;

    ii. $\tau_{\max} = \max(\tau_1,\ \tau_2)$ and $\tau_{\min} = \min(\tau_1,\ \tau_2)$ are Markov times;

---

[8] The notation $\tau \wedge n$ means $\min(\tau, n)$.

iii. if $\tau_1 \leq \tau_2$ a.c. (i.e., with probability one,) then the σ-algebras generated by them, $\mathcal{A}_1^*$, $\mathcal{A}_2^*$, respectively, obey $\mathcal{A}_1^* \subset \mathcal{A}_2^* \ (\subset \mathcal{A})$.

Proof: The proof of i. is quite evident since ϕ is a measurable function. As for the proof of ii., we note that if we put

$$A_{1n} = \{\omega : \tau_1(\omega) \leq n\}, \qquad A_{2n} = \{\omega : \tau_2(\omega) \leq n\}, \qquad (5.45)$$

$$A_{3n} = \{\omega : \tau_{\min}(\omega) \leq n\}, \qquad A_{4n} = \{\omega : \tau_{\max}(\omega) \leq n\}, \qquad (5.46)$$

then we find that $A_{3n} = A_{1n} \cup A_{2n}$ and $A_{4n} = A_{1n} \cap A_{2n}$. Since τ_1 and τ_2 are $\mathcal{A}$-measurable, it follows that $A_{3n}, A_{4n} \in \mathcal{A}$, for all n, which completes the proof of ii.

As for iii., since $\tau_1 \leq \tau_2$ a.c., it follows immediately that

$$A_{2n} \subset A_{1n}.$$

We note that $A_{1n}, A_{2n} \in \mathcal{A}_n$ and that, see the discussion at the end of Example 4,

$$\mathcal{A}_i^* = \{B : B \in \mathcal{A}, B \cap A_{in} \in \mathcal{A}_n, \ n \in N\}, \ i = 1, 2.$$

Let $B \in \mathcal{A}_1^*$; then, $B \in \mathcal{A}$ and $B \cap A_{1n} \in \mathcal{A}_n$. On the other hand,

$$B \cap A_{2n} = (B \cap A_{1n}) \cap A_{2n}.$$

Since $(B \cap A_{1n}) \in \mathcal{A}$ and, evidently, $A_{2n} \in \mathcal{A}_n$, it follows that $B \cap A_{2n} \in \mathcal{A}_n$, $n \in N$, which shows that $B \in \mathcal{A}_2^*$.

$$\text{q.e.d.}$$

Proposition 5. Let $(\Omega, \mathcal{A}, \mathcal{P})$ be a probability space, $\{\mathcal{A}_n : n \in N\}$ be a stochastic basis, [i.e., a sequence of (sub) σ-algebras such that $\mathcal{A}_{n-1} \subset \mathcal{A}_n \subset \mathcal{A}$,] $\{X_n : n \in N\}$ be a sequence of $\mathcal{A}_n$-measurable L^1 random variables, and τ_i, $i = 1, 2$, be Markov times such that $\tau_1 \leq \tau_2$ a.c. Define

$$h_1 = \sum_{j=0}^{\tau_1} X_j, \qquad h_2 = \sum_{j=0}^{\tau_2} X_j.$$

Then, the following statements are true:

i. if $E(X_{n+1} \mid \mathcal{A}_n) \geq 0$, $n \in N$, then, for any $A \in \mathcal{A}_1^*$,

$$\int_A h_1 \, d\mathcal{P} \leq \int_A h_2 \, d\mathcal{P};$$

ii. if $E(X_{n+1} \mid \mathcal{A}_n) = 0$, then, for any $A \in \mathcal{A}_1^*$, $\int_A h_1 \, d\mathcal{P} = \int_A h_2 \, d\mathcal{P}$.

Proof: Define $A_{ij} = \{\omega : \tau_i(\omega) = j\}$, $i = 1, 2$, $j = 0, 1, 2, \ldots, n$, put $B_{ij} = A \cap A_{ij}$, and note that we have the decompositions $A = \bigcup_{j=0}^{n} B_{ij}$, $i = 1, 2$. It will suffice to deal with the case that τ_1 is fixed on A, since this is the case on the components of the decomposition. Thus, suppose that, on A, $\tau_1 = j$ and $\tau_2 > j$, so that

$$h_1 = \sum_{k=0}^{j} X_k, \qquad h_2 = h_1 + \sum_{k=j+1}^{\tau_2} X_k. \qquad (5.47)$$

We further note that

$$\bigcup_{k=j+1}^{n} B_{2k} = A \bigcap_{k=0}^{j} \bar{B}_{2k} \in \mathcal{A}_j. \qquad (5.48)$$

Consequently,

$$\int_A h_2 \, d\mathcal{P} = \int_A h_1 \, d\mathcal{P} + \int_A \left(\sum_{k=j}^{n-1} X_{k+1} \right) d\mathcal{P} = J_1 + J_3. \qquad (5.49)$$

But,

$$\int_A \left(\sum_{k=j}^{n-1} X_{k+1} \right) d\mathcal{P} = \sum_{k=j}^{n-1} \int_{\bigcup_{s>k} B_{2s}} X_{k+1} \, d\mathcal{P}.$$

Since $\bigcup_{s>k} B_{2s} \in \mathcal{A}_k$ we have, by the definition of conditional expectation,

$$\int_{\bigcup_{s>k} B_{2s}} X_{k+1} \, d\mathcal{P} = \int_{\bigcup_{s>k} B_{2s}} E(X_{k+1} \mid \mathcal{A}_k) \, d\mathcal{P} \geq 0. \qquad (5.50)$$

This implies that, in Eq. (5.49), $J_3 \geq 0$, so that i. is proved.

As for ii., we may repeat all arguments until Eq. (5.50) and, given the condition in ii., we must conclude that $J_3 = 0$, which establishes the validity of ii.

q.e.d.

Corollary 1. In the context of Proposition 5, the following statements are true:

    i. if $S = \{(S_n, \mathcal{A}_n) : n \geq 0\}$ is a submartingale, with $S_n = \sum_{j=0}^{n} X_j$, then i. of Proposition 5 holds;

    ii. if S is a martingale then ii. of Proposition 5 holds.

Proof: The entities h_i of Proposition 5 now become the "observations" of the stochastic sequence, S, at the random times τ_i. We need to prove that, for any $A \in \mathcal{A}_1^*$,

$$\int_A S_{\tau_2} \, d\mathcal{P} \geq \int_A S_{\tau_1} \, d\mathcal{P} \quad \text{or} \quad \int_A S_{\tau_2} \, d\mathcal{P} = \int_A S_{\tau_1} \, d\mathcal{P},$$

according to whether S is a submartingale or a martingale, respectively. Now, if S is a **submartingale**, we have

$$E(X_{k+1} \mid \mathcal{A}_k) = E(S_{k+1} \mid \mathcal{A}_k) - S_k \geq 0, \tag{5.51}$$

so that the condition in i. of Proposition 5 is satisfied, and part i. of the corollary is proved. Similarly, if S is a **martingale**, then

$$E(X_{k+1} \mid \mathcal{A}_k) = E(S_{k+1} \mid \mathcal{A}_k) - S_k = 0 \tag{5.52}$$

so that the condition in ii. of Proposition 5 is satisfied and, thus, part ii. of the Corollary is proved.

q.e.d.

Corollary 2. In the context of Corollary 1, consider the sequence of Markov times $\tau_1 \leq \tau_2 \leq \cdots \leq \tau_q$. Let $\mathcal{A}_i^*$ be the σ-algebra induced by τ_i, $i = 1, 2, \ldots q$, and define $h_i = S_{\tau_i}$. The sequence of observations on S at the random times τ_i, i.e., the sequence $h = \{(h_i, \mathcal{A}_i^*) : i = 1, 2, \ldots q\}$, is

    i. a submartingale if S is submartingale;

    ii. a martingale if S is a martingale.

Proof: To prove the corollary we need to show if S is a submartingale then

$$h_{n+1} = h_n + \sum_{j=1}^{\tau_{n+1} - \tau_n} X_{\tau_n + j} \qquad (5.53)$$

is also a submartingale, while if S is a martingale then Eq. (5.53) represents a martingale. But this is straightforward since if S is a submartingale then $E(X_{\tau_n + j} \mid \mathcal{A}_s) \geq 0$, for $s < \tau_n + j$, while if S is a martingale that quantity would be zero. In the first instance, Eq. (5.53) represents a submartingale, while in the second it represents a martingale.

q.e.d.

We conclude this section with a number of useful inequalities.

Remark 5. In Proposition 5 and its corollary, the proofs implicitly assume that N is a finite set, although generally we take it to be the set $N = \{0, 1, 2, \ldots\}$. We gave the proof in the context of a finite index set in order to simplify its exposition. In the of a countable index set, we may proceed as follows. Redefine $h_n = \sum_{j=0}^{n} X_j$ and suppose it is either a martingale or a submartingale. In such a case, the term h_i of Proposition 5 becomes h_{τ_i}, $i = 1, 2$. We need to assume that $E \mid h_{\tau_i} \mid < \infty$ and, moreover, that the tails of their distribution are not too "thick", i.e.,

$$\liminf_{n \to \infty} \int_{\bigcup_{s > n} B_{is}} \mid h_n \mid d\mathcal{P} = 0, \qquad i = 1, 2. \qquad (5.54)$$

In such a case, the result still holds, i.e., $E(h_{\tau_2}) \geq E(h_{\tau_1})$ if $h = (h_n, \mathcal{A}_n)$ is a submartingale and $E(h_{\tau_2}) = E(h_{\tau_1})$ if h is a martingale. A sketch of the argument is as follows: proceeding exactly as in the Proof of the Proposition, arrive at Eq. (5.49); take $A = \Omega$ and use Fatou's theorem obtain the desired result.

Proposition 6. Let $(\Omega, \mathcal{A}, \mathcal{P})$ be a probability space, $\{\mathcal{A}_k : k \in N\}$ be a stochastic basis, [i.e., a sequence of (sub) σ-algebras such that $\mathcal{A}_{k-1} \subset \mathcal{A}_k \subset \mathcal{A}$,] and $X = \{(X_k, \mathcal{A}_k) : k \in N\}$ be a submartingale. Finally, suppose N is a finite index set with maximal element n, $E(X_n^+)^p < \infty$, for $p \geq 1$, and define

$$X_n^*(\omega) = \max_{1 \leq k \leq n} X_k^+(\omega).$$

The following statements are true:

   i. given any integer r,

$$\mathcal{P}(A_n^*) \le r E(X_n^+), \tag{5.55}$$

     where $A_n^* = \{\omega : X_n^*(\omega) > \frac{1}{r}\}$;

  ii. for $p > 1$,

$$E(X_n)^p \le E(X_n^*)^p \le \left(\frac{p}{p-1}\right)^p E(X_n^+)^p. \tag{5.56}$$

Proof: Let $\tau_1 = \min(j \le n : X_j^+(\omega) > \frac{1}{r})$, i.e., τ_1 is the smallest (integer) index $j \ (\le n)$ for which $X_j^+(\omega) > (1/r)$; if no such index exists, set $\tau_1 = n$. Moreover, define $\tau_2 = n$ and note that if we put

$$B_t = \{\omega : \tau_1 = t\}, \quad t = 0, 1, \ldots, n, \tag{5.57}$$

then

$$A_n^* = \bigcup_{t=0}^{n} B_t, \tag{5.58}$$

so that $A_n^* \in \mathcal{A}_1^*$, the latter being the σ-algebra induced by τ_1. Thus, the conditions of Proposition 5 (and its corollaries) are satisfied, and we therefore conclude that

$$\begin{aligned} \frac{1}{r}\mathcal{P}(A_n^*) &\le \int_{A_n^*} X_{\tau_1}^+ \, d\mathcal{P} \le \int_{A_n^*} X_{\tau_2}^+ \, d\mathcal{P} \\ &= \int_{A_n^*} X_n \, d\mathcal{P} \le \int_{A_n^*} X_n^+ \, d\mathcal{P} \le E(X_n^+). \end{aligned}$$

Hence, $\mathcal{P}(A_n^*) \le r E(X_n^+)$, which concludes the proof of i.

As for the proof of ii., let $A_t^* = \{\omega : X_n^* > t\}$ and note [9] that, for $p > 1$,

$$E(X_n^*)^p = p \int_0^\infty t^{p-1} \mathcal{P}(A_t^*) \, dt. \tag{5.59}$$

---

[9] If X is a nonnegative random variable with cumulative distribution function F, then we may write $EX^p = -\int_0^\infty t^p \, d[1 - F(t)]$; integrating by parts, we find $EX^p = p \int_0^\infty t^{p-1}[1 - F(t)] \, dt = p \int_0^\infty t^{p-1} \mathcal{P}(A_t^*) \, dt$.

Substituting from Eq. (5.54) we have

$$
\begin{aligned}
E(X_n^*)^p &= p\int_0^\infty t^{p-2}\left[\int_{A_t^*} X_n^+ \, d\mathcal{P}\right] dt = p\int_0^\infty t^{p-2}\left[\int_\Omega X_n^+ I_t \, d\mathcal{P}\right] dt \\
&= p\int_\Omega X_n^+ \left[\int_0^\infty t^{p-2} I_t \, dt\right] d\mathcal{P} = p\int_\Omega X_n^+ \left[\int_0^{X_n^*} t^{p-2} \, dt\right] d\mathcal{P} \\
&= \left(\frac{p}{p-1}\right)\int_\Omega X_n^+ (X_n^*)^{p-1} \, d\mathcal{P} = qE(X_n^+ X_n^{*(p-1)}). \qquad (5.60)
\end{aligned}
$$

The proof of the proposition may be concluded by using Holder's inequality on Eq. (5.61).

q.e.d.

Corollary 3. If the submartingale is assumed to be **nonnegative** then the following statements are true:

   i. $P(A_n^*) \leq rE(X_n)$;

  ii. for $p > 1,$[10] and with $\frac{1}{p} + \frac{1}{q} = 1$,

$$
\|X_n\|_p \leq \|X_n^*\|_p \leq q\|X_n\|_p. \qquad (5.61)
$$

Proof: This is obvious by exponentiating, to $(1/p)$, the terms in Eq. (5.55).

Corollary 4. If X is a **square integrable** martingale, then the following statements are true:

   i. given any integer r,

$$
P(A_n^*) \leq r^2 E(X_n^2), \qquad A_n^* = \left\{\omega : \max_{j\leq n} |X_j(\omega)| > \frac{1}{r}\right\};
$$

  ii.

$$
E\left(\max_{j\leq n} X_j^2\right) \leq 4E(X_n^2).
$$

---

[10] We remind the reader that $\| X \|_p = - \left(\int_\Omega | X |^p \, d\mathcal{P}\right)^{\frac{1}{p}}$.

Proof: We note that, given the conditions in part i., $\{(X_n^2, \mathcal{A}_n) : n \geq 1\}$ is a nonnegative submartingale; consequently, from Corollary 3, $\mathcal{P}(A_n^*) \leq r^2 E(X_n^2)$, where

$$A_n^* = \left\{\omega : \max_{j \leq n} X_j^2 > \frac{1}{r^2}\right\} = \left\{\omega : \max_{j \leq n} \mid X_j \mid > \frac{1}{r}\right\}, \qquad (5.62)$$

which proves part i.

As for part ii., $\{(X_n^2, \mathcal{A}_n) : n \geq 1\}$ is a nonnegative submartingale, and again by Corollary 3 (part ii.), taking $p = 2$ and exponetiating, we find

$$E(\max_{j \leq n} X_j^2) \leq 4 E(X_n^2).$$

q.e.d.

Corollary 5. If, in the context of Proposition 6, N is a countable index set and $\sup_{n \geq N} E(X_n^+) < \infty$, then

$$\mathcal{P}(A^*) \leq r \sup_{n \geq N} E(X_n^+), \qquad (5.63)$$

where

$$A^* = \left\{\omega : \sup_{n \geq N} X_n^+(\omega) \geq \frac{1}{r}\right\}. \qquad (5.64)$$

Proof: We note that from Proposition 6, Eq. (5.54), $\mathcal{P}(A_n^*) \leq r E(X_n^+)$. But, this implies that, for any n,

$$\mathcal{P}(A_n^*) \leq r \sup_{n \geq N} E(X_n^+). \qquad (5.65)$$

Noting that

$$A^* = \bigcup_{n=0}^{\infty} A_n^*, \qquad A_n^* \subset A_{n+1}^* \qquad (5.66)$$

and that

$$A_m^* = \bigcup_{j=0}^{m} A_j^*, \qquad (5.67)$$

we conclude that

$$\mathcal{P}(A^*) = \lim_{m \to \infty} \mathcal{P}(A_m^*) \leq \sup_{n \geq N} E(X_n^+).$$

q.e.d.

Another useful set of inequalities is given in

Proposition 7. Let $(\Omega, \mathcal{A}, \mathcal{P})$ be a probability space, $\{\mathcal{A}_k : k \in N\}$ be a stochastic basis, and $X = \{(X_k, \mathcal{A}_k) : k \in N\}$ be a nonnegative stochastic sequence dominated by the increasing predictable sequence $a = \{(a_n, \mathcal{A}_{n-1}) : n \in N\}$. Given any r, $c > 0$, and stoppping time τ, define

$$X_\tau^* = \sup_{n \le \tau} X_n, \tag{5.68}$$

$$A_\tau^* = \{\omega : X_\tau^* \ge \frac{1}{r}\}, \tag{5.69}$$

$$b_\tau^* = \{\omega : a_\tau(\omega) \ge c\}. \tag{5.70}$$

Then, the following statements are true:

  i. $\mathcal{P}(A_\tau^*) \le rE(a_\tau)$;

 ii. $\mathcal{P}(A_\tau^*) \le rE(a_\tau \wedge c) + \mathcal{P}(b_\tau^*)$;

iii. statements i. and ii. remain valid even if the sequence a is nonnegative increasing but **not predictable**, provided there exists some $c_1 \in R^+$ such that $\mathcal{P}(D) = 1$, where $D = \{\omega : \sup_{k \ge 1} | \Delta a_k | \le c_1\}$, except that the statement in ii. should be modified to read

$$\mathcal{P}(A_\tau^*) \le rE[a_\tau \wedge (c + c_1)] + \mathcal{P}(b_\tau^*);$$

 iv. $\|X_\tau^*\|_p \le (\frac{2-p}{1-p})^{\frac{1}{p}} \|a_\tau\|_p$, $\quad 0 < p < 1$.

Proof: For fixed n, put $s_n = \min(j : j \le \tau \wedge n, X_j \ge \frac{1}{r})$. If no such index exists, set $s = \tau \wedge n$; also, define $X_{\tau \wedge n}^* = \max_{1 \le k \le \tau \wedge n} X_k$ and $A_{\tau \wedge n}^* = \{\omega : X_{\tau \wedge n}^*(\omega) \ge \frac{1}{r}\}$. An immediate consequence of these definitions is [11]

$$E(a_\tau) \ge E(a_{s_n}) \ge E(X_{s_n}) \ge \int_{A_{\tau \wedge n}^*} X_{s_n} \, d\mathcal{P} \ge \frac{1}{r} \mathcal{P}(A_{\tau \wedge n}^*). \tag{5.71}$$

Thus, we have established that $\mathcal{P}(A_{\tau \wedge n}^*) \le rE(a_\tau)$. Next, note that

$$\mathcal{P}(A_{\tau \wedge n}^*) = E(I_{\tau \wedge n}),$$

---

[11] The first inequality follows because $\tau \ge s_n$ and the fact that the sequence is increasing; the second inequality follows because a is a dominating sequence.

where $I_{\tau \wedge n}$ is the indicator function of the set $A^*_{\tau \wedge n}$. Since $A^*_{\tau \wedge n} \subset A^*_{\tau \wedge n+1}$, it follows that

$$\lim_{n \to \infty} A^*_{\tau \wedge n} = A^*_\tau, \qquad \lim_{n \to \infty} \mathcal{P}(A^*_{\tau \wedge n}) = \mathcal{P}(A^*_\tau).$$

Consequently, and since $I_{\tau \wedge n} \leq 1$, for all n, it follows by the dominated convergence theorem (Proposition 19 of Chapter 1) that

$$\mathcal{P}(A^*_\tau) = \lim_{n \to \infty} \mathcal{P}(A^*_{\tau \wedge n}) \leq r E(a_\tau), \tag{5.72}$$

which completes the proof of i.

As for ii., note that

$$\begin{aligned} \mathcal{P}(A^*_\tau) &= \mathcal{P}(A^*_\tau \cap \bar{b}^*_\tau) + \mathcal{P}(A^*_\tau \cap b^*_\tau) \\ &\leq \mathcal{P}(A^*_\tau \cap \bar{b}^*_\tau) + \mathcal{P}(b^*_\tau) \end{aligned}$$

and define $\alpha = \inf(j : a_{j+1} \geq c)$. Since $I_{a_\tau < c} X^*_\tau \leq X^*_{\tau \wedge \alpha}$, we have that

$$A^*_\tau \cap b^*_\tau = \left\{ \omega : I_{a_\tau < c}(\omega) X^*_\tau(\omega) \geq \frac{1}{r} \right\} \subset \left\{ \omega : X^*_{\tau \wedge \alpha}(\omega) \geq \frac{1}{r} \right\} = B^*_{\tau \wedge \alpha}.$$

Consequently,

$$\begin{aligned} \mathcal{P}(A^*_\tau) &\leq \mathcal{P}(B^*_{\tau \wedge \alpha}) + \mathcal{P}(b^*_\tau) \leq r E(a_{\tau \wedge \alpha}) + \mathcal{P}(b^*_\tau) \\ &\leq r E(a_\tau \wedge c) + \mathcal{P}(b^*_\tau), \end{aligned} \tag{5.73}$$

which completes the proof of ii.

To show the validity of iii., we note that the proof of i. does not depend on the fact that a is a predictable sequence, only that it is dominating, which it continues to be. To show that ii. continues to hold, redefine α so that

$$\alpha = \inf(j : a_j \geq c).$$

With this definition, $a_{\tau \wedge \alpha} \leq (c + c_1)$; this is so since at the "previous value of the index" the process a assumed a value less that c and by the condition in iii., $\sup_{k \geq 1} |\Delta a_k| \leq c_1$, with probability one. Consequently, $a_{\tau \wedge \alpha}$ must obey the condition just stated. Thus, Eq. (5.73) may be restated as

$$\begin{aligned} \mathcal{P}(A^*_\tau) &\leq \mathcal{P}(B^*_{\tau \wedge \alpha}) + \mathcal{P}(b^*_\tau) \leq r E(a_{\tau \wedge \alpha}) + \mathcal{P}(b^*_\tau) \\ &\leq r E[a_\tau \wedge (c + c_1)] + \mathcal{P}(b^*_\tau), \end{aligned}$$

and the proof of iii. is complete.

As for iv., note that

$$\|X^*_\tau\|^p_p = E(X^*_\tau)^p = \int_0^\infty \mathcal{P}[(X^*_\tau)^p \geq t]\, dt = \int_0^\infty \mathcal{P}[X^*_\tau \geq t^{\frac{1}{p}}]\, dt.$$

Using the results of ii. and taking A^*_τ to mean the set $\{\omega : X^*_\tau(\omega) \geq t^{\frac{1}{p}}\}$, we find that

$$
\begin{aligned}
\int_0^\infty \mathcal{P}\left[X^*_\tau \geq t^{\frac{1}{p}}\right] dt &\leq \int_0^\infty \left\{ t^{-\frac{1}{p}} \left[\int_\Omega \left(a_\tau \wedge t^{\frac{1}{p}}\right) d\mathcal{P}\right] + \mathcal{P}\left(a_\tau \geq t^{\frac{1}{p}}\right) \right\} dt \\
&= \int_\Omega \left[\int_0^{a_\tau} dt + a_\tau \int_{a_\tau}^\infty t^{-\frac{1}{p}}\, dt \right] d\mathcal{P} + \int_\Omega a^p_\tau\, d\mathcal{P} \\
&= \left(\frac{2-p}{1-p} \right) E(a^p_\tau).
\end{aligned}
$$

q.e.d.

Corollary 6. Let $\{X^n, a^n : n \geq 1\}$ be **sequences** satisfying their respective conditions as stated in Proposition 7, and suppose that for some **sequence** of stopping times, $\{\tau_n : n \geq 1\}$,

$$a^n_{\tau_n} \xrightarrow{\text{P}} 0 \quad \text{as} \quad n \to \infty.$$

Then, $(X^n)^*_{\tau_n} \xrightarrow{\text{P}} 0$ as $n \to \infty$.

Proof: We remind the reader that

$$(X^n)^*_{\tau_n} = \max_{1 \leq k \leq \tau_n} X^n_k.$$

Since $a^n_{\tau_n} \xrightarrow{\text{P}} 0$, choose a sequence $\{c_n : n \geq 1,\ c_n > 0\}$ such that $c_n \to 0$, define the sets

$$A^*_{1n} = \left\{ \omega : (X^n)^*_{\tau_n}(\omega) \geq \frac{1}{r} \right\}, \quad A^*_{2n} = \{ \omega : a^n_{\tau_n}(\omega) \geq c_n \},$$

and note that $E(a^n_{\tau_n} \wedge c_n) \leq c_n$. But, from the proposition, we immediately conclude

$$\mathcal{P}(A^*_{1n}) \leq r E(a_\tau \wedge c_n) + \mathcal{P}(A^*_{2n}) \leq \mathcal{P}(A^*_{2n}) + r c_n. \tag{5.74}$$

Letting $n \to \infty$, we have that $\mathcal{P}(A^*_{1n}) \to 0$.

q.e.d.

It is interesting that, under slightly altered conditions, we can also prove the converse of the corollary, i.e., if $(X^n)^*_{\tau_n} \overset{P}{\to} 0$ then $a^n_{\tau_n} \overset{P}{\to} 0$ as $n \to \infty$.

Corollary 7. Let $X = \{(X_n, \mathcal{A}_n) : n \geq 1\}$ be a **nonnegative** stochastic sequence, $a = \{(a_n, \mathcal{A}_{n-1}) : n \geq 1\}$ be a (nonnegative) increasing predictable sequence, defined on the probability space $(\Omega,\ \mathcal{A},\ \mathcal{P})$, [with $\mathcal{A}_0 = (\emptyset, \Omega)$,] and such that, for every stopping time τ, $E(X_\tau) \geq E(a_\tau)$. Then, the following statements are true:

i. for arbitrary integer r and $c > 0$,

$$P\left(a_\tau \geq \frac{1}{r}\right) \leq r E(X^*_\tau), \quad P\left(a_\tau \geq \frac{1}{r}\right) \leq r E(X^*_\tau \wedge c) + P(X^*_\tau \geq c);$$

ii. if X^n, a^n, $n \geq 1$, are **sequences** satisfying their respective conditions as stated above and if for some **sequence** of stopping times, $\tau_n : n \geq 1$,

$$(X^n)^*_{\tau_n} \overset{P}{\to} 0 \quad \text{as} \quad n \to \infty,$$

then,

$$a^n_{\tau_n} \overset{P}{\to} 0 \quad \text{as} \quad n \to \infty.$$

Proof: As in the proof of Proposition 7, define, *mutatis mutandis*, and for fixed n,

$$s_n = \min\left(j : j \leq \tau \wedge n,\ a_j \geq \frac{1}{r}\right)$$

$$s = \tau \wedge n \quad \text{if no such integer exists.}$$

Then,[12]

$$E(X^*_\tau) \geq E(X_{s^*_n}) \geq E(X_{s_n}) \geq E(a_{s_n})$$

$$\geq \int_{\{\omega : a_\tau \wedge n \geq \frac{1}{r}\}} a_{s_n}\, dP \geq rP\left(a_{\tau \wedge n} \geq \frac{1}{r}\right),$$

---

[12] In the chain of inequalities, the first is valid since s_n is a truncated stopping time; the second because X^* is a maximum; the third follows from the condition of the corollary; the fourth from the fact that a_n is nonnegative and the integral is taken over a reduced region; the last follows because a_n is an **increasing sequence** and the index $\tau \wedge n$ is, by contruction, equal to or greater than s_n.

or $\mathcal{P}(a_{\tau\wedge n} \geq \frac{1}{r}) \leq rE(X_\tau^*)$. As in the proof of Proposition 7, using Fatou's Lemma establishes the validity of the first statment of part i.

As for the second statement of part i., define

$$\alpha = \inf\left(j : X_{j+1}^* \geq c\right)$$
$$= \infty \quad \text{if no such integer exists.}$$

We then have the following chain of reasoning

$$
\begin{aligned}
\mathcal{P}\left(a_\tau \geq \frac{1}{r}\right) &= \mathcal{P}\left(a_\tau \geq \frac{1}{r},\ X_\tau^* < c\right) + \mathcal{P}\left(a_\tau \geq \frac{1}{r},\ X_\tau^* \geq c\right) \\
&\leq \mathcal{P}\left[I(X_\tau^* < c)a_\tau \geq \frac{1}{r}\right] + \mathcal{P}(X_\tau^* \geq c) \\
&\leq \mathcal{P}\left(a_{\tau\wedge\alpha} \geq \frac{1}{r}\right) + \mathcal{P}(X_\tau^* \geq c).
\end{aligned}
$$

Using the first part of i., we thus conclude

$$\mathcal{P}\left(a_\tau \geq \frac{1}{r}\right) \leq rE(X_{\tau\wedge\alpha}^*) + \mathcal{P}(X_\tau^* \geq c) \leq rE(X_\tau^* \wedge c) + \mathcal{P}(X_\tau^* \geq c), \tag{5.75}$$

which completes the proof of part i.

As for part ii., we proceed, *mutatis mutandis*, exactly as in the proof of Corollary 6, defining the sets A_{in}^*, $i = 1, 2$, by

$$A_{1n}^* = \{\omega : (X^n)_{\tau_n}^*(\omega) \geq c_n\}, \quad A_{2n}^* = \{\omega : a_{\tau_n}^n(\omega) \geq \frac{1}{r}\}$$

and noting that $E(X_\tau^* \wedge c_n) \leq c_n$. Consequently, we find

$$\mathcal{P}(A_{2n}^*) \leq \mathcal{P}(A_{1n}^*) + rE(X_\tau^* \wedge c_n) \leq rc_n + \mathcal{P}(A_{1n}^*). \tag{5.76}$$

Since the rightmost member of Eq. (5.76) converges to zero with n, the proof of the corollary is completed.

$$\text{q.e.d.}$$

5.6   Upcrossings

In this section, we take up the concept of upcrossings and the basic martingale convergence results. We begin with

Definition 6. Let $\{(X_n, \mathcal{A}_n) : n \geq 0\}$ be a **submartingale stochastic sequence** and let $[a, b] \subset (-\infty, \infty)$. The random variable

$\gamma : \Omega \longrightarrow N$,

such that $\gamma_n(a, b)$ denotes the number of times that the submartingale made a transition from a value equal to or less than a to a value equal to or greater than b, over the interval $(0, n]$,[13] is said to be the **number of upcrossings of the submartingale** over the compact interval $[a, b]$. More precisely, it is the number, s, of occurrences of the event $S_{n_{i-1}} \leq a$, $S_{n_i} \geq b$, $n_i \leq n$, $i = 1, 2, \ldots, s$.

An immediate consequence of the definition is

Proposition 8. Let $X = \{(X_n, \mathcal{A}_n) : n \geq 1\}$ be a submartingale defined on the probability space $(\Omega, \mathcal{A}, \mathcal{P})$ and let $\gamma_n(a, b)$ be the number of upcrossings over the interval $[a, b]$. Then,

$$E[\gamma_n(a, b)] \leq \frac{E(X_n - a)^+}{b - a}. \tag{5.77}$$

Proof: Define $Y_n = (X_n - a)^+$ and note that $Y = \{(Y_n, \mathcal{A}_n) : n \geq 1\}$ is a nonnegative submartingale. In the context of this submartingale, the interval in question becomes $[0, c]$, where $c = b - a$, and the number of upcrossings is denoted by $v_n(0, c)$, although, of course, we have that $v_n(0, c) = \gamma_n(a, b)$. Define the Markov times $\tau_0 = 0$, $\tau_1 = \min(n > 0 : X_n \leq a$, or $Y_n = 0)$, $\tau_2 = \min(n > \tau_1 : Y_n \geq c)$; $\tau_3 = \min(n > \tau_2 : Y_n = 0)$; $\tau_4 = \min(n > \tau_3 : Y_n \geq c)$; $\ldots$; $\tau_{2m-1} = \min(n > \tau_{2(m-1)} : Y_{2m-1} = 0)$; $\tau_{2m} = \min(n > \tau_{2m-1} : Y_{2m} \geq c)$ and suppose that τ_{2m} is the last time, in the interval $[0, n]$, that the submartingale attains a value equal to or greater than c. For all other remaining indices, say $j = 2m + 1, 2m + 2, \ldots, n$, set the value $\tau_j = n$. A little reflection will show that

$$cv_n(0, c) \leq \sum_{i=1}^{n} \chi_i(Y_i - Y_{i-1}), \tag{5.78}$$

where

$$\chi_i = 1 \quad \text{if} \quad \tau_{2j+1} < i \leq \tau_{2(j+1)} \tag{5.79}$$

$$= 0 \quad \text{if} \quad \tau_{2j} < i \leq \tau_{2j+1}. \tag{5.80}$$

---

[13] If, for example, X_j denotes the value assumed by the submartingale **at the** j^{th} **Bernoulli trial** then $\gamma_n(a, b)$ represents the number of times an upcrossing has occurred in n trials.

This is so since

$$A_i = \{\omega : \chi_i = 1\} = \left[\bigcup_{j=0}^{i-1} \{\omega : \tau_{2j+1}(\omega) < i\}\right] \cap \{\omega : \tau_{2(j+1)}(\omega) \geq i\}$$

$$= \left[\bigcup_{j=0}^{i-1} \{\omega : \tau_{2j+1}(\omega) < i\}\right] \cap \overline{\{\omega : \tau_{2(j+1)}(\omega) < i\}} \in \mathcal{A}_{i-1}, \quad (5.81)$$

and when we have an upcrossing, $\chi_i = 1$. In addition, the term corresponding to it, in the right member of Eq. (5.78), is $Y_{\tau_{2(j+1)}} - Y_{i-1}$ such that $Y_{\tau_{2(j+1)}} \geq c$ and $Y_{i-1} = 0$. Thus, upon summation, we have Eq. (5.78). To evaluate its expectation we note that

$$\begin{aligned}
cE[v_n(0,c)] &\leq E\left[\sum_{i=1}^{n} \chi_i(Y_i - Y_{i-1})\right] = \sum_{i=1}^{n} \int_{A_i} (Y_i - Y_{i-1}) \, d\mathcal{P} \\
&= \sum_{i=1}^{n} \int_{A_i} E(Y_i - Y_{i-1} \mid \mathcal{A}_{i-1}) \, d\mathcal{P} \\
&= \sum_{i=1}^{n} \int_{A_i} [E(Y_i \mid \mathcal{A}_{i-1}) - Y_{i-1}] \, d\mathcal{P} \\
&\leq \sum_{i=1}^{n} \int_{\Omega} [E(Y_i \mid \mathcal{A}_{i-1}) - Y_{i-1}] \, d\mathcal{P} \\
&= \sum_{i=1}^{n} [E(Y_i) - E(Y_{i-1})] = E(Y_n).
\end{aligned}$$

The second equality above follows from the basic definition of conditional expectations, and the other relations are self evident. Noting that $c = b - a$, $v_n(0,c) = \gamma_n(a,b)$, and $Y_n = (X_n - a)^+$, we have that

$$E[\gamma_n(a,b)] \leq \frac{E(X_n - a)^+}{b - a}.$$

q.e.d.

5.7 Martingale Convergence

In this section, we present a number of important martingale convergence results that will be found useful at a later stage of our discussion. We begin with the fundamental martingale convergence theorem.

Proposition 9 (Doob). Let $(\Omega, \mathcal{A}, \mathcal{P})$ be a probability space and let $X = \{(X_n, \mathcal{A}_n) : n \geq 1\}$ be an L^1-bounded submartingale, i.e., one obeying $\sup_{n \geq 1} E \mid X_n \mid < \infty$. Then, there exists a random variable, say X_∞, such that $X_n \overset{\text{a.c.}}{\to} X_\infty$ and $E \mid X_\infty \mid < \infty$.

Proof: For the first part, we proceed by contradiction; thus, suppose not and note that if we define the set

$$A = \{\omega : \limsup_{n \to \infty} X_n(\omega) > \liminf_{n \to \infty} X_n(\omega)\} \tag{5.82}$$

then it must obey $\mathcal{P}(A) > 0$. Since, evidently, between any two numbers, say $x < y$, we can place at least two rational numbers, say $c < d$, let $\{(a_i, b_i) : a_i < b_i, i \geq 1\}$ be the collection of all rational numbers that fit between the limit inferior and limit superior of Eq. (5.82), define

$$A_i = \{\omega : \liminf_{n \to \infty} X_n(\omega) < a_i < b_i < \limsup_{n \to \infty} X_n(\omega)\}, \tag{5.83}$$

and note that $A = \bigcup_{i=1}^{\infty} A_i$. Let $\gamma_n(a, b)$ be the number of upcrossings over the interval $[a, b]$, where the latter may be **any** of the intervals $[a_i, b_i]$. Since, obviously, $\gamma_n(a, b) \leq \gamma_{n+1}(a, b)$, it follows that the limit of the upcrossing sequence exists and is given by

$$\lim_{n \to \infty} \gamma_n(a, b) = \gamma_\infty(a, b). \tag{5.84}$$

Moreover,

$$E[\gamma_n(a, b)] \quad \leq \quad \frac{E(X_n - a)^+}{b - a} \leq \frac{EX_n^+ + \mid a \mid}{b - a}$$
$$\leq \quad \frac{E \mid X_n \mid + \mid a \mid}{b - a} \leq \frac{\sup_{n \geq 1} E \mid X_n \mid + \mid a \mid}{b - a}.$$

Consquently,

$$E[\gamma_\infty(a, b)] = \lim_{n \to \infty} E[\gamma_n(a, b)] < \infty, \tag{5.85}$$

which contradicts the statement $\mathcal{P}(A) > 0$. This is so since if Eq. (5.85) holds then we could choose an infinite sequence of terms converging to the limit inferior and an infinite number of terms converging to the limit superior, thus inducing an infinite number of upcrossings. Hence, $\mathcal{P}(A) = 0$ and $X_n \overset{\text{a.c.}}{\to} X_\infty$, as required. By Fatou's lemma (Proposition 18 in Chapter 1), we further conclude that $\lim_{n \to \infty} E(X_n) = E(\lim_{n \to \infty} X_n) = E(X_\infty)$.

q.e.d.

Corollary 8. Let X be a nonpositive submartingale; then, the following statments are true:

    i. there exists a random variable, X_∞, such that $X_n \overset{\text{a.c.}}{\to} X_\infty$ and X_∞ is a.c. finite;

    ii. the stochastic sequence $X^* = \{(X_n, \mathcal{A}_n) : 1 \le n \le \infty\}$, where $\mathcal{A}_\infty = \sigma(\bigcup_{n=1}^\infty \mathcal{A}_n)$ is a **submartingale**.

Proof: To prove i., we note that since $E(X_{n+1}) \ge E(X_n) \cdots \ge E(X_1) > -\infty$ and $X_n \le 0$, it follows that $E(-X_n) \le E(-X_1)$; this, in turn, implies that $\sup_{n \ge 1} E(-X_n) \le \infty$; by Proposition 9, its limit, $-X_\infty$, exists a.c. and it is finite a.c., which completes the proof.

    As for ii., let m be any integer and use Fatou's lemma to obtain

$$E[X_\infty \mid \mathcal{A}_m] = E[\lim_{n \to \infty} X_n \mid \mathcal{A}_m] \ge \limsup_{n \to \infty} E[X_n \mid \mathcal{A}_m] \ge X_m.$$

q.e.d.

Corollary 9. If X is a nonnegative martingale, then there exists an a.c. finite random variable, say X_∞, such that $X_n \overset{\text{a.c.}}{\to} X_\infty$.

Proof: By the definition of a martingale process, $E(X_n) = E(X_1) < \infty$. Thus, $\sup_{n \ge 1} E \mid X_n \mid < \infty$. The result then follows immediately by Proposition 9.

q.e.d.

Remark 6. The question may now be raised as to whether or not the condition of Proposition 9 implies L^1-convergence as well, i.e., whether it implies $\lim_{n \to \infty} E \mid X_n - X_\infty \mid = 0$. This may be a particularly appealing proposition since we have already established that $E \mid X_\infty \mid < \infty$. The answer, however, is in the negative, as the following simple counterexample will indicate. Let X be a martingale, such that $X_n = \prod_{i=1}^n \xi_i$, the $\xi's$ are i.i.d., and

$$
\begin{aligned}
\xi_i \quad &= \quad 0 \quad \text{with probability } \frac{1}{2} \\
&= \quad 2a \quad \text{with probability } \frac{1}{2}.
\end{aligned}
$$

By Corollary 9, this converges with probability one to $X_\infty \equiv 0$. On the other hand, $E(X_n) = 1$, for all n, and moreover, $E \mid X_n - X_\infty \mid = 1$, which shows that this martingale does not converge in L^1 mode, even though it satisfies the conditions of the proposition above. What is required for L^1 convergence is spelled out in the following proposition.

Proposition 10. As in Proposition 9, let X be a **uniformly integrable submartingale.** Then, there exists a random variable, say X_∞, such that

$$E \mid X_\infty \mid < \infty, \quad X_n \overset{a.c.}{\to} X_\infty, \quad X_n \overset{L^1}{\to} X_\infty.$$

Moreover, the stochastic sequence $X^* = \{(X_n, A_n) : 1 \le n \le \infty\}$ is also a submartingale.

Proof: By uniform integrability, [14] we infer that $\sup_{n \ge 1} E \mid X_n \mid < \infty$. Hence, by Proposition 9, there exists an a.c. finite random variable, say X_∞, such that $X_n \overset{a.c.}{\to} X_\infty$. To show L^1 convergence, let $m \ge n$ and note that for any $A \in A_n$, convergence with probability one and uniform integrability imply that $\int_A \mid X_m - X_\infty \mid dP \longrightarrow 0$, or that $\lim_{m \to \infty} \int_A X_m \, dP = \int_A X_\infty \, dP$. Moreover, since X is a submartingale, for $m \ge n$ and $A \in A_n$, we have

$$\int_A X_m \, dP = \int_A E(X_m \mid A_n) \, dP \le \int_A X_n \, dP. \tag{5.86}$$

Consequently, we must have, for all $A \in A_n$,

$$\int_A X_n \, dP \le \int_A X_\infty \, dP = \int_A E(X_\infty \mid A_n) \, dP,$$

which implies $E(X_\infty \mid A_n) \ge X_n$, thus showing X^* to be a supermartingale.

q.e.d.

---

[14] Uniform integrability means the following: define

$$A_n = \{\omega : \mid X_n \mid > c, c \in R^+\}.$$

A sequence of random variables is said to be u.i. if and only if

$$\sup_n \int_{A_n} \mid X_n \mid dP \longrightarrow 0,$$

as $c \to \infty$.

Corollary 10. If X is a submartingale such that, for some $p > 1$,

$$\sup_n E \mid X_n \mid^p < \infty,$$

then there exists a random variable, say X_∞, such that

$$E \mid X_\infty \mid < \infty, \quad X_n \overset{\text{a.c.}}{\to} X_\infty, \quad X_n \overset{L^1}{\to} X_\infty.$$

Proof: It will suffice to show that the condition of the corollary implies the uniform integrability of the random variables of the submartingale.

Proof: Let $K = \sup_{n \geq 1} E \mid X_n \mid^p$; by the condition of the corollary, $K < \infty$. Let $c \in R^+$ be arbitrary and consider the sets

$$A_n = \{\omega : \mid X_n(\omega) \mid > c\}, \quad n = 1, 2, \ldots \tag{5.87}$$

We must show that

$$\lim_{c \to \infty} \sup_{n \geq 1} \int_{A_n} \mid X_n \mid d\mathcal{P} = 0.$$

To do so, we first note that

$$\begin{aligned} E \mid X_n \mid^p &= \int_{A_n} \mid X_n \mid^p d\mathcal{P} + \int_{\bar{A}_n} \mid X_n \mid^p d\mathcal{P} \\ &\geq \int_{A_n} \mid X_n \mid^p d\mathcal{P} \geq c^{p-1} \int_{A_n} \mid X_n \mid d\mathcal{P}. \end{aligned} \tag{5.88}$$

But, the relation in Eq. (5.88) may also be rewritten as

$$\int_{A_n} \mid X_n \mid d\mathcal{P} \leq c^{1-p} E \mid X_n \mid^p \leq c^{1-p} K. \tag{5.89}$$

Since $1 - p < 0$, we conclude that

$$\lim_{c \to \infty} \sup_{n \geq 1} \int_{A_n} \mid X_n \mid d\mathcal{P} \leq \lim_{c \to \infty} c^{1-p} K = 0.$$

q.e.d.

5.8   Convergence Sets

In previous discussions, we have considered conditions under which a martingale stochastic sequence converged with probability one. As the term implies, this means that the set over which (pointwise) convergence occurs is the reference set Ω, with the possible exception of subsets of measure zero. When, however, this is not the case, an interesting question is: how can the set over which convergence occurs be characterized? It is this question we shall now address.

Definition 7. Let $\xi = \{\xi_n : n \geq 1\}$ be a sequence of random variables defined on the probability space $(\Omega, \mathcal{A}, \mathcal{P})$. The set

$$CS(\xi) = \{\omega : \lim_{n \to \infty} \xi_n(\omega) = \xi_\infty(\omega) < \infty\}$$

is said to be the **convergence set** of the sequence ξ, i.e., it is the set over which the random variable ξ_∞ is finite and it is the pointwise limit of the sequence $\xi_n(\omega)$.

The previous discussion had also established that for submartingales obeying $\sup_{n \geq 1} E \mid X_n \mid < \infty$ the convergence set is essentially the reference set Ω. What if this condition does not hold?

Definition 8. Let $X = \{(X_n, \mathcal{A}_n) : n \geq 0\}$, such that $\mathcal{A}_0 = (\emptyset, \Omega)$, be a stochastic sequence defined on the probability space $(\Omega, \mathcal{A}, \mathcal{P})$. It is said to belong to the class $\mathcal{D}^+$, i.e., $X \in \mathcal{D}^+$, if and only if

$$E[(\Delta X_{\tau_j})^2 I(\tau_j < \infty)] < \infty,$$

for every integer $j > 0$, where $\Delta X_n = X_n - X_{n-1}$, $X_0 = 0$ and [15]

$$\tau_j = \inf(n \geq 1 : X_n > j)$$
$$= \infty \quad \text{if no such integer exists.}$$

Proposition 11. Let $X = \{(X_n, \mathcal{A}_n) : n \geq 1\}$ be a submartingale defined on the probability space $(\Omega, \mathcal{A}, \mathcal{P})$. If, in addition, $X \in \mathcal{D}^+$, then $CS(X) = A^*$, where

$$A^* = \{\omega : \sup_{n \geq 1} X_n(\omega) < \infty\}.$$

---

[15] We remind the reader that the shorthand notation $I(\tau_j < \infty)$ denotes the indicator function of the set $\{\omega : \tau_j(\omega) < \infty\}$.

Proof: If $\omega \in CS(X)$, then

$$\infty > X_\infty(\omega) = \lim_{n \to \infty} X_n(\omega) = \limsup_{n \to \infty} X_n(\omega).$$

But, this implies $\sup_{n \geq 1} X_n(\omega) < \infty$, so that $\omega \in A^*$ and $CS(X) \subseteq A^*$.
    Next, suppose $\omega \in A^*$. We note that

$$A^* = \bigcup_{j=1}^{\infty} B_j, \quad B_j = \{\omega : \tau_j(\omega) = \infty\}. \tag{5.90}$$

This is so since the event $\sup_{n \geq 1} X_n < \infty$ is, evidently, the union

$$\{\omega : \sup_{n \geq 1} X_n(\omega) < \infty\} = \bigcup_{j=1}^{\infty} \{\omega : \sup_{n \geq 1} X_n(\omega) < j\}$$

$$= \bigcup_{j=1}^{\infty} B_j. \tag{5.91}$$

Thus, $\omega \in A^*$ implies $\omega \in B_j$ for one or more indicies j; suppose then $\omega \in B_j$ and consider the stopped process $X^s = \{(X_{\tau_j \wedge n}, \mathcal{A}_n) : n \geq 1\}$. Evidently,

$$\begin{aligned} X_{\tau_j \wedge n}^+ &= X_{\tau_j \wedge n}^+ I(\tau_j = \infty) + X_{\tau_j \wedge n}^+ I(\tau_j < \infty) \\ &\leq j + X_{\tau_j \wedge n}^+ I(\tau_j < \infty). \end{aligned} \tag{5.92}$$

Consequently, for every n, we have

$$\begin{aligned} E(X_{\tau_j \wedge n}^+) &\leq j + E[X_{\tau_j}^+ I(\tau_j < \infty)] \\ &= E[\Delta X_{\tau_j}^+ I(\tau_j < \infty) + X_{\tau_j - 1}^+ I(\tau_j < \infty)] \\ &\leq 2j + E[\Delta X_{\tau_j}^+ I(\tau_j < \infty)] \\ &\leq 2j + E[(\Delta X_{\tau_j})^+ I(\tau_j < \infty)] \\ &< \infty. \end{aligned} \tag{5.93}$$

But, Eq. (5.93) implies that

$$\sup_{n \geq 1} E(X_{\tau_j \wedge n}^+) < \infty. \tag{5.94}$$

Since $X_n^+ \leq |X| \leq 2X_n^+ - X_n$, we see that, for submartingales,

$$E(X_n^+) \leq E(|X|) \leq 2E(X_n^+) - E(X_n) \leq 2E(X_n^+) - E(X_1), \tag{5.95}$$

so that Eq. (5.94) implies

$$\sup_{n\geq 1} E(|X_{\tau_j \wedge n}|) < \infty. \tag{5.96}$$

We thus conclude, by Proposition 9, that the sequence converges with probability one to an a.c. finite random variable. But, this means that $A^* \subseteq CS(X)$ and, consequently, $A^* = CS(X)$.

q.e.d.

Corollary 11. Let X be a martingale and define the sets

$$A^+ = \{\omega : \limsup_{n\to\infty} X_n(\omega) = \infty\}, \quad A^- = \{\omega : \liminf_{n\to\infty} X_n(\omega) = -\infty\}.$$

If

$$E\left(\sup_{n\geq 1} |\Delta X_n|\right) < \infty$$

then

$$CS(X) \cup (A^+ \cap A^-) = \Omega. \tag{5.97}$$

Proof: We note that, by Proposition 11, $X \in \mathcal{D}^+$; consequently, if $\sup_{n\geq 1} X_n < \infty$ then $A^* = CS(X)$; moreover, if we define $Y_n = -X_n$ then $Y \in \mathcal{D}^+$, and we have $B^* = CS(X)$, where $B^* = \{\omega : \sup_{n\geq 1} Y_n < \infty\}$. But, we also note that

$$B^* = \{\omega : \inf_{n\geq 1} X_n > -\infty\}. \tag{5.98}$$

Consequently, we have $A^* \cup B^* = CS(X)$ and $\Omega = CS(X) \cup \overline{CS(X)}$. But,

$$\Omega = CS(X) \cup (\bar{A}^* \cap \bar{B}^*).$$

The proof will be complete if we note that $\bar{A}^* = A^+$ and $\bar{B}^* = A^-$.

q.e.d.

Remark 7. The import of the corollary is that martingales are either well behaved, in which case $CS(X) = \Omega$, or not. When they are not, they are very poorly behaved indeed, since then their limsup is at ∞ and their liminf is at $-\infty$.

Another useful result is

Proposition 12. Let X be a submartingale and let

$$X_n = m_n + a_n$$

be its Doob decomposition. The following statments are true:

  i. if X is a nonnegative submartingale then

$$C^* = \{\omega : a_\infty(\omega) < \infty\} \subseteq CS(X) \subseteq A^* = \{\omega : \sup_{n \geq 1} X_n(\omega) < \infty\};$$

  ii. if $X \in \mathcal{D}^+$, then $CS(X) = A^* \subseteq C^*$;

  iii. if $X \in \mathcal{D}^+$ **and** it is also a nonnegative submartingale, then $CS(X) = A^* = C^*$.

Proof: For $\omega \in A^*$, Proposition 9 implies $\omega \in CS(X)$, thus establishing the second inclusion of part i. As for the first inclusion, we note that defining

$$C_j = \{\omega : a_\infty(\omega) \leq j\} \tag{5.99}$$

we have that

$$C^* = \bigcup_{j=1}^{\infty} C_j. \tag{5.100}$$

Hence, if $\omega \in C^*$, then $\omega \in C_j$ for one or more values of the index j. We further observe that, defining

$$\begin{aligned} \tau_j &= \inf(n \geq 1 : a_{n+1} > j) \\ &= \infty \quad \text{otherwise, i.e., when no such integer exists,} \end{aligned} \tag{5.101}$$

we can also write $C_j = \{\omega : \tau_j(\omega) = \infty\}$. Thus, if ω is such that $\tau_j(\omega) = \infty$ then $a_n(\omega) \leq j$, for all n, and hence, $a_\infty(\omega) \leq j$. Defining the stopped sequence [16] $X_{\tau_j \wedge n}$, we obtain

$$E(X_{\tau_j \wedge n}) = E(a_{\tau_j \wedge n}) \leq j. \tag{5.102}$$

Since we are dealing with a nonnegative submartingale, we thus have

$$\sup_{n \geq 1} E(X_{\tau_j \wedge n}) \leq j < \infty,$$

---

[16] Note that for ω such that $\tau_j(\omega) = \infty$, in effect, $X_{\tau_j \wedge n}(\omega) = X_n(\omega)$.

and Proposition 9 implies that the sequence converges. Thus, we have shown that if $\omega \in C^*$ then $\omega \in CS(X)$, which is the first inclusion of i.

To prove part ii., note that the first inclusion follows from Proposition 11; as for the second inclusion, define, as in Proposition 11,

$$\tau_s = \inf(n \geq 1 : X_n > s) \qquad (5.103)$$
$$= \infty \quad \text{otherwise, i.e., when no such integer exists,}$$

and note that in the notation of that proposition

$$A^* = \bigcup_{s=1}^{\infty} B_s, \quad B_s = \{\omega : \tau_s(\omega) = \infty\}, \quad A^* = \{\omega : \sup_{n \geq 1} X_n(\omega)\}.$$

We must show that $A^* \subseteq C^*$. Now, if $\omega \in A^*$ then $\omega \in B_s$ for one or more values of the index s. Consider the Doob decomposition of the stopped sequence

$$X_{\tau_s \wedge n} = m_{\tau_s \wedge n} + a_{\tau_s \wedge n}$$

and note that

$$E(a_{\tau_s \wedge n}) = E(X_{\tau_s \wedge n} \leq E(X_{\tau_s \wedge n}^+).$$

Since $X \in \mathcal{D}^+$, we conclude that, for every n,

$$E(a_{\tau_s \wedge n}) \leq E(X_{\tau_s \wedge n}^+) \leq 2s + E[(\Delta X_{\tau_s})^+ I(\tau_s < \infty)] < \infty. \qquad (5.104)$$

Moreover, since for $\omega \in B_s$, $X_{\tau_j \wedge n} = X_n$, it follows that

$$X_{\tau_s \wedge n}(\omega) \longrightarrow X_\infty(\omega) < \infty,$$

and thus, $a_\infty(\omega) < \infty$. Hence, $\omega \in A^*$ implies that $\omega \in C^*$, or that $A^* \subseteq C^*$, which establishes the second inclusion of ii.

As for part iii., we have by part i.

$$C^* \subseteq CS(X) \subseteq A^*,$$

while by part ii. we have

$$CS(X) = A^* \subseteq C^*.$$

Together these relations imply $CS(X) = A^* = C^*$.

q.e.d.

Corollary 12. Let $X = \{(X_n, \mathcal{A}_n) : n \geq 0\}$ be a stochastic sequence such that $\mathcal{A}_0 = (\emptyset, \Omega)$, $X_n = \sum_{j=1}^{n} \xi_j$, $\xi_j \geq 0$, and $E(\xi_j) < \infty$. Suppose, further, that $X_0 = \xi_0 = 0$. The following statements are true:

   i. $\{\omega : \sum_{j=1}^{\infty} E(\xi_j \mid \mathcal{A}_{j-1})(\omega) < \infty\} \subseteq CS(X)$;

   ii. if, in addition,

$$E(\sup_{n \geq 1} \xi_n) < \infty,$$

   then $\{\omega : \sum_{j=1}^{\infty} E(\xi_j \mid \mathcal{A}_{j-1})(\omega) < \infty\} = CS(X)$.

Proof: Since

$$E(X_{n+1} \mid \mathcal{A}_n) = X_n + E(\xi_{n+1} \mid \mathcal{A}_n) \geq X_n, \qquad E(X_n) < \infty,$$

it follows that X is a nonnegative submartingale. Let its Doob decomposition be

$$X_n = m_n + a_n, \quad a_n = \sum_{j=0}^{n-1}[E(X_{j+1} \mid \mathcal{A}_j) - X_j] = \sum_{j=0}^{n-1} E(\xi_{j+1} \mid \mathcal{A}_j).$$

$$(5.105)$$

It is evident, from Eq. (5.105) that

$$\{\omega : a_\infty(\omega) < \infty\} = \left\{\omega : \sum_{j=0}^{\infty} E(\xi_{j+1} \mid \mathcal{A}_j)\right\}.$$

Consequently, the validity of part i. follows from part i. of Proposition 12.

As for part ii., note that $\Delta X_n = \xi_n$ and that, consequently,

$$E\left(\sup_{n \geq 1} |\Delta X_n|\right) < \infty$$

implies

$$E\left[(\Delta X_{\tau_j})^+ I(\tau_j < \infty)\right] \leq E\left(\sup_{n \geq 1} |\Delta X_n|\right) < \infty.$$

Hence, $X \in \mathcal{D}^+$, where τ_j is a stopping time as defined in Eq. (5.103). Thus, by part ii. of Proposition 12, $\{\omega : \sum_{j=0}^{\infty} E(\xi_{j+1} \mid \mathcal{A}_j)(\omega)\} = CS(X)$.

$$\text{q.e.d.}$$

Corollary 13. In the context of Corollary 12, let $\{A_n : A_n \in \mathcal{A}_n, n \geq 1\}$ be a sequence of sets, and $\{I_n : n \geq 1\}$ a sequence of their indicator functions. Then,

$$\left\{\omega : \sum_{j=0}^{\infty} \mathcal{P}(A_{j+1} \mid \mathcal{A}_j)(\omega) < \infty\right\} = \left\{\omega : \sum_{j=1}^{\infty} I_n(\omega) < \infty\right\}.$$

Proof: Put $X_n = \sum_{j=1}^{n} I_j$; note that $I_j \geq 0$, $E(I_j) = \mathcal{P}(A_j)$, and, moreover, that $X = \{(X_n, \mathcal{A}_n) : n \geq 1\}$ is a nonnegative submartingale obeying

$$\Delta X_n = I_n \leq 1, \qquad E(\sup_{n \geq 1} \mid \Delta X_n \mid) < \infty.$$

Since

$$\left\{\omega : \sum_{j=1}^{\infty} I_n(\omega) < \infty\right\} = \{\omega : \lim_{n \to \infty} X_n(\omega) = X_\infty(\omega) < \infty\} = CS(X),$$

the conclusion follows immediately from part ii of Corollary 11.

$$\text{q.e.d.}$$

Proposition 13. Let $Y = \{(Y_n, \mathcal{A}_n) : n \geq 1\}$ be a square integrable martingale. The following statements are true:

i. $A^* = \{\omega : CV(Y)(\omega) < \infty\} \subseteq CS(Y)$;

ii. if, in addition,

$$\sup_{n \geq 1} E(\mid \Delta Y_n \mid^2) < \infty, \quad \text{then} \quad A^* = CS(Y).$$

Proof: We consider the two submartingales [17] Y_n^2 and $(Y_n + 1)^2$ together with their Doob decompositions

$$Y_n^2 = m_{1n} + a_{1n}, \qquad (Y_n + 1)^2 = m_{2n} + a_{2n}.$$

---

[17] The reason we consider both these submartingales is that $(Y_n+1)^2 - Y_n^2 = 2Y_n + 1$, so that **if both submartingales** converge, then Y_n must also converge, on the **intersection of their convergence sets**, to an a.c. finite random variable, say Y_∞.

Since $E[(\Delta Y_n)^2] = E\{[\Delta(Y_n + 1)]^2\}$, we would expect the conditional (quadratic) variations[18] of the two martingales to be the same. Moreover, from the properties of the Doob decomposition, we have that, for the reason just noted, $a_{1n} = a_{2n}$, and moreover, that $CV(Y) = a_{1\infty}$. By part i. of Proposition 12, we also have that $A^* \subseteq CS(Y_n^2)$ **and** $A^* \subseteq CS[(Y_n + 1)^2]$. Consequently, $A^* \subseteq CS(Y_n^2) \cap CS[(Y_n + 1)^2] = CS(Y)$, which concludes the proof of part i.

As for part ii., the condition therein implies that $Y_n^2 \in \mathcal{D}^+$. To see this, let j be any integer, define the stopping time

$$
\begin{aligned}
\tau_j &= \inf(n \geq 1 : Y_n > j) \\
&= \infty \quad \text{otherwise, i.e., if no such integer exists,}
\end{aligned}
$$

and notice that for ω such that $\tau_j(\omega) < \infty$ we have the following:

$$
\begin{aligned}
\mid \Delta Y_{\tau_j}^2 \mid &= \mid Y_{\tau_j}^2 - 2Y_{\tau_j} Y_{\tau_j - 1} + Y_{\tau_j - 1}^2 + 2Y_{\tau_j} Y_{\tau_j - 1} - 2Y_{\tau_j - 1}^2 \mid \\
&\leq (\Delta Y_{\tau_j})^2 + 2 \mid Y_{\tau_j - 1} \mid \Delta Y_{t_j} \mid .
\end{aligned}
$$

Since, by Liapounov's inequality,

$$
(E \mid t \mid^p)^{\frac{1}{p}} \leq (E \mid t \mid^q)^{\frac{1}{q}}, \quad \text{for } p \leq q,
$$

it follows that

$$
\begin{aligned}
E \mid \Delta Y_n^2 \mid I(\tau_j < \infty) &\leq E \Delta Y_{\tau_j})^2 I(\tau_j < \infty) + 2j^{\frac{1}{2}} E \mid \Delta Y_{t_j} \mid I(\tau_j < \infty) \\
&\leq E \sup_{n \geq 1} \mid \Delta Y_n \mid^2 + 2j^{\frac{1}{2}} \left(E \sup_{n \geq 1} \mid \Delta Y_n \mid^2 \right)^{\frac{1}{2}} < \infty.
\end{aligned}
$$

Thus, $Y^2 \in \mathcal{D}^+$, and by part ii. of Proposition 12,

$$
\{\omega : a_{1\infty}(\omega)\} = CS(Y^2),
$$

---

[18] We remind the reader that if $X = \{(X_n, \mathcal{A}_n) : n \geq 1\}$ is a square integrable martingale then its **conditional (quadratic) variation** is given by

$$
CV(X) = \sum_{j=1}^{\infty} E[(\Delta X_j)^2 \mid \mathcal{A}_{j-1}] = \sum_{j=1}^{\infty} E(\Delta X_j^2 \mid \mathcal{A}_{j-1}).
$$

Whether the series is truncated or not, note that $CV(X)$, or $CV_n(X)$, is a **random variable**, since the conditional expectations, $E[(\Delta X_j)^2 \mid \mathcal{A}_{j-1}]$, are random variables.

as well as

$$\{\omega : a_{1\infty}(\omega)\} = CS(Y^2).$$

By the same argument as above, we conclude $\{\omega :< CV(Y)(\omega) < \infty\} = CS(Y)$.

q.e.d.

Another important result is

Proposition 14. Let $X = \{(X_n, \mathcal{A}_n) : n \geq 0\}$ be a square integrable martingale defined on the probability space $(\Omega, \mathcal{A}, \mathcal{P})$ such that $\mathcal{A}_0 = (\emptyset, \Omega)$, $X_0 = 0$; in addition, let $\{(a_n, \mathcal{A}_{n-1}) : n \geq 1\}$ be a predictable increasing sequence such that almost certainly $a_1 \geq 1$ and $a_\infty = \infty$. If, almost certainly,

$$\sum_{j=1}^{\infty} \frac{E[(\Delta X_j)^2 \mid \mathcal{A}_{j-1}]}{a_j^2} < \infty,$$

then

$$\frac{X_n}{a_n} \xrightarrow{\text{a.c.}} 0.$$

Alternatively, if X is a square integrable martingale and a.c. $CV(X) = \infty$, then

$$\frac{X_n}{CV(X)} \xrightarrow{\text{a.c.}} 0.$$

Proof: Define

$$m_n = \sum_{j=1}^{n} \frac{\Delta X_j}{a_j} \tag{5.106}$$

and notice that m_n is $\mathcal{A}_n$-measurable, square integrable, and moreover, that $E(m_n \mid \mathcal{A}_{n-1}) = m_{n-1}$, i.e., $m = \{(m_n, \mathcal{A}_n) : n \geq 1\}$ is a **square integrable** martingale. In addition, rewrite Eq. (5.107) as

$$X_n = X_{n-1} + a_n \Delta m_n.$$

Take $m_0 = X_0 = 0$ to obtain

$$\frac{X_n}{a_n} = \frac{1}{a_n} \sum_{j=1}^{n} a_j \Delta m_j. \tag{5.107}$$

We note that, by construction, $(\Delta m_n)^2 = \frac{(\Delta X_n)^2}{a_n^2}$, so that

$$CV(m) = \sum_{j=1}^{\infty} \frac{E[(\Delta X_j)^2 \mid \mathcal{A}_{j-1}]}{a_j^2} < \infty \,\text{a.c.} \qquad (5.108)$$

Consequently, by Proposition 13, [19]

$$m_n \overset{\text{a.c.}}{\to} m_\infty. \qquad (5.109)$$

From Toeplitz' lemma (Lemma 2 of Chapter 3), we thus conclude from Eq. (5.108) that

$$\frac{X_n}{a_n} \overset{\text{a.c.}}{\to} 0.$$

The case where X is specified to be a square integrable martingale with $<X>_\infty = \infty$ a.c. is handled in exactly the same manner. Thus, take $<X>_n = a_n$ and note that all conditions regarding the sequence $\{(a_n, \mathcal{A}_{n-1}) : n \geq 1\}$ are satisfied. Consequently,

$$\frac{X_n}{CV_n(X)} \overset{\text{a.c.}}{\to} 0.$$

q.e.d.

5.9 WLLN and SLLN for Martingales

Of considerable interest in econometrics is the applicability of the various versions of laws of large numbers to martingale sequences, since such problems occur quite frequently.

This issue is addressed by the following very basic results.

Proposition 15. Let $\{(\xi_n, \mathcal{A}_n) : n \geq 0\}$ be a stochastic sequence, with $\mathcal{A}_0 = (\emptyset, \Omega)$, defined on the probability space $(\Omega, \mathcal{A}, \mathcal{P})$ and such that $E(\xi_{n+1} \mid \mathcal{A}_n) = 0$, $E \mid \xi_n \mid < \infty$. Let $b = \{b_n : n \geq 1\}$ be a sequence of real numbers such that $0 < b_n < b_{n+1}$, $\lim_{n \to \infty} b_n = \infty$,

---

[19] Actually, Proposition 13 merely states that

$$\{\omega : CV(m)(\omega) < \infty\} \subseteq CS(m).$$

However, in this case, it is given that $CV_n(m)$ converges a.c., so that, with the possible exception of sets of measure zero, $CS(m) = \Omega$.

and define [20] $X_n = \sum_{j=1}^n \xi_j$, $A_{in} = \{\omega : |\xi_i(\omega)| \ge b_n\}$; let I_{in} be the indicator function of A_{in} and $\xi_{in} = \xi_i I_{in}$. If

i. $\sum_{j=1}^n \mathcal{P}(A_{jn}) \longrightarrow 0$;

ii. $\frac{1}{b_n} \sum_{j=1}^n E(\xi_{jn} | \mathcal{A}_{j-1}) \overset{P}{\to} 0$;

iii. $\frac{1}{b_n^2} \sum_{j=1}^n \mathrm{Var}(\xi_{jn} | \mathcal{A}_{j-1}) \overset{P}{\to} 0$,

then

$$\frac{X_n}{b_n} \overset{P}{\to} 0.$$

Proof: Put $X_{nn} = \sum_{j=1}^n \xi_{jn}$ and consider

$$\frac{X_n - X_{nn}}{b_n} = \frac{1}{b_n} \sum_{j=1}^n \xi_j (1 - I_{jn}) = \frac{1}{b_n} \sum_{j=1}^n \xi_j I(|x_j| > b_n).$$

Since

$$B_n = \left\{ \omega : \left| \frac{X_n - X_{nn}}{b_n} \right| > 0 \right\} \subseteq \left\{ \omega : \frac{1}{b_n} \left| \sum_{j=1}^n \xi_j (1 - I_{jn}) \right| > 0 \right\}$$

$$\subseteq \left\{ \omega : \sum_{j=1}^n (1 - I_{jn}) > 0 \right\} = C_n = \bigcup_{j=1}^n A_{jn},$$

and

$$\mathcal{P}(B_n) \le \mathcal{P}(C_n) \le \sum_{j=1}^n \mathcal{P}(A_{jn}) \longrightarrow 0,$$

we conclude that it will be sufficient to show that

$$\frac{X_{nn}}{b_n} \overset{P}{\to} 0.$$

Moreover, in view of condition ii., it will be sufficient to show that

$$Z_n = \frac{X_{nn}}{b_n} - \frac{\sum_{j=1}^n E(\xi_{jn} | \mathcal{A}_{j-1})}{b_n} = \frac{\sum_{j=1}^n \zeta_{jn}}{b_n} \overset{P}{\to} 0,$$

---

[20] If we wished, we could have begun by stating that $X = \{(X_n, \mathcal{A}_n) : n \ge 1\}$ is a martingale and defining all other entities in terms of the differences ΔX_n; the result would be identical to the one appearing in the text if we make the identification $\Delta X_n = \xi_n$.

where $\zeta_{jn} = \xi_{jn} - E(\xi_{jn} \mid \mathcal{A}_{j-1})$. Finally, it is easy to determine that

$$\operatorname{Var}(Z_n) = \sum_{j=1}^{n} \operatorname{Var}(\zeta_{jn}) + 2 \sum_{i<j} \operatorname{Cov}(\zeta_{in}\zeta_{jn}) = \sum_{j=1}^{n} \operatorname{Var}(\zeta_{jn}) \xrightarrow{P} 0.$$

Consequently,

$$P\left(\mid Z_n \mid \geq \frac{1}{r} \mid \mathcal{A}_{n-1} \right) \leq r \sum_{j=1}^{n} \operatorname{Var}(\zeta_{jn}) \longrightarrow 0.$$

q.e.d.

For SLLN, we present a more general result than that given for WLLN.

Proposition 16. Let $\{(\xi_n, \mathcal{A}_n) : n \geq 0\}$ be a stochastic sequence, with $\mathcal{A}_0 = (\emptyset, \Omega)$, defined on the probability space $(\Omega, \mathcal{A}, \mathcal{P})$, and $c \in R^+$, but otherwise arbitrary. Let

$$A_{ic} = \{\omega : \mid \xi_i(\omega) \mid \geq \mid c\}, \qquad \xi_{ic} = \xi_i I_{ic},$$

where, I_{ic} is the **indicator function** of $\bar{A}_{ic}$. In addition, define

$$B_1 = \left\{ \omega : \sum_{j=1}^{\infty} P(A_{jc} \mid \mathcal{A}_{j-1}) < \infty \right\}, \quad B_2 = \left\{ \omega : \sum_{j=1}^{\infty} E(\xi_{jc} \mid \mathcal{A}_{j-1}) < \infty \right\},$$

$$B_3 = \left\{ \omega : \sum_{j=1}^{\infty} \operatorname{Var}(\xi_{jc} \mid \mathcal{A}_{j-1}) < \infty \right\}, \quad B = B_1 \cap B_2 \cap B_3.$$

Then, $X_n = \sum_{j=1}^{n} \xi_j$ converges on B, i.e., for any $\omega \in B$,

$$X_n(\omega) \longrightarrow X_\infty(\omega).$$

Proof: Let $CS(X)$ be the convergence set of the stochastic sequence $X = \{(X_n, \mathcal{A}_n) : n \geq 0\}$. We are required to prove that $B \subseteq CS(X)$. This will be accomplished if we show that $CS(X) \cap B = B$. Since $\sum_{j=1}^{n} P(A_{jc} \mid \mathcal{A}_{j-1})$ converges, we conclude, by Corollary 13, that the event $\mid \xi_i \mid \geq c$ occurs only **finitely many times**. Since

$$X_n = \sum_{j=1}^{n} \xi_j = \sum_{j=1}^{n} \xi_{jc} + \sum_{j=1}^{n} \xi_i I(\mid \xi_i \mid \geq c),$$

it follows that, **restricted to** B, **the convergence set of** X **coincides with that of** $\sum_{j=1}^{n} \xi_{jc}$. More precisely, what we want to convey is that

$$B \cap CS(X) = B \cap CS\left(\sum_{j=1}^{n} \xi_{jc}\right), \qquad (5.110)$$

where the last symbol indicates the convergence set of the entity in parentheses. Because of the condition in ii., the latter convergence set, restricted to B, coincides with that of

$$z_n = \sum_{j=1}^{n} \zeta_{jc}, \qquad \zeta_{jc} = \xi_{jc} - E(\xi_{jc} \mid \mathcal{A}_{j-1}).$$

Next, we note that $z = \{(z_n, \mathcal{A}_n) : n \geq 0\}$ is a **square integrable martingale** obeying

$$|\Delta z_n| = |\xi_{nc} - E(\xi_{nc} \mid \mathcal{A}_{n-1})| \leq 2c. \qquad (5.111)$$

By Proposition 13, part ii., Eq. (5.111) implies that

$$CS(z) = \{\omega : CV(z) < \infty\} = \left\{\omega : \sum_{j=1}^{\infty} \mathrm{Var}(\xi_{jc} \mid \mathcal{A}_{j-1}) < \infty\right\} = B_3.$$
$$(5.112)$$

What Eqs. (5.110) and (5.113) imply is that

$$B \cap CS(X) = B \cap CS\left(\sum_{j=1}^{n} \xi_{jc}\right) = B \cap B_3 = B.$$

q.e.d.

5.10 Martingale CLT

In this section, we shall present some major results and, as we have done in Chapter 4, we shall use the indices t, T, which are more customary in econometrics, in lieu of j, n. We begin with a general equivalence result.

Proposition 17. Let $\{(X_{tT}, \mathcal{A}_{tT}) : t = 1, 2, \ldots, T\}$, for each $T \geq 1$, be a stochastic sequence defined on the probability space $(\Omega, \mathcal{A}, \mathcal{P})$ such

that $\mathcal{A}_{t-1,T} \subseteq \mathcal{A}_{tT} \subseteq \mathcal{A}$, with $\mathcal{A}_{0T} = (\emptyset, \Omega)$ and $X_{0T} = 0$, for all T. [21]
Furthermore, define

$$a*. \quad A_{tT} = \left\{ \omega : |X_{tT}(\omega)| > \frac{1}{r} \right\},$$

$$a. \quad P_T = \sum_{t=1}^{T} \mathcal{P}(A_{tT} \mid \mathcal{A}_{t-1T}),$$

$$b. \quad X_T^* = \max_{1 \le t \le T} |X_{tT}|,$$

$$c. \quad m_T(1) = \sum_{t=1}^{T} E\left[X_{tT} I\left(|X_{tT}| \le \frac{1}{r}\right) \mid \mathcal{A}_{t-1,T}\right] = \sum_{t=1}^{T} m_{tT}(1),$$

$$d. \quad \sigma_T^2 = \sum_{t=1}^{T} \operatorname{Var}\left[X_{tT} I\left(|X_{tT}| \le \frac{1}{r}\right) \mid \mathcal{A}_{t-1,T}\right],$$

$$e. \quad s_T^{*2} = \sum_{t=1}^{T} \{X_{tT} - E[X_{tT} I(|X_{tT}| \le 1) \mid \mathcal{A}_{t-1,T}]\}^2,$$

$$f. \quad \mathcal{L}_T = \sum_{t=1}^{T} E\left[X_{tT}^2 I\left(|X_{tT}| \ge \frac{1}{r}\right) \mid \mathcal{A}_{t-1,T}\right]. \tag{5.113}$$

The following statements are true:

i. $P_T \overset{P}{\to} 0$ and $X_T^* \overset{P}{\to} 0$ are equivalent, i.e., **convergence in probability for a. and b. are equivalent statements;**

ii. if the conditions listed in i. hold, then $\sigma_T^2 \overset{P}{\to} \sigma^2 \ge 0$ [22] and $s_T^{*2} \overset{P}{\to} \sigma^2$ are equivalent statements, i.e., **if the entities in a. or b. converge in probability to zero, then the entities in d. and e. are equivalent in the sense that if one converges in probability to a limit the other converges as well, and to the same limit.**

Proof: Although aspects of the proof of i. were given in preceding discussions, we give here a fresh proof. Thus, write

$$|X_{tT}| = |X_{tT}| I\left(|X_{tT}| \le \frac{1}{r}\right) + |X_{tT}| I\left(|X_{tT}| > \frac{1}{r}\right)$$

and note that

$$X_T^* = \max_{1 \le t \le T} |X_{tT}| \le \frac{1}{r} + \sum_{j=1}^{T} |X_{tT}| I\left(|X_{tT}| > \frac{1}{r}\right).$$

___
[21] It is also understood that, for fixed $t \le T$, $\mathcal{A}_{tT} \subseteq \mathcal{A}_{t,T+1}$.
[22] Note that $\sigma^2 = 0$ is not excluded.

For arbitrary integer q, define

$$B_T = \left\{\omega : \left[\sum_{t=1}^{T} |X_{tT}| \, I\left(|X_{tT}| > \frac{1}{r}\right)\right] > \frac{1}{q}\right\},$$

$$C_T = \left\{\omega : \left[\sum_{t=1}^{T} I\left(|X_{tT}| > \frac{1}{r}\right)\right] > \frac{1}{q}\right\},$$

and note that $B_T \subseteq C_T$, in fact, $B_T = C_T$. Thus, the statements $X_T^* \xrightarrow{\text{P}} 0$ and $\sum_{t=1}^{T} I\left(|X_{tT}| > \frac{1}{r}\right) \xrightarrow{\text{P}} 0$ are equivalent. Now define

$$u_{sT} = I\left(|X_{sT}| > \frac{1}{r}\right), \qquad U_{tT} = \sum_{s=1}^{t} u_{st}$$

$$v_{sT} = \mathcal{P}(A_{sT} \mid A_{s-1,T}), \qquad V_{tT} = \sum_{s=1}^{t} v_{sT}, \tag{5.114}$$

and note that, for each $T \geq 1$, V_{tT} is $A_{t-1,T}$-measurable and obeys $0 \leq V_{tT} \leq V_{t+1,T}$, i.e., it is an increasing predictable sequence. Similarly, for each $T \geq 1$, U_{tT} is A_{tT}-measurable, and moreover, we have $E(V_{tT}) \geq E(U_{tT})$, in fact, $E(V_{tT}) = E(U_{tT})$. Hence, both sequences fulfill the conditions of Corollary 6; thus, we conclude that $P_T \xrightarrow{\text{P}} 0$, implies that $\sum_{t=1}^{T} I\left(|X_{tT}| > \frac{1}{r}\right) \xrightarrow{\text{P}} 0$, and consequently, that $X_T^* \xrightarrow{\text{P}} 0$. For the converse, we note that since for all t, T, $E(U_{tT}) = E(V_{tT})$ and otherwise the sequences satisfy all the requirements of Corollary 7, we conclude that $X_T^* \xrightarrow{\text{P}} 0$ implies $P_T \xrightarrow{\text{P}} 0$, which completes the proof of part i.

As for part ii., define

$$s_T^2 = \sum_{t=1}^{T} \left[X_{tT} I\left(|X_{tT}| \leq \frac{1}{r}\right) - E_r\right]^2,$$

$$E_1 = E[X_{tT} I(|X_{tT}| \leq 1) \mid A_{t-1,T}],$$

$$E_D = E[X_{tT} I(|X_{tT}| \in (\frac{1}{r}, 1]) \mid A_{t-1,T}],$$

$$E_r = E\left[X_{tT} I\left(|X_{tT}| \leq \frac{1}{r}\right) \mid A_{t-1,T}\right], \tag{5.115}$$

and note that $s_T^{*2} = s_T^2 + s_{T1}$, where

$$s_{T1} = \sum_{t=1}^{T} \left[X_{tT}^2 - X_{tT}^2 I\left(|X_{tT}| \leq \frac{1}{r}\right) - 2X_{tT} E_1\right]$$

$$+ 2 \sum_{t=1}^{T} \left[X_{tT} I\left(|X_{tT}| \leq \frac{1}{r}\right) E_r + E_1^2 - E_r^2\right]$$

$$= \sum_{t=1}^{T} \left[X_{tT}^2 u_{tT} - 2X_{tT} u_{tT} E_r - 2X_{tT} E_D + 2E_D E_r + E_D^2\right].$$

Consequently,

$$|s_{T1}| \leq \sum_{t=1}^{T} \left| X_{tT}^2 u_{tT} - 2X_{tT} u_{tT} E_r - 2X_{tT} E_D + 2E_D E_r + E_D^2 \right|$$

$$\leq \sum_{t=1}^{T} \left[\left(\max_{1 \leq t \leq T} | X_{tT} |^2 + 2 \max_{1 \leq t \leq T} | X_{tT} | \right) u_{tT} \right]$$

$$+ \left(2 \max_{1 \leq t \leq T} | X_{tT} | + 3 \right) \sum_{t=1}^{T} \mathcal{P}(| X_{tT} | \in (\frac{1}{r}, 1])$$

$$\leq \left(\max_{1 \leq t \leq T} | X_{tT} |^2 + \max_{1 \leq t \leq T} | X_{tT} | \right) \sum_{t=1}^{T} u_{tT}$$

$$+ \left(2 \max_{1 \leq t \leq T} | X_{tT} | + 3 \right) \sum_{t=1}^{T} \mathcal{P}(A_{tT} | A_{t-1,T}). \qquad (5.116)$$

Since by i. $\sum_{t=1}^{T} u_{tT} \overset{P}{\to} 0$ and $P_T \overset{P}{\to} 0$, it follows that $| s_{T1} | \overset{P}{\to} 0$. In turn, this implies that to prove ii. we need only show that σ_T^2 and s_T^2 are equivalent, in the sense that if one converges in probability, the other converges, also, and to the same limit.

To pursue this, define

$$\zeta_{tT} = X_{tT} I \left(| X_{tT} | \leq \frac{1}{r} \right) - m_{tT}, \quad \zeta_{tT}^* = \sum_{s=1}^{t} \zeta_{tT}, \quad z_{tT}^2 = E(\zeta_{tT}^2 | A_{t-1,T}),$$
$$(5.117)$$

and note that, for each T, $\{(\zeta_{tT}, A_{tT}) : t \leq T\}$ is a square integrable martingale difference and, moreover,

$$QV_t(\zeta_T^*) = \sum_{s=1}^{t} (\Delta \zeta_{sT})^2 = \sum_{s=1}^{t} \zeta_{sT}^2$$

$$CV_t(\zeta_T^*) = \sum_{s=1}^{t} E[(\Delta \zeta_{sT})^2 | A_{s-1,T}] = \sum_{s=1}^{t} z_{tT}^2. \qquad (5.118)$$

Notice, further that $QV_T(\zeta_T^*) = s_T^2$, $CV_T(\zeta_T^*) = \sigma_T^2$, and define

$$W_{tT} = \sum_{s=1}^{t} w_{sT}, \qquad w_{sT} = \zeta_{sT}^2 - z_{sT}^2. \qquad (5.119)$$

We note that, for each T, $\{(W_{tT}, A_{tT}) : t \leq T\}$ is a **square integrable martingale difference** and, moreover, that

$$W_{TT} = s_T^2 - \sigma_T^2.$$

Thus, another way of stating what is required of us in order to prove ii. is that we must prove that $| W_{TT} | \xrightarrow{P} 0$ or, equivalently, that $W_{TT}^2 \xrightarrow{P} 0$, whenever either s_T^2 or σ_T^2 converge to zero in probability. The quadratic variation of the martingale difference in Eq. (5.119) is given by

$$QV_t(W_T) = \sum_{s=1}^{t} (\Delta W_{sT})^2 = \sum_{s=1}^{t} w_{sT}^2,$$

and it obeys

$$
\begin{aligned}
QV_T(W_T) &= \sum_{t=1}^{T} w_{tT}^2 = \sum_{t=1}^{T} | w_{tT} | \, | w_{tT} | \\
&\leq \max_{1 \leq t \leq T} | w_{tT} | \sum_{t=1}^{T} (\zeta_{tT}^2 + z_{tT}^2) \\
&\leq \frac{4}{r^2} [QV_T(\zeta_T^*) + CV_T(\zeta_T^*)].
\end{aligned}
\tag{5.120}
$$

Since the two stochastic sequences in the rightmost member of Eq. (5.120), dominate each other, i.e., for arbitrary stopping time τ, we have **both**

$$E[QV_\tau(\zeta_T^*)] \geq E[CV_\tau(\zeta_T^*)] \quad \text{and} \quad E[CV_\tau(\zeta_T^*)] \geq E[QV_\tau(\zeta_T^*)],$$

it follows that $QV_T(\zeta_T^*)$ is dominated by

$$\frac{8}{r^2} QV_T(\zeta_T^*) \quad \text{or by} \quad \frac{8}{r^2} CV_T(\zeta_T^*).$$

Finally, it will suffice to show that $QV_T(\zeta_T^*)$ converges in probability to zero, when the conditions in i. are satisfied and either $s_T^2 \xrightarrow{P} \sigma^2$ or $\sigma_T^2 \xrightarrow{P} \sigma^2$. This follows from the fact that $W_{TT} \leq QV_T(\zeta_T^*)$, a.c. There are two ways we can approach this. One is to exploit the relations in Eq. (5.120) and show directly that if $\frac{8}{r^2} QV_T(\zeta_T^*) \xrightarrow{P} 0$ then $QV_T(W_T)$, and hence, W_{TT}^2 converge to zero as well, etc. The other approach is simply to use Proposition 7 and Corollary 6. We shall employ the latter. If $\sigma_T^2 = CV_T(\zeta_T^*)$ converges to $\sigma^2 \in [0, \infty)$, we note that $Z_{tT} = \frac{8}{r^2} CV_t(\zeta_T^*)$ is, for each T, a nonnegative increasing predictable sequence that dominates $QV_t(\zeta_T^*)$, which is a nonnegative stochastic sequence. Since $Z_{TT} \xrightarrow{P} 0$, it follows by Corollary 6 that $QV_T(\zeta_T^*) \xrightarrow{P} 0$. In turn, this implies that $| W_{TT} | \xrightarrow{P} 0$. Thus, we conclude that if $\sigma_T^2 \xrightarrow{P} \sigma^2$, then $s_T^2 \xrightarrow{P} \sigma^2$ as well. On the other hand, suppose that $s_T^2 \xrightarrow{P} \sigma^2$; this means that $QV_T(\zeta_T^*) \overset{P}{\to} \sigma^2$ and, consequently, that $Y_{tT} = \frac{8}{r^2}QV_T(\zeta_T^*)$ converges to zero in probability. The latter is, for each T, a nonnegative increasing sequence that dominates $QV_t(W_T)$. We cannot, however, invoke Corollary 6, as we did just above, because Y_{tT} is not a **predictable** sequence. On the other hand, we see that $| \Delta Y_{tT} | = \frac{8}{r^2}\zeta_{tT}^2 \leq \frac{32}{r^4}$; consequently,

$$\sup_{T \geq 1} \sup_{t \leq T} | \Delta Y_{tT} | \leq \frac{32}{r^4},$$

and the implication of Corollary 6 holds by virtue of the discussion surrounding the proof of part iii. of Proposition 7 and the nature of the bound established above. This means that $QV_T(W_T)$ converges to zero in probability and so does $| W_{TT} |$, which completes the proof of ii.

q.e.d.

When the stochastic sequence of Proposition 17 is a **square integrable martingale difference** or when the **Lindeberg** condition holds, i.e., when the entity in Eq. (5.113) obeys $\mathcal{L}_T \overset{P}{\to} 0$, then certain special conclusions follow, which are stated in the proposition below.

Proposition 18. Let the conditions and definitions of Proposition 17 hold; in addition, **in suppose that the processes therein are square integrable and the Lindeberg condition holds, i.e.,**

$$\mathcal{L}_T \overset{P}{\to} 0.$$

Then, the following statements are true:

i. $P_T \overset{P}{\to} 0$;

ii. $X_T^* \overset{P}{\to} 0$;

iii. if $X^T = \{(X_{tT}, \mathcal{A}_{tT}) : t = 1, 2, \ldots, T\}$ is, in addition, for each $T \geq 1$, a (**square integrable**) **martingale difference**, then

1. $\sum_{t=1}^{T} | E[X_{tT}I(| X_{tT} | > \frac{1}{r}) | \mathcal{A}_{t-1,T}] | \overset{P}{\to} 0$;

2. $\sum_{t=1}^{T} | E[X_{tT}I(| X_{tT} | \leq \frac{1}{r}) | \mathcal{A}_{t-1,T}] | \overset{P}{\to} 0$;

3. $\sum_{t=1}^{T} \left| E[X_{tT} I(\mid X_{tT} \mid > \frac{1}{r}) \mid \mathcal{A}_{t-1,T}] \right|^2 \overset{\text{P}}{\to} 0$;

4. $\sum_{t=1}^{T} \left| E[X_{tT} I(\mid X_{tT} \mid \leq \frac{1}{r}) \mid \mathcal{A}_{t-1,T}] \right|^2 \overset{\text{P}}{\to} 0$;

5. $\sigma_T^2 \overset{\text{P}}{\to} \sigma^2$ is equivalent to $\sum_{t=1}^{T} E(X_{tT}^2 \mid \mathcal{A}_{t-1,T}) \overset{\text{P}}{\to} \sigma^2$;

6. $s_T^{*2} \overset{\text{P}}{\to} \sigma^2$ is equivalent to $\sum_{t=1}^{T} X_{tT}^2 \overset{\text{P}}{\to} \sigma^2$.

Proof: To prove i., we note that

$$\mathcal{L}_T \quad \geq \quad \frac{1}{r^2} \sum_{t=1}^{T} E[I(\mid X_{tT} \mid > \frac{1}{r}) \mid \mathcal{A}_{t-1,T}]$$

$$= \quad \frac{1}{r^2} \sum_{t=1}^{T} \mathcal{P}(A_{tT} \mid \mathcal{A}_{t-1,T}) = \frac{1}{r^2} P_T.$$

Thus, $P_T \leq r^2 \mathcal{L}_T$ and, consequently, $P_T \overset{\text{P}}{\to} 0$.

The validity of ii. is proved in view of i. and part i. of Proposition 17.

To prove iii., part 1, put $m_{tT}^* = \mid E[X_{tT} I(\mid X_{tT} \mid > \frac{1}{r}) \mid \mathcal{A}_{t-1,T}] \mid$ and note that

$$m_{tT}^* \quad = \quad \mid E[X_{tT} I(\mid X_{tT} \mid \in (\frac{1}{r}, 1]) \mid \mathcal{A}_{t-1,T}]$$

$$+ E[X_{tT} I(\mid X_{tT} \mid > 1) \mid \mathcal{A}_{t-1,T}] \mid$$

$$\leq \quad E[I(\mid X_{tT} \mid \in (\frac{1}{r}, 1]) \mid \mathcal{A}_{t-1,T}] + E[X_{tT}^2 I(\mid X_{tT} \mid > 1) \mid \mathcal{A}_{t-1,T}]$$

$$\leq \quad \mathcal{P}(A_{tT} \mid \mathcal{A}_{t-1,T}) + E[X_{tT}^2 I(\mid X_{tT} \mid > \frac{1}{r}) \mid \mathcal{A}_{t-1,T}].$$

Consequently,

$$\sum_{t=1}^{T} \left| E\left[X_{tT} I\left(\mid X_{tT} \mid > \frac{1}{r} \right) \mid \mathcal{A}_{t-1,T} \right] \right| \leq P_T + \mathcal{L}_T \overset{\text{P}}{\to} 0.$$

The proof of iii., part 2, follows immediately if we note that

$$E\left[X_{tT} I\left(\mid X_{tT} \mid > \frac{1}{r} \right) \mid \mathcal{A}_{t-1,T} \right] = -E\left[X_{tT} I\left(\mid X_{tT} \mid \leq \frac{1}{r} \right) \mid \mathcal{A}_{t-1,T} \right]$$

because the processes are martingale differences, and hence, $E(X_{tT} \mid \mathcal{A}_{t-1,T}) = 0$.

To prove iii., part 3, we note that by Liapounov's inequality, Proposition 14 of Chapter 2,

$$m_{tT}^* \leq E\left[|X_{tT}| \, I\left(|X_{tT}| > \frac{1}{r}\right) \mid \mathcal{A}_{t-1,T}\right]$$

$$\leq \left\{E\left[|X_{tT}|^2 \, I\left(|X_{tT}| > \frac{1}{r}\right) \mid \mathcal{A}_{t-1,T}\right]\right\}^{\frac{1}{2}};$$

consequently, $\left|E[X_{tT} I(|X_{tT}| > \frac{1}{r}) \mid \mathcal{A}_{t-1,T}]\right|^2 \leq \mathcal{L}_T \xrightarrow{P} 0$.

The proof of iii., part 4, follows immediately from part 3, in the same manner as the proof of part 2 follows from the proof of part 1.

To prove iii., part 5, we note that

$$\sigma_T^2 = \sum_{t=1}^{T} E\left[X_{tT}^2 I\left(|X_{tT}| \leq \frac{1}{r}\right) \mid \mathcal{A}_{t-1,T}\right]$$

$$- \sum_{t=1}^{T} \left|E\left[X_{tT} I\left(|X_{tT}| \leq \frac{1}{r}\right) \mid \mathcal{A}_{t-1,T}\right]\right|^2,$$

and consequently, the conclusion is evident in view of part 4.

Finally, to prove iii., part 6, we note that by part ii. of Proposition 17, s_T^{*2} is equivalent to s_T^2, in the sense they both have the same probability limit. Consequently, we need only consider

$$D_T = \sum_{t=1}^{T} X_{tT}^2 - s_T^2 = 2 \sum_{t=1}^{T} \left[X_{tT} I\left(|X_{tT}| \leq \frac{1}{r}\right) E_r - E_r^2\right],$$

where E_r is as defined in the last equation of Eq. (5.115). Thus, the conclusion

$$|D_T| \leq \frac{2}{r} \sum_{t=1}^{T} \left|E\left[X_{tT} I\left(|X_{tT}| > \frac{1}{r}\right) \mid \mathcal{A}_{t-1,T}\right]\right|$$

$$+ \sum_{t=1}^{T} \left|E\left[X_{tT} I\left(|X_{tT}| > \frac{1}{r}\right) \mathcal{A}_{t-1,T}\right]\right|^2 \xrightarrow{P} 0$$

follows immediately from parts 2 and 4.

q.e.d.

Before we take up the discussion of CLT for martingales, it is extremely useful to produce the following result.

Proposition 19. Let $\{X_{tT} : t < T\}$ be, for each $T \geq 1$, a stochastic sequence defined on the probability space $(\Omega,\ \mathcal{A},\ \mathcal{P})$ and put

$$Z_{tT} = \sum_{s=1}^{t} X_{tT}, \quad g_T(\theta) = \prod_{t=1}^{T} E(e^{i\theta X_{tT}} \mid \mathcal{A}_{t-1,T}), \quad \theta \in R.$$

Moreover, let Z be a random variable such that

$$E(e^{i\theta Z}) = g(\theta) \neq 0.$$

If

$$g_T(\theta) \overset{\mathrm{P}}{\to} g(\theta),$$

then

$$E(e^{i\theta Z_{TT}}) \longrightarrow E(e^{i\theta Z}), \quad \text{i.e.,} \quad \sum_{t=1}^{T} X_{tT} = Z_{TT} \overset{\mathrm{d}}{\to} Z.$$

Proof: Define

$$h_T(\theta) = \frac{e^{i\theta Z_{TT}}}{g_T(\theta)}$$

and note that $\mid h_T(\theta) \mid < q(\theta) < \infty$, where q is nonrandom. This is so by the requirement that $\mid g(\theta) \mid > 0$ and the fact that $g_T(\theta) \overset{\mathrm{P}}{\to} g(\theta)$. Next, [23] we observe that $E[h_T(\theta)] = 1$, and consequently,

$$
\begin{aligned}
E(e^{i\theta Z_{TT}}) - E(e^{i\theta Z}) &= E[e^{i\theta Z_{TT}} - g(\theta)] = E\{h_T(\theta)[g_T(\theta) - g(\theta)]\} \\
&= E\{h_T(\theta)[g_T(\theta) - g(\theta)] + g(\theta)[h_T(\theta) - 1]\} \\
&= E\{h_T(\theta)[g_T(\theta) - g(\theta)]\}.
\end{aligned}
$$

Thus,

$$\mid E(e^{i\theta Z_{TT}}) - E(e^{i\theta Z}) \mid \leq q(\theta) E \mid g_T - g(\theta) \mid.$$

---

[23] This becomes quite evident if we take conditional expectations, first with respect to $\mathcal{A}_{T-1,T}$, then with respect to $\mathcal{A}_{T-2,T}$ etc. When we terminate this, we shall have

$$h_T^* = \frac{g_T(\theta)}{g_T(\theta)} = 1.$$

Hence, when we complete the expectation process, we find

$$\int_{\Omega} h_T \, d\mathcal{P} = \int_{\Omega} h_T^* \, d\mathcal{P} = 1.$$

It should be pointed out, if the reader has not already surmised this fact from the preceding discussion, that $E(e^{i\theta Z_{TT}}) = E[g_T(\theta)]$.

To complete the argument, we must show that $E \mid g_T(\theta) - g(\theta) \mid \longrightarrow 0$, with T. Since $\mid g_T(\theta) - g(\theta) \mid$ is bounded by some (nonrandom) function, say $c(\theta) < \infty$, we obtain

$$
\begin{aligned}
E[k_T(\theta)] &= E\left[k_T(\theta)I\left(k_T \leq \frac{1}{r}\right)\right] + E\left[k_T(\theta)I\left(k_T > \frac{1}{r}\right)\right] \\
&\leq \frac{1}{r} + c(\theta)\mathcal{P}(A_T),
\end{aligned}
\tag{5.121}
$$

where $A_T = \{\omega : k_T(\theta,\omega) > \frac{1}{r}\}$, and we have put, for convenience, $k_T(\theta) = \mid g_T(\theta) - g(\theta) \mid$. By the conditions of the proposition and for given $\theta \in R$, the rightmost member of Eq. (5.121) converges to $\frac{1}{r}$ as $T \to \infty$; since r is arbitrary, we conclude that

$$
E(e^{i\theta Z_{TT}}) \longrightarrow E(e^{i\theta Z}) \quad \text{or that} \quad Z_{TT} \xrightarrow{d} Z.
$$

q.e.d.

Proposition 20. Let $\{X_{tT} : t \leq T\}$ be, for each $T \geq 1$, a square integrable stochastic sequence defined on the probability space $(\Omega, \mathcal{A}, \mathcal{P})$ and put

$$
X_T = \sum_{t=1}^{T} X_{tT}.
$$

If

i. $P_T = \displaystyle\sum_{t=1}^{T} \mathcal{P}(A_{tT} \mid \mathcal{A}_{t-1T}) \xrightarrow{\text{P}} 0;$

ii. $m_T(c) = \displaystyle\sum_{t=1}^{T} E[X_{tT}I(\mid X_{tT} \mid \leq c) \mid \mathcal{A}_{t-1,T}] \xrightarrow{\text{P}} 0$, for fixed $c \in R^+$;

iii. $\sigma_T^2 = \displaystyle\sum_{t=1}^{T} \text{Var}[X_{tT}I(\mid X_{tT} \mid \leq \frac{1}{r}) \mid \mathcal{A}_{t-1,T}] \xrightarrow{\text{P}} \sigma^2 \geq 0,$

$$\tag{5.122}$$

then [24]

$$
X_T \xrightarrow{d} X \sim N(0, \sigma^2).
$$

Proof: Since c is fixed, we can divide and restate condition ii. as

$$
\sum_{t=1}^{T} E[X'_{tT}I(\mid X'_{tT} \mid \leq 1) \mid \mathcal{A}_{t-1,T}] \xrightarrow{\text{P}} 0, \quad \text{where} \quad X'_{tT} = \frac{X_{tT}}{c}.
$$

---

[24] Note that degenerate distributions are **not** excluded, i.e., it is admissible that $\sigma^2 = 0$.

Thus, without loss of generality, we shall interpret the condition in ii. to mean $m_T(1) \xrightarrow{P} 0$. Consider, then

$$
\begin{aligned}
X_T &= \sum_{t=1}^{T} X_{tT} = \sum_{t=1}^{T} X_{tT} u_{tT} + \sum_{t=1}^{T} X_{tT} u_{tT}^* \\
&= \sum_{t=1}^{T} [X_{tT} u_{tT} + X_{tT} u_{tT}^* - m_{tT}(r) + m_{tT}(r)] \\
&= \sum_{t=1}^{T} \zeta_{tT} + \sum_{t=1}^{T} X_{tT} u_{tT} + m_T(r),
\end{aligned}
\tag{5.123}
$$

where

$$
\zeta_{tT} = X_{tT} u_{tT}^* - m_{tT}(r), \quad m_{tT}(r) = E(X_{tT} I(|X_{tT}| \le \tfrac{1}{r}) \mid \mathcal{A}_{t-1,T})
$$
$$
u_{tT}^* = I(|X_{tT}| \le \tfrac{1}{r}), \qquad u_{tT} = I(|X_{tT}| > \tfrac{1}{r}).
\tag{5.124}
$$

By Proposition 16, $\sum_{t=1}^{T} X_{tT} u_{tT}^* \xrightarrow{P} 0$; by condition ii., the discussion surrounding Eq. (5.116) and the fact that $m_T(r) = m_T(1) - E_D$, with E_D as defined in Eq. (5.115), we conclude that $m_T(r) \xrightarrow{P} 0$. Thus,

$$
X_T \sim \zeta_{tT}^* \quad \text{and we need only deal with} \quad \zeta_{tT}^* = \sum_{s=1}^{t} \zeta_{sT},
$$

which is actually a martingale difference. Moreover, in view of the fact that, for any given r, all terms other than ζ_{tT}^* converge in probability to zero, we may choose a sequence $\{r_T : T \ge 1, \ r_{T+1} \ge r_T, \ r_\infty = \infty\}$ and interpret ζ_{tT}^* as

$$
\zeta_{tT}^* = \sum_{s=1}^{t} \zeta_{sT}, \quad \zeta_{sT} = X_{sT} I\left(|X_{sT}| \le \frac{1}{r_T}\right) - m_{sT}(r_T).
$$

Put

$$
g_T(\theta) = \prod_{t=1}^{T} E(e^{i\theta \Delta \zeta_{tT}^*} \mid \mathcal{A}_{t-1,T}) = \prod_{t=1}^{T} E(e^{i\theta \zeta_{tT}} \mid \mathcal{A}_{t-1,T})
$$

and note that in order to complete the proof, we need only show, in view of Proposition 19, that

$$
g_T(\theta) \xrightarrow{P} g(\theta) = e^{-\frac{1}{2}\theta^2 \sigma^2}.
$$

Thus, let

$$
1 + P_{tT} = E(e^{i\theta \zeta_{tT}} \mid \mathcal{A}_{t-1,T}) \quad \text{or} \quad P_{tT} = E[(e^{i\theta \zeta_{tT}} - 1) \mid \mathcal{A}_{t-1,T}]
$$

and observe that

$$
\begin{aligned}
R_T &= \left| \sum_{t=1}^{T} \left[P_{tT} + \frac{1}{2}\theta^2 \mathrm{Var}(\zeta_{tT} \mid \mathcal{A}_{t-1,T}) \right] \right| \\
&= \left| \sum_{s=1}^{T} \left[E(e^{i\theta\zeta_{sT}} - 1 - i\theta\zeta_{sT} + \frac{1}{2}\theta^2\zeta_{sT}^2 \mid \mathcal{A}_{s-1,T}) \right] \right| \\
&\le \frac{1}{6} \sum_{s=1}^{T} E(\mid \zeta_{sT} \mid^3 \mid \mathcal{A}_{s-1,T}) \\
&\le \frac{1}{3r_T} \sum_{s=1}^{T} \mathrm{Var}(\zeta_{sT} \mid \mathcal{A}_{s-1,T}).
\end{aligned}
\tag{5.125}
$$

Consequently, [25] since

$$
\prod_{t=1}^{T} E(e^{i\theta\zeta_{tT}} \mid \mathcal{A}_{t-1,T}) = \prod_{t=1}^{T} e^{P_{tT}}(1 + P_{tT})e^{-P_{tT}},
$$

in order to complete the proof of the Proposition we need only verify the conditions placed on the P_{tT} in the discussion of footnote 25. We note that

$$
\mid P_{tT} \mid \le \frac{1}{2}\theta^2 \mathrm{Var}(\zeta_{tT} \mid \mathcal{A}_{t-1,T}) \le \frac{\theta^2}{r_T^2},
$$

---

[25] In this argument, we are using the following result, a suggestive sketch of whose proof is given below. Let

$$
y_T = \prod_{t=1}^{T} (1 + x_{tT})e^{-x_{tT}},
$$

where the x_{tT} are complex random variables obeying

$$
\sum_{t=1}^{T} \mid x_{tT} \mid \le K, \quad \text{and} \quad \mid x_{tT} \mid \le c_T,
$$

such that K and c_T are not random, and the latter is a monotone sequence converging to zero; then,

$$
y_T \overset{\text{a.c.}}{\longrightarrow} 1.
$$

The proof of this statement is as follows: since $\log y_T = \sum_{t=1}^{T}[\log(1 + x_{tT}) - x_{tT}]$, we find, by the properties of alternating series,

$$
\begin{aligned}
\mid \log y_T \mid &\le \sum_{t=1}^{T} \mid \log(1 + x_{tT}) - x_{tT} \mid \le \frac{1}{2}\sum_{t=1}^{T} \mid x_{tT} \mid^2 \\
&\le \frac{1}{2}c_T \sum_{t=1}^{T} \mid x_{tT} \mid \le \frac{1}{2}Kc_T \longrightarrow 0, \quad \text{with } T.
\end{aligned}
$$

Thus, $\log y_T \overset{\text{a.c.}}{\longrightarrow} 0$, which implies that $y_T \overset{\text{a.c.}}{\longrightarrow} 1$.

which, evidently, declines monotonically to zero. We further note that

$$\sum_{t=1}^{T} | P_{tT} | \leq \theta^2 \sum_{t=1}^{T} \mathrm{Var}(\zeta_{tT} \mid \mathcal{A}_{t-1,T}) = \theta^2 \sigma_T^2. \qquad (5.126)$$

If it were known that, say $\sigma_T^2 < K$, for some nonrandom K, the proof would have been completed. Since it is not, let us first impose the required condition on Eq. (5.126), i.e., let us suppose that, for all T, $\sigma_T^2 < K$. Since when this is so we can, **with probability one, determine the limiting behavior of** $g_T(\theta)$**, by determining the limiting behavior of** $\exp\left(\sum_{t=1}^{T} P_{tT}\right)$, we conclude that

$$\exp\left(\sum_{t=1}^{T} P_{tT}\right) = e^{-\frac{1}{2}\theta^2\sigma_T^2} \overset{\mathrm{P}}{\to} e^{-\frac{1}{2}\theta^2\sigma^2},$$

which completes the proof, on the condition that the bound above is valid. To remove the condition, consider the hypothetical bound, say $K_* = \sigma^2 + 1$, the stopping time

$$\begin{aligned} \tau_T &= \inf(t \leq T, \ \sigma_t^2 \geq \sigma^2 + 1) \\ &= \infty, \quad \text{otherwise, i.e., if} \quad \sigma_T^2 \leq \sigma^2 + 1, \end{aligned}$$

and the truncated sequence

$$\zeta_{t\wedge\tau_T}^* = \sum_{s=1}^{t\wedge\tau_T} \zeta_{sT}.$$

Proceeding in exactly the same manner as above, we must now see whether the bounds are observed. Evidently, we still have $| P_{sT} | \leq \frac{2}{r_T}$; moreover, we note that

$$\sum_{t=1}^{T\wedge\tau_T} | P_{tT} | \leq \sigma^2 + 1 + \frac{2}{r_T} \leq \sigma^2 + 1 + \frac{2}{r_1} \leq K,$$

where, now, K is a true bound valid for all T. Hence, the truncated process satisfies the required conditions, and we conclude that, **with probability one, we can determine the limiting behavior of** $g_T(\theta)$**, by determining the limiting behavior of**

$$\exp\left(\sum_{t=1}^{T\wedge\tau_T} P_{tT}\right).$$

Moreover, it is evident that as $T \to \infty$,

$$\exp\left(\sum_{t=1}^{T \wedge \tau_T} P_{tT}\right) \xrightarrow{\mathrm{P}} e^{-\frac{1}{2}\theta^2 \sigma^2}.$$

To add a somewhat redundant refinement to the argument above, and noting that the characteristic function of ζ_{TT}^* is actually $E(g_T(\theta))$, we consider ES_T, where

$$S_T = \exp\left(\sum_{t=1}^{T} P_{tT}\right) - \exp\left(\sum_{t=1}^{T \wedge \tau_T} P_{tT}\right).$$

Let, for given θ,

$$B_T = \{\omega : \mid S_T(\omega, \theta) \mid > 0\}$$

and note that this is equivalent to the set

$$C_T = \{\omega : \tau_T(\omega) \le T\}.$$

Hence,

$$\lim_{T \to \infty} E(S_T) \le 2 \lim_{T \to \infty} \mathcal{P}(C_T) = 2 \lim_{T \to \infty} \mathcal{P}(\tau_T < \infty) = 0,$$

in view of the fact that the $\exp\left(\sum_{t=1}^{T \wedge \tau_T} P_{tT}\right)$ and $\exp\left(\sum_{t=1}^{T} P_{tT}\right)$ converge to the same probability limit. Thus,

$$X_T \sim \sum_{t=1}^{T} \zeta_{tT} = \zeta_{TT}^*, \quad \text{and} \quad E(e^{i\theta\zeta_{TT}^*}) \longrightarrow e^{-\frac{1}{2}\theta^2\sigma^2}.$$

q.e.d.

Remark 8. A careful reading of the last proposition discloses that the CLT we have proved applies to individually uniformly infinitesimal variables. This is so since the conditions under which we have operated have enabled us, in the end, to reduce the problem to one involving martingale differences, where the individual terms are bounded by $(1/r)$ and r is arbitrary! One would surmise, then, that if we begin with sequences that are square integrable martingale differences, obeying the Lindeberg condition, then the assertions under which a CLT may be proved will be considerably simplified. This is indeed the case, as the following result makes plain.

Proposition 21. Let $\{X_{tT} : t \leq T\}$ be, for each $T \geq 1$, a square integrable martingale difference defined on the probability space $(\Omega, \mathcal{A}, \mathcal{P})$ and put

$$X_T = \sum_{t=1}^{T} X_{tT}.$$

Suppose, further, that the Lindeberg condition holds, i.e.,

$$\mathcal{L}_T \xrightarrow{P} 0.$$

Then, the following statements are true:

    i.   if $\sum_{t=1}^{T} E(X_{tT}^2 \mid \mathcal{A}_{t-1,T}) \xrightarrow{P} \sigma^2$ then $X_T \xrightarrow{d} X \sim N(0, \sigma^2)$

    ii.   if $\sum_{t=1}^{T} X_{tT}^2 \xrightarrow{P} \sigma^2$ then $X_T \xrightarrow{d} X \sim N(0, \sigma^2)$.

Proof: To prove part i., we note that conditions i. and ii. of Proposition 20 are satisfied, in view of Proposition 18 and the fact that the Lindeberg condition holds. The remaining condition of Proposition 20 (i.e., condition iii.) is reduced, again by condition iii. part 2 of Proposition 18, to the requirement that

$$\sum_{t=1}^{T} E(X_{tT}^2 \mid \mathcal{A}_{t-1,T}) \xrightarrow{P} \sigma^2,$$

which is asserted by part i. of this proposition; hence, its proof follows immediately from Proposition 20.

As for the proof of part ii., we note that by Proposition 17, part ii., the condition

$$\sigma_T^2 = \sum_{t=1}^{T} \text{Var}(X_{tT} \mid \mathcal{A}_{t-1,T}) \xrightarrow{P} \sigma^2$$

is equivalent to $s_T^* \xrightarrow{P} \sigma^2$; by condition iii, part 6 of Proposition 18, the latter is equivalent to

$$\sum_{t=1}^{T} X_{tT}^2 \xrightarrow{P} \sigma^2,$$

which is asserted by part ii. of this proposition. Hence, conditions i., ii., and iii., of Proposition 20 are satisfied and the proof of part ii. follows immediately from Proposition 20.

                                                    q.e.d.

5.11   Mixing and Stationary Sequences

5.11.1   Preliminaries and Definitions

In this section, we examine other forms of dependence that are important in the development of econometric theory. We begin with the question of how to frame the degree of dependence amongst elements of a stochastic sequence; for example, suppose $\{\xi_n : n = 0, \pm 1, \pm 2, \ldots\}$ is a sequence of random variables defined on the probability space $(\Omega, \mathcal{A}, \mathcal{P})$. How can we describe the degree to which elements of the sequence exhibit dependency? Well, a simple idea occurs almost immediately. Why not separate or partition the sequence in two components, for example, one containing the elements $\{\ldots, \xi_{-r}, \xi_{-r+1}, \ldots, \xi_0, \xi_1, \ldots, \xi_s\}$ and the other containing the elements $\{\xi_{s+n}, \xi_{s+n+1}, \ldots\}$. In this case, the two components are separated by n elements and generate the two σ-algebras, respectively, $\mathcal{A}_{-\infty,\,s} = \sigma(\xi_r : r \leq s)$ and $\mathcal{A}_{s+n,\,\infty} = \sigma(\xi_r : r \geq s+n)$. To gauge the degree of dependence between events (i.e., measurable sets) in the two σ-algebras, we may compare the unconditional and conditional probabilities of a set, say $A_2 \in \mathcal{A}_{s+n,\,\infty}$, given another set, say $A_1 \in \mathcal{A}_{-\infty,\,s}$. If the two are the same, then the two sets of variables are independent or at least uncorrelated. If the difference is not null, but it shrinks as $n \to \infty$, then the farther apart two elements of the sequence become the less information they convey about each other, i.e., the remote past does not give much information about the present, and the present does not give us much information about the distant future. Thus, what we seek is a gauge on the difference $\mid \mathcal{P}(A_2 \cap A_1) - \mathcal{P}(A_2)\mathcal{P}(A_1) \mid$. The smaller the bound on the difference above, the smaller is the "degree" of dependence. Thus, what we seek is the **smallest possible bound** on the entity above, modified by $\mathcal{P}(A_1)$, i.e., we wish to determine the smallest ϕ_n such that

$$\mid \mathcal{P}(A_2 \cap A_1) - \mathcal{P}(A_2)\mathcal{P}(A_1) \mid \, \leq \phi_n \mathcal{P}(A_1), \qquad (5.127)$$

holds. The modification by $\mathcal{P}(A_1)$ is essential because, otherwise, the magnitude of the difference can be increased by taking larger sets A_1, without in any way affecting the manner in which elements of the sequence may exhibit dependence. In fact, if we agree that **the difference** is to be considered null, whenever $\mathcal{P}(A_1) = 0$, then we can formulate the measure of dependency in terms

Definition 9. Let $\xi = \{\xi_n : n = 0, \pm 1, \pm 2, \ldots\}$ be a sequence of random variables defined on the probability space $(\Omega, \mathcal{A}, \mathcal{P})$. Let $\mathcal{A}_{-\infty, s} = \sigma(\xi_r : r \leq s)$, $\mathcal{A}_{s+n, \infty} = \sigma(\xi_r : r \geq s + n)$, be the σ-algebras generated, respectively, by the random variables ξ_r, $r \leq s$, ξ_r, $r \geq s+n$, and let ϕ be a nonnegative function defined on the integers such that

$$\phi_0 = 1 \geq \phi_1 \geq \phi_2 \geq \phi_3 \geq \ldots, \qquad \lim_{n \to \infty} \phi_n = 0.$$

On the understanding that if $\mathcal{P}(A_1) = 0$ the left member of Eq. (5.127) vanishes, we say that ξ is ϕ-mixing if an only if for all $s \in (-\infty, \infty)$, $n \geq 1$,

$$\sup_{A_1 \in \mathcal{A}_{-\infty, s}, A_2 \in \mathcal{A}_{s+N, \infty}} | \mathcal{P}(A_2 \mid A_1) - P(A_2) | \leq \phi_n. \qquad (5.128)$$

Another class of sequences, not necessarily dependent, that is of considerable interest in econometrics is the class of **stationary processes**, which has the two subclasses: processes that are **stationary in the strict sense** and processes that are **stationary in the wide sense.** The first subclass, also termed **strictly stationary**, is defined by

Definition 10. Let $\xi = \{\xi_n : n = 0, \pm 1, \pm 2, \ldots\}$ be a sequence of random variables defined on the probability space $(\Omega, \mathcal{A}, \mathcal{P})$. Denote by $\xi_{(k)} = \{\xi_{k+1}, \xi_{k+2}, \ldots\}$, so that in this notation the sequence ξ, above, should be denoted by $\xi_{(0)}$, and let $B \in \mathcal{B}(R^\infty)$. The sequence $\xi_{(0)}$ is said to be **strictly stationary**, or stationary in the strict sense, if and only if, for every $k \geq 1$,

$$\mathcal{P}(\xi_{(0)} \in B) = \mathcal{P}(\xi_{(k)} \in B). \qquad (5.129)$$

Remark 9. Since by the Kolmogorov convention the probability characteristics of a sequence are uniquely determined if we can determine them for any finite number of (consecutive) terms, we see that what the definition implies is that for a sequence to be strictly stationary we require that, for any $n \geq 1$ and $s, k \in (-\infty, \infty)$, the joint distributions of $(\xi_{s+1}, \xi_{s+2}, \ldots, \xi_{s+n})$ and $(\xi_{k+1}, \xi_{k+2}, \ldots, \xi_{k+n})$ are identical.

While this is a rather stringent requirement, the conditions for wide sense stationarity are somewhat more loose, as the following definition indicates.

Definition 11. Let $\xi = \{\xi_n : n = 0, \pm 1, \pm 2, \ldots\}$ be a sequence of square integrable random variables defined on the probability space (Ω, $\mathcal{A}$, $\mathcal{P}$). The sequence ξ is said to be **stationary in the wide sense**, or **covariance stationary**, if and only if for every s, k, and n, as in Definition 10,

$$E(\xi_s) = E(\xi_1), \quad \text{Cov}(\xi_{s+n}, \xi_s) = \text{Cov}(\xi_{k+n}, \xi_k), \quad (5.130)$$

i.e., if the process has a **constant mean** and its (auto) covariance function depends only on the **(absolute) difference of the indices** of the two elements whose covariance is taken.

Remark 10. The requirement $E(\xi_n) = E(\xi_1)$, for all n, is quite an important one and should not be overlooked. For example, some authors define covariance stationarity solely in terms of the second moment property, it being implied that the first moment is null. It is important to realize that the sequence ξ^*, whose elements consist of $\xi_s + m(s)$, where $m(s)$ is a nontrivial function, would not be covariance stationary even if ξ were a zero mean covariance stationary process!

Example 5. Let $\epsilon = \{\epsilon_s : s = 0, \pm 1, \pm 2, \ldots\}$ be a sequence of i.i.d. random variables and let g be a measurable function,

$g : R^n \longrightarrow R,$

and put $\xi_s = g(\epsilon_s, \epsilon_{s+1}, \ldots, \epsilon_{s+m})$. Then, the sequence $\xi = \{\xi_s : s = 0, \pm 1, \pm 2, \ldots\}$ has the following properties: first, any two elements ξ_k and ξ_{k+n} are mutually independent, provided $n > m$. Such sequences are said to be m-**dependent**. In this terminology, an i.i.d. sequence, like ϵ, is said to be 0-**dependent**. A little reflection will show that m-dependent sequences are also ϕ-**mixing**, since $\phi_n = 0$ when $n >$

m, owing to the fact that random variables more than m units of the index apart are mutually independent. Second, the sequence is **strictly stationary** or **stationary in the strict sense** since the collections $\{\xi_r : r = s, s+1, s+2, \ldots, s+n\}$ and $\{\xi_r : r = k, k+1, k+2, \ldots, k+n\}$ are, even for arbitrary indices s, k, identical functions of random variables having the same distribution. Third, if the sequence is square integrable, then it is evidently also **stationary in the wide sense** or **covariance stationary**.

Example 6. Consider a special case of Example 5, viz., a moving average of order q. Here, $\epsilon = \{\epsilon_s : s = 0, \pm 1, \pm 2, \ldots\}$ is as in Example 5, but the function g is now **linear**. Thus, we put $\xi_s = \epsilon_s + \theta_1 \epsilon_{s-1} + \theta_2 \epsilon_{s-2} + \cdots + \theta_q \epsilon_{s-q}$ and obtain the sequence $\xi = \{\xi_s : s = 0, \pm 1, \pm 2, \ldots\}$. Define the $q+1$-element (row) vector, $r(\theta) = (\theta_q, \theta_{q-1}, \theta_{q-2}, \ldots, 1)$, and the matrix

$$A = \begin{bmatrix} r(\theta) & 0 & \cdots & 0 \\ 0 & r(\theta) & \cdots & 0 \\ \vdots & & & \\ 0 & 0 & \cdots & r(\theta) \end{bmatrix}. \tag{5.131}$$

Putting $\epsilon_{(s-q)} = (\epsilon_{s-q}, \epsilon_{s-q+1}, \epsilon_{s-q+2}, \ldots, \epsilon_{s-q+n})$, it is easily seen that the collections $\{\xi_r : r = s, s+1, \ldots, s+n\}$ and $\{\xi_r : r = k, k+1, \ldots, k+n\}$ have the representation $A\epsilon_{(s-q)}$ and $A\epsilon_{(k-q)}$, respectively. Thus, the two collections have, for arbitrary k, s, and q, the same joint distribution. Hence, ξ is **strictly stationary**. Moreover, if ϵ is a square integrable sequence then ξ is **covariance stationary** as well.

Example 7. With the same sequence ϵ as in Example 6, consider the autoregression

$$u_s = \rho u_{s-1} + \epsilon_s, \quad |\rho| < 1, \quad s = 0, \pm 1, \pm 2, \ldots$$

We first note that we have a simple stochastic difference equation, which can be solved to yield

$$u_s = \sum_{j=0}^{\infty} \rho^j \epsilon_{s-j}. \tag{5.132}$$

Assuming that ϵ is a square integrable sequence with variance σ^2, we conclude immediately from Eq. (5.132) that

$$\mathrm{Cov}(u_s, u_{s+n}) = \rho^{|n|}\frac{\sigma^2}{1 - \rho^2}, \quad \mathrm{Corr}(u_s, u_{s+n}) = \rho^{|n|}.$$

The sequence $u = \{u_s : s = 0, \pm 1, \pm 2, \ldots\}$ has a declining autocorrelation function converging to zero with n. Consequently, it is a ϕ-mixing sequence, but **it is not** an m-dependent sequence.

On the other hand, it is easy to see that it is a **stationary sequence both in the strict and the wide sense.**

5.11.2   Measure Preserving Transformations

Definition 12. Let $(\Omega, \mathcal{A}, \mathcal{P})$ be a probability space and

$$T : \Omega \longrightarrow \Omega.$$

Then, T is said to be a measure preserving **transformation** if and only if it is measurable, and in addition, for any $A \in \mathcal{A}$,

$$\mathcal{P}(A) = \mathcal{P}[T^{-1}(A)]. \tag{5.133}$$

Example 8. It is rather simple to construct stationary sequences using measure preserving transformations. Thus, let η be a random variable, T a measure preserving transformation, and consider the sequence $\xi = \{\xi_s : \xi_s = \eta[T^{s-1}(\omega)], \ s = 1, 2, \ldots\}$. We claim that this is a stationary sequence in the strict sense. To verify the claim it is simpler to proceed as follows: let $\xi_{(k-1)}$ denote the subsequence [26] of ξ, whose first element is $\eta[T^{k-1}(\omega)]$; let $B \in \mathcal{B}(R^\infty)$, and define

$$A_{j-1} = \{\omega : \xi_{(j-1)} \in B\}, \quad j = 1, 2, 3, \ldots$$

Consider first the pair A_0 and A_1 and inquire: when does $\omega \in A_1$? We note that $\omega \in A_1$ means $\{\eta[T(\omega)], \eta[T^2(\omega)], \eta[T^3(\omega)], \ldots)\} \in B$. This holds if and only if $T(\omega) \in A$, in which case, by the definition of A, we must have $\{\eta[T(\omega)], \eta[T^2(\omega)], \eta[T^3(\omega)], \ldots)\} \in B$, and hence,

---

[26] Note that, in this notational framework, the sequence itself ought to be denoted by $\xi_{(0)}$.

that $\omega \in A_1$, and conversely. But, this means that $A_1 = T^{-1}(A)$, which, since B is arbitrary, establishes that $\xi_{(0)}$ and $\xi_{(1)}$ have the same distribution. Repeating the procedure for as many values of the index j as desired we can show that $\xi_{(k)}$ and $\xi_{(s+k)}$ have the same distribution.

Having seen that, for a measure preserving transformation T, the measure of a set $A \in \mathcal{A}$ is equal to the measure of its inverse image under T, it would not be surprising to find that T transforms every set almost into itself. This is the import of

Proposition 22. Let $(\Omega, \mathcal{A}, \mathcal{P})$ be a probability space,

$$T : \Omega \longrightarrow \Omega$$

a **measure preserving** transformation, and $A \in \mathcal{A}$. Then, for almost all $\omega \in A$ and infinitely many $n \geq 1$, $T^n(\omega) \in A$.

Proof: Let

$$B = \{\omega : \omega \in A \text{ and } T^n(\omega) \notin A, \text{ for all } n \geq 1\}.$$

Notice that, by definition, $T^{-1}(B) = \{\omega : T(\omega) \in B\}$; but $T(\omega) \in B$, in conjunction with the definition of B, implies that $\omega \notin B$, so that $B \cap T^{-1}(B) = \emptyset$. The argument may be repeated, thus showing that, for any $n \geq 1$, $B \cap T^{-n}(B) = \emptyset$. In addition, note that

$$T^{-m}(B) \cap T^{-(m+n)}(B) = T^{-m}[B \cap T^{-n}(B)] = \emptyset,$$

which shows that the sequence $\{T^{-n}(B) : n \geq 0\}$ is one of **disjoint sets, all having the same measure.** [27] Since the sets in question are disjoint, we must also have

$$1 = \mathcal{P}(\Omega) \geq \sum_{j=0}^{\infty} \mathcal{P}(T^{-j}(B)) = \sum_{j=0}^{\infty} \mathcal{P}(B),$$

---

[27] Since T is measure preserving, we have

$$\mathcal{P}(B) = \mathcal{P}[T^{-1}(B)] = \mathcal{P}\{T^{-1}[T^{-1}(B)]\} = \cdots = \mathcal{P}[T^{-n}(B)], \quad \text{for all } n \geq 1.$$

which implies $\mathcal{P}(B) = 0$. This establishes that, for almost all $\omega \in A$ and at least one n, say n_0, $T^{n_0}(\omega) \in A$. Eliminating n_0 and repeating the process we can show that, for almost all $\omega \in A$ and infinitely many $n \geq 1$, $T^n(\omega) \in A$.

q.e.d.

Corollary 14. Let $\zeta(\omega) \geq 0$ be a nonnegative random variable defined on the probability space $(\Omega, \mathcal{A}, \mathcal{P})$ and define the set $A = \{\omega : \zeta(\omega) > 0\}$. Then, for almost all $\omega \in A$,

$$\sum_{j=0}^{\infty} \zeta[T^j(\omega)] = \infty. \tag{5.134}$$

Proof: For any integer r, define the set

$$A_r = \left\{ \omega : \zeta(\omega) \geq \frac{1}{r} \right\}$$

and let ω be any point in A_r. By the preceding proposition, for almost all $\omega \in A_r$ and for infinitely many n, $T^n(\omega) \in A_r$. Consequently, for infinitely many j, $\zeta[T^j(\omega)] \geq \frac{1}{r}$, and thus,

$$\sum_{j=0}^{\infty} \zeta[T^j(\omega)] = \infty, \quad \text{for almost all} \quad \omega \in A_r.$$

Letting $r \to \infty$ completes the proof.

q.e.d.

5.12   Ergodic Theory

Ergodicity, as the following discussion will set forth, is a property of measure preserving transformations that can be thought of, intuitively, as governing the manner in which the realization of a sequence proceeds through "time". For example, imagine that once each day, beginning in the indefinite past and continuing into the indefinite future, the following game is played. A die is thrown and the outome (face showing) is recorded. In this reference space, Ω, an element $\omega \in \Omega$, consists of the (doubly) infinite sequence

$$[\ldots, y_{-1}(\omega), y_0(\omega), y_1(\omega), \ldots],$$

where $y_{-1}(\omega)$ indicates the outcome in "yesterday's" throw, $y_0(\omega)$ the outcome of today's throw, and so on. If I were to shift the position of the entities $y_i(\omega)$ to the left or to the right, i.e., if $y_{-1}(\omega)$ were to occupy "today's" position, y_0 "tomorrow's" position, and so on, one would not expect that the probability attached to the sequence would be altered. This is so since we have in mind a sequence of Bernoulli trials, and no particular significance accrues to "today's" or "tomorrow's" outcome .

We have given in this example an instance of a "measure" preserving transformation, say T. For the latter to be also **ergodic**, we must have, in some sense, that the relative frequence of a 5, for example, in $[\omega, T(\omega), T^2(\omega), T^3(\omega), \ldots]$ is what it is in Ω, viz., $\mathcal{P}(\{5\}) = \frac{1}{6}$, since, evidently,

$$\Omega = \cdots \times S \times S \times S \times \cdots, \qquad S = \{1, 2, 3, 4, 5, 6\}.$$

This is, in fact, implied by Eq. (5.148) in Proposition 30 of this chapter, if the reader will take the set $B = \{5\}$ and interpret $T^{-k}(B)$ as the outcome $\{5\}$, k "days" ahead. One then finds that the expected frequency of a $\{5\}$ occurrence is $\mathcal{P}(\{5\})$!

Definition 13. Let $(\Omega, \mathcal{A}, \mathcal{P})$ be a probability space and

$$T : \Omega \longrightarrow \Omega$$

a **measure** preserving transformation. A set $A \in \mathcal{A}$ is said to be **invariant** if and only if $T^{-1}(A) = A$. It is said to be **almost invariant** if and only if [28] the symmetric difference, $A \triangle T^{-1}(A)$, has measure zero.

A random variable, X, defined on the measure space above is said to be **invariant** if and only if for all $\omega \in \Omega$, $X(\omega) = X[T(\omega)]$, and it is said to be **almost invariant** if and only if, for almost all [29] $\omega \in \Omega$,

$$X(\omega) = X[T(\omega)].$$

---

[28] The symmetric difference of two sets A and B is defined by $A \triangle B = (A - B) \cup (B - A)$ or, in the alternative notation, $A \triangle B = (A \cap \bar{B}) \cup (B \cap \bar{A})$.

[29] This is a shortcut for the statement, "except possibly for sets of $\mathcal{P}$-measure zero."

Definition 14. A measure preserving transformation, as in Definition 13, is said to be **ergodic** if and only if **every invariant set has measure either zero or one.**

Proposition 23. In the context of Definition 13, the following statements are true:

    i. if $B \in \mathcal{A}$ is almost invariant, then there exists an invariant set, $A \in \mathcal{A}$, such that $\mathcal{P}(A \bigtriangleup B) = 0$;

  ii. if

$$\mathcal{I}_a = \{B : B \in \mathcal{A} \text{ and is almost invariant under } T\},$$
$$\mathcal{I} = \{A : A \in \mathcal{A} \text{ and is invariant under } T\}, \qquad (5.135)$$

    then both $\mathcal{I}$ and $\mathcal{I}_a$ are σ-algebras.

Proof: If B is almost invariant, let $A = \limsup T^{-n}(B)$ and note that $T^{-1}(A) = \limsup T^{-(n+1)}(B) = A$, which shows A to be invariant. It is also evident that $A \bigtriangleup B \subseteq \bigcup_{n=0}^{\infty} [T^{-n}(B) \bigtriangleup T^{-(n+1)}(B)]$. Since
$$T^{-n}(B) \bigtriangleup T^{-(n+1)}(B) = [T^{-n}(B) - T^{-(n+1)}(B)] \cup [T^{-(n+1)}(B) - T^{-n}(B)],$$
we have

$$\mathcal{P}[T^{-n}(B) \bigtriangleup T^{-(n+1)}(B)] = \mathcal{P}(B) - \mathcal{P}[T^{-1}(B)] + \{\mathcal{P}[T^{-1}(B)] - \mathcal{P}(B)\}$$
$$= \mathcal{P}[B \bigtriangleup T^{-1}(B)] = 0.$$

To prove part ii., we note that if $A, B \in \mathcal{I}$, then, since $T^{-1}(A \cup B) = T^{-1}(A) \cup T^{-1}(B)$, it follows that $A \cup B \in \mathcal{I}$. Similarly, since $T^{-1}(\bar{A}) = \overline{T^{-1}(A)}$, we have that $\bar{A} \in \mathcal{I}$. Finally, if $\{A_i : A_i \in \mathcal{I}, i \geq 1\}$ is a disjoint sequence, then by the monotone property we conclude $\bigcup_{i=1}^{\infty} A_i \in \mathcal{I}$. If it is not a disjoint sequence, it may be rendered disjoint by the redefinition $B_1 = A_1$ and $B_j = A_j - (\bigcup_{i=1}^{j-1} A_i)$, for $i \geq 2$. It may then be verified that $\bigcup_{j=1}^{n} B_j = \bigcup_{j=1}^{n} A_j$. An entirely similar argument can be made regarding $\mathcal{I}_a$, which thus completes the proof.

                                                   q.e.d.

The following is an operational characterization of ergodicity.

Proposition 24. In the context of Definition 13, a transformation T is **ergodic**, if and only if **every** almost invariant set, $B \in \mathcal{A}$, has measure either zero or one.

Proof: From the previous proposition, given any almost invariant set, $B \in \mathcal{A}$, there exists an invariant set A, such that $\mathcal{P}(A \triangle B) = 0$. If T is ergodic, then $\mathcal{P}(A)$ is either zero or one, which implies that $\mathcal{P}(B)$ is either zero or one. Conversely, suppose every almost invariant set has measure either zero or one. Again, by the preceding proposition, it would follow that every invariant set has measure either zero or one, and consequently, that T is ergodic.

q.e.d.

The implications of ergodicity for random variables are given in the following proposition.

Proposition 25. Let T be a measure preserving transformation in the context of Definition 13. The following statements are equivalent:

i. T is ergodic;

ii. every almost invariant (under T) random variable is constant a.c., i.e., with probability one;

iii. every invariant (under T) random variable is constant a.c.

Proof: We prove first that i. implies ii. Thus, let T be ergodic and let X be a random variable almost invariant under T, i.e., for almost all $\omega \in \Omega$, $X(\omega) = X[T(\omega)]$. If $k \in R$ is any number, then the set $A_k = \{\omega : X(\omega) \leq k\}$ is almost invariant, and hence, $\mathcal{P}(A_k)$ is equal to zero or one, according to Proposition 24. Now, let $K = \sup\{k : \mathcal{P}(A_k) = 0 \text{ or } 1\}$ and note that $| K | < \infty$. Moreover, consider the sets $B = \{\omega : X(\omega) < K\}$, $B_n = \{X(\omega) \leq K - \frac{1}{n}\}$, $n \geq 1$, and observe that

$$\mathcal{P}(B) = \mathcal{P}\left(\bigcup_{n=1}^{\infty} B_n\right) \leq \sum_{n=1}^{\infty} \mathcal{P}(B_n) = 0.$$

This follows from the fact that for each n, $B_n = A_k$, with $k = K - \frac{1}{n}$. We may repeat exactly the same construction with the collection $C =$

$\{\omega : X(\omega) > K\}$ and $C_n = \{\omega : X(\omega) \geq K + \frac{1}{n}\}$, thus showing that $P(C) = 0$. But, this means that $P(\{\omega : X(\omega) = K\}) = 1$, which shows that if X is almost invariant under T and if the latter is ergodic, then X is constant a.c.

The fact that ii. implies iii. is, of course, quite evident.

To prove that iii. implies i., let $A \in \mathcal{A}$; we shall show that if A is invariant (under T) then either $P(A) = 0$ or $P(A) = 1$. Let I_A be the characteristic or indicator function of the set A, and thus an invariant random variable. This means either $I_A = 0$ or $I_A = 1$. Since $P(A) = E(I_A) = I_A$, we conclude that for every $A \in \mathcal{I}$, i.e., for every set, A, invariant under T, $P(A) = 0$ or $P(A) = 1$.

q..e.d.

The question now arises as to whether there exist other criteria or characterisitcs by which we can determine whether a measure preserving transformation is ergodic. The answer is yes and a determinative property or characteristic of such transformations is the **property of mixing**. We have

Definition 15. In the context of Definition 13, a measure preserving transformation, T, is said to be **mixing** or to have the **mixing property** [30] if and only if, for all sets $A, B \in \mathcal{A}$,

$$\lim_{n \to \infty} P[A \cap T^{-n}(B)] = P(A)P(B). \tag{5.136}$$

An immediate consequence is

Proposition 26. In the context of Definition 15, every **mixing transformation** is **ergodic**.

Proof: Let T be an arbitrary mixing transformation and let $\mathcal{I} \subset \mathcal{A}$ be the class of sets that are invariant under T. We shall show that if $B \in \mathcal{I}$, then either $P(B) = 1$ or $P(B) = 0$. Let $A \in \mathcal{A}$ and $B \in \mathcal{I}$. By invariance, we have $T^{-1}(B) = B$; hence $T^{-n}(B) = B$. But then,

$$\lim_{n \to \infty} P[A \cap T^{-n}(B)] = P(A \cap B) = P(A)P(B).$$

---

[30] This property is also referred to by some authors as **strong mixing**.

Taking the case $A = B$, we have $\mathcal{P}(B) = [\mathcal{P}(B)]^2$, which implies either $\mathcal{P}(B) = 1$, or $\mathcal{P}(B) = 0$.

q.e.d.

5.13 Convergence and Ergodicity

In this section, we take up the dicussion of sequences involving entities of the form

$$\{X(\omega), X[T(\omega)], X[T^2(\omega)], X[T^3(\omega)], \ldots\}$$

and the conditions under which convergence is obtained.

Proposition 27 (Maximal Ergodic Theorem). Let $(\Omega, \mathcal{A}, \mathcal{P})$ be a probability space, T a measure preserving transformation, and X a random variable such that $E \mid X \mid < \infty$. In addition, define

$$
\begin{aligned}
S_m(\omega) &= X(\omega) + X[T(\omega)] + X[T^2(\omega)] + \cdots + X[T^{m-1}(\omega)] \\
M_n(\omega) &= \max\{0, S_1(\omega), S_2(\omega), \ldots, S_n(\omega)\} \\
I_{M_n>0}(\omega) &= 1, \quad \text{if } M_n(\omega) > 0 \\
&= 0, \quad \text{otherwise.}
\end{aligned}
$$

Then, for every $n \geq 1$, $E[X(\omega)I_{M_n>0}(\omega)] \geq 0$.

Proof: If $n \geq k$, then we have, by construction, $M_n[T(\omega)] \geq S_k[T(\omega)]$, and therefore

$$X(\omega) + M_n[T(\omega)] \geq X(\omega) + S_k[T(\omega)] = S_{k+1}(\omega).$$

Note, also, that

$$M_n[T(\omega)] = \max\{0, S_1[T(\omega)], S_2[T(\omega)], \ldots, S_n[T(\omega)]\},$$

and, consequently, that

$$
\begin{aligned}
X(\omega) + M_n[T(\omega)] &= \max\{X(\omega), S_2(\omega), S_3(\omega), \ldots, S_{n+1}(\omega)\} \\
&= \max\{S_1(\omega), S_2(\omega), \ldots, S_{n+1}(\omega)\},
\end{aligned}
$$

which implies

$$X(\omega) + M_n[T(\omega)] \geq \max\{S_1(\omega), S_2(\omega), \ldots, S_n(\omega)\}.$$

It follows, therefore, that

$$EXI_{M_n>0} \geq E\{\max\{S_1, S_2, \ldots, S_n\} - M_n[T(\omega)]\}I_{M_n>0}.$$

But, over the set $\{\omega : M_n(\omega) > 0\}$, we must have

$$\max\{S_1(\omega), S_2(\omega), \ldots, S_n(\omega)\} = M_n(\omega).$$

Hence, we may rewrite [31]

$$
\begin{aligned}
E\left[X(\omega)I_{M_n(\omega)>0}(\omega)\right] &= E\{M_n(\omega) - M_n[T(\omega)]\}\,I_{M_n(\omega)>0}(\omega) \\
&\geq E\{M_n(\omega) - M_n[T(\omega)]\} = 0.
\end{aligned}
$$

q.e.d.

A natural consequence of this discussion, is a string of remarkable convergence results, referred to as ergodic theorems, due to the early (1931) work of Birkoff, Khinchin, and others. We have

Proposition 28 (Mean Ergodic Theorem). In the context of Proposition 27, let T be a measure preserving transformation, X an integrable random variable, i.e., $E\,|\,X\,| < \infty$, and $\mathcal{I} \subset \mathcal{A}$ the class of sets that are invariant under T. Then,

$$\frac{1}{n}\sum_{j=0}^{n-1} X[T^k(\omega)] \overset{\text{a.c.}}{\to} E(X \mid \mathcal{I}). \tag{5.137}$$

---

[31] The last equality below is valid as follows: if it is given that $E\,|\,X\,| < \infty$, then we may represent the integrals in question as

$$\int_\Omega X(w)\mathcal{P}(dw) = \lim_{n\to\infty}\sum_{i=1}^{n} a_i \mathcal{P}(B_i), \qquad \int_{T(\Omega)} X[T(\omega)]\mathcal{P}\,dT(\omega) = \lim_{n\to\infty}\sum_{i=1}^{n} a_i \mathcal{P}(A_i),$$

where $A_i = \{T(\omega) : X[T(\omega)] \in L_i\}$, $B_i = \{\omega : X(\omega) \in L_i\}$, $\{L_i : i \geq 1\}$ is, for each n, a collection of half open intervals covering the range of the random variable, and the a_i are suitable points in L_i. We note that for each $i \geq 1$, $B_i = T^{-1}(A_i)$, and $\mathcal{P}(A_i) = \mathcal{P}[T^{-1}(A_i)] = \mathcal{P}(B_i)$, since T is measure preserving. Thus,

$$E[X(\omega)] = E\{X[T(\omega)]\}.$$

If, in addition, T is ergodic, then

$$\frac{1}{n} \sum_{j=0}^{n-1} X[T^k(\omega)] \overset{\text{a.c.}}{\to} E(X). \tag{5.138}$$

Proof: We may assume that $E(X \mid \mathcal{I}) = 0$; if not, then redefine X to be $X - E(X \mid \mathcal{I})$ so that, in the context of this proof, $E(X \mid \mathcal{I}) = 0$. Define now

$$S_n(\omega) = X(\omega) + X[T(\omega)] + X[T^2(\omega)] + X[T^3(\omega)] + \cdots + X[T^{n-1}(\omega)]$$

and note that if we put

$$\bar{a}(\omega) = \limsup_{n \to \infty} \frac{S_n(\omega)}{n} \tag{5.139}$$

we have that $\bar{a}(\omega) = \bar{a}[T(\omega)]$, so that the random variable $\bar{a}$ is invariant under T. Similarly, if we define

$$\underline{a}(\omega) = \liminf_{n \to \infty} \frac{S_n(\omega)}{n}, \tag{5.140}$$

the random variable $\underline{a}$ is also invariant under T. Consequently, the sets $A_r = \{\omega : \bar{a}(\omega) > \frac{1}{r}\}$ and $B_r = \{\omega : -\underline{a}(\omega) > \frac{1}{r}\}$, where r is an arbitrary integer, are also invariant. We shall now show that $0 \leq \underline{a} \leq \bar{a} \leq 0$, thus concluding the proof of part i. Let

$$M_{k*}^0 = -M_{k*} = -\min\{0, S_{1*}(\omega), S_{2*}(\omega), \ldots, S_{k*}(\omega)\};$$

$$M_{k*} = \max\{0, S_{1*}(\omega), S_{2*}(\omega), \ldots, S_{k*}(\omega)\};$$

$$M_k^* = \max\{0, S_1^*(\omega), S_2^*(\omega), \ldots, S_k^*(\omega)\};$$

$$S_{k*}(\omega) = \sum_{j=0}^{k-1} Z[T^{j-1}(\omega)]; \quad S_k^*(\omega) = \sum_{j=0}^{k-1} Y[T^{j-1}(\omega)];$$

$$Z(\omega) = Y_*(\omega)I_r^*(\omega); \quad Y(\omega) = Y_*(\omega)I_r(\omega); \quad Y_*(\omega) = X(\omega) - \frac{1}{r};$$

$$I_r^*(\omega) = 1, \quad \text{if} \quad \omega \in B_r, \quad I_r(\omega) = 1, \quad \text{if} \quad \omega \in A_r,$$

$$= 0, \quad \text{otherwise}; \qquad\qquad = 0, \quad \text{otherwise}; \tag{5.141}$$

and note that since $\mid Y \mid < \mid X \mid + \frac{1}{r}$, and similarly for Z, then, by the dominated convergence theorem, we find that

$$E(YI_{M_n^*>0}) \longrightarrow E(YI_r), \quad E(ZI_{M_n^0>0}) \longrightarrow E(ZI_r^*). \tag{5.142}$$

This is so since, for example,

$$\{\omega:\ M_n^*(\omega) > 0\}\quad = \quad \left\{\omega:\ \max_{1 \le k \le n} S_k^* > 0\right\} = \left\{\omega:\ \max_{1 \le k \le n} \frac{S_k^*}{k} > 0\right\}$$

$$\uparrow\quad \left\{\omega: \sup_{k \ge 1} \frac{S_k^*}{k} > 0\right\} = \left\{\omega: \sup_{k \ge 1} \frac{S_k}{k} > 0\right\} \cap A_r$$

$$= \quad A_r. \tag{5.143}$$

Similarly,

$$\{\omega:\ M_n^0(\omega) > 0\} = \{\omega:\ -M_{n*}(\omega) > 0\} = \left\{\omega:\ -\min_{1 \le k \le n} \frac{S_{k*}}{k} > 0\right\}$$

$$\downarrow\quad \left\{\omega:\ -\inf_{k \ge 1} \frac{S_{k*}}{k} > 0\right\} = \left\{\omega:\ -\inf_{k \ge 1} \frac{S_k}{k} > 0\right\} \cap B_r$$

$$= \quad B_r. \tag{5.144}$$

Evaluating the limits of the two integrals in Eq. (5.142) we find

$$0 \le E(YI_r) \quad = \quad E\left(X - \frac{1}{r}\right) I_r = E(XI_r) - \frac{1}{r}\mathcal{P}(A_r),$$

$$0 \le E(ZI_r^*) \quad = \quad E\left(X - \frac{1}{r}\right) I_r^* = E(XI_r^*) - \frac{1}{r}\mathcal{P}(B_r). \tag{5.145}$$

Since we can always write $E(X) = E[E(X \mid \mathcal{I})]$ and since we have assumed $E(X \mid \mathcal{I}) = 0$, Eq. (5.145) implies that $\mathcal{P}(A_r) = 0$ and $\mathcal{P}(B_r) = 0$. These, in turn, imply that

$$\mathcal{P}(\{\omega:\ \bar{a}(\omega) \le 0\}) = 1,\quad \mathcal{P}(\{\omega:\ -\underline{a}(\omega) \le 0\}) = 1. \tag{5.146}$$

Eq. (5.146) states that, with probability one $0 \le \underline{a} \le \bar{a} \le 0$, which completes the proof of part i.

As for part ii., we note that $E(X \mid \mathcal{I})$ is an invariant random variable; if T is also ergodic, then such random variables are constant.; thus, we must have, in the ergodic case,

$$\frac{S_n}{n} \overset{a.c.}{\to} E(X).$$

q.e.d.

It is interesting to note that under the same conditions as in Proposition 28 we can, in addition to a.c. convergence, also show convergence in mean, i.e., convergence in L^1. Thus, we have

Proposition 29. In the context of Proposition 28, the following statements are also true:

i. $\frac{S_n}{n} \xrightarrow{L^1} E(X \mid \mathcal{I})$, i.e.,

$$\lim_{n \to \infty} E \left| \frac{1}{n} \sum_{k=0}^{n-1} X[T^k(\omega)] - E(X \mid \mathcal{I}) \right| = 0;$$

ii. if T is also **ergodic**, then

$$\lim_{n \to \infty} E \left| \frac{1}{n} \sum_{k=0}^{n-1} X[T^k(\omega)] - E(X) \right| = 0.$$

Proof: Since X is an a.c. finite random variable, there exists (Proposition 10 of Chapter 1) a **bounded** random variable, say Y, such that for $K < \infty$ and arbitrary integer r, $|Y| \le K$ and $E \mid X - Y \mid < (1/r)$. Therefore, we have

$$E \left| \frac{S_n}{n} - E(X \mid \mathcal{I} \mid) \right| \le E \left| \frac{1}{n} \sum_{k=0}^{n-1} \{ X[T^k(\omega)] - Y[T^k(\omega)] \} \right|$$

$$+ E \left| \frac{1}{n} \sum_{k=0}^{n-1} Y[T^k(\omega)] - E(Y \mid \mathcal{I}) \right|$$

$$+ E \mid E(X \mid \mathcal{I}) - E(Y \mid \mathcal{I}) \mid.$$

By construction,

$$E \left| \frac{1}{n} \sum_{k=0}^{n-1} \{ X[T^k(\omega)] - Y[T^k(\omega)] \} \right| \le \frac{1}{r}, \quad E \mid E(X \mid \mathcal{I}) - E(Y \mid \mathcal{I}) \mid \le \frac{1}{r}.$$

Moreover, by Proposition 28, the middle term obeys

$$\frac{1}{n} \sum_{k=0}^{n-1} Y[T^k(\omega)] \xrightarrow{a.c.} E(Y \mid \mathcal{I}).$$

Consequently, by the dominated convergence theorem, Proposition 19 of Chapter 1,

$$\lim_{n \to \infty} E \left| \frac{1}{n} \sum_{k=0}^{n-1} Y[T^k(\omega)] - E(Y \mid \mathcal{I}) \right| = 0,$$

which completes the proof of part i.

As for part ii., we need only replace, in the argument above, $E(X \mid \mathcal{I})$ and $E(Y \mid \mathcal{I})$ by $E(X)$ and $E(Y)$, respectively, in view of the fact that Proposition 28 implies that when T is ergodic

$$\frac{1}{n}\sum_{k=0}^{n-1} Y[T^k(\omega)] \xrightarrow{\text{a.c.}} E(Y).$$

Again, invoking the dominated convergence theorem the proof is complete.

q.e.d.

An important consequence of the preceding is

Proposition 30. In the context of Proposition 28, a mean preserving transformation, T, is **ergodic** if and only if, for all $A, B \in \mathcal{A}$,

$$\lim_{n\to\infty} \frac{1}{n}\sum_{k=0}^{n} P[A \cap T^{-k}(B)] = P(A)P(B). \qquad (5.147)$$

Proof: Let $\mathcal{I}$ be the class of sets $A \in \mathcal{A}$ that are invariant under T, let $B \in \mathcal{I}$, and suppose Eq. (5.147) holds. Now, by definition, $T^{-1}(B) = B$, and consequently, $T^{-k}(B) = B$. Therefore, for any $A \in \mathcal{A}$, we have

$$P(A)P(B) = \lim_{n\to\infty}\sum_{k=0}^{\infty} P[A \cap T^{-k}(B)] = P(A \cap B).$$

If, in addition, $A = B$, we find

$$P(A) = P(A \cap A) = P(A)^2,$$

which implies either $P(A) = 1$ or $P(A) = 0$. This means that **for all** $A \in \mathcal{I}$, their measure is either one or zero; hence, T is ergodic.

Conversely, suppose T is ergodic and let

$$
\begin{aligned}
I_{T^{-k}(B)}(\omega) &= 1, \quad \text{if } \omega \in T^{-k}(B) \\
&= 0, \quad \text{otherwise.}
\end{aligned}
$$

Define also the random variables

$$
\begin{aligned}
X(\omega) = I_B(\omega) &= 1, \quad \text{if } \omega \in B \\
&= 0, \quad \text{otherwise;} \\
X(T^k)(\omega) &= 1, \quad \text{if } T^k(\omega) \in B \\
&= 0, \quad \text{otherwise,}
\end{aligned}
$$

so that, for example, $X[T(\omega)] = I_{T^{-1}(B)}$ and, in general, for $k \geq 1$, $X[T^k(\omega)] = I_{T^{-k}(B)}$. By Proposition 28 and since T is ergodic,

$$\lim_{n \to \infty} \frac{1}{n} \sum_{k=0}^{n-1} X[T^k(\omega)] = \lim_{n \to \infty} \frac{1}{n} \sum_{k=0}^{n-1} I_{T^{-k}(B)} = E(X) = E(I_B) = \mathcal{P}(B).$$
(5.148)

If $A \in \mathcal{A}$, then integrating, over the set A, the relation in Eq. (5.148) yields

$$\mathcal{P}(A)\mathcal{P}(B) = \lim_{n \to \infty} \frac{1}{n} \sum_{k=0}^{n-1} \int_A I_{T^{-k}(B)} \, d\mathcal{P}.$$

Noting that

$$\int_A I_{T^{-k}(B)} \, d\mathcal{P} = \int_\Omega I_{T^{-k}(B)} I_A \, d\mathcal{P} = \int_\Omega I_{A \cap T^{-k}(B)} \, d\mathcal{P} = \mathcal{P}[A \cap T^{-k}(B)],$$

we conclude that

$$\lim_{n \to \infty} \frac{1}{n} \sum_{k=0}^{n} \mathcal{P}[A \cap T^{-k}(B)] = \mathcal{P}(A)\mathcal{P}(B).$$

q.e.d.

5.14   Stationary Sequences and Ergodicity

5.14.1   Preliminaries

The perceptive reader may have been somewhat puzzled as to the practical implications of Proposition 28, it being quite unclear as to what circumstances may call for the utilization of the results in Eqs. (5.137) and (5.138). We shall now make the connection between econometric problems and the results therein somewhat more transparent. To this end, let $\xi = \{\xi_i : i \geq 1\}$ be a stationary sequence of random variables defined on the probability space $(\Omega, \mathcal{A}, \mathcal{P})$. We recall from Chapter 2 that by the Kolmogorov construction we completely determine the distribution of the random sequence, if we are able to specify the entities $\mathcal{P}(\xi \in B)$, where

$$B \;=\; \{x : \; x = (x_1, x_2, \ldots, x_k, R, R, \ldots), \; (x_1, x_2, \ldots, x_k) \in B^*\}$$

$$B \;\in\; \mathcal{B}(R^\infty), \quad B^* \in \mathcal{B}(R^k),$$
(5.149)

i.e., when we are able to specify the probability attaching to events described by cylinder sets with a k-dimensional base. In this connection, note that $x \in R^\infty$, and thus, for every i, x_i is a real number. Since in our discussions the sample space, Ω, is not explicitly specified, it is not clear whether or not it is able to support measure preserving transformations. Thus, it is not clear to what use we can put the result of Proposition 28. While this may well appear quite correct on the surface, in fact, we can proceed as follows. Given the sequence ξ, we can consider the probability space $(\Omega^*, \mathcal{A}^*, \mathcal{P}^*)$, which is induced by ξ, and such that $\Omega^* = R^\infty$, $\mathcal{A}^* = \mathcal{B}(R^\infty)$, and $P = \mathcal{P}^*$. The induced probability measure P is defined by the condition that $P(B) = \mathcal{P}(A)$, where $A = \{\omega : \omega \in \Omega, \; \xi(\omega) \in B\}$. On this space, we can define a transformation

$$T^* : \Omega^* \longrightarrow \Omega^*$$

such that if $\omega^* = (x_1, x_2, x_3, \ldots)$ then

$$T^*(\omega^*) = (x_2, x_3, x_4, \ldots),$$

i.e., the transformation is such that it drops the first element of the sequence (of real numbers). Define now the random variable X,

$$X : R^\infty \longrightarrow R,$$

by the condition

$$X(\omega^*) = x_1,$$

i.e., is the (measurable) function that, when evaluated at a point of the space R^∞, picks out the first element of the sequence (of real numbers). In this context, then, the transformation, T^*, noted above, makes a great deal of sense, since

$$X(\omega^*) = x_1, \quad X[T^*(\omega^*)] = x_2, \ldots, \quad X[T^{*k-1}(\omega^*)] = x_k, \ldots$$

It should, perhaps, be easy to see that if ξ is a **strictly stationary** stochastic sequence then T^* is a **measure preserving** transformation since, under strict stationarity, $\xi_{(1)} = \{\xi_i : i \geq 1\}$ and $\xi_{(k)} = \{\xi_i : i \geq k\}$ have the same distribution, for $k \geq 2$.

5.14.2 Convergence and Strict Stationarity

The preceding discussion suggests that the property of being ergodic ought to be defined for stochastic sequences as well. We have

Definition 16. Let $\xi = \{\xi_i : i \geq 1\}$ be a stochastic sequence defined on the probability space $(\Omega,\ \mathcal{A},\ \mathcal{P})$. A set $A \in \mathcal{A}$ is said to be **invariant relative to the sequence** if and only if there exists a set, say $B \in \mathcal{B}(R^\infty)$, such that for all $k \geq 1$,

$$A = \{\omega : \xi_{(k)}(\omega) \in B\},$$

where $\xi_{(k)} = \{\xi_i : i \geq k\}$.

Remark 11. Notice the stringent requirements that are placed on invariant sets, i.e., for every $\omega \in A$, **every member of the sequence** must be able to assume a value in **every coordinate component** of B! For example, for $k = 1$, we have that ξ_i assumes a value in the ith coordinate component. When $k = 2$, ξ_{i+1} assumes a value in the ith coordinate component and generally when $k = r$, ξ_{i+r-1} assumes a value in the ith coordinate component, and so on. Moreover, all this must hold simultaneously!

Incidentally, it can easily be verified that the collection of all invariant sets relative to a sequence ξ, forms a σ-algebra.

Definition 17. In the context of Definition 16, the sequence ξ is said to be **ergodic** if and only if every invariant set has $\mathcal{P}$-measure either one or zero.

An almost immediate consequence of the preceding discussion is

Proposition 31 (Mean Ergodic Theorem). Let $\xi = \{\xi_i : i \geq 1\}$ be a stochastic sequence defined on the probability space $(\Omega,\ \mathcal{A},\ \mathcal{P})$; suppose further that ξ is **strictly stationary** and integrable, i.e., $E \mid \xi_1 \mid < \infty$. Then, the following statements are true:

  i. for $S_n = \sum_{j=1}^{n} \xi_j$,

$$\frac{S_n}{n} \overset{\text{a.c.}}{\to} E(\xi_1 \mid \mathcal{I}), \qquad (5.150)$$

where $\mathcal{I} \subset \mathcal{A}$ is the σ-algebra of sets that are invariant with respect to the sequence ξ;

ii. if, in addition, the sequence ξ is **ergodic** then

$$\frac{S_n}{n} \overset{\text{a.c.}}{\to} E(\xi_1). \tag{5.151}$$

Proof: We shall carry out our proof using the apparatus of the coordinate probability space developed just above. In that context, we make the identification

$$\frac{S_n}{n} = \frac{1}{n} \sum_{k=0}^{n-1} X[T^{*k-1}(\omega^*)]. \tag{5.152}$$

By Proposition 28, then, it follows that

$$\frac{S_n}{n} \overset{\text{a.c.}}{\to} E(X \mid \mathcal{I}),$$

and the only remaining problem is to determine what is $\zeta = E(X \mid \mathcal{I})$ in the present context. Since the sequence is integrable and

$$E\left| \frac{1}{n} \sum_{k=1}^{n} \xi_k - \zeta \right| \longrightarrow 0,$$

it follows that, for any $A \in \mathcal{I}$,

$$\frac{1}{n} \sum_{k=1}^{n} \int_A \xi_k d\mathcal{P} \longrightarrow \int_A \zeta d\mathcal{P},$$

where $\mathcal{I}$ is the σ-algebra of invariant sets relative to the sequence. To determine the nature of ζ, we note that for $B \in \mathcal{B}(R^\infty)$ and such that $A = \{\omega : \xi_{(k)} \in B\}$, for all $k \geq 1$,

$$\int_{\{\omega : \xi_{(k)}(\omega) \in B\}} \xi_k d\mathcal{P} = \int_{\{\omega : \xi_{(1)}(\omega) \in B\}} \xi_1 d\mathcal{P}.$$

The equality above is valid in view of the fact that ξ is **stationary**. Thus, for every set invariant relative to the sequence, we have

$$\int_A \zeta d\mathcal{P} = \int_A \xi_1 d\mathcal{P}. \tag{5.153}$$

But, from the discussion of Chapter 2, it follows immediately that $\zeta = E(\xi_1 \mid \mathcal{I})$.

As for the proof of ii., we note that if the sequence is ergodic then all sets $A \in \mathcal{I}$ obey either $\mathcal{P}(A) = 1$ or $\mathcal{P}(A) = 0$. It follows then that when ξ is ergodic $E(\xi_1 \mid \mathcal{I})$ is a constant, and since $E[E(\xi_1 \mid \mathcal{I})] = E(\xi_1)$, we conclude that $\zeta = E(\xi_1)$.

q.e.d.

One may also prove second moment ergodic theorems, but this is best dealt with in conjunction with our discussion of such matters in the context of stationarity in the wide sense or covariance stationarity.

5.14.3   Convergence and Covariance Stationarity

In this section, we shall confine our attention to proving first and second moment ergodic theorems for covariance stationary sequences. Evidently, such results apply equally well to **square integrable** strictly stationary sequences. The mode of convergence in this discussion will be **convergence in mean square, L^2**.

Remark 12. Although the context was never appropriate, the following is a very useful point and should have been made a long time ago. **It is always possible to show a.c. convergence of (appropriate) sequences of random variables, provided that one allows for the existence of higher order moments and certain other conditions.** To illustrate this, suppose in Proposition 30 we allowed for the existence of second moments, it was given that $E(\xi_1 \mid \mathcal{I}) = 0$, and moreover,

$$\mathrm{Var}\left(\frac{S_n}{n}\right) \leq c^n, \quad |c| < 1. \tag{5.154}$$

Given any integer r, let

$$A_{n,r} = \left\{ \omega : \left|\frac{S_n}{n}\right| > \frac{1}{r} \right\}.$$

By Chebyshev's inequality, $\mathcal{P}(A_{n,r}) \leq rc^n$. Since

$$\sum_{n=1}^{\infty} rc^n = \frac{r}{1-c} < \infty,$$

it follows from the Borel-Cantelli lemma that $\mathcal{P}(A_{n,r}, i.o.) = 0$, i.e.,

$$\frac{S_n}{n} \xrightarrow{a.c.} 0.$$

Actually, we had been very conservative in assigning the order of magnitude of the variance of (S_n/n); clearly, it must approach zero at a rate faster than $(1/n)$ since the series $\sum_{n=1}^{N} \frac{1}{n}$, diverges. On the other hand, for any $\delta > 1$, we have convergence, i.e, $\sum_{n=1}^{\infty} \frac{1}{n^{\delta}} < \infty$, so that if $\text{Var}(\frac{S_n}{n}) \leq \frac{K}{n^{\delta}}$, the result established above remains!

Evidently, we can make the same argument about second order moments, third order moments, and so on. In general, if we wish to prove convergence of the kth order "sample moment", we need to assume the existence of $(2k)^{th}$ order moments and the observance of certain conditions on their order of magnitude.

Such an approach, of course, requires rather stringent conditions, the satisfaction of which puts severe limits on the potential applicability of the results in applied work.

The convergence issue for first order moments is settled in

Proposition 32. Let $\xi = \{\xi_i \cdot i \geq 1\}$ be a zero mean stochastic sequence defined on the probability space $(\Omega, \mathcal{A}, \mathcal{P})$; suppose further that ξ is **square integrable** and **stationary in the wide sense**, or covariance stationary, i.e., $E(\xi_n^2) < \infty$, for all n, and in addition, $E(\xi_{n+k}\xi_k) = R(n)$. Then, with $S_n = \sum_{i=1}^{n} \xi_i$,

$$\frac{S_n}{n} \xrightarrow{L^2} 0,$$

if and only if [32]

$$\lim_{n\to\infty} \frac{1}{n} \sum_{j=0}^{n-1} R(j) = 0. \tag{5.155}$$

Proof: To prove sufficiency, we need to show that

$$J_n = \frac{1}{n^2} E(S_n^2) = \frac{1}{n^2} \sum_{k=1}^{n} \sum_{r=1}^{n} R(k-r) \longrightarrow 0. \tag{5.156}$$

---

[32] If we had developed the theory of spectral representation for covariance stationary processes, which unfortunately lies beyond the current scope of this volume, the condition in Eq. (5.155) would have been replaced by the condition that the spectrum of the sequence is **continuous at zero**. Continuity of the spectral density at zero is equivalent to the condition in Eq. (5.155).

We may render the rightmost member of Eq. (5.156) as

$$
\begin{aligned}
J_n &= \frac{1}{n}R(0) + \frac{1}{n^2}\sum_{k=1}^{n}\sum_{r\neq k} R(k-r) \\[2mm]
&= \frac{1}{n}\sum_{j=-(n-1)}^{n-1}\left(1 - \frac{|j|}{n}\right) R(j) \\[2mm]
&= \frac{1}{n}\sum_{j=0}^{n-1} R(j) - \frac{2}{n}\sum_{j=1}^{n-1}\frac{j}{n} R(j).
\end{aligned}
$$

The last equality, above, follows from the fact that for covariance stationary sequences $R(j) = R(-j)$. Moreover, by the conditions of the proposition, the first term of the last relation converges to zero with n; hence, the second vanishes as well, which completes the proof of sufficiency.

To prove necessity, we note that [33]

$$
\left|\frac{1}{n}\sum_{j=0}^{n-1} R(j)\right|^2 = \left|E\left[\xi_1\left(\frac{1}{n}\sum_{k=1}^{n}\xi_k\right)\right]\right|^2
$$

$$
\leq E(\xi_1^2)E\left|\frac{1}{n}\sum_{k=1}^{n}\xi_k\right|^2. \tag{5.157}
$$

Hence, if $\frac{S_n}{n} \xrightarrow{L^2} 0$, i.e.,

$$
E\left|\frac{1}{n}\sum_{k=1}^{n}\xi_k\right|^2 \longrightarrow 0,
$$

then, since **the sequence is square integrable**, i.e., $E(\xi_1^2) < \infty$, we conclude

$$
\left|\frac{1}{n}\sum_{j=0}^{n-1} R(j)\right|^2 \longrightarrow 0, \quad \text{or} \quad \lim_{n\to\infty}\frac{1}{n}\sum_{j=0}^{n-1} R(j) = 0.
$$

q.e.d.

Notwithstanding the import of Remark 11, it turns out that a slight modification of the procedure employed therein and a very slightly more

---

[33] The last inequality in Eq. (5.157) is essentially the Cauchy inequality for integrals.

restrictive set of conditions than those of Proposition 32 yield convergence with probability one ! In particular, we have

Proposition 33. Let $\xi = \{\xi_i : i \geq 1\}$ be a zero mean stochastic sequence defined on the probability space $(\Omega, \mathcal{A}, \mathcal{P})$; suppose further that ξ is **square integrable** and **stationary in the wide sense**, or covariance stationary, i.e., $E(\xi_n^2) < \infty$, for all n, and $E(\xi_{n+k}\xi_k) = R(n)$. Let

$$S_n = \sum_{i=1}^{n} \xi_i$$

and suppose that, for some $\delta > 0$,

$$\mathrm{Var}\left(\frac{S_n}{n}\right) \leq \frac{c}{n^\delta}, \quad c > 0.$$

Then,

$$\frac{S_n}{n} \xrightarrow{\text{a.c.}} 0.$$

Proof: We use essentially the same type of proof as utilized in Proposition 17 of Chapter 4. We first prove the result for a subsequence, and then we show that every element of the sequence $\{\frac{S_n}{n} : n \geq 1\}$ is sufficiently close to an element of the subsequence in question, and hence, the result holds for the original sequence as well. Since $\delta > 0$, we shall deal only with the case $\delta \in (0, 1]$; the case $\delta > 1$ is fairly trivial and has been dealt with in Remark 11.

Define the sequence of indices

$$k(n) = \inf\{k : k \geq n^\gamma, \quad \text{such that } k \text{ is an integer and } \delta\gamma > 1\}.$$

We note, in passing, that $n^\gamma \leq k(n) \leq n^\gamma + 1$ and that $\gamma > 1$, since we deal with the case $\delta \in (0, 1]$. Consider the sequence of sets

$$A_{k(n),r} = \left\{\omega : \left|\frac{S_{k(n)}}{k(n)}\right| \geq \frac{1}{r}\right\}.$$

By the standard Chebyshev inequality, we find

$$\mathcal{P}(A_{k(n),r}) \leq \frac{c}{k(n)^\delta} \leq \frac{c}{n^{\gamma\delta}}.$$

Since, $\sum_{n=1}^{\infty} \mathcal{P}(A_{k(n),r}) < \infty$, it follows by the Borel-Cantelli theorem that

$$\mathcal{P}(A_{k(n),r}, \ i.o.) = 0, \quad \text{or, equivalently,} \quad \frac{S_{k(n)}}{k(n)} \xrightarrow{\text{a.c.}} 0.$$

Next, put

$$D_n = \max_{k(n-1) < n \leq k(n)} | \ S_n - S_{k(n)} \ |,$$

and note that

$$D_n \ \leq \ \left| \sum_{j=k(n-1)+1}^{k(n)} X_j \right|;$$

moreover,

$$B_{n,r} = \left\{ \omega : \frac{D_n}{k(n)} > \frac{1}{r} \right\} = \left\{ \omega : \frac{D_n^2}{k(n)^2} > \frac{1}{r^2} \right\}.$$

Evaluating the expectation $J_{k(n)} = E \ | \ \sum_{j=k(n-1)+1}^{k(n)} X_j \ |^2$, we find

$$\begin{aligned} J_{k(n)} \ &= \ \sum_{j=k(n-1)}^{k(n)} \sum_{j'=k(n-1)}^{k(n)} R(j - j') \\ &\leq \ R(0)[k(n) - k(n-1)]^2 \ \leq \ n^\gamma \left\{ \frac{1}{n^\gamma} + \left[1 - \left(1 - \frac{1}{n} \right)^\gamma \right] \right\}. \end{aligned}$$

Consequently, using a Chebyshev inequality, again, we find [34]

$$\sum_{n=1}^{\infty} \mathcal{P}(B_{n,r}) \leq K \sum_{n=1}^{\infty} \frac{1}{n^\gamma} < \infty,$$

which, therefore, establishes that

$$\mathcal{P}(B_{n,r}, \ i.o.) = 0, \quad \text{or, equivalently, that} \quad \frac{D_n}{k(n)} \xrightarrow{\text{a.c.}} 0.$$

Since, $S_n = S_{k(n)} + S_n - S_{k(n)}$ and $k(n) \geq n$, it follows that

$$\left| \frac{S_n}{n} \right| \leq \frac{| \ S_{k(n)} \ |}{k(n)} + \frac{D_n}{k(n)}.$$

---

[34] In the inequality below, we make use of the following relations:

$$\begin{aligned} \frac{k(n) - k(n-1)}{k(n)} \ &\leq \ \frac{k(n) - k(n-1)}{n^\gamma} \ \leq \ \frac{n^\gamma + 1 - (n-1)^\gamma}{n^\gamma} \\ &\leq \ \frac{1}{n^\gamma} + \left[1 - \left(1 - \frac{1}{n} \right)^\gamma \right] \ \leq \ \frac{K}{n^\gamma}. \end{aligned}$$

The last inequality is valid since, for sufficiently large n, $1 - (1 - \frac{1}{n})^\gamma \approx \frac{1}{n^\gamma}$.

Moreover, since the two components of the right member **converge a.c.**, it follows that the left member converges a.c. as well.

q.e.d.

Using basically the same techniques as in Proposition 32, we may prove an ergodic result for second moments. Thus, we have

Proposition 34. Let $\xi = \{\xi_i : i \geq 1\}$ be a zero mean stochastic sequence defined on the probability space $(\Omega, \mathcal{A}, \mathcal{P})$; suppose also that ξ is at least **stationary in the wide sense**, i.e., covariance stationary, and possesses finite **fourth order** moments. Define, further,

$$\hat{R}(n) = \frac{1}{N} \sum_{k=1}^{N-n} x_{n+k} x_k, \tag{5.158}$$

where $\{x_j : j = 1, 2, \ldots, N\}$ are observations, respectively, on the elements of the sequence $\{\xi_j : j = 1, 2, \ldots, N\}$. Then, the following statements are true:

i. a necessary and sufficient condition for

$$\hat{R}(n) \xrightarrow{L^2} R(n), \quad n \geq 0,$$

is that, for $n \geq 0$,

$$\lim_{N \to \infty} \frac{1}{N} \sum_{k=1}^{N} E\left\{[\xi_{n+k}\xi_k - R(n)][\xi_{n+1}\xi_1 - R(n)]\right\} = 0; \tag{5.159}$$

ii. if the elements of the sequence have a jointly normal distribution, i.e., the sequence is Gaussian, then

$$\hat{R}(n) \xrightarrow{L^2} R(n), \quad n \geq 0,$$

if and only if

$$\lim_{N \to \infty} \frac{1}{N} \sum_{j=0}^{N-1} R(j)^2. \tag{5.160}$$

Proof: We note that

$$
\begin{aligned}
H_N &= (N-n)E\mid \hat{R}(n) - R(n)\mid^2 \\[2mm]
&= \frac{1}{(N-n)} \sum_{k=1}^{N-n} \sum_{k'=1}^{N} E\left\{[\xi_{n+k}\xi_k - R(n)][\xi_{n+k'}\xi_{k'} - R(n)]\right\} \\[2mm]
&= \frac{1}{N-n} \sum_{k=1}^{N-n} E[\xi_{n+k}\xi_k - R(n)][\xi_{n+1}\xi_1 - R(n)] \\[2mm]
&\quad + \frac{1}{N-n} \sum_{k=1}^{N-n} E[\xi_{n+k}\xi_k - R(n)][\xi_{n+2}\xi_2 - R(n)] \\
&\quad \cdots\cdots \\
&\quad \cdots\cdots \\
&\quad \cdots\cdots \\
&\quad + \frac{1}{N-n} \sum_{k=1}^{N-n} E[\xi_{n+k}\xi_k - R(n)][\xi_N \xi_{N-n} - R(n)].
\end{aligned}
$$

Thus, we see that L^2-convergence of $\hat{R}(n)$ to $R(n)$ involves the $N-n$ conditions:

$$
\lim_{N\to\infty} \frac{1}{N} \sum_{k=1}^{N} E\left\{[\xi_{n+k}\xi_k - R(n)][\xi_{n+i}\xi_i - R(n)]\right\} = 0, \qquad (5.161)
$$

for $i = 1, 2, \ldots, N-n$. Since the process is stationary, however, this is essentially the same condition given in Eq. (5.159); this means that $\lim_{N\to\infty} H_N = 0$, which completes the proof of part i.

As for part ii., we note that from the properties of the normal distribution

$$
\begin{aligned}
L_k &= E[\xi_{n+k}\xi_k - R(n)][\xi_{n+1}\xi_1 - R(n)] \\
&= E(\xi_{n+k}\xi_k \xi_{n+1}\xi_1) - R(n)^2 \\
&= R(n)^2 + R(k-1)^2 + R(n+k-1)R(n-k+1) - R(n)^2 \\
&= R(k-1)^2 + R(n+k-1)R(n-k+1).
\end{aligned}
$$

Since, evidently, $\mid R(s)R(k)\mid^2 \le R(s)^2 R(k)^2$, it follows that

$$
\frac{1}{N-n} \sum_{k=1}^{N-n} L_k \le \frac{1}{N-n} \sum_{j=0}^{N-n-1} \left[R(j)^2 + R(n+j)^2 + R(n-j)^2\right].
$$

$$(5.162)$$

Thus, if $\hat{R}(n) \overset{L^2}{\to} R(n)$, the conidition in Eq. (5.160) must be satisfied, and if the condition in Eq. (5.160) is satisfied, then $\hat{R}(n) \overset{L^2}{\to} R(n)$.

q.e.d.

5.15   Miscellaneous Results and Examples

The purpose of this section is to provide some applications for the results of the previous sections and to present some new results that are not of sufficient importance to justify their presentation as propositions.

We begin by asking is there no test to determine whether a measure preserving transformation is mixing, relative to a sequence of random variables, beyond that inherent in the definition? The answer is that there does exist such a test. We have in particular,

Assertion 1. Let $\xi = \{\xi_i : i \geq 1\}$ be an integrable sequence defined on the probability space $(\Omega, \mathcal{A}, \mathcal{P})$ and let T be a measure preserving transformation,

$$T : \Omega \longrightarrow \Omega.$$

Then, T is mixing relative to the sequence ξ if for any two variables in ξ, say ξ_1 and ξ_2,

$$\lim_{n\to\infty} E\left\{\xi_1[T^n(\omega)]\xi_2(\omega)\right\} = E\left[\xi_1(\omega)\right] E\left[\xi_2(\omega)\right]. \tag{5.163}$$

Proof: The proof of this is usually given by construction, first for simple random variables, then for bounded random variables, and finally for a.c. finite random variables. For simplicity, we give only the first step, the rest being simply a matter of approximations. Let $\{B_i : i = 1, 2, \ldots, m\}$ be a **finite partition** of Ω and suppose the two variables are given, in canonical form, by

$$\xi_1(\omega) = \sum_{i=1}^m a_i I_{B_i}(\omega), \quad \xi_2(\omega) = \sum_{j=1}^m b_j I_{B_j}(\omega).$$

Then, [35]

$$\xi_1[T^n(\omega)] = \sum_{i=1}^m a_i I_{B_i}[T^n(\omega)] = \sum_{i=1}^m a_i I_{T^{-n}(B_i)}(\omega). \qquad (5.164)$$

Consequently,

$$
\lim_{n\to\infty} E\left\{\xi_1[T^n(\omega)]\xi_2(\omega)\right\} = \lim_{n\to\infty} \sum_{i=1}^m \sum_{j=1}^m a_i b_j E\left[I_{T^{-n}(B_i)}(\omega) I_{B_j}(\omega)\right]
$$

$$
= \lim_{n\to\infty} \sum_{i=1}^m \sum_{j=1}^m a_i b_j E\left[I_{B_j \cap T^{-n}(B_i)}(\omega)\right]
$$

$$
= \sum_{i=1}^m \sum_{j=1}^m a_i b_j \left\{\lim_{n\to\infty} \mathcal{P}[B_j \cap T^{-n}(B_i)]\right\}.
$$

Thus, if T is mixing then the last member above can be written as

$$
\sum_{i=1}^m \sum_{j=1}^m a_i b_j \left\{\lim_{n\to\infty} \mathcal{P}[B_j \cap T^{-n}(B_i)]\right\} = \sum_{i=1}^m \sum_{j=1}^m a_i b_j \mathcal{P}(B_j)\mathcal{P}(B_i)
$$

$$
= \left[\sum_{i=1}^m a_i \mathcal{P}(B_i)\right]\left[\sum_{j=1}^m b_j \mathcal{P}(B_j)\right]
$$

$$
= E(\xi_1)E(\xi_2).
$$

On the other hand, if Eq. (5.163) holds, then from

$$
0 = \lim_{n\to\infty} E\left\{\xi_1[T^n(\omega)]\xi_2(\omega)\right\} - E\left[\xi_1(\omega)\right]E\left[\xi_2(\omega)\right]
$$

$$
= \sum_{i=1}^m \sum_{j=1}^m \{\lim_{n\to\infty} \mathcal{P}[B_j \cap T^{-n}(B_i)] - \mathcal{P}(B_j)\mathcal{P}(B_i)\},
$$

we conclude that $\lim_{n\to\infty} \mathcal{P}[B_j \cap T^{-n}(B_i)] = \mathcal{P}(B_j)\mathcal{P}(B_i)$, which shows that T is mixing, thus concluding the proof.

In earlier discussion, we have argued that a stochastic sequence, $\xi = \{\xi_i : i \geq 1\}$, consisting of i.i.d. random variables is **strictly stationary**; is it also **ergodic**? The answer is given in

---

[35] The last equality in Eq. (5.164) is justified as follows: $I_{B_i}[T^n(\omega)] = 1$, if and only if $T^n(\omega) \in B_i$ and is zero otherwise; but, this is simply another way of saying that it is equal to 1 if and only if $\omega \in T^{-n}(B_i)$, i.e., we have the identification

$$
I_{T^{-n}(B_i)}(\omega) = I_{B_i}[T^n(\omega)],
$$

as claimed.

Assertion 2. Let $\xi = \{\xi_i : i \geq 1\}$ be a sequence of i.i.d. (integrable) random variables defined on the probability space $(\Omega, \mathcal{A}, \mathcal{P})$. Then, the sequence is ergodic.

Proof: First note that in view of the i.i.d. property, the sequence is strictly stationary. Consider now the equivalent coordinate space, as at the beginning of the previous section, and let that coordinate space be denoted by $(\Omega^*, \mathcal{A}^*, \mathcal{P}^*)$, so that $\Omega^* = R^\infty$, and $\mathcal{A}^* = \mathcal{B}(R^\infty)$. Define the probability measure on the coordinate space, $\mathcal{P}^*$ by the condition: if $A = \{\omega : \xi(\omega) \in B\}$, with $B \in \mathcal{B}(R^\infty)$, then $\mathcal{P}^*(B) = \mathcal{P}(A)$. In this probability space, consider the transformation

$$T : \Omega^* \longrightarrow \Omega^*$$

such that for any $\omega^* = (x_1, x_2, \ldots) \in \Omega^*$, $T(\omega^*) = (x_2, x_3, \ldots)$. Consider, further, the random variable

$$X_* : \Omega^* \longrightarrow R,$$

defined by the condition that its value at ω^* is equal to the first entry in the sequence that is ω^*. Thus, for example, we have

$$X_*(\omega^*) = x_1, \quad X_*[T(\omega^*)] = x_2, \quad X_*[T^2(\omega^*)] = x_3, \ldots$$

Define now the random variables

$$X_1(\omega^*) = X_*(\omega^*), \quad X_2(\omega^*) = X_*(T[\omega^*]), \quad X_3(\omega^*) = X_*[T^2(\omega^*)], \ldots,$$

and note that we have the identification

$$\xi_i \sim X_i, \quad i = 1, 2, 3, \ldots$$

Thus, the sequence $X = \{X_i : i \geq 1\}$ is one of independent identically distributed random variables. Note, further, that

$$X_k[T^n(\omega^*)] = X_*[T^k T^n(\omega^*)] = X_*[T^{k+n}(\omega^*)] = X_{k+n+1}(\omega^*).$$

Since, for n sufficiently large and any indices r, s,

$$E\left(X_r[T^n(\omega^*)]X_s(\omega^*)\right) = E(X_{n+r+1})E(X_s),$$

the conclusion follows immediately, from Assertion 1.

Another interesting result is

Assertion 3. Let $\xi = \{\xi_i : i \geq 1\}$ be a zero mean stationary sequence of jointly normal random variables with autocovariance function

$$R(n) = E(\xi_{n+k}\xi_k).$$

A sufficient condition for the sequence to be ergodic is that $R(n) \longrightarrow 0$.

Proof: Without loss of generality, we may simplify matters by taking $R(0) = 1$ and considering the coordinate probability space constructed above. In that context, we obtain

$$J_{n,s,k} = E\{X_s[T^n(\omega^*)]X_k(\omega^*)\}$$

$$= \frac{1}{2\pi v}\int_{-\infty}^{\infty}\left\{\int_{-\infty}^{\infty}\exp -\frac{1}{2v}[x - R(s + k + n)]^2 dx\right\}\exp -\frac{1}{2}y^2 dy,$$

where $v = 1 - R(s + k + n)^2$. Letting $n \longrightarrow \infty$ yields

$$E\{X_s[T^n(\omega^*)]X_k(\omega^*)\} = E(X_s)E(X_k).$$

The conclusion, then, follows from Assertion 1.

Further, it is rather easy to show that finite moving averages, stable autoregression, or stable ARMA sequences are all stationary. Take, for example, what is occasionally called the **general linear sequence**, i.e., the sequence $u = \{u_t : t \geq 1\}$, where

$$u_t = \sum_{j=0}^{\infty}a_j\epsilon_{t-j}, \qquad \sum_{j=1}^{\infty}|a_j| < \infty, \tag{5.165}$$

and the ϵ's are i.i.d. random variables with mean zero and finite variance. Notice that this is a more restrictive class of sequences relative to sequences that merely obey

$$\sum_{j=0}^{\infty}|a_j|^2 < \infty,$$

since

$$\sum_{j=0}^{\infty}|a_j| \geq \left(\sum_{j=1}^{\infty}|a_j|^2\right)^{\frac{1}{2}},$$

and thus, if

$$\sum_{j=0}^{\infty} |a_j| < \infty, \quad \text{then} \quad \sum_{j=1}^{\infty} |a_j|^2 < \infty,$$

but the converse need not be true. Notice, further, that general linear sequences are essentially extensions of moving average sequences and thus, behave essentially like moving average sequences. It may be easily verified that they are at least **wide sense stationary** (covariance stationary) as well as **ergodic**. They are covariance stationary, since they are zero mean sequences and a little calculation will show that they satisfy Definition 11 of this Chapter, i.e.,

$$E(u_t u_{t+\tau}) = E(u_s u_{s+\tau}) = K(\tau) = \sum_{j=0}^{\infty} a_j a_{j+\tau}.$$

They are also ergodic, since

$$\lim_{T \to \infty} \frac{1}{T} \sum_{\tau=0}^{T} K(\tau) = 0.$$

To see that this is, indeed, the case observe that

$$\lim_{T \to \infty} \frac{1}{T} \sum_{\tau=0}^{T} K(\tau) \leq \lim_{T \to \infty} \frac{1}{T} \sum_{\tau=0}^{T} |K(\tau)| \leq \lim_{T \to \infty} \frac{1}{T} \left(\sum_{j=0}^{\infty} |a_j| \right)^2,$$

so that the conclusion is immediate from Eq. (5.165).

Bibliography

Billingsley, P. (1968) *Convergence of Probability Measures*, Wiley, New York.

———————————— (1986) *Probability and Measure*, (second edition), Wiley, New York.

Breiman, L. (1968) *Probability*, Addison-Wesly, Reading, Massachusetts.

Chow, Y.S. and H. Teicher (1988) *Probability Theory*, (second edition), Springer-Verlag, New York.

Chung, K.L. (1974) *A Course in Probability Theory*, (second edition), Academic Press, New York.

Gihman, I.I. and A.V. Skorohod (1974) *The Theory of Stochastic Processes I*, Springer-Verlag, Heidelberg; reprinted by Springer-Verlag, New York, 1980.

Gnedenko, B.V. and A.N. Kolmogorov (1954) *Limit Distributions for Sums of Independent Random Variables*, Addison-Wesley, Reading, Massachusetts.

Halmos, P. (1950) *Measure Theory*, Van Nostrand, New York; reprinted by Springer-Verlag, New York, 1974.

Hall, P and C.C. Heyde (1980) *Martingale Limit Theory and Its Applications*, Academic Press, New York.

Hannan, E.J. (1970) *Multiple Time Series*, Wiley, New York.

Hogg, R.V. and A.T. Craig (1970) (third edition) *Introduction to Mathematical Statistics*, Macmillan, New York.

Loeve, M. (1977) *Probability Theory I*, (fourth edition), Springer-Verlag, New York.

——————————— (1978) *Probability Theory II*, (fourth edition), Springer-Verlag, New York.

Padgett, W.J. and R.L. Taylor (1973) *Laws of Large Numbers for Normed Linear Spaces and Certain Frechet Spaces*, Lecture Notes in Mathematics No. 360, Springer-Verlag, New York.

Parthasarathy, K. R. (1967) *Probability Measures on Metric Spaces*, Academic Press, New York.

Renyi, A. (1970) *Foundations of Probability*, Holden-Day, San Francisco.

Royden, H. L. (1968) *Real Analysis*, (second edition), Macmillan, New York.

Siryayev, A. N. (1978) *Optimal Stopping Rules*, Springer-Verlag, New York.

——————————— (1984) *Probability*, Springer-Verlag, New York.

Yaglom, A. M. (1962) *Stationary Random Functions*, Prentice-Hall, New York.

Index

absolutely continuous
  distribution function, 89
  measure, 61
abstract space, 2
  see also space
additive (set function)
  finitely additive, 18
  σ-additive, 18
algebra, 10
  generated by, 78
almost invariant
  random variable, 344
  set, 344
  see also invariant
ARMA sequence, 368
asymptotically equivalent, 151
asymptotically negligible, 269
axiom of countability
  first, 71
  second, 71

Banach space, 73, 159
  separable, 205
base (basis), 70, 71
  countable, 200
basic (*or* elementary) set, 77
Berry-Essen theorem, 275
Bochner (B-)integral, 214
Borel
  -Cantelli theorem, 136
  for independent case, 136
  set, 11, 79
  σ-algebra, 11, 79
  (measurable) space, 11, 79
    one dimensional, 11, 79

    infinite dimensional, 81
    n-dimensional, 81
bounded convergence theorem, 43

canonical representation
  (of function), 30
Caratheodory extension theorem, 88
Cartesian product, 64
  see direct product
Cauchy
  convergence, 72
    see also complete normed linear space
  inequality, 106
central limit theorem (CLT)
  for martingales, 322
  Liapounov, 274
  Lindberg(-Feller), 270
  for random variables, 257
    i.i.d., 263
    independent, 257
change of variable, 102
characteristic function (CF), 246
  for normal distribution, 259
generalized Chebyshev inequality, 105
class
  λ-class, 126
  π-class, 126
classical strong law of large numbers, 153
classical weak law of large numbers, 153
closed set, 66

373